IRELAND UNDER THE TUDORS

RICHARD BAGWELL
VOLUME I

PREFACE.

'Irish policy,' said Mr. Disraeli in the House of Commons, 'is Irish history, and I have no faith in any statesman, who attempts to remedy the evils of Ireland, who is either ignorant of the past or who will not take lessons from it.' This is most true, and history, if it is to be of any use, should be written for instruction, and not merely for the confirmation of existing prejudices. This is especially so in the present case, for, as Sir George Stanley told Cecil in 1565, 'the practises of Ireland be great, and not understood to all men that seem to have knowledge thereof.' The writer who enters the arena as an advocate may produce an interesting party pamphlet, but he will hardly make the world either wiser or better. The historian's true office is that of the judge, whose duty it is to marshal all the material facts with just so much of comment as may enable his hearers to give them their due weight. The reading public is the jury.

Starting with this conception of the task before me, I have not attempted to please any party or school. The history of Ireland is at the best a sad one; but its study, if it be really studied for the truth's sake, can hardly fail to make men more tolerant. In Ireland, as in other countries, a purely Celtic population was unable to resist the impact of the Teutonic race. First came the pagan Northmen, with power to ruin, but without power to reconstruct. Then followed the Anglo-Normans, seeking for lands and lordships, but seeking them under the patronage of the Catholic Church.[Pg vi] For a time it seemed as though the conquest would be complete; but the colony proved too weak for its work, and the mail-clad knights failed almost as completely as the Scandinavian corsairs.

The main cause of this second failure was the neglect or jealousy of the kings. They feared the growth of an independent power within sight of the English shore, and they had neither means nor inclination to do the work of government themselves. Little gain and less glory were to be had in Ireland, and Scotch, Welsh, or Continental politics engrossed their attention in turn. They weakened the colony, partly of set purpose, and partly by drawing men and supplies from thence. In short, they were absentees; and, to use an expression which has gained currency in modern times, they were generally content to look upon Ireland as a mere drawfarm.

The Wars of the Roses almost completed the ruin of the work which Henry II. had begun. For a moment it seemed as if the colony was about to assert its independence. But this could not have been done without an understanding with the native race, and it does not appear that any such understanding was possible. The upshot was that Yorkist and Lancastrian parties were formed in Ireland, that the colony was thus still further weakened, and that the English language and power seemed on the point of disappearing altogether.

The throne of Henry VIII. was erected on the ruins of mediæval feudalism, and guarded by a nation which longed for rest, and which saw no hope but in a strong monarchy. The King saw that he had duties in Ireland. Utterly unscrupulous where his own passions were concerned, the idea of a patriot King was not altogether strange to him. Irish chiefs were encouraged to visit his court, and were allowed to bask in the sunshine of royal favour; and it is conceivable that the 'Defender of the Faith,' had he con[Pg vii]tinued to defend it in the original sense, might have ended by attaching the native Irish to the Crown. By respecting for a time their tribal laws, by making one chief an earl and another a knight, by mediating in their quarrels, and by attending to their physical and spiritual wants, a Catholic Tudor might possibly have succeeded where Anglican and Plantagenet had failed. The revolution in religion changed everything, and out of it grew what many regard as the insoluble Irish question.

Henry II. had found Ireland in the hands of a Celtic people, for the intermixture of Scandinavian blood was slight and partial. Henry VIII. found it inhabited by a mixed race. From the beginning there had been rivalry and ill-feeling between men of English blood born in Ireland, and those of English birth who were sent over as officials or who went over as adventurers. During the fifteenth century England did nothing to preserve the ties of kinship, and the Celtic reaction tended to swallow up the interlopers. The degenerate English proverbially became more Irish than the Irish themselves, but the distinction would scarcely have been so nearly obliterated had it not been for the change in religion. The nobles of the Pale, the burghers of the walled towns, and the lawyers in Dublin were equally disinclined to accept the new model. Neither Irish chieftains nor Anglo-Irish lords found much difficulty in acknowledging Henry's supremacy both in Church and State; but further than that they would not go. The people did not go so far, and, in the words of the annalists, regarded the Reformation simply as a 'heresy and new error.'

Religion itself was at an extremely low ebb, and only the friars preserved the memory of better days. Henry may have imagined that he could lead the people through the bishops and other dignitaries: if so, he was entirely mistaken. The friars defied his power, and the hearts of the poor were with them. In Ireland, at least, it was Rome that under[Pg viii]took the work of popular reformation. The Franciscans and Jesuits endured cold and hunger, bonds and death, while courtly prelates neglected their duties or were distinguished from lay magnates only by the more systematic nature of their oppressions. And thus, as the hatred of England daily deepened, the attachment of the Irish to Rome became daily closer. Every effort of Henry to conciliate them was frustrated by their spiritual guides, who urged with perfect truth that he was an adulterer, a tyrant, and a man of blood. Holding such cards as these, the friars could hardly lose the game, and they had little difficulty in proving to willing ears that the King's ancestors received Ireland from the Pope, and that his apostasy had placed him in the position of a defaulting vassal.

Henry's vacillations and the early deaths of Edward and Mary for a time obscured the true nature of the contest, but it became apparent in Elizabeth's time. She was an excommunicated Queen. From a Catholic point of view she was clearly illegitimate. Many English Catholics ignored all this and served her well and truly, but those who carried dogmas to their logical conclusions flocked to the enemy's camp. Spain, Belgium, and Italy were filled with English refugees, who were willing enough that the Queen should be hurt in Ireland, since England was beyond their reach. But even here national antipathies were visible, and Irish suitors for Spanish help came constantly into collision with Englishmen bent upon the same errand.

Desmond, Shane O'Neill, and Hugh O'Neill seem to have cared very little for religion themselves. The first was a tool of Rome; the two latter rather made the Church subservient to their own ambition. But in these cases, and in a hundred others of less importance, the religious feeling of the people was always steadily opposed to the English Crown. Elizabeth was by nature no persecutor, yet she persecuted. Her advisers always maintained, and her apologists may still[Pg ix] maintain, that in hanging a Campion or torturing an O'Hurley she did not meddle with freedom of conscience, but only punished those who were plotting against her crown. The Catholics, on the other hand, could plead that they had done nothing worthy of death or of bonds, nor against lawful authority, and that they suffered for conscience' sake. And the Continental nations, who were mainly Catholic, sided on the whole with the refugees. Ireland, it is true, was only a pawn in their game, and Philip II. was probably wrong in not making her much more. At Cork or Galway the Armada might have met with scarcely any resistance, and a successful descent would have taxed Elizabeth's resources to the utmost.

The poverty of the Crown is the key to many problems of the Elizabethan age. The Queen had to keep Scotland quiet, to hold Spain at bay, and to maintain tolerable relations with France. She saw what ought to be done in Ireland, but very often could not afford to do it. The tendency to temporise was perhaps constitutional, but it was certainly much increased by want of money. Her vacillating policy did much harm, but it was caused less by changes of opinion than by circumstances. When the pressure at other points slackened she could attend to her troublesome kingdom; when it increased she was often forced to postpone her Irish plans. Ireland has always suffered, and still suffers sorely, from want of firmness. In modern times party exigencies work mischief analogous to that formerly caused by the sovereign's necessities.

The dissolution of the monasteries was followed by no proper provision for education. In the total absence of universities and grammar-schools, certain monks and nuns had striven nobly to keep the lamp of knowledge burning, but they were ruthlessly driven from house and home. Elizabeth was alive to all this, but she could not give Ireland her undivided attention, and such remedies as were applied[Pg x] came too late. The oppressed friars kept possession of the popular ear, and the Jesuits found the crop ready for their sickle. Denied education at home, many sons of good families sought it abroad, and the natural leaders of the Irish acquired habits of thought very different from those of English gentlemen. Archbishop Fitzgibbon, one of the most important champions of Catholic Ireland, saw clearly that his country could not stand alone. He would have preferred the sovereignty of England, but she had become aggressively Protestant, and he turned to Spain, to France, to Rome, anywhere rather than to the land whence his own ancestors had sprung. The lineage of the United Irishmen and their numerous progeny may be easily traced back to Tudor times.

A few words now to the critics whom every writer hopes to have. The spelling both of Irish names and English documents has throughout been modernised, from regard to the feelings of the public. Irish history is already sufficiently repulsive to that great unknown quantity the general reader, and it would be cruel to add to its horrors. Etymologists will always go for their materials to originals, and not to modern compositions. When, therefore, such names as Clandeboye or Roderic O'Connor are met with in the text, it is not to be supposed that I have never heard of Clann-Aedha-Buidhe or Ruaidhri O'Conchobair.

Of the first 123 pages of this book, I need only say that original authorities have as much as possible been consulted. In the third and four following chapters, much use has been made of Mr. Gilbert's 'Viceroys,' a debt which I desire to acknowledge once for all.

In so succinct a review of more than three centuries, it has not been thought necessary to quote the authority for every fact.

For the reign of Henry VIII. I have chiefly relied on the second and third volumes of the 'State Papers,' published in 1834. They are sometimes cited as 'S. P.' or 'State Papers,[Pg xi]' and when only the date of a letter or report is given it must be understood that this collection is referred to. The great calendar of letters and papers begun by Dr. Brewer and continued by Mr. Gairdner contains some items not included in the older publication; it is referred to as Brewer. Other sources of information have not been neglected, and are indicated in the footnotes.

The account of the reigns of Edward VI., Mary, and Elizabeth is chiefly drawn from the 'State Papers, Ireland'—all documents preserved in the Public Record Office and calendared by Mr. Hans Claude Hamilton. How excellently the editor has done his work can only be appreciated by one who has entered into his labours as closely as I have done. Except where a document has already been printed, I have nearly always referred to the original MS. All documents cited by date or number without further description must be understood as being in this collection. The late Dr. Brewer's calendar of the Carew MSS. at Lambeth often fills up gaps in the greater series; it is referred to as Carew. Many papers, both in Fetter Lane and at Lambeth, are copies; but their authenticity is not disputed. The Carew calendar is on so full a plan that it has not been thought necessary to consult the manuscripts; indeed, except for local purposes, it is not likely that they will be much consulted in the future. Other collections are referred to in their places, but it may be well to mention specially the journal of the Irish (Kilkenny) Archæological Society, whose editor, the Rev. James Graves, has done as much as any man to lay a broad foundation for Irish history.

O'Donovan's splendid edition of the 'Four Masters' has generally been consulted for the Irish version of every important fact. O'Clery and his fellow-compilers wrote under Charles I., and are not therefore strictly contemporary for the Tudor period. They appear to have faithfully transcribed original annals, but to this one important exception must be[Pg xii] made. The old writers never hesitated to record facts disagreeable to the Church; the later compilers were under the influence of the counter-reformation which produced Jesuitism. Making some allowance for this, the 'Four Masters' must be considered fair men. Michael O'Clery spent much time at Louvain, but he wrote in Ireland, and had native assistants. Philip O'Sullivan, on the other hand, was a Spanish officer, and published his useful but untrustworthy 'Compendium' at Lisbon. The 'Annals of Lough Cé' are preferable in some ways to the 'Four Masters,' but they do not cover so much ground. All the native annalists are jejune to an exasperating degree. Genealogy seems to have been the really important thing with them, and they throw extremely little light on the condition of the people. We are forced therefore to rely on the accounts, often prejudiced and nearly always ill-informed, of English travellers and officials.

The Anglo-Irish chronicles in 'Holinshed' were written by Richard Stanihurst, who dedicated his work to Sir Henry Sidney, for the reign of Henry VIII., and after that by John Hooker. Stanihurst, a native of Dublin, was not born till 1545. He has been thought an unpatriotic writer, and excited the violent antipathy of O'Donovan; but he appears to have been pretty well informed. The speeches which he puts into the mouths of his characters must be considered apocryphal, but as much may be said of like compositions in all ages. Hooker was an actor in many of the events he describes. He was a Protestant and an Englishman, prejudiced no doubt, but not untruthful, and his statements are often borne out by independent documents. Edmund Campion, the Jesuit, wrote in Ireland under Sidney's protection; his very interesting work is less a history than a collection of notes.

Other books, ancient and modern, are referred to in the footnotes. Among living scholars, I desire to thank[Pg xiii] Dr. W. K. Sullivan, of Cork, who had the great kindness to correct the first chapter, and to furnish some valuable notes. Hearty thanks are also due to the gentlemen at the Public Record Office, and especially to Mr. W. D. Selby and Mr. J. M. Thompson.

In making the index a few errors were discovered in the text, and these have been noted as errata. Some mistakes may still remain uncorrected, but I am not without hope that they are neither many nor of much importance.

Marlfield, Clonmel:
August 13, 1885.

CHAPTER I.

INTRODUCTORY.

Scope of the work.
The main object of this book is to describe in some detail, and as impartially as possible, the dealings of England with Ireland during the reigns of Henry VIII. and his three children. As an introduction to the study of that period, it seemed desirable to give some account of the course of government during those 340 years which had elapsed since the first Anglo-Norman set foot upon the Irish shore. And, seeing that Teutonic invaders had effected a lodgment about three centuries and a half before Henry II.'s accession, it was hardly possible to avoid saying something about the men who built the towns which enabled his subjects to keep a firm grip upon the island. Lastly, it seemed well at the very outset to touch lightly upon the peculiarities of that Celtic system with which the King of England found himself suddenly confronted.

The Roman period.
Agricola took military possession of south-western Scotland partly in the hope of being able to invade Ireland. He had heard that the climate and people did not differ much from those of Britain, and he knew that the harbours were much frequented by merchants. He believed that annexation would tend to consolidate the Roman power in Britain, Gaul, and Spain, and kept by him for some time a petty Irish king who had been expelled by his own tribe, and to whom he professed friendship on the chance of turning him to account.[Pg 2] Agricola thought there would be no great difficulty in conquering the island, which he rightly conjectured to be smaller than Britain and larger than Sicily or Sardinia.

'I have often,' says Tacitus, 'heard him say that Ireland could be conquered and occupied with a single legion and a few auxiliaries, and that the work in Britain would be easier if the Roman arms could be made visible on all sides, and liberty, as it were, removed out of sight.' Agricola, like many great men after him, might have found the task harder than his barbarous guest had led him to suppose; and in any case fate had not ordained that Ireland should ever know the Roman Peace. It was reserved for another petty king, after the lapse of nearly 1,100 years, to introduce an organised foreign power into Ireland, and to attach the island to an empire whose possessions were destined to be far greater than those of Imperial Rome.

The Celtic polity.
Setting aside all ethnological speculations as foreign to the scope of this work, it may be sufficient to say that the inhabitants of Ireland at the dawn of authentic history were Celts, of the same grand division as the bulk of the Scots Highlanders, but differing considerably from the people of Wales. Their organisation in the twelfth century had not passed beyond the tribal stage.[1]

[Pg 3]

The Irish Monarchy or Pentarchy.
There was a monarch of all Ireland, who had Meath—the Middle—as his official appanage, and who reigned originally at Tara. There were provincial kings of Ulster, Munster, Leinster, and Connaught. A primacy was given to the race of Niall, who lived presumably in the fourth and fifth centuries, and from whom the O'Neills, O'Donnells, and others trace their descent. The theory is thought to have been pretty closely adhered to until the desertion of Tara in the sixth century of our era. After that the over-king lived in his own territory; but his authority was often disputed, especially by Munster, the revolt of which province finally broke up the old order.[2]

Weakness of the Brehon law.
Wars were frequent, and Irish Brehons, who were rather legal experts than judges, exerted themselves to define rights and liabilities, and to establish a peaceful polity. Perhaps in laying down the law they sometimes rather stated their own conception of what it ought to be than described the actual state of things; much as Brahminical writers propounded a theory of caste which cannot be reconciled with historical truth. Neither the Church nor the Law had always original power sufficient to enforce steady obedience. The Law might be clear enough, but the central government was often too weak to secure respect for the opinion of experts. Portia might have argued like a very Daniel, but she could have done nothing without the Duke behind her. In the absence[Pg 4] of such an overpowering authority, the decisions of the Brehons were little more than arbitrations which might be, and probably often were, accepted as final, but on which neither party could be compelled to act.[3]

Ireland was outside the imperial system.
In the treatise called the 'Senchus Mór' there is a passage which may be as old as the fourteenth century, in which it is allowed that the nature of Irish royalty varied considerably from time to time. 'The King of Erin without opposition,' says the writer or interpolator, 'received stock from the King of the Romans; or it was by the successor of

Patrick the stock is given to the King of Erin, that is, when the seaports of Dublin, and Waterford, and Limerick, and the seaports in general, are subject to him.' There is here an attempt at once to bring Ireland within the pale of the Empire, and to show that the Irish Church was independent. It was natural that the Brehons should seek to introduce their country into the circle of nations, but we know as a matter of fact that the Empire never had anything to do with Ireland. The passage quoted may have been inspired by a wish to deny English supremacy by attorning, as it were, to the superior lord. It is a tribute to the greatness of the[Pg 5] Empire more than anything else, and it was not thought of until the Brehon law schools had fallen from their high estate.

The tribal system. The chief.

It was by giving stock that an Irish chief showed his power and added to his wealth. There were lands attached to his office, but his capital consisted of kine, and he extracted a sort of rent by obliging his inferiors to give them pasture. The number of cattle which he 'grazed without loss' upon other people's ground was the measure of his power and popularity. There were free tribesmen the amount of whose obligation to their chief was strictly laid down, though a greater quantity of stock might be voluntarily taken under certain restrictions. But there were also servile or semi-servile classes whose comparatively unprotected condition placed them more or less in the power of the chief to whose sept they were attached. An ambitious chief would always have opportunities of aggrandisement, and his wealth enabled him to support a mercenary force, and to grow strong at the expense of his own and other tribes. Broken men who had lost their own tribal position would always flock to an ambitious chief, and the disturbing influence of such retainers was often too strong for Brehons or priests. But the growth of power by means of mercenaries was not peculiar to Ireland, and was perhaps less frequent than is commonly supposed.[4]

[Pg 6]

Frequency of war.

Whatever the advantages of a pure Celtic system, it did not secure general peace. There is no period of which Celtic Ireland may be more justly proud than that between the death of St. Columba in 597 and the death of St. Gall about 640. It was the age in which the Irish saint Columbanus bearded Thierri and Brunehaut, in which Ireland herself was a noted seat of learning, and in which the monasteries of Luxueil, of St. Gall, and of Bobbio were founded by Irishmen. Yet, under thirty years out of forty-four either battle or murder is recorded in the Chronicon Scotorum. In some years there were several battles and several murders.

In 628 Leinster was devastated. Quarrels between near relations were frequent, and often ended in murder. When we consider that the deaths of important people only are recorded, we cannot pronounce the Ireland which sent forth Aidan, and Adamnan, and Columbanus to have been at all a peaceful country. Christianity was then established, and no Scandinavian irruption had yet hindered the development of purely native ideas. But Irish chroniclers, perhaps owing to their genealogical turn, give a disproportionate space to deaths; and it may be admitted that the number of homicides was not greater in Ireland than in some parts of Germany in feudal times.[5]

[Pg 7]

Celtic law of succession.

Primogeniture, which is practically incompatible with the tribal stage of political organisation, was perhaps formally acknowledged at a very remote period, but was unknown as a rule of succession to Irish chiefries in the ages with which this book chiefly deals. In those comparatively modern times a vacancy was filled from the same family, but the person chosen was generally a brother or a cousin of the deceased. It seldom happened, perhaps, that an Irish chief, who was necessarily a warrior, attained threescore and ten years, and on an average a son would be less likely to make an able leader than one of an older generation. To avoid disputed successions, an heir-apparent, called the tanist, was chosen before a vacancy actually occurred, and sometimes probably against the wish of the reigning chief. Very often the sons refused to accept the tanist, and bloody quarrels followed. This system stank in the nostrils of the Tudor lawyers; but in the twelfth century the true principle of hereditary succession was not fully understood. It was, perhaps, a suspicion that his eldest son might not succeed him quietly that induced Henry II. to crown him in his lifetime. A later and much stronger analogy may be found in the history of the Empire. Charles V. procured the election of his brother Ferdinand as king of the Romans, and he was actually crowned. Many years later Charles wished to substitute his son Philip; but Ferdinand refused to yield, and he was sustained by the electors, who had no mind to see the Empire become an appendage of the Spanish monarchy. The influence of the Irish Brehons probably tended to prevent chiefries from becoming hereditary. In such cases as the earldom of Desmond we have a mixture of the two systems; the earls were chiefs as regarded the Irish; but their succession to the honour, and through it to the quasi-chiefry, was regulated by feudal rules.

Tudor view of the Celtic land law.

As the chief was elected by his tribe from among a limited number, so was the land distributed among the tribesmen[Pg 8] within certain fixed limits. As it is with England's treatment of Ireland that we have to do, it may be as well to let Sir John Davies himself say how the matter appeared to the Tudor lawyers:—

Septs.

'First be it known that the lands possessed by the mere Irish in this realm were divided into several territories or countries; and the inhabitants of each Irish country were divided into several septs or lineages.'

Lord and tanist.

'Secondly, in every Irish territory there was a lord or chieftain, and a tanist who was his successor apparent. And of every Irish sept or lineage there was also a chief, who was called Canfinny, or head of a "cognatio."'

Tanistry and gavelkind.

'Thirdly, all possessions in these Irish territories (before the common law of England was established through all the realm as it now is) ran at all times[6] in course of tanistry, or in course of gavelkind. Every lordship or chiefry, with the portion of land that passed with it, went without partition to the tanist, who always came in by election, or by

8

the strong hand, and never by descent.[7] But all the inferior tenancies were partible among the males in gavelkind.'[8]

No estate of inheritance.

'Again, the estate which the lord had in the chiefry, or that the inferior tenants had in gavelkind, was no estate of inheritance, but a temporary or transitory possession. For[Pg 9] just as the next heir of the lord or chieftain would not inherit the chiefry, but the eldest and worthiest of the sept (as was before shown in the case of tanistry), who was often removed and expelled by another who was more active or stronger than he: so lands in the nature of gavelkind were not partible among the next heirs male of him who died seised, but among all the males of his sept, in this manner:—

Partitions of tribal land.

'The Canfinny, or chief of a sept (who was commonly the most ancient of the sept) made all the partitions at his discretion. This Canfinny, after the death of each tenant holding a competent portion of land, assembled all the sept, placed all their possessions in hotchpotch, and made a new partition of the whole; in which partition he did not assign to the sons of the deceased the portion which their father held, but allotted the better or larger part to each one of the sept according to his antiquity.'[9]

Effect of frequent partitions.

'These portions being thus allotted and assigned were possessed and enjoyed accordingly until the next partition, which, at the discretion or will of the Canfinny, might be made at the death of each inferior tenant. And thus by these frequent partitions and the removals or translations of the tenants of one portion or another, all the possessions were uncertain, and the uncertainty of possession was the very cause that no civil habitations were erected, and no enclosure or improvement of lands made, in the Irish countries where that custom of gavelkind was in use; especially in Ulster, which seemed everywhere a wilderness before this new plantation made there by the English undertakers. And this was the fruit of this Irish gavelkind.'

Position of daughters and of bastard sons.

'Also by this Irish custom of gavelkind bastards took their shares with the legitimate, and wives, on the other hand, were quite excluded from dower, and daughters took nothing, even if their father died without issue male. So[Pg 10] that this custom differed from Kentish gavelkind in four points.'[10]

Four points peculiar to Irish gavelkind.

The four points were the certainty of estate in each share, the exclusion of bastards, the admission of a widow to one moiety, and the admission of females in default of issue male. For which reasons, says Sir John, the Kentish custom was always held good and lawful by the law of England. He admits, however, that the Irish custom had a counterpart in North Wales, which had been totally abolished by Henry VIII., along with other usages resembling those of Ireland. Edward I. had only ventured to exclude bastards, and to give widows their dowry.[11]

Sir John Davies did not exhaust the subject.

Notwithstanding the above decision, it is probable that a description of tanistry and gavelkind does not exhaust the subject. The theoretical division among all the males of a sept is not at all likely to have been carried out, except in very early times. Human nature was against it. From the twelfth century the example of the Anglo-Normans, which cannot have been altogether without weight, was against it. The interest of the chief was everywhere against it, because it would deprive him of the means of rewarding his friends, and because he was always tempted to seize lands to his own use. The tendency to private property would be always asserting itself, but the exact historical truth can never be known. Before the close of the mediæval period, a great part of Ireland had been reconquered by the tribes from Anglo-Norman hands. Is it possible that the Irish land system can have been anywhere restored in its integrity? On the whole,[Pg 11] it is at least probable that English statesmen in the sixteenth century made as many mistakes about tenures in Ireland as their representatives in the eighteenth and part of the nineteenth made about tenures in India. Good faith may be generally granted in both cases, but the blunders made were no less disastrous. It is at all events clear that primogeniture was no Celtic usage, that it is no part of the law of nature, and that the Tudor lawyers treated it as an end in itself, and almost as a necessary element in the eternal fitness of things. In the twelfth century Irish practice may have come much nearer to theory than in the sixteenth; at all events, Henry II.'s grants to individuals were absolutely opposed to Celtic notions of justice.

Composition for murder.Celtic usages part of the common Aryan stock.The conflict of laws is the key to Anglo-Irish history.

The Irish admitted composition for murder. This blood-fine, called an eric, was an utter abomination to the English of the sixteenth century, who had quite forgotten the laws and customs of their own Teutonic ancestors. To men long used to a strong central government such a custom seemed impious. It was nevertheless part of the common heritage of the Aryan race, and had been in vogue among the peoples from whom the later English sprung. The Njal Saga illustrates its use among the Icelanders by many famous cases strictly in point. The feudal system and the canon law had caused the Teutonic nations to abandon a usage which they once had in common with the Irish. Celtic Ireland had never had a very strong central government, and such as it was it had sustained serious damage. Homicide was still considered a personal injury. The rule was not a life for a life, but adequate damages for the loss sustained. The idea of public justice, irrespective of private interests, was far in advance of the stage which had been reached by the Irish Celts. Irish history cannot be understood unless the fact is clearly grasped, that the development of the tribal system was violently interrupted by a feudal half-conquest. The Angevin and Plantagenet kings were strong enough to shake and discredit the native polity; but they had neither the power nor the inclination to feudalise a people which had never gone through the preliminary stages. When the Tudors[Pg 12] brought a more steadfast purpose and better machinery to the task, they found how hard it was to evolve order out of the shattered remnants of two systems which had the same origin, but which had been so brought together as to make complete fusion impossible. From the first the subjects of England and the natives of Ireland had been on entirely different planes. Even for us it is extremely difficult to avoid confusion by applying modern terms to ancient things. The Tudor lawyers and statesmen could hardly even attempt to look at jarring systems from the outside. They saw that the common law was more advanced than that of the Brehons, but they could not see that they were really the same thing at different stages. In fact, plain Englishmen in the sixteenth century could not do what only the most enlightened Anglo-Indians can do in the nineteenth. They were more civilised than the Irish, but they were not educated enough to recognise the common ancestor. That there was a common ancestor, and that neither party could recognise him, is the key to Anglo-Irish history both before and after the Tudor times.

Origin of the Irish Church. Patrick and Columba.Exile of Columba.Saint Bridget.

The early history of the native Irish Church is shrouded in much obscurity. The best authorities are disposed to accept St. Patrick as the apostle of Ireland, the fifth century as the period of his labours, and Armagh as his chief seat. He was not a native of Ireland; so much seems certain. A more interesting, because a more clearly defined figure, is that of Columba or Columkille, who was born in Donegal in 521. The churches of Derry, Durrow, Kells, Swords, Raphoe, Tory Island, and Drumcliff, claim him as their founder; but it is as the apostle of North Britain that he is best known. He was religious from his youth, but a peculiarly serious tinge was given to his mind by a feeling of remorse for bloodshed which he had partly caused. He had surreptitiously transcribed a psalter belonging to another saint, who complained of this primitive infringement of copyright. A royal decision that 'to every cow belongs her calf' was given, and was followed by an appeal to arms. Exile was then imposed as a penance on Columba, whose act had been the[Pg 13] original cause of offence. Such was long the received legend, but perhaps the exile was voluntary.[12] Whether his departure was a penance or the result of a vow, tradition says that he was bound never to see Ireland again, that he landed first on Oronsay, but found that Erin was visible from thence, and refused to rest until he had reached Iona. His supposed feelings are recorded in a very ancient poem:—

'My vision o'er the brine I stretch
From the ample oaken planks;
Large is the tear of my soft grey eye
When I look back upon Erin.
Upon Erin my attention is fixed.'

Columba was the Paul of Celtic Christianity. By him and his disciples a great part of Scotland was evangelised, and it was to him that the British Church looked as a founder when the time came to decide between the relative pretensions of the Celtic and the Norman type of religion. St. Bridget or Bride, who died four years after Columba's birth, is scarcely less celebrated. She was born near Dundalk, and her chief seat was at Kildare. She was the mother of Irish female monachism, and in popular estimation is not less famous than Patrick, and perhaps more so than Columba.[13]

The Irish Church was originally monastic.

Irish Christianity was at first monastic. A saint obtained a grant of land from a chief. A church was built, and a settlement sprung up round it. The family, as it was called, consisted partly of monks and partly of dependents, and the abbot ruled over all as chief of a pseudo-tribe. Like a lay chiefry the abbacy was elective, and the abbots wielded considerable power. These ecclesiastical clans even made war with each other. Thus, it is recorded that in 763 the family of St. Ciaran of Clonmacnoise fought with the family of St. Columba of Durrow, and that 200 of the Columbides fell.[Pg 14] The head of such a confraternity was called coarb, or successor of the founder, and Irish writers sometimes called the Pope 'coarb of Peter.' In course of time the coarb of Patrick crystallised into the Archbishop of Armagh, and the coarb of Columba into the Bishop of Derry. Other saints were revered as the founders of other sees. Very often at least the abbot was chosen from among the founder's kin.

The early Church was episcopal, but not territorially so.

Episcopal orders were acknowledged from the first, but it was long before the notion of a territorial bishop prevailed. In early days there were many bishops, wanderers sometimes, and at other times retained by the abbot as a necessary appendage to his monastery. The bishop was treated with great respect, but was manifestly inferior to the head of a religious house. St. Patrick was said to have consecrated 350 bishops, founded 700 churches, and ordained 5,000 priests; a mere legend, but perhaps tending to show that the episcopal order was very numerous in Ireland. Travelling bishops without definite duties, and with orders of doubtful validity, became a scandal to more regularly organised churches, and drew down a rebuke from Anselm as late as the beginning of the twelfth century. At an earlier period impostors pretending to be Irish bishops were not uncommon.[14]

Ireland gradually conformed to Roman usage.

The Irish Church long continued to keep Easter on a different day from that sanctioned by Rome, and to use a different form of tonsure. But the inconvenience of such dissidence from the general body of Western Christendom was soon felt. About 630 Pope Honorius I. addressed a letter to the[Pg 15] Irish Church, in which he reminded the clergy that they were a scanty company inhabiting a remote region, and that it could not be for their interest to remain isolated. Cummian, afterwards seventh abbot of Iona, warmly espoused the papal cause. 'Rome errs,' he said with great scorn, 'Jerusalem errs, Alexandria errs, Antioch errs, the whole world errs—the Britons and Irish are the only right-minded people.' The southern Irish followed Cummian, but the northern rejected his advice, and some even called him a heretic; yet this did not prevent his being elected to fill Columba's chair. Adamnan, ninth abbot of Iona, and biographer of the great founder, was no less earnest on the Roman side than Cummian had been. At the Synod of Whitby in 664 Wilfred discomfited Colman of Lindisfarne, and settled the question so far as England was concerned. Adamnan lived till 704, and succeeded in converting nearly all the Irish churches, except those subject to his own monastery.

Close of the Paschal controversy, 716.

In 716, under Duncadh, the eleventh abbot, Iona conformed, and the Paschal controversy came to an end, after lasting 150 years. The coronal tonsure was adopted three years later. The supremacy of Rome was thus acknowledged, but circumstances long prevented the Irish from adopting the Roman plan of Church organisation.

Influence of the Scandinavian invasions on the Church.The Eugenian Constitution, 1151.

The Scandinavian inroads began towards the close of the century which witnessed the submission of Iona. It is probable that the influx of pagan Northmen kept Ireland apart from the rest of Christendom. The ninth century produced Erigena and other eminent Irishmen, but a country in which Christianity was fighting for bare life was not a promising field for Church reformers or systematisers. It was not until Clontarf had finally decided the cause in favour of Christianity that Ireland had again leisure to think of ecclesiastical polity. Gillebert of Limerick, an Ostman, was the first papal legate, and as such presided at the synod of Rathbreasil in or about 1118, where the first serious attempt was made to divide all Ireland into dioceses. The great influence of Malachi of Armagh was exerted in the same direction. He was the friend of Bernard of Clairvaux, and he introduced the[Pg 16] Cistercian order into Ireland. Pope Eugenius III., himself a Cistercian, finished the work, and in 1151 Ireland accepted four archiepiscopal palls from Rome. From that date the Irish Church must be held to have fully accepted not only papal supremacy but Roman organisation. That she had not done so long before seems due to accident more than anything else. From mere remoteness of position Ireland had escaped the dominion of Imperial Rome. From the same remoteness she was comparatively slow to feel the influence of Papal Rome. Still, it can scarcely be doubted that had it not been for the Scandinavian intrusion, the Ireland which adopted the Roman Easter and the Roman tonsure before the middle of the eighth century, would have gladly accepted the palls long before the middle of the twelfth.[15]

FOOTNOTES:

[1] As to the divisions and sub-divisions of the ancient Irish people, I prefer to give the following statement of Dr. Sullivan:—'The unit territory was the Tuath, each of which had a Ri, or chief. Three, four, or even more Tuatha were connected together for military and other purposes as a Mór Tuath; the king or chief of the confederacy, who acted as Commander-in-Chief, was the Ri Mór Tuatha, or great chief. This group corresponded to the Gothic Thiuda, old Norse Thjoth. The Irish unit Tuath corresponded to the Norse Fylk, the Teutonic Gavi or Gau, the Greek Phyle, and the old Latin Tribus; it was at first genealogical, but acquired a geographical and political signification. The tribe or Tuath consisted in some cases of a Clann, the progeny or descendants of a chief. Sometimes a Clann embraced several Tuatha. Clann was strictly genealogical, Tuath both genealogical and geographical. The Clann consisted of families or houses called Fine, equivalent to Cognatio—the Anglo-Saxon Maegth. The head of a Fine was the Cendfinne or chieftain. The Fine was a sept. The Clann therefore consisted of several septs, and the land of the tribe or Tuath was divided between the septs or Fine composing it. The Fine or sept is one of the most important parts of the Irish organisation, but the word is used in several senses: thus, the relatives of a chief or other tribesman to the fifth degree constituted the true Cognatio or Geilfine, i.e. Hand-fine. The Fine or sept was in fact an independent unit, which paid Erics for all its members, and received Erics or fines for the killing of one of its own members, and also took possession of the Dibad or property of its deceased members. But when the sept did not fulfil its obligations, the Ri of the Tuath was bound to enforce justice. So when the Tuath itself failed in its obligations and duties, the Ri Mór Tuatha or superior chief was bound to enforce justice in the recalcitrant tribe. The Ri Mór Tuatha, or Ri buiden, or king of companies, corresponded to the Anglo-Saxon Heretoga or Dux. The King of the Great Tribe received hostages from the sub-reguli of his territory for their Ceílsine or fealty, and he might call upon them to support him with a levy of their tribes.'

[2] 'The existence of the Irish Pentarchy,' says Dr. Sullivan, 'was as real as that of any similar confederacy among nations in a tribal stage, and the means of enforcing the orders of the over-king were not very different or less effective than in many federal states—ancient, mediæval, and modern.'

[3] 'It is quite true,' says Dr. Sullivan, 'that the central power was not always strong enough to enforce rights, and in many instances was defeated in its attempt to do so. But in what does this differ from other federal states, ancient and modern? The Emperors of Germany were not always able to subdue and to enforce their decrees against the princes and nobles of the Empire, and in numerous instances the decisions of the imperial chancery might be regarded in precisely the same light—as mere arbitrations. To say there was no law, properly speaking, seems to me wholly irreconcilable with actual facts, and especially with the existence of a rich and elaborate nomenclature of native terms not borrowed from Roman law. This nomenclature implies an equally elaborate machinery. It was the existence of this legal system which kept out the canon law, which never, for instance, succeeded in suppressing or even modifying the marriage customs. In discussing the laws and institutions of early nations we are liable to go to one or other of two extremes:—(1) We represent the laws, &c., in terms of modern law, by which we make inchoate institutions full-grown, while the germs of a legal system are represented as a fully developed code; or (2) we deny the existence of all law and legislation. You are right I think as regards the Church; for owing to the organisation of the old Celtic Church it was perfectly acephalous. Whatever influence it did exert was individual and never official, and, therefore, not continuous—it might be described in fact as sporadic influence.'

[4] 'All through the laws,' says Dr. Sullivan, 'there is ample evidence to prove that the tribesmen, or Aires, were bound to take stock from the Ri, or chief, only. The amount of this stock, called Saer, or free-stock, is strictly laid down, and the amount of the tribute payable for this stock, called Bestigi, or house-refection, or tribute, is also strictly laid down. But if the Ri were wealthy he might offer more stock to his Ceiles, clients or vassals, on condition of paying him certain dues, called Biatad. The stock so given was called Daer, or base-stock; and its acceptance by a tribesman made a Daer-ceilé of him, and placed him very much in the power of the Ri, or chief. No tribesman could accept Daer-stock without the consent of his Fine, or sept, which would be bound by the acts of its members. A tribesman, with the consent of his Fine, might accept Daer-stock from any Flath, or lord, in his own Tuath, or tribe. All the above applies to the tribesmen, or Aires, who alone constituted the free class. But besides the Ceiles, or clients, or free tribesmen, or Aires, there was another class, called Fuidirs. The markland of the tribe and the land held in severalty of the Ri, and the similar land of the Cendfinne, or chieftain (or captain, as he is called in the Scottish Highlands) of a sept was let out to various classes of Fuidirs. Some were Saer, or free Fuidirs, and others Daer, or base Fuidirs. The Saer-fuidirs, again, were of two sorts—broken tribesmen who went into another Tuath and got stock as well as land from a Ri, or Flath, and Saer-fuidirs who possessed some stock of their own which they grazed on land of a chief or of a Flath. Some of these free Fuidirs entered into daer, or servitude, by accepting stock under certain conditions. The Fuidir classes were the true tenants at will. The Aires were of the clan, the Fuidirs, Bottachs, or cottiers, and other servile classes, belonged to the clan. The giving and taking of Daer-stock depended upon the impoverishment of a sept through cattle murrain, the levying of blood-fines on account of the misconduct of some of its members, &c. But the whole thing was voluntary, and depended on the poverty of a sept and the wealth and ability of the Ri, or Flath.'

[5] Dr. Sullivan does not think Christianity was fully established by the middle of the seventh century. 'The Irish Church organisation,' he says, 'was ill calculated to influence the social habits and the political life of the people; unlike the diocesan and centralised system of the Latin Church. Hence a high spiritual life and intellectual cultivation within the numerous cœnobiums was quite compatible with practical paganism and disorder outside.'

[6] 'At all times' must be understood to refer only to those comparatively modern ages above mentioned.

[7] 'The election,' says Dr. Sullivan, 'was always from the Geilfine, or relatives within the fifth degree. Should the Geilfine fail, or be all killed in battle, the Derbfine, or relatives from the fifth to the ninth degree, came in.'

[8] 'This,' says Dr. Sullivan, 'is not right. There was the "joint undivided family" formed by the Bo-aire class, or freemen possessed of cattle. The poorer Flaths, or heads of septs, did not gavel their possessions, but either elected a tanist or formed a "joint undivided family." When the property of an Aire was not sufficient to gavel, so as to qualify one or more Aires, the division of the inheritance did not take place, but the parties agreed to form a "joint undivided family." In such a family one was head, and as such was an Aire. Bo-aires of this class, to avoid the gavelling of their property, elected a Tanist—the Tanaise Bo-aire. Poor and broken tribesmen, not having sufficient wealth to qualify them as Aires, formed a "joint-family," or Congilda. Every Flath, or head of a sept, had a tanist also. The Irish "joint-family" was an institution of great importance and of surpassing interest in the comparative history of the Aryan family.'

[9] 'This account of Davies,' says Dr. Sullivan, 'is entirely wrong. The law of the distribution of the property of a deceased tribesman was most carefully laid down. No doubt then as now, and naturally more frequently then than now, a chief, or head of a sept, or of a Treb (homestead) might usurp power he did not possess, and do wrong.'

[10] 'Marriages in Ireland,' says Dr. Sullivan, 'were not regulated by canon law. The Irish marriage customs were in full force long after the Norman conquest. According to these customs, which appear to have been wholly uninfluenced by the canon law, bastardy was entirely different from what that term implied in countries under canon law, and in modern times. The Irish marriage customs should consequently be taken into account here, as they sanctioned a kind of polygamy, divorce, &c. See also the excommunication in 1282, by the Archbishop of Canterbury against Llewellyn, Prince of Wales, at the request of Edward I., in which the marriage customs of the Welsh, identical with those of the Irish, constitute one of the charges.'

[11] Le Résolution des justices touchant le Irish custome de gavelkind. Reported by Sir John Davies, A.G., 3 Jac. i.

[12] Dr. Sullivan believes the story of the decision against Columba to be a mere myth.

[13] 'The Irish Church,' says Dr. Sullivan, 'had undoubtedly two distinct phases of monasticism: one that of the Patrician period—an obscure but highly important and interesting phase; the other, that of the sixth and subsequent centuries, to which the Irish missionaries belonged.'

[14] 'Besides,' says Dr. Sullivan, 'the monastic bishop proper, who furnished the wandering Scotic bishops of the Middle Ages, there is a later development of a higher church organisation in the tribal bishop, who was a close approximation to a diocesan bishop. The tribal bishop was a bishop who had jurisdiction over the whole of a Tuath, and sometimes even a Mór Tuath. The growth of territorial jurisdiction is well marked by the prestige attached to the office—the bishop ranked in fact almost on a level with the chief, and was entitled to the same legal retinue. Many of the ancient dioceses, and some of the existing ones, e.g. Ross, Kilmacduagh, Kilfenora, represent ancient Tuaths, or tribe territories. Several deaneries were former dioceses, and are co-extensive with ancient Tuatha.

[15] Dr. Sullivan warns me not to attribute too much influence to the Danish Church. 'The tribe-bishop,' he says, 'was a much earlier development, and proves the growth of diocesan jurisdiction and the consequent merging of the Irish Church in the Latin Church. The acceptance of the Roman time for celebrating Easter by the Irish Church and the constant intercourse between Ireland and the Continent had brought the Irish Church fully under Roman supremacy three and a half centuries earlier. What really took place in the early part of the twelfth century was the more complete adoption of the organisation of the Western Church, and of the principles of the canon law; and especially the granting of lands and charters to the Church in the same way as in feudal lands. The marriage of Irish princes with Saxon and other foreign princesses, and the growth of towns which helped to relax its rigid tribal system, did more than the Danish Church.' The chief towns were, however, of Danish origin.

[Pg 17]

CHAPTER II.

THE SCANDINAVIAN ELEMENT.

First appearance of the Northmen, 795.
Norwegian ships began to appear on the Irish coast in 795, one year after the destruction of the church at Lindisfarne. The islands were harried, Lambay being perhaps the first to suffer; everything of value was taken, and the hermits and anchorites were killed or carried away. Iona, where the greatest of Irish saints had founded a new Church, was burned or plundered in 802 and 806. About twelve years after their first visit the Scandinavians began to venture inland, sacking the monasteries, which contained such wealth as Ireland then possessed, and slaughtering the monks. The famous religious community at Bangor, in Down, was thus destroyed about 824. The first permanent settlement of the northern invaders was perhaps in the neighbourhood of Limerick. They had a fort at Cork before 848, and at Dublin before 852. There were also forts on Lough Foyle and at Waterford. The flat coast between Dublin and the borders of Meath lay open to a floating enemy, and early obtained the name of Fingal, or the land of the stranger.

Turgesius, 830.

In or about 830 a chief arrived who pursued a more ambitious policy. He is called Turgeis or Turgesius by the Irish, and by the Irish only: this may be a form of Thorkils or Trygve, and may perhaps be a name applied to the mysterious hero whom the Scandinavians call Ragnar Lodbrok. Turgesius landed in Ulster, and planned the complete subjugation of Ireland. He burned Armagh and drove out St. Patrick's successor, and then took up a central position near Athlone, whence his flotillas could act on Lough Ree and Lough Dearg. We know that the Northmen dragged ships or boats overland to Loch Lomond, and similar feats[Pg 18] may have been performed in Ireland. There was another plundering station on Lough Neagh about the same time.

Turgeis mastered the northern half of Ireland, and made frequent incursions into the other half. Against the Church he showed peculiar animosity, and his wife used the high altar at Clonmacnoise as a throne when she gave audience; perhaps she uttered oracular responses from it. In the south Turgeis was less powerful, for the dispossessed abbot of Armagh took refuge at Emly in Tipperary. But the whole coast was attacked by innumerable corsairs, who sometimes made raids far into the central districts. Dublin was fortified by the Norwegians about 840, and became the chief seat of the Scandinavian power. Turgeis did not live to unite the various bands, but fell into the hands of Malachi, King of Meath, in 845, and was drowned in Lough Owel. The Northmen of Limerick were defeated in the same year at Roscrea, and their earl, Olfin, was slain.[16]

A.D. 852.

The Black and White Gentiles.

Seven years after the death of Turgeis came the Black Gentiles, who are generally supposed to have been Danes, as the White Gentiles were certainly Norwegians. Whether the colour of their armour or their complexion was referred to is doubtful. The newcomers made themselves masters of Dublin, and of the plunder which the first invaders had accumulated from all the Irish churches. Before one of the battles fought to decide whether Black or White Pagans were to enjoy this property, Horm, or Gorm, the Danish chief, is said to have invoked St. Patrick, a singular confusion of ideas, which may have resulted from intercourse with Christians in England. Victory followed. The Black Gentiles seem to have retained their supremacy; but the distinction becomes partly obliterated, and the Danes, of whom we read later, were probably intermingled with Norwegians. It is recorded that Amlaf, son of the King of Norway, came to Ireland in 852 or 853, that all the foreigners of Erin submitted to him, and that the Irish also paid tribute. The[Pg 19] name of the Black Gentiles is believed to be preserved in the little town of Baldoyle.

Forty years' peace.

Amlaf and his sons were not satisfied with the spoils of thrice plundered churches, but everywhere violated tombs in search of gold ornaments. Another great chief was Ivar, who appears to have been Ivar Beinlaus, son of Ragnar Lodbrok, and founder of the Northumbrian kingdom, which was afterwards closely connected with the Irish Danes. To the Norwegians who fled to Ireland from the iron rule of Harold Harfager, the King of Dublin was one of the chief sovereigns on earth. Carrol, lord of Ossory, was in alliance with Amlaf and Ivar, and ruled Dublin after their deaths; but he died about 885, and a Norse dynasty was then re-established by force. A dozen years later another Carrol drove the foreigners across the Channel, but Sitric, king of Northumberland, regained the fortress in 919, and the Celts do not appear to have recaptured it. For a period of some forty years, ending about 916, Ireland is said to have had a little rest. The enemy may have had enough to do elsewhere, but their predatory expeditions did not entirely cease. There were perhaps no fresh invasions in force, but former settlers held their own against the Irish, with whom they were generally at war.

Renewed invasions, 916.Severe treatment of the natives.

Whatever may have caused the period of comparative rest, the Danish incursions began again with renewed vigour. A great host came to Waterford in 916, defeated the men of Leinster, and harried all the south of Ireland; churches, as usual, attracting their special attention. Ragnal, Ivar's grandson, represented by the Ulster annalists as king of all the Irish Scandinavians, was the chief leader, and he afterwards led his men to Scotland, where the great but indecisive battle of Tynemoor was fought.[17] Sitric, Ragnal's brother, took Dublin from the Irish, who had, perhaps, held it since 902, and on Ragnal's death succeeded to the royal title. The natives had occasional successes, but on the whole they were conspicuously inferior in the field, and Nial Glundubh, King of Ireland, who headed a great confederacy, fell in the attempt[Pg 20] to recover Dublin. Twelve chiefs or kings of northern and central tribes are said to have died at the same time. After this reverse all serious attempt to check the invaders seems to have been given up, and fleet after fleet brought hordes of oppressors to the ill-fated island. Munster suffered especially, and the general nature of a Danish invasion cannot be better apprehended than by transcribing the chronicler's words:—'And assuredly the evil which Erin had hitherto suffered was as nothing compared to the evil inflicted by these parties. All Munster was plundered by them on all sides and devastated, and they spread themselves over Munster and built earth-works and towers and landing-places over all Erin, so that there was no place in Erin without numerous fleets of Danes and pirates; so that they made spoil-land and sword-land and conquered-land of her throughout her breadth and generally; and they ravaged her chieftainries, privileged churches, and sanctuaries, and demolished her shrines, reliquaries, and books. They wrecked her beautiful ornamental temples: for neither veneration, nor honour, nor mercy for holy ground, nor protection for church or sanctuary, for God or man, was felt by this furious, ferocious, pagan, ruthless, wrathful people. In short, until the sand of the sea, the grass of the field, or the stars of heaven are counted it will not be easy to recount or enumerate or relate what the Gaedhil, all, without distinction, suffered from; whether men or women, boys or girls, laics or clerics, freemen or serfs, young or old; indignity, outrage, injury, and oppression. In a word, they killed the kings and the chieftains, the heirs to the crown, and the royal princes of Erin. They killed the brave and the valiant, the stout knights, champions, soldiers, and young lords, and most of the heroes and warriors of all Ireland; they brought them under tribute and reduced them to bondage and slavery. Many were the blooming, lively women; the modest, mild, comely maidens; the pleasant, noble, stately, blue-eyed young women; the gentle, well-brought-up youths; and the intelligent, valiant champions, whom they carried to oppression and bondage over the broad green sea. Alas! many and frequent were the bright eyes that were suffused[Pg 21] with tears and dimmed with grief and despair at the separation of son from father, and daughter from mother, and brother from brother, and relatives from their race and from their tribe.'[18]

The Northmen fail to found a permanent kingdom.

The Irish Danes became strong enough to interfere with effect in English politics, and Olaf Cuaran, or Sitricson, King of Dublin, was a general of the great Scandinavian army which Athelstane overthrew at Brunanburgh. The Danes were much fewer than the Irish, but their general superiority during the tenth century was incontestable; and had the invaded people been of kin to them the kingdom of Canute might have had a counterpart in Ireland. Irish Celts were only too ready to call in Scandinavian allies in their internal quarrels, but they could never amalgamate with them. Occasionally a confederation of tribes would gain a great success, as at the battle of Tara, where King Malachi defeated the Dublin Danes under Athelstane's old opponent, Olaf Cuaran. After great slaughter on both sides the Dublin men had the worst, and were forced to release Donnell, King of Leinster, who was then in their hands. A great part of Ireland was at this time subject to the Danes, and the battle of Tara has been called the end of the 'Babylonish captivity of Ireland, inferior only to the captivity of hell.' King Olaf went on a pilgrimage to Iona, where he died in the following year. Thirty-seven years had passed since his acceptance of Christianity, at least in name; yet the Danes plundered the sacred isle only five years later, in 986, and killed the abbot and fifteen of his monks. It is to be noted that the Scandinavian treatment of churches reacted on the Irish, and that many native warriors came to regard saints and sanctuaries with as little respect as Turgesius himself.

Their strongest power in Munster.

Munster seems to have been more completely subdued than any other part of Ireland. The Danish stations at Waterford, Cork, and Limerick made invasion at all times easy, and the sons of Ivar bid fair to found a lasting dynasty at the latter place. There was a tax-gatherer in every petty district, a receiver to intercept the dues of every church, a[Pg 22] soldier billeted in every house, 'so that none of the men of Erin ... had power to give even the milk of his cow, nor as much as the clutch of eggs of one hen in succour or in kindness to an aged man, or to a friend, but was forced to preserve them for the foreign steward, or bailiff, or soldier. And though there were but one milk-giving cow in the house she durst not be milked for an infant of one night, nor for a sick person, but must be kept for the steward, or bailiff, or soldier of the foreigners. And however long he might be absent from his house, his share or his supply durst not be lessened; although there was in the house but one cow, it must be killed for the meal of the night, if the means of a supply could not be otherwise procured.'[19]

Succession to the kingdom of Cashel.

At last a deliverer arose. According to the will of Olioll Olum, King of Munster in the third century—such is the theory—the sovereignty of Cashel, that is of Munster, was to belong alternately to the races of his two sons, Eoghan Mor and Cormac Cas. The Eoghanachts and Dal Cais are generally Anglicised as the Eugenians and Dalcassians; the strength of the former and much stronger tribe being in Cork, Limerick, and Kerry—that of the latter in Clare. The Eugenian Fergraidh was king in 967, when he was murdered by his own people. Mahon the Dalcassian then became king, in compliance with the constitutional theory, but not without a struggle. Urged on by his brother Brian, he attacked the Danish settlements up and down the country, and became master of Cashel, when Ivar, finding his supremacy threatened, summoned all that would obey him to root out utterly the whole Dalcassian race.

Molloy, Mahon, and Brian.

The tribes of Western Munster generally were disposed to follow Mahon, but Molloy, King of Desmond, and some others, adhered to the Dane rather than admit the supremacy of a local rival. A pitched battle took place at Solloghead, near Tipperary, in which the foreigners and their allies were totally defeated. Molloy and other chiefs who had taken the losing side were forced to give hostages to the victor. Mahon burned Limerick and drove away Ivar, who returned[Pg 23] after a year with a great fleet, and fixed his head-quarters on Scattery Island, where St. Senanus had so sternly resisted the blandishments of a female saint.

Murder of Mahon. Brian succeeds him.

For some years Mahon reigned undisputed King of Munster, but his successes only stimulated the jealousies of Molloy and the other Eugenian chiefs, who saw their race reduced to play an inferior part. They accordingly conspired with Ivar, and Molloy procured the treacherous murder of Mahon. The crime was useless, for Brian was left, and he immediately succeeded both to the leadership of his own tribe and to the kingdom of Munster, Molloy having certainly forfeited all moral claim to the alternate succession. Brian pursued the Danes to their strongholds, slew Ivar and his sons, and carried off the women and the treasure. There was, however, still a Scandinavian settlement at Limerick, and we find a grandson of Ivar afterwards in Brian's service as one of the ten Danish stewards whom he employed. He was ambitious, and he had experience of the skill of such officers in extorting contributions from unwilling subjects. Molloy and his chief allies were slain; and Brian, having reduced the Limerick Danes to insignificance, turned his arm against those of Waterford, whose territory he ravaged, and whose Celtic allies, inhabiting the modern county of Waterford, he easily subdued. Brian was acknowledged as supreme in Munster, and took security from the principal churches not to give sanctuary to thieves or rebels. As the consequence of further expeditions Leinster also became tributary; and thus, in eight years after his brother's death, Brian was admitted to be supreme in the southern half of Ireland.

Brian aims at being King of all Ireland.

In his further expeditions, undertaken with a view of becoming King of all Ireland, the Danes of Waterford sometimes accompanied Brian; but his progress towards the desired goal was arrested for a while by a prudent treaty with Malachi II., head King of Ireland, whom he acknowledged as undisputed sovereign of the northern half, and by a revolt of the Leinster men, who were allied with the Danes of Dublin, the united forces of Brian and Malachi having overthrown the Leinster Danes at Glenmama, near Dunlavin,[Pg 24] Dublin fell an easy prey. The spoils taken are represented as enormous, and the mention of carbuncles and other precious stones, of buffalo-horns, goblets, and many-coloured vestures, betoken some degree of luxury and much commercial activity among the Danes. It is to be observed that Brian and his followers, though Christians, had no scruple about making slaves. His panegyrists simply say that the Danes by their cruelty and oppression had deserved no better treatment. Threshing and other rough work was done by the male prisoners. Menial work, including the severe labour of the hand-mill, was done by the women. 'There was not,' we are told, 'a winnowing sheet from Howth to the furthest point of Kerry that had not a foreigner in bondage on it, nor was there a quern without a foreign woman.' The fairer and more accomplished of the Danish women of course underwent the fate of Chryseis.

Brian and the Danes, Gormflaith.
Having in vain sought a refuge with the northern Irish, Sitric was forced to submit to Brian, who reinstated him at Dublin as a tributary king. Sitric's mother, Gormflaith, or Kormlada, was sister to Maelmordha, King of Leinster, and her husband, King Olaf, having been dead many years, she was free to marry Brian, which she did soon after, while Brian's daughter married Sitric. Wielding thus the whole force of southern Ireland, Brian called upon Malachi to acknowledge his supremacy. The King of Ireland sought aid in vain from his kinsmen, the northern Hy Neill, whose king Aedh, or Hugh, sarcastically remarked that when his clan had held the chief kingship they had known how to defend their own. No help coming from Connaught either, Malachi was forced to submit to Brian's power, and though no formal cession took place the King of Ireland quietly subsided into King of Meath.

Brian, King of all Ireland, 1002.
Brian was henceforth reckoned as monarch of Ireland. He invaded Connaught with a flotilla on the Shannon and an army marching on land, and the chiefs of the western province were glad to give hostages. The Ulster potentates falling out among themselves, the north also was easily subdued, and Brian became the actual lord paramount of Ireland.[Pg 25] After this he made a tour round the island, starting from the Shannon and marching through Roscommon and over the Curlew mountains into Sligo. Hugging the coast by Ballyshannon to Donegal, he crossed Barnesmore Gap into Tyrone, and then passing the Foyle, near Lifford, he went through Londonderry, Antrim, Down, and Louth, to the neighbourhood of Kells. In a previous expedition he had visited Armagh and laid twenty ounces of gold on the altar. A fleet, manned by the Danes of Dublin, Limerick, and Waterford, seems to have circumnavigated Ireland while he was making the circuit by land.

Brian's supremacy a loose one. Gormflaith's intrigues.
The supremacy of Brian was no doubt an extremely loose one. He had made no real impression on the northern tribes, and they only waited a favourable opportunity to cast off the nominal yet galling yoke. But for about seven years there seems to have been no serious attempt against him, and he was able to turn his attention to the building of churches and bridges. It was during this period that a lone woman is said to have walked unmolested from the Bloody Foreland to Glandore with a gold ring at the end of a wand. Peace, however, there was not; for Brian was engaged in at least two warlike expeditions to Ulster, and there was a fair amount of murder and private war among the minor chiefs. Brian had repudiated Gormflaith, Maelmordha's sister and Sitric's mother, and probably not without good reason, for her moral character was by no means on a par with her beauty and talents, since she had been married successively to Olaf Cuaran and to Malachi II., and had been repudiated by both. 'She was,' says the Saga, 'the fairest of all women, and best gifted in everything that was not in her power, but it was the talk of men that she did all things ill over which she had any power.' Brian afterwards married a daughter of the King of Connaught, and when she died, Gormflaith may have sought to be reinstated. At all events she was at Kincora when her brother arrived, bringing with him the tribute of Leinster. Her taunts, and a quarrel which he had with Murrough, Brian's eldest son,

provoked Maelmordha to leave Kincora in anger, and to raise the standard of revolt.[Pg 26] 'Gormflaith,' says the Saga, 'was so grim against King Brian after their parting, that she would gladly have him dead, and egged on her son Sitric very much to kill him.' Sitric readily agreed to Maelmordha's proposal, and so did the northern Hy Neill, who had never been really conquered, and who at once invaded Meath. After a gallant struggle against Leinster and Ulster, Malachi was overpowered, and called upon Brian for help. The King of Ireland, to whom the men of Connaught remained faithful, accordingly ravaged the country between his own district and Dublin, but was obliged to retire from before its walls for want of provisions.[20]

Alliance of Sitric and Gormflaith against Brian.

Sitric and Gormflaith made use of the breathing space allowed them to organise a powerful confederacy against Brian. Sitric himself went to Sigurd, Earl of Orkney, who, after many refusals, at last agreed to join, on condition of receiving the Crown of Ireland and Gormflaith's land. 'All his men,' says the Saga, 'besought Earl Sigurd not to go into the war, but it was all to no good.' Gormflaith was well pleased at the prospect before her, and advised large preparations for the inevitable struggle.

Sitric's allies. Sigurd. Brodir.

Sigurd was nominally a Christian, but he reposed his chief trust in the raven banner which his mother had woven with mighty spells; and many Scandinavian warriors were still fanatically attached to Thor and Woden. The Vikings, Ospak and Brodir, were lying off Man, and to them Sitric next addressed himself in person. The Norsemen do not seem to have insisted on youth in their wives, for Brodir was induced to join by the same promises which had been made to Sigurd, and Gormflaith's first husband had been dead thirty-three years. 'Brodir,' says the Icelandic account, 'had been a Christian man and a mass deacon, but he had thrown off his faith and become God's dastard, and now worshipped heathen fiends, and was of all men most skilled in sorcery. He had the coat of mail on which no steel would bite. He was both tall and strong, and had such long[Pg 27] locks that he tucked them under his belt. His hair was black.'[21]

Conflict between Christianity and Paganism.

Ospak, who had leanings towards Christianity, refused to attack Brian; indeed, he went over to him, and, according to Norse accounts, was baptized. An immense force was, however, gradually collected, and Scandinavian contingents are mentioned from Northumbria, under two Earls, from Norway, from Orkney and Shetland, Skye and Lewis, from Cantire, Argyle, and Galloway. Welshmen from Pembrokeshire and Cornwall, Frenchmen, that is in all probability French Normans, under Karl and Ebric, and some Flemings under a knight are also spoken of. Romans even are mentioned, but this may be mere magniloquence. To oppose this motley host Brian had the men of Munster, Meath, and South-eastern Connaught, and the Danes of Limerick and probably of Waterford. He may have had the numerical superiority, for Sigurd told his mother, the wise woman, that he expected to be outnumbered seven to one. The eve of the battle of Clontarf was signalised, according to the annalists, by various supernatural occurrences. A messenger from St. Senanus appeared to the king, and prophesied his death as the penalty due for violating the sanctuary on Scattery Island thirty-seven years before. The interests and prejudices of monastic chroniclers may account for this story, but it is not so easy to explain the firm belief in pagan deities, in fairies, in demons, and in satyrs shown by two independent historians. It is evident that the oracles of heathenism were not supposed to have been dumb more than 500 years after the death of Patrick, and 400 after that of Columba. Nor was there any lack of marvels on the Danish side. Brodir, who had already been plagued by showers of boiling blood, by supernatural noises, by deaths among his men, and by ravens with beaks and claws of iron, 'tried by sorcery how the fight would go. And the answer ran, that if the fight were on Good Friday, King Brian would fall but win the day; but if they fought before, they would all fall that were against him.'[22]

[Pg 28]

Battle of Clontarf, 1014.

The battle was fought upon the fateful Friday, and Brian refused to take part in it because the day was holy. He remained in the rear protected by a ring of soldiers with their shields locked together. It was observed that the successive bearers of the raven banner all fell, and Hrafn the red, who was called by Sigurd to the dangerous duty, refused, saying, 'Bear thine own devil thyself.' "'Tis fittest that the beggar should bear the bag,' answered the Earl, and put the banner under his cloak. Sigurd fell, and Sitric had to retire before Ospak. Hrafn the red flew to a river into which the devils wished to drag him, but a spoken spell dispersed them. 'Thy dog,' he cried, 'Apostle Peter, hath run twice to Rome, and he would run the third time if thou gavest him leave.' Of Thorstein we are told that he interrupted his flight to tie his shoe. Kerthialfad, Brian's foster son, asked him why he lingered at such a critical moment, and the Northman returned an answer worthy of Sparta's best days—'Because I can't get home to-night, since I am at home out in Iceland.'[23]

Death of Brian.

In the moment of victory Brian was left behind, and Brodir, who had lingered for a time in a thicket, broke through the line of shields and hewed off the king's head. The Viking was taken and disembowelled alive, according to the Norse account, but the Irish writers say that he fell by Brian's hands. Sigurd being already dead, Gormflaith lost all chance of a royal husband, and it is only further recorded of her that she died sixteen years later. Many other chiefs fell, including Maelmordha, and Murrough, Brian's favourite son, and the fight was followed, as it had been heralded, by many signs and wonders both in the Celtic and in the Scandinavian world.

The Danes were not expelled.

The popular delusion that the battle of Clontarf caused the expulsion of the Danes from Ireland must be pretty well dissipated by this time. Sitric remained with reserves within the fortress, and thus saved his kingdom; nor do the annalists cease to make frequent mention of the foreigners. But the defeat was great, and may have had considerable in[Pg 29]fluence in deciding those who were already hovering between Woden and Jesus. Fourteen years after Clontarf we find Sitric going to Rome, and his son Olaf was killed in England when attempting the same pilgrimage. These facts lend some countenance to the legend that Sitric founded Christ Church in 1038; for the Roman court well knew how to impress the rude northern warriors, and to profit in various ways by their simple faith. We are told that Flosi the Icelander went to Rome to cleanse himself from the stain of blood-guiltiness, 'where,' says the Njal-Saga, 'he gat so great honour that he took absolution from the Pope himself, and for that he gave a great sum of money.'

But they soon accepted Christianity.

Without actually amalgamating, the Danes seem to have drawn gradually closer to the native Irish. A royal heir of Ulster received the name of Ragnal less than half a century after Clontarf, and in 1121 a bishop seems to have been temporarily appointed at Dublin by the joint election of Irish and Danes. But quarrels were frequent even after the Danes had become fully Christianised; and when the men of Munster invaded Fingal in 1133, they burned the church of Lusk when it was full of people and treasures. Nor did fresh invasions quite cease, for Magnus, King of Norway, made two expeditions to Ireland, in the latter of which, in 1103, he lost his life. The separate history of the Irish Ostmen was drawing to a close, even at the date of the Anglo-Norman invasion; but they have left indelible traces upon the map of Ireland and on the traditional lore of her people.

The Danes were traders.

Giraldus informs us that the Scandinavians who settled at Dublin, Waterford, and Limerick, came under pretence of peaceful trading. The Irish, he says, were prevented by their innate sloth from going down to the sea in ships, but were ready to welcome those who would trade for them, and thus allowed the fierce strangers to get a strong footing. However this may be, it is certain that the Irish are deficient in maritime enterprise, and equally certain that the Northmen had a constant eye to trade as well as to war and plunder. Unerring instinct pointed out the best stations, and on the sites thus chosen the chief cities of Ireland were reared. The[Pg 30] Kaupmannaeyjar or merchant isles, probably those now called the Copelands, may have been a rendezvous for passing vessels. Arabic coins, of which more than 20,000 pieces from more than 1,000 different dies are preserved at Stockholm, have been found in Ireland, and the Irish Northmen certainly had a coinage of their own, when the native princes had none. Pieces have been found which were struck by, or at least for, a Scandinavian king of Dublin as early as the ninth century, and all coins minted in Ireland up to the Anglo-Norman invasion were perhaps of similar origin. Many such pieces have been found in the Isle of Man, and some as far off as Denmark.[24]

They were superior to the Irish in peaceful arts.

The Irish annalists constantly dwell on the superiority of Norse arms and armour as a reason for their success in war. Ringmail in particular shows a high degree of manufacturing skill, and they wore it at Clontarf both in brass and iron, while none is mentioned in the pompous Irish catalogue of the arms worn by Brian's troops. Nor was this costly harness worn only by the Scandinavian leaders, for they are said to have had 1,000 coats of mail in that one battle. Danish swords which have survived from Brian's days are of superior workmanship to Irish blades of the same date; and the Northmen had perhaps a superiority in bows also, though on this point the annalists are less explicit. The turgid verbosity of these writers makes it doubtful whether the Danes used poisoned arrows, but no such thing is mentioned in the Saga.

They built the first cities. Dublin, Waterford.

The flotillas which Brian maintained on inland waters, and the sea-going vessels which attended his army in the North, were all manned by Danes, and a mercantile marine has in every age been the best nursery of naval power. No doubt the Irish felt the advantage of having commercial emporiums on their coast, as other shore-going people profited by Greek and Phœnician colonies. The analogy might easily be carried further, and Dublin and Waterford might be represented as standing between the Anglo-Normans and Celts of Ireland, as Massilia stood between the Romans and Celts of[Pg 31] Gaul. It is at all events clear that the Scandinavians built the first cities and coined the first money in Ireland.

Brian's monarchy soon fell to pieces.

High as Brian towers above other mediæval Celts—one annalist calls him the Charlemagne of North-western Europe—it cannot be said that he laid the foundation of an Irish monarchy. He lived to be eighty, yet none of his work lasted. Malachi received the honorary office of chief king, from which his rival's personal prowess had driven him, and the years of his reign are counted by some annalists without noticing Brian's intervention, as in the modern case of Charles II. Brian was indeed doubly a usurper, in wresting Munster from the race of Eoghan, and in wresting Ireland from the race of Nial, in whom royalty had been vested for centuries. With all his ceaseless exertions he was little more than a levier of black mail, who left intact the internal government of weaker princes. Borumha, or the tribute-taker, if that be really the meaning of the term, describes his position with sufficient accuracy. When he died Donnchadh, or Donogh, his son by Gormflaith, became head of his tribe, and claimed the succession to the Irish monarchy. The Eugenians repudiated his claim, alleging that their turn, which had been wrongfully passed over, had now come to reign in Munster. Not satisfied with this, their two principal chiefs fell out among themselves. The Ossorian followed suit, and thus Brian's creation crumbled at once into dust.

More than 150 years elapsed between the battle of Clontarf and the landing of the first Anglo-Norman, and they were years of almost constant war and confusion. Had Ireland been left to herself a prince might in time have arisen strong enough to establish such a monarchy as Brian failed to found. The Danes had ceased to be a seriously disturbing influence, but there is no evidence that any such process of consolidation was going on, and a feudal system, which had lost none of its vigour, was at last confronted with a tribal system which had lost none of its inherent weakness.

Progress of Christianity.

It is impossible to fix the exact date when Christianity began to make head against the Irish Ostmen. When St. Anschar obtained from the Swedes a place for his God in[Pg 32] the northern pantheon, and when Guthrum and his officers submitted to baptism in Wessex, a foundation had been laid for a general Scandinavian conversion. But neither Norway nor the Norwegian colonies in Iceland, Shetland, Orkney, or the Hebrides, yielded so soon. Irish anchorites spent some time in Iceland about 795, and when Ingulf and Lief landed in 870 they found that Irish priests had lately been there, and had left behind them books, bells, and croziers. The second batch had probably fled from Ingulf's congeners in Ireland. Olaf Trygvesson, the first Christian king of Norway, was educated at Athelstane's court, and the nominal conversion of Norway may date from the year of his accession. Five years later, in 1000, Christianity was established by law in Iceland. Removed as she was from English or Roman influences, Ireland remained a stronghold of paganism after the Danes of England had been generally converted; and the Irish being on the whole weaker in war, were scarcely in a position to prove that Woden and Thor had nothing to say for themselves. Olaf Cuaran was baptized in England. It is clear that the Irish Danes remained generally pagan throughout the tenth century, and that the confederacy which failed at Clontarf had to a great extent been formed against Christianity. The story of Ospak and Brodir shows that some of the fiercest Danes were beginning to waver, the question at issue being the relative power of two deities, rather than the relative merit of two systems. After Clontarf Woden seems to have been looked upon as beaten. He had been tried and found wanting, like Baal on Mount Carmel, and the defeated party went over to the stronger side.

The Danish church of Dublin.

The connection of the Dublin Danes with their brethren in England had long been very close, and it was to Canterbury and Rome rather than to Armagh that they naturally turned. Sitric and Canute were perhaps in the Eternal City together; their visit was at least almost simultaneous, and we cannot doubt that every means were taken to prejudice the powerful neophyte against the pretensions of St. Patrick's successor. An Ostman named Dunan or Donat is reckoned the first Bishop of Dublin, and is credited with the foundation of Christ[Pg 33] Church. A tradition which may be true, but which is not supported by contemporary evidence, makes Sitric the joint founder. From an expression in the celebrated letter of the Dublin burgesses to Archbishop Ralph d'Eures it may be fairly inferred that Donat had his succession from Canterbury, and he certainly corresponded with Lanfranc on the subject of infant baptism. He was succeeded by Patrick or Gillapatrick, an Ostman, who was consecrated by Lanfranc in St. Paul's at the instance of Godred Crovan, king of Man, who was then supreme at Dublin. Godred's reign is rather shadowy, but Lanfranc's letter to him has always been considered genuine, and it addresses him as king not only of Dublin, but of Ireland. Lanfranc also wrote to Tirlogh, who had acquired the supreme kingship, like his father, Brian Borumha. It is not unlikely that the curious poem which represents St. Patrick as blessing Dublin and its Danish inhabitants, and cursing the Hy Neill, was forged at this time, partly in the Munster interest and partly to prove that Dublin was not subject to Armagh.[25]

Dublin acknowledges Canterbury and repudiates Armagh.

In his letters Lanfranc insists much upon Catholic unity. According to modern ideas, the heaviest of the charges which he brings against the Irish Church is the levity with which they regarded the marriage tie. It appears that men even exchanged wives. Bishop Patrick promised ecclesiastical fealty to the Archbishop of Canterbury, as Primate of the British Isles. Lanfranc had obeyed the order of his old pupil Alexander II., who was prompted by the deacon Hildebrand, and had gone to Rome to receive his pall. But in his dealings with Dublin he acted independently, and he was ready to give advice to Irish prelates, though without claiming direct jurisdiction over them. In doctrinal matters he was an ally of Rome. Himself an Italian, he espoused the dogma of transubstantiation in opposition to the Irishman Erigena, and the Frenchman Berengarius; and on the great question of clerical celibacy he was a follower, though not an extreme one, of the uncompromising Hildebrand. The ever-watchful Roman Court probably espied the germ of a Western[Pg 34] patriarchate, and was thus moved to annex Armagh as a counterpoise to the dangerous primacy claimed under a grant of Gregory the Great by the successors of Augustine. Gregory VII., in addressing the kings, nobles, and prelates of Ireland, took care to claim absolute sovereignty by divine right; and here he ran little risk of such a rebuff as William the Conqueror administered.[26]

Lanfranc and Anselm.

Patrick's successor was Donat O'Haingly, an Irishman, but a Benedictine monk of Canterbury, who was consecrated by Lanfranc, to whom he had been recommended by King Tirlogh. He was succeeded by his nephew Samuel, a Benedictine of St. Albans, who was consecrated by Anselm. That great archbishop was not altogether pleased with his Irish brother, whom he chid for alienating vestments bestowed on the Church of Dublin by Lanfranc, and for having the cross borne before him, although he had never received the pall. A further element of confusion was introduced, probably in 1118, by the Irish synod of Rathbreasil, which declared Dublin to be in the diocese of Glendalough; and it seems that the Irish inhabitants submitted, while those of Danish origin refused to do so.

Ralph of Canterbury consecrates Gregory, who receives the pall from Pope Eugenius.

On the death of Bishop Samuel O'Haingly, the Irish annals inform us that 'Cellach, comarb of Patrick, assumed the bishopric of Ath-cliath,[27] by the choice of foreigners and Gaeidhil.' If there be any truth in this it was a bold stroke on the part of Armagh to exercise jurisdiction in Dublin, and was probably the act of the Irish as opposed to the Danish party. In the same year, or the next, the burgesses and clergy of Dublin wrote to Ralph of Canterbury, begging him to consecrate their nominee Gregory. They reminded him that their bishops originally derived their dignity from his predecessors, and that the bishops of Ireland were very jealous of them; and especially he of Armagh, because they preferred the rule of Canterbury. Ralph consecrated Gregory, and he[Pg 35] governed the see for forty years. To his lot it fell to receive the pall sent by Pope Eugenius, who was too politic to insist on a visit to Rome. For the moment it was enough to assert the necessity of the pallium and its papal origin. The legate Paparo ignored the pretensions of the bishop whose church in the mountains had the name of city, and divided the diocese into two parts: the bishop with the Cantuarian succession being made Metropolitan, and the Irishman at Glendalough being reduced to the position of a suffragan. St. Lawrence O'Toole, who was the second Archbishop of Dublin, derived his succession from Armagh, and the Scandinavian Church of Dublin ceases to have a separate history.

See of Waterford.

Of far less importance than that of Dublin, the early history of the see of Waterford is proportionately obscure. Malchus, a Benedictine of Winchester, who seems to have been the first bishop elected by the Ostmen, was consecrated by Anselm; to whom he promised canonical obedience, and with whom he corresponded. It seems likely that he was afterwards translated to Lismore, or he may have held both sees together, as they were held in after years. It is probable that the great Malachi of Armagh studied under him. Maelisa O'Hanmire appears next in succession, but we know nothing of him. He may have represented a reaction against the dominion of Canterbury. The next name preserved is that of Tosti, who was, of course, a Dane, and who assisted in the establishment of the papal or Eugenian constitution. Tosti's successor, Augustine O'Sealbhaigh, was practically appointed by Henry II., and he attended the Lateran Council in 1179.

See of Limerick. Gillebert.

The tradition which connects St. Patrick with Limerick is of the vaguest kind: practically, the first recorded bishop is Gillebert. He was an Irishman. Cellach of Armagh acted with the Bishop of Limerick on this occasion; but while both were anxious to parcel out Ireland into dioceses, neither ventured to interfere with Dublin, which was under the powerful patronage of Canterbury. Gillebert resigned both the legatine authority and his own bishopric before his death, which took place in or about 1145. His successor[Pg 36] Patrick, having been elected by the Ostmen, was consecrated in England by Theobald, Archbishop of Canterbury, to whom he promised canonical obedience. The three following bishops, Harold, Turgeis, and Brictius, who may be Elbric or Eric, were doubtless all Ostmen. Very little is known of them, except that the last named attended the Lateran Council in 1179 and 1180.

See of Cork.

Cork was often plundered by the Northmen, and they settled there permanently early in the eleventh century. But they found themselves confronted by a strong monastic organisation, under the successor of St. Finbar, whereas at Dublin, Waterford, and Limerick the field had been clear. Around the abbey a native town had sprung up, which was strong enough to maintain itself by the side of the Scandinavian garrison. Once, with the help of a force from Carbery, they defeated a confederacy of Danes belonging to Cork, Waterford, and Wexford. The Ostmen were in quiet possession of Cork for a period long preceding the Anglo-Norman invasion, but they were probably content to take their Christianity from their neighbours, for we do not find that any bishop of this see sought consecration at Canterbury.[28]

FOOTNOTES:

[16] The account which Giraldus gives of Turgesius is funny, but worthless.

[17] Reeves's Adamnan, p. 332 n.

[18] Wars of the Gaedhill with the Gaill, chap. xxxvi.

[19] Wars of the Gaedhill with the Gaill, chap. xl.

[20] The quotations are from Burnt Njal, chap. cliii.

[21] Burnt Njal, chap. cliv.

[22] Ibid., chap. clvi. Wars of the Gaedhill with the Gaill, chaps. xcviii. and xcix. Annals of Lough Cé, pp. 7-13.

[23] Burnt Njal, chap. clvi.

[24] Many details about the Hiberno-Norse coins are to be found in Worsaae.

[25] Book of Rights, pp. 225 sqq., and O'Donovan's preface.

[26] See Hook's Lives of Lanfranc, Anselm, and Ralph d'Eures. Translations of the letters mentioned in the text may be found in King's Primer of the Irish Church; most of the originals are printed in Ussher's Sylloge.

[27] The Irish always called Dublin Ath-cliath, or the Ford of Hurdles.

[28] The great mine of knowledge about the Irish Scandinavians is Todd's Wars of the Gaedhill with the Gaill, in the Record series. I have also used Dasent's Story of Burnt Njal, and Anderson's Orkneyinga Saga. Haliday's Scandinavian Kingdom of Dublin, edited by Mr. J. P. Prendergast, is a good modern book. Worsaae's Danes and Norwegians is said to be somewhat fanciful, but it contains information not readily accessible elsewhere.

[Pg 37]

IRELAND IN 1172
CHAPTER III.

THE REIGN OF HENRY II.

England lays claim to Ireland, 1155.

The claims of the Kings of England to Ireland were very vague. They sometimes acted as patrons of the Irish Ostmen, who were not unwilling to follow the example of their Northumbrian kinsmen, but they performed no real function of sovereignty. William the Conqueror and his sons had not time to attend to Ireland, and this applies in an even greater degree to Stephen. Henry II. ascended an undisputed throne, and in the first year of his reign turned his thoughts to the fertile island of the West. Being badly in want of a title, he sent John of Salisbury to Rome for leave to conquer Ireland, to root up the saplings of vice there, and to bring the wild Irish into the way of the true faith. The Pope was Nicholas Breakspeare, known in history as Adrian IV., the only Englishman who ever filled the papal chair. The popes were usually ready to grant boons to kings, if by so doing they could extend their own power, and an English pope must have felt a double pride in conferring favours on a king of England. The mission of John of Salisbury was successful. He brought back the Bull Laudabiliter and a gold ring containing a very fine emerald, intended to be used in Henry's investiture. Empress Maude objected to an Irish expedition, and nothing was done until long after Adrian's death. Henry took the precaution of having the grant confirmed by Alexander III., and there is ample evidence that he annexed Ireland with the entire approbation of that Pope.[29]

Adrian IV grants Ireland to Henry II.

Irish scholars, torn asunder by their love of Rome and their love of Ireland, formerly attempted to prove that[Pg 38] Adrian's bull was not genuine; but its authenticity is no longer disputed. The momentous document runs as follows:—

Adrian's bull.

'Hadrian the bishop, servant of the servants of God, to his very dear son in Christ, the illustrious King of the English, health and apostolic benediction:

'Your magnificence praiseworthily and profitably takes thought how to increase a glorious name on earth and how to lay up a reward of everlasting happiness in heaven, while you are intent, like a Catholic prince, on enlarging the bounds of the Church, on declaring the truth to unlearned and rude peoples, and on uprooting the seedlings of vice from the Lord's field. The better to attain that end you have asked counsel and favour of the apostolic see. In which action we are sure that, with God's help, you will make happy progress in proportion to the high design and great discretion of your proceedings, inasmuch as undertakings which grow out of ardour for the faith and love of religion are accustomed always to have a good end and upshot. There is no doubt and your nobility acknowledges that Ireland, and all islands upon which Christ the sun of justice has shone, and which have received the teachings of the Christian faith, rightfully belong to the blessed Peter and the most holy Roman Church. We have, therefore, the more willingly made a faithful plantation among them, and inserted a bud pleasing to God, in that we foresee that it will require a careful internal watch at our hands. However, you have signified to us, my dear son in Christ, that you wish to enter the island of Ireland, in order to reduce that people to law, and to uproot the seedlings of vice there, and to make a yearly payment of a denarius to the blessed Peter out of each house, and to preserve the rights of the churches of that land whole and undiminished.

'We, therefore, seconding your pious and laudable desire with suitable favour, and giving a kindly assent to your petition, do hold it for a thing good and acceptable that you should enter that island for the extension of the Church's borders, for the correction of manners, for the propagation[Pg 39] of virtue, and for increase of the Christian religion; and that you should perform that which you intend for the honour of God and for the salvation of that land; and let the people of that land receive you honourably and venerate you as their lord; the ecclesiastical law remaining whole and untouched, and an annual payment of one denarius being reserved to the blessed Peter and to the most holy Roman Church. But if you shall complete the work which you have conceived in your mind, study to mould that race to good morals, and exert yourself personally and by such of your agents as you shall find fit in faith, word, and living, to honour the Church there, and to plant and increase the Christian faith, and strive to ordain what is for the honour of God and the safety of souls in such a manner that you may deserve at God's hands a heap of everlasting treasure, and on earth gain a glorious name for ages yet to come.'

The papal title.
The right of the Pope to dispose of islands rested upon the donation of Constantine, which is now admitted to be as certainly spurious as Adrian's bull is certainly genuine. Adrian may have believed the donation authentic, but in any case, as Irish scholars point out, Constantine could not give what he had never possessed. It is true that Ireland never really formed part of the Roman Empire, but so strong was the idea of an œcumenical sovereignty that Celtic lawyers imagined a state of things in which Ireland would be tributary to the King of the Romans. This was a mere fiction, but it was one of which Rome would readily take advantage, and the Pope who insisted so sturdily on Barbarossa holding his stirrup was not the one in whose hands any available weapon would be allowed to rust.[30]

Henry II. finds a pretext for interference.
Henry II. was the most powerful prince in Europe, and sooner or later he was almost sure to have a reason for interfering in Ireland. The opportunity was at last afforded by Dermod MacMurrough, King of Leinster, who aspired to reign over all Ireland with the help of Anglo-Norman arms. As early as 1152 Dervorgil O'Melaghlin,

wife of Tiernan O'Rourke, Prince of Brefny, being ill-treated by her husband,[Pg 40] left him, and placed herself, her cattle, and her furniture under the protection of Dermod. Dervorgil was forty-four and Dermod sixty-two, so that the affair, in spite of a beautiful poem on the subject, was not what would be commonly called romantic. Yet Cleopatra was thirty-nine, when Antonius, at the age of fifty-three, refused to survive her. O'Rourke felt the insult and the loss of the lady, or, at least, of her property, and appealed to Tirlogh O'Connor, King of Connaught and titular King of Ireland. Dermod was compelled to abandon Dervorgil, who survived her husband eleven years, and died as late as 1193, during a pilgrimage to Mellifont Abbey. On the death of Tirlogh O'Connor his son Roderic became a candidate for the chief sovereignty, but Dermod espoused the cause of the O'Neill candidate, who was successful. The flight or abduction of Dervorgil was certainly not the proximate cause of the Norman invasion, but by placing Dermod in permanent opposition to O'Connor and O'Rourke, it probably contributed to bring it about.

Dermod MacMurrough.

In 1166 Dermod, who had made himself odious by his tyranny, was expelled from Leinster by O'Connor and O'Rourke, who demolished his stronghold at Ferns, and transferred his kingship to the next-of-kin. The clergy appear to have been generally favourable to Dermod; and as Adrian's bull, even if not published, could hardly be a secret, it may have been their advice which induced him to go to Henry II. Dermod, though seventy-seven years old, was still active and enterprising, and he sought the king in Aquitaine or Guienne. Henry was too busy to think of going to Ireland himself, but he gave the suppliant a kind of letter of marque in the following terms:—'Henry, King of England, Duke of Normandy and Aquitaine, and Count of Anjou, to all his faithful English, Norman, Welsh, and Scots, and to all nations subject to his jurisdiction, greeting: When these present letters reach you you will know that we have received into the bosom of our grace and favour Dermod, prince of the Leinstermen. If anyone, therefore, within the bounds of our power wishes to help his restoration[Pg 41] as our man and liege subject, let him know that he has our licence and favour for the purpose.'[31]

Dermod seeks allies in England.

Thus armed, Dermod returned to Bristol, which was much frequented by ships from Leinster, and he appears to have been supplied with money by his partisans there. His promise of gold and land at first attracted little attention, but after two or three weeks he was visited by Richard Fitz-Gilbert de Clare, Earl of Chepstow. Earl Richard, whose father had lost most of his lands, lent a favourable ear to Dermod, and undertook to bring an army to Ireland in the spring of 1169. The Irishman promised to give him his daughter Eva, his only legitimate child. According to Norman law Eva would bring the kingdom of Leinster to her husband and children. According to Celtic law the lands belonged to the tribe, and the royal dignity was elective. In this singular contract between MacMurrough and Fitz-Gilbert, we have the key to most of the problems which have made Ireland the despair of statesmen.

Earl Richard and his friends.

Dermod, however, did not rest his hopes of success upon Earl Richard alone. He went to St. David's, so as to be as near Ireland as possible, and made friends with the bishop, who had two brothers admirably suited for the work in hand. Nesta, the beautiful daughter of Rice ap Tudor, Prince of South Wales, is reported to have been the mistress of Henry I., and to have had two sons by him. The younger of these had also two sons, the Robert and Meiler Fitz-Henry who played a prominent part in the conquest of Ireland. Nesta afterwards married Gerald of Windsor, by whom she had three sons and one or two daughters, and from one or other of her children all the Fitzgeralds, Barrys, Carews, and Cogans are descended. After the death of Gerald, Nesta married Stephen, the castellan of Abertivy, and by him had one son, the famous Robert Fitz-Stephen. Giraldus, who must have known, twice states expressly that Fitz-Stephen had no legitimate child. The historian himself was Nesta's grandson, through her daughter Angareta, who married William de Barry. Robert Fitz-Stephen, and his half-[Pg 42]brother, Maurice Fitzgerald, listened readily to MacMurrough, who promised them Wexford and two cantreds of land, if they would help him conquer Leinster.[32]

Fitz-Stephen and others land in Ireland, 1169.

Robert Fitz-Stephen was a desperate man. Betrayed by his own followers, he had suffered three years' imprisonment among the Welsh, had been released on promising to serve Rice Fitz-Griffith against Henry II., and had agreed to hold Abertivy for the Cambrian and not for the Angevin. Dermod now offered him a loophole to escape from, and he agreed to accept his offers and to invade Ireland. His half-brother, Maurice Fitzgerald, consented to accompany him. Dermod then slipped over to Ireland and sought a refuge among the clergy of Ferns, who entertained him, as the Archdeacon of St. David's carefully notes, to the best of their small ability. It was in the winter of 1168 that MacMurrough returned to Ireland, and in May 1169 Fitz-Stephen and his brother followed with thirty knights of their own kinfolk, sixty men-at-arms, and 300 archers, picked, as Giraldus says, from among the youth of Wales. Three ships carried them all, and they landed safely in Bannow Bay, a shallow inlet which they had probably mistaken either for Waterford or Wexford. The brothers were accompanied by Hervey de Montmorency, who was sent by his nephew, Earl Richard, rather as a spy than as a soldier. On the following day Maurice de Prendergast, whose name still lives at Haverfordwest, brought ten knights and a number of archers from Milford, and landed not far from the same place. As soon as Dermod heard of the adventurers' arrival he sent his son Donald with 500 men to welcome them, and soon followed himself. Donald, surnamed Kavanagh, from having been fostered at Kilcavan, was illegitimate; but that was a matter little considered among the old Irish, and he became the ancestor of those Kavanaghs or MacMurroughs who afterwards claimed the kingship of Leinster and even of Ireland, and who baffled Richard II. and his great army.

[Pg 43]

They win Wexford.

After a smart conflict Fitz-Stephen and MacMurrough mastered Wexford, which was a Danish town. The Irishman's readiness to grant Wexford to the adventurers was very probably caused by the fact that the town had never been really in his power. Perhaps he hoped to get rid of the Normans when he had used them to subdue his enemies. It was evident that Fitz-Stephen and his company could do little more than hold Wexford. If Leinster was to be conquered it could only be by a much larger force. Nevertheless, Fitz-Stephen decided to advance into the country, and was joined by the Wexford Danes, who probably were not slow to learn that the Normans were their kinsmen. With a heterogeneous army of 3,000 men, Dermod and his allies marched towards Ossory. There was a battle in open ground with the Ossorians, and the mail-clad stranger had an easy victory. Among the slain was a personal enemy of Dermod, and we are told that that savage, 'lifting up the dead man's head by hair and ears, cruelly and inhumanly tore away the nostrils and lips with his teeth.' In the meantime King Roderic had set his army in motion against the invaders, and easily penetrated to the neighbourhood of Ferns. The monastery was surrounded by woods and bogs, and Fitz-Stephen, who was an adept in Welsh warfare, taught the Leinstermen how to make it impregnable with ditches and abattis. Neither party were very anxious to fight, and Dermod made a treaty with Roderic, in which he acknowledged him as chief king, in consideration of being allowed to enjoy Leinster in peace. Giraldus says there was a secret understanding that the adventurers should be sent home as soon as they had pacified Leinster, and that no reinforcements should be brought over.

Earl Richard hesitates. His friends take Waterford.

Whatever understanding he might have with O'Connor, Dermod did not soon abandon the hope of more help from Wales. 'We have,' he wrote to Earl Richard, 'observed the storks and swallows; the summer birds have come, and with this west wind have returned. Neither Favonius nor Eurus has brought us your much-desired and long-expected presence.' The Earl had waited for the return of Hervey de[Pg 44] Montmorency, and when he brought a favourable report it was still necessary to make at least some show of consulting Henry II. The King had forbidden him to go to Ireland, but he now sought an audience and begged either the restoration of his estates or leave to carve out a new one for himself. Henry gave an ambiguous answer, which the Earl chose to interpret in his own favour. In May 1170 he sent out Hervey again, accompanied by Raymond Fitzgerald, called Le Gros, a creature of Fitz-Stephen and Maurice, with twenty knights and seventy archers. Raymond landed at the south-eastern angle of the modern county of Kilkenny, just at the point where the united Nore and Barrow flow into the Suir. He intrenched himself at once, and was soon attacked by the Waterford Danes. If Giraldus is to be believed, a panic seized the assailants, of whom 500 were killed, and many taken. Among Raymond's followers was a leper named William Ferrand, who performed prodigies of valour, 'choosing rather to die gloriously than to endure the burden of his disease.' A question arose as to the disposal of the prisoners. Raymond was for sparing, Hervey for slaying. 'The opinion of the latter,' says Giraldus, 'prevailed; the citizens were condemned, and, their limbs having been broken, they were cast headlong into the sea.'

Earl Richard lands, 1170.

Earl Richard landed near Waterford on August 23, 1170. The city was taken soon afterwards, and Reginald's tower is particularly mentioned as forming part of the defences. That tower still stands with one of Cromwell's cannon balls sticking in the wall—a monument of three distinct invaders: the Pagan Northman, the Catholic Anglo-Norman, and the Puritan Englishman. 'Earl Strongbow,' say the Lough Cé annalists with pathetic brevity, 'came into Erin to Dermod MacMurrough to avenge his expulsion by Roderic, son of Tirlogh O'Connor; and Dermod gave him his own daughter and a part of his patrimony; and Saxon foreigners have been in Erin since then.'

The adventurers take Dublin.

Waterford and Wexford having fallen, and his daughter Eva having been married to Earl Richard, Dermod, who now aspired to the crown of all Ireland, felt himself strong enough[Pg 45] to attack Dublin. The Earl had brought 200 knights and 1,000 other soldiers, so that the allied force was a considerable one. MacMurrough led the army safely through the Wicklow mountains, which were the scene of more than one disaster to Elizabeth's officers. Dermod's auxiliaries had been trained in Wales; and probably understood mountain warfare much better than those who had served in the Netherlands, or even on the Scottish border. Lawrence O'Toole, Archbishop of Dublin, a man revered both by Danes and Irishmen, attempted to make peace between the citizens and their assailants; but Raymond and Milo de Cogan, while their elders parleyed, led a chosen band to the assault. They soon mastered the place; and Hasculph, with a number of followers and some treasure, escaped to the Orkneys, whence he went to Norway for help. Meath, which for some unexplained reason was in O'Rourke's possession, was next invaded, and Roderic then wrote to upbraid Dermod with having broken his oath by interfering outside the bounds of Leinster. MacMurrough shortly answered that he meant to be monarch of Ireland, and Roderic then killed his son, who was with him as a hostage. The clergy of Armagh assembled in their synod saw or suspected that the invasion was different from all former invasions. They agreed that Ireland had brought a curse on herself by keeping Englishmen in slavery, and they ordered the liberation of all such bondsmen. Henry II. also saw that something extraordinary had happened. He had no fancy for having an independent Norman principality within sight of Snowdon, and he ordered the adventurers to return, strictly forbidding all communication with them in the meantime. Fitz-Gilbert wrote to the King, who was in Aquitaine, protesting that he believed he had the royal licence for what he had done, and that he was ready to be his vassal for all he might gain in Ireland. Raymond was sent with the letter, but Henry kept him a long time in suspense.

The Danes vainly attempt to retake Dublin.
At Whitsuntide, 1171, while Earl Richard was waiting for the King's answer, Hasculph returned with sixty ships, containing a well-armed force, under a berserker called John the Mad. Milo de Cogan had been left governor of Dublin,[Pg 46] and he and his brother Richard succeeded after a short fight in routing their assailants. John the Mad was killed, and Hasculph taken while trying to escape across the slob to his ships. The prisoner annoying him by threats of another and more formidable attempt, Milo ordered him to be beheaded. He had, however, spoken truth, for Godred, King of Man, soon appeared with thirty ships, and blocked the mouth of the Liffey, while Roderic, having collected a great army from all parts of Ireland, except the extreme north and south, besieged the city by land. The Earl and his followers being thus shut up in Dublin, Dermod's local enemies besieged Fitz-Stephen in the castle which he had built at Wexford. No help, as the Irish well knew, could be expected from England while Henry II. frowned, and the Normans at Dublin resolved on a great effort to relieve Fitz-Stephen. A sally was arranged, and Roderic's army was dispersed. The Irish had trusted entirely to their numbers, and kept no watch and no order. Such stores of provisions fell into the victors' hands that there was no need to victual Dublin for a year afterwards. Fitz-Stephen, however, was not relieved. By force or stratagem, Giraldus says it was by perjury, the Wexford people obtained possession of his person, and killed or captured his men. Hearing of the disaster at Dublin, the victors burned their town and withdrew with their prisoners to an island in the middle of the harbour. Earl Richard arrived too late for his

immediate purpose, and continued his journey to Waterford, whence he made his way to the King, whom he met near Gloucester. Henry was at first obdurate, but it was finally agreed that Dublin and all other port towns, with the lands adjoining, should be handed over to the King, and that the Earl and his heirs should hold all their other conquests of him and his heirs. While preparations were being made for a royal expedition, O'Rourke once more attacked Dublin, but the Cogans again surprised the Irish camp, and the city was never again seriously threatened by the natives.

Henry II. lands in Ireland, 1171.

The last attack on Dublin was about September 1, 1171, and on October 16 the King sailed from Milford Haven with 400[Pg 47] ships, containing 4,000 men, of whom 400 or 500 were knights. He landed next day at Crook, on the right bank of the Suir, some miles below Waterford, which he entered on the 18th. The Wexford men saw that the game was up, and brought Fitz-Stephen to the King, expecting thanks for surrendering the man who had dared to make war without the royal licence. Henry spoke sharply to the prisoner, and ordered him to be kept safely in Reginald's tower. Dermod MacCarthy, chief of Desmond and Cork, did homage at Waterford. Thence Henry went to Lismore, where he stayed two days. From Lismore he went to Cashel, where Donald O'Brien, chief of Thomond and Limerick, followed MacCarthy's example. The minor chiefs of Munster also made their submission, the only one mentioned by Giraldus being O'Phelan, who ruled a great part of the county of Waterford. Dermod's old antagonist, Donald of Ossory, also did homage. Henry placed governors both in Cork and Limerick, but it is not clear that he visited either of those cities. He then returned along the Suir to Waterford, where he took Fitz-Stephen into favour, and restored Wexford to him. During this progress the King selected three sites for fortresses, which were afterwards built by his son John—Lismore on the Blackwater, and Ardfinnan and Tibraghny on the Suir. The first and last were intended to command the upper tidal waters of the Blackwater and Suir; Ardfinnan secured a passage from the southern sea-board into Central Ireland, and Cromwell recognised its importance nearly five hundred years afterwards.

Henry II. winters at Dublin.

Leaving a governor in Waterford, Henry then led the bulk of his army to Dublin, where he received the submissions of O'Rourke and of the chiefs of Leinster and Uriel. Hugo de Lacy and William Fitz-Adelm were sent to meet Roderic at the Shannon, and the monarch of Ireland acknowledged himself a tributary and vassal of the King of England. Ulster still held out; for the submission of the nominal head king can in no way be held to bind the chiefs, much less the people, of his own province, and certainly not those of all Ireland. Giraldus does not venture to advance any such theory, and yet Hooker, who translated his work in Elizabeth's[Pg 48] time, coolly interpolates the statement that 'by him and his submission all the residue of the whole land became the King's subjects, and submitted themselves.' The synod which met at Cashel under the legate's presidency did what was possible for the Church to do in strengthening Henry's pretensions. The King held a court at Dublin during the winter of 1171 and 1172. His temporary palace, erected outside the walls on the ground now occupied by the southern side of Dame Street, was built of polished wicker-work, after the manner of the country. Here he kept Christmas in state, and invited the Irish chiefs to share his feast. They admired the King's grandeur, and were by him persuaded to eat crane's flesh, which the Normans thought a delicacy, but which the Irish had hitherto loathed. The winter was so stormy that there was scarcely any communication with England, and Henry's pleasure in his new acquisition must have been darkened by the sense of impending retribution for the recent murder of Becket.

Henry's warlike preparations. He distrusts the adventurers.

From the preparation which he made for the invasion of Ireland, it seems clear that the King profoundly distrusted the adventurers who had insisted on winning him a new realm. Vast stores of provisions, a great number of hand-mills, artisans for building bridges, horses, and tools for building or trenching, might indeed have been required for a war against the natives. But the Irish had no fortresses, and wooden castles, of which we also read, can only have been intended for attacking the port-towns which Earl Richard had promised to give the King, and which were already in Norman hands. Henry saw enough of Ireland to know that he had really nothing to fear from the adventurers. Dermod MacMurrough was dead before his arrival, and it was clear that Earl Richard would have enough to do in maintaining his wife's monstrous claim without doing anything to offend his own sovereign.

When, therefore, shortly before Easter, 1172, news came from Aquitaine and Normandy that the legates were on their way to inquire into the Canterbury tragedy, Henry lost no time in appointing Hugo de Lacy his representative at Dublin,[Pg 49] and in arranging for the safe keeping of Waterford and Wexford. He sailed from the latter port on Easter Monday 1172, having been in Ireland exactly six months.[33]

Henry leaves Ireland. He grants Meath to De Lacy.

Before leaving the country Henry granted to Hugo de Lacy all the territory of Meath, by the service of fifty knights. This included Westmeath, with parts of King's County and Longford, and was about 800,000 acres in extent. De Lacy, to whom Hoveden gives the title of justiciar, must be considered as the first Viceroy of Ireland, and he lost no time in advancing a claim which, if successful, would make him one of the most important vassals of the Crown. Tiernan O'Rourke, the one-eyed King of Meath, consented to meet the Pretender at the Hill of Ward. The conference ended in a quarrel, and O'Rourke was killed. Giraldus charges treason upon the Irishman, and the Irish annalists charge it upon the Norman. The important point is that De Lacy was able to make head against the Irish, and that a powerful Norman colony was established by him in the fertile central tract of Ireland. Earl Richard was rather less successfully engaged in fighting for Leinster, which Henry had granted him by the service of one hundred knights, when he was summoned to Normandy, where he did such good service that the King made him Viceroy in De Lacy's room. This was in 1173. It was in the next year, or perhaps in 1175, that Henry had the bulls or privileges of Adrian IV. and Alexander III. promulgated in Ireland. We can hardly suppose that they were previously unknown to the clergy, who so manifestly favoured the Anglo-Normans all through. Perhaps the King's main object in publishing them at this time was to make his own peace with Rome, by ostentatiously announcing that he held Ireland of the tiara, and not in right of his own sword.

Difficulties of the adventurers.

When Earl Richard returned to Ireland he found that he had lost ground. The Irish were beginning to recover confidence, and Hervey and Raymond were quarrelling bitterly. The latter was the favourite of the soldiers, who insisted on having him for leader, and he gained some[Pg 50] successes over the Danes of Cork and over the MacCarthys. Believing himself worthy of the highest rewards, Raymond asked for the Constableship of Leinster, and for the hand of Basilia, the earl's sister. The new Viceroy was disinclined to grant these terms, and Raymond, whose father had just died, went over to Wales to look after his old inheritance. Hervey thus became second in command, and planned a campaign in concert with the Dublin garrison. Earl Richard accompanied him to Cashel, but the intended junction was not effected. Donald O'Brien's homage to Henry II. did not prevent him from hindering his representative, and at Thurles he surprised and totally defeated the Dublin division. No less than 400 Danes are said by Giraldus to have fallen, which shows that a portion of that nation had accepted the alliance of their Teutonic kindred. The O'Briens were aided by a large contingent from Connaught, but it does not appear that Roderic was himself present. The immediate result of this defeat was the recall of Raymond and his marriage to Basilia. He easily put down a partial revolt of the Waterford and Wexford Danes; and, finding himself indispensable, remained at Wexford until his bride was brought to him. The honeymoon was scarcely begun when news came that Roderic was wasting Meath, and had penetrated nearly to Dublin. Raymond hastened thither, and the Connaught men retired before him. Castles, according to Giraldus, were already built at Trim and Duleek; but they had not proved strong enough to resist Roderic, and Raymond's first care was to restore and strengthen them. The adventurers, most of whom were already nearly related, were still more closely united by the marriage of Hervey to Raymond's sister Nesta, and of Earl Richard's daughter Aline to William Fitzgerald.

The adventurers fail to hold Limerick. William Fitz-Adelm made Viceroy. Death of Strongbow, 1176.

Donald O'Brien was not left long to enjoy his victory. Limerick was taken by a sudden onslaught under Raymond, and the bounds of the colony were advanced as far as they had yet been. Raymond still lingered on the Shannon, where he received a loving letter from his wife, in which she informed him 'that the great molar tooth, which had been[Pg 51] hurting her so much, had now fallen out.' He could not read, but his chaplain secretly imparted the contents of the paper, and he guessed that Basilia alluded to the death of her brother, who had been for some time ill. He hurried to Dublin, and found that Earl Richard was indeed dead. Deprived of their leader, and probably hard pressed by the Irish, the Normans thought it prudent to evacuate Limerick. It was surrendered to Donald O'Brien, who set fire to the city in four places as soon as they were gone. When the King heard of this he remarked that the abandonment of Limerick was the only wise thing that had been done concerning it. The Normans chose Raymond their governor in Earl Richard's room; but he was quickly superseded by William Fitz-Adelm de Burgh, whom Henry sent over as Viceroy with large powers.

Fitz-Adelm depresses the adventurers.

According to Giraldus, the new governor did all in his power to depress the adventurers of Nesta's stock. Raymond came to meet him with a chosen band of his relations and friends finely mounted and armed. Instead of being conciliated, the Viceroy muttered to his suite, 'I will soon cut short this pride and disperse these shields.' According to the same authority, he took advantage of the death of Maurice Fitzgerald to defraud that leader's children. Giraldus is partial, but it is easy to see that official governors were from the first jealous of the local magnates, and were disposed to engross all influence. Fitz-Adelm did little or nothing to increase the Norman power in Ireland, and he was recalled in 1177.

Treaty between Henry II. and Roderic O'Connor.
In October 1175, not long before the death of Earl Richard, Henry II. made a treaty with Roderic O'Connor, which must be understood as a kind of declaration of policy. The commissaries who attended at Windsor on Roderic's part were Catholicus, or Keyly O'Duffy, Archbishop of Tuam, the Abbot of Ardfert, and the King of Connaught's Brehon, whom Giraldus calls his Chancellor. The Archbishop of Dublin, St. Lawrence O'Toole, was among the witnesses to the instrument by which Henry granted 'to his liege man Roderic, King of Connaught, as long as he should serve[Pg 52] faithfully, to be King under him, ready to serve him as his man, and to hold his land well and peacefully, as he held it before the King of England's entry into Ireland, paying him tribute.' Should he be unable to maintain his authority, the King's forces were to help him. The tribute was to be one in every ten marketable hides. Roderic was not to meddle with those lands which the King held in his own hands, or in those of his barons: that is to say, Dublin with its appurtenances; Meath with its appurtenances, in as ample a manner as Murchat O'Melaghlin had held it; Wexford with its appurtenances, and all Leinster; Waterford and Dungarvan with its appurtenances, and all the lands between the two places. Irish fugitives willing to return into the King's land were to have peace on paying the aforesaid tribute, 'or by performing the ancient accustomed services for their lands.' Those who would not return were to be coerced by the King of Connaught, who was to take hostages from all whom the King granted to him, and to give hostages on his own part wherever the King required him. No refugees from the King's lands were to be entertained by Irishmen under any pretence. At the same time, as if to mark the fact that Irishmen were his own subjects as well as Normans, Henry appointed Augustine O'Sealbhaigh to the bishopric of Waterford, and sent him, in charge of the Archbishop of Dublin, to be consecrated by the Archbishop of Cashel. This was a confirmation of the Eugenian constitution, and put an end to the succession of the Danish bishops through Canterbury. Henry had no wish to have future Beckets interfering in Ireland. Canterbury was near and Rome was far.

Henry's original policy frustrated by De Courcy.
The treaty with Roderic, if we accept it as Hoveden and Benedict have handed it down, shows that a full conquest of Ireland was not intended by Henry II. The possession of the port-towns gave him the command of St. George's Channel, and a control over the trade of the island. He had seen enough to know that a permanent conquest was beyond the power of a feudal army, and his policy was to balance the adventurers, his own creation De Lacy, and the native princes against each other. Fitz-Adelm, a subtle[Pg 53] intriguer with an eye for money, probably seemed a fitter instrument for his purpose than any enterprising soldier. But Fitz-Adelm brought with him to Ireland one of those restless and unscrupulous men of action, who sometimes disconcert the best laid plans of statesmen. John De Courcy is represented by Giraldus as a tall, fair man, of immense strength and extraordinary audacity, an experienced warrior, though often more of a partisan than a general; but religious in his way, and ever ready to ascribe to God the glory of any successful exploit. He was the patron of the monk Jocelin, who wove such a tangled web about St. Patrick, and he carried with him everywhere a tract of St. Columba, which was supposed to point him out as the destined conqueror of

Ulster. Seeing that neither gain nor glory could be had under the Viceroy, De Courcy, in January 1177, boldly marched into Ulster with twenty-two knights and 300 chosen men. Among the knights were Almaric St. Lawrence, ancestor of the Howth family, and Roger le Poer, apparently a collateral ancestor of the Powers and Eustaces. In the course of a year or two, though by no means always successful in battle, De Courcy made himself supreme in eastern Ulster. Where they had the advantage of the ground, the natives were too much for the adventurers; but in a fair field a hundred Normans, at least under such a leader as De Courcy, were more than a match for 1,000 Irish. Discipline and steadiness soon gave them the coast, and the castles which they built everywhere enabled them to make war or peace as they pleased. Downpatrick was John de Courcy's capital.

De Courcy and De Lacy. Castle-building.

O'Donlevy, chief king of Uladh, or that part of Ulster now comprised in Antrim and Down, had done homage to Henry II., and imagined that he would be thus secured from invasion. But the King evidently understood the matter differently, for De Courcy had a grant from him of such northern lands as he could conquer. Fitz-Adelm having failed as a Viceroy, Henry now fell back upon Hugo de Lacy, who perhaps dreamed of making himself independent. He distinguished himself by good government from 1177 to 1181, and by showing[Pg 54] favour to the Irish; and he married a daughter of Roderic O'Connor without the King's consent. Henry accordingly sent for De Lacy to England, and gave the viceregal authority to John, Constable of Chester. The Lord of Meath succeeded in making his peace, and was soon restored to the government; Robert of Salisbury, a priest, being sent as a spy upon him. De Lacy covered his own district with castles, Trim being his capital. Delvin he granted to William Nugent, his sister Rose's husband, who became the ancestor of the Earls of Westmeath. Other estates he gave to his friends and followers, who founded many of the families of the Pale. The Flemings, Lords of Slane, became the most important of these. Other barons followed the example of De Lacy; and Giraldus mentions that by the year 1182 castles were built at or near Newtown Barry, Castle Dermot, Leighlin, Timahoe, Athy, Narragh, and other places. The Meath castles, says the chronicler, were too many to mention by name.

John designated as King of Ireland.

As early as 1177 Henry had nominated his son John King of Ireland. For this he had the leave of Alexander III., and in 1186 Urban III. actually sent a crown of peacock's feathers set in gold for the King to crown one of his sons, the choice being left to him. The intervening Pope, Lucius III., had opposed the plan, and this may have been the reason why it was never carried out. Or the King may have hesitated to repeat even in John's favour an experiment which had succeeded so ill in the case of his eldest son. The Oxford nomination of 1177 was allowed to take effect only so as to constitute John Lord of Ireland, and this title was afterwards assumed by the Kings of England. In the sixteenth century it was by some taken as evidence that the crown in Ireland was subject to the popes. But the idea of a separate, though subordinate, kingdom was very nearly realised. The acts of the colony were from the date of the Oxford Council executed in the name of 'John, Lord of Ireland, son of the King of England,' and the first Anglo-Norman coinage bore his face.

John sent to Ireland as Viceroy.

On March 31, 1185, the King knighted John at Windsor, and on April 24 the latter, who was in his nineteenth year,[Pg 55] sailed from Milford Haven, with 300 knights and a large body of troops. The expedition reached Waterford in safety next day, and the neighbouring chiefs flocked to do honour to the King's son, and to give him the kiss of peace. The Anglo-Norman courtiers—young men mostly—pulled their long beards, and they at once departed to the hostile chiefs, Roderic O'Connor, Donnell O'Brien, and Dermod MacCarthy. All chance of conciliating the more powerful and distant potentates was thus taken away. Giraldus Cambrensis was present at Waterford, and he likens John to Rehoboam. The Irish, who had adhered to the invaders since Fitz-Stephen's first landing, were deprived of their lands; the castles were given up to favourites, who did nothing but eat, drink, and plunder; the worst officers were put in the best places, and the men, as a natural consequence, were as bad as their masters, devoted to Venus and Bacchus, but neglectful of Mars. Hoveden adds that John put all the profits of government into his own pocket, and that his soldiers being unpaid were useless in war. The three castles projected by his father were built; but he lost many to the Irish, and De Lacy was suspected of intriguing against him. It is clear that there could be no confidence in a prince whose chief care was to rob and displace the men who had won his principality for him. The disastrous experiment lasted only eight months, when John returned to England, leaving the government to John de Courcy, who retained power until the death of Henry II. The Lough Cé annalists, who wrote beyond the Shannon, give the following account of John's expedition:—'The son of the King of the Saxons came to assume the sovereignty of Erin ... afterwards he went across to complain of Hugo de Lacy to his father; for it was Hugo de Lacy that was King of Erin when the son of the King of the Saxons came, and he permitted not the men of Erin to give tribute or hostages to him.' To the Irish bordering on Meath no doubt De Lacy seemed a veritable king. The Four Masters, who were better acquainted with the English theory of government, repeat this; but soften Hugo's title of king into that of the King of England's deputy.[Pg 56]

Murder of Hugh de Lacy. The colony continues to extend.

In or out of office, De Lacy continued to increase his dominion in Meath, but his career was cut short not long after John's departure. Having encroached upon the lands of the O'Caharneys, he was murdered while building a castle at Durrow by a foster-relation of the injured clan. His death was a great blow to the colonists, but his son Hugo succeeded to scarcely diminished power, and is accused by Giraldus of systematically thwarting De Courcy. Fitz-Stephen meanwhile was carving out a principality in Munster, where he would be tolerably free from official interference. He and Milo de Cogan were joint grantees of Cork, and the latter married his daughter Catherine to Maurice, son of Raymond le Gros, to whom Dermod MacCarthy had given a portion of North Kerry. From this alliance the Fitzmaurices sprung. It is probable that in granting the land of the O'Connors to a stranger, Dermod gave that over which he had no real authority. The territory immediately round the city of Cork was divided between Fitz-Stephen and Cogan, the former taking that lying to the east, and the latter that lying to the west. Fitz-Stephen's share passed to his sister's son, Philip de Barry. Before the death of Henry II. the country about Cork was studded with castles, but it is impossible to say how far it was really conquered. Intermarriages with the Irish were no doubt common from the first. The example set by Strongbow and by Hugo de Lacy was not likely to want imitators.

No conquest of Ireland under Henry II.

The conquest of Ireland by Henry II., as it used to be called, amounts on the whole to this. The coast from Larne to Cork harbour was, at the date of the King's death, strongly held by the invaders, all the ports being in their hands, and the principal points being defended by castles. They were also pretty firmly established on the south side of the Shannon estuary. The rivers of Leinster were in their hands, and the central plain almost, if not quite as far west as the Shannon. De Courcy had begun to assert his dominion over Monaghan and Armagh. All the Danish towns except Limerick were fully possessed by the conquerors. On the other hand, the Irish were not expelled from any part of the[Pg 57] island. The mountains which extend almost uninterruptedly from Dublin to Waterford still sheltered the O'Tooles, the O'Byrnes, the MacMurroughs, the O'Nolans, and other clans. Fitz-Stephen had begun the conquest of what is now the county of Cork, but the Irish were still in force on all sides of the city. The natives generally had recovered in some degree from their first alarm. The first invaders had been trained in mountain warfare, but those who succeeded them were often quite unfit to dispute the possession of hills and woods with the light-armed natives. And there were jealousies between Normans, English, and Welsh, which went far to neutralise the strength of the colony. Had it not been for the dissensions of the Irish themselves, it is probable that they would have confined the invaders to the east coast. It was a quarrel between Dermod MacCarthy and his son which brought the Geraldines to Kerry; disputes among the O'Connors introduced De Cogan, De Lacy, and De Courcy into Connaught; and, though they effected nothing, they paved the way for the De Burgos, to whose founder, William Fitz-Adelm, Henry granted the whole of the western province. The King's troubles with his own sons, with the Holy See, and with France, prevented him from attending to Ireland. It would have been better for the peace of mankind had he made a real conquest, instead of leaving it to barons, who lost much of their old civilisation, and who disdained to learn anything from the weaker people whom they oppressed.[34]

FOOTNOTES:

[29] Matthew Paris calls the Irish 'bestiales.'

[30] See the Senchus Mór, ii. 225.

[31] Giraldus, Ex. Hib. lib. i. cap. 2.

[32] In Webb's Compendium of Irish Biography is a carefully compiled catalogue of Nesta's children and grandchildren. I have generally followed it, noting, however, that Fitz-Stephen's children cannot be held legitimate in the face of Giraldus' distinct statement.

[33] The details of Henry's preparations may be studied in Sweetman's Calendar of Documents.

[34] In narrating the events of Henry II.'s reign, I have generally followed Giraldus Cambrensis, checking him by references to Hoveden and Regan. The Expugnatio may be considered a fanciful book in some ways. But if we eliminate everything supernatural, and make some allowance for the writer's prejudices, I see no reason to question his good

faith. Of the native Irish he knew little, but the invaders were his neighbours, friends, and relations. Fitz-Stephen and the other descendants of Nesta may be unduly praised, Fitz-Adelm perhaps unduly blamed; but, after all, this is no more than may be said against most historians of their own times. Giraldus was undoubtedly an observer of first-rate power.

[Pg 58]

CHAPTER IV.

FROM JOHN'S VISIT IN 1210 TILL THE INVASION BY THE BRUCES IN 1315.

John acts as lord of Ireland under his father and brother.

Richard I. did not interfere with his brother's jurisdiction over Ireland, and this may be the reason why the records of the colony during his reign are so scanty. The invaders, though they fought a good deal among themselves, continued to extend their power, and gained a firm footing in Connaught. Some years before the death of Henry II., Roderic's sons had invited the Anglo-Normans into his kingdom, and in 1183 the last monarch of Ireland retired to the abbey of Cong, where he died in 1198. His brother Cathal Crovdearg, or Charles of the Red Hand, about whom many marvellous stories are told, ultimately made himself supreme; but not without the help of William Fitz-Adelm, who lost no opportunity of advancing the claim given him by Henry's thoroughly unjustifiable grant. Fitz-Adelm, who had made himself master of Limerick, at first opposed Cathal Crovdearg, but joined him in 1201 and enabled him to triumph over all competitors. The accession of John to the crown of England put an end to the separate lordship of Ireland, but his successors, until the time of Henry VIII., continued to call themselves only lords of Ireland. If Berengaria had had children, it is possible, and even probable, that Ireland would have passed to John's issue as a separate, or at the most a tributary kingdom. The early years of John's reign were much disturbed by a violent feud between the De Lacies and De Courcy. The King favoured the former party, and in 1205 created the younger Hugo Earl of Ulster and Viceroy. He proved an oppressive governor, over-taxing the King's subjects to provide means for his foreign enterprises.[Pg 59] The southern colonists, in alliance with some of the natives, defeated the Viceroy near Thurles, and the King began to fear that he had given too much power to one family; for Walter de Lacy continued to rule Meath, while his brother was all-powerful in the north and east. A royal army was accordingly levied, and John prepared to revisit the lordship where he had so signally failed twenty-five years before.

King John visits Ireland.

The excommunicated King sailed from Milford Haven with a motley army of mercenaries, under command of Fair Rosamond's son, William Long-sword, and landed on June 20, 1210, at the same place as his father had done. Among his train were John de Grey, Bishop of Norwich, whom Innocent III. had refused to make Archbishop of Canterbury, and John de Courcy, who had been captured and given up by the De Lacies, and who had suffered a rigorous imprisonment, but was now again in favour with the King. John did not let the grass grow under his feet. On the eighth day after his arrival he was at Dublin, having travelled by Ross, Thomastown, Kilkenny, and Naas. The first effect of his presence was to separate the two De Lacies, and the Lord of Meath sent him the following message:—'Walter salutes the King as his liege lord, of whom he holds all he possesses; and prays the King to relax his ire, and suffer Walter to approach his presence; Walter will not plead against the King, but places all his castles and lands in the hands of the King as his lord, to retain or restore as he pleases.' The messenger added that Walter had lost much by his brother Hugo, and that he left him to the King's pleasure. It is possible that this was said in consequence of an arrangement between the two brothers. John was not pacified, and prepared to invade both Meath and Ulster. Trim was reached by July 2, and Kells by the 4th, and the Kings of Connaught and Thomond were summoned to take part in the expedition to Ulster. Cathal Crovdearg and Donough O'Brien both obeyed the King's order, and the royal army proceeded by Dundalk, Carlingford, and Downpatrick to Carrickfergus. The latter place was taken and garrisoned. Hugo de Lacy had already fled into Scotland.[Pg 60] The King stayed eight or nine days at Carrickfergus, where he was visited by Hugh O'Neill, who does not appear to have made any real submission, and then marched by Holywood, Downpatrick, Banbridge, and Carlingford to Drogheda. From Drogheda he again entered Meath, visited Duleek and Kells, and seems to have penetrated as far west as Granard. He was in Dublin by August 18, and back to England before the end of the month, having spent sixty-six days in Ireland. On his return from Ulster he had summoned Cathal Crovdearg a second time, bidding him bring his son 'to receive a charter for the third part of Connaught.' Over-persuaded by his wife, Cathal went to the King alone. John's object may have been to make a hostage of the boy, and he seized instead MacDermot of Moylurg, O'Hara of Sligo, and two other men of importance in Connaught. Carrying these chiefs with him to England, the King left the government of Ireland to Bishop de Grey, who signalised his advent to power by building a castle and bridge at Athlone. William de Braose, who had enormous estates in Ireland, was driven into exile by John, who starved his wife and son to death, and gave his castle of Carrigogunnel on the Shannon to Donough O'Brien.

The Anglo-Normans flock to the King. He erects twelve shires.

The Anglo-Norman barons of Ireland flocked to Dublin while John was there, and swore to obey the laws of England. The King divided their country into twelve counties: Dublin, Kildare, Meath, Uriel or Louth, Carlow, Kilkenny, and Wexford in Leinster; and Waterford, Cork, Kerry, Limerick, and Tipperary in Munster. Every knight's fee was bound to supply a well-armed horseman, and inferior tenants were bound to provide foot-soldiers. The Viceroy was to give a notice of forty days when the feudal array was to muster at Dublin, and serve against the King's enemies for forty days in each year. Ulster and Connaught were not shired, but were afterwards sometimes regarded as counties. Perhaps the nobles of these provinces were supposed to be constantly employed against the Irish. The native chiefs were considered as tributary subjects, but not as tenants. In 1215 John ordered the Archbishop of Dublin to buy enough scarlet[Pg 61] cloth to make robes for the Kings of Ireland; and it is clear that they were expected to serve, though the exact measure of the aid rendered may have been left to themselves.

Leinster is divided after Earl Richard's death.

When Strongbow died without a son the principality of Leinster fell to his eldest daughter Isabel, who became a ward of the Crown. In 1189 the minor was given in marriage to William Earl Marshal, who thus became Earl of Pembroke and Strigul, and lord of a territory in Ireland, corresponding nearly to the counties of Wexford, Kildare,

Carlow, Kilkenny, and part of the Queen's County. He built a castle and incorporated a town at Kilkenny, and died in 1219, transmitting his honours and great power to his son William. The younger William was Viceroy in 1224, and depressed the De Lacies, allying himself generally with Cathal Crovdearg O'Connor. He died in 1231, leaving all to his brother Richard, who made good his position, although Henry III.'s foreign advisers plotted his destruction. Strongbow's grandson was killed in 1234 by the feudatories who were bound to defend him, and the colony never recovered the blow.

The De Burgos in Connaught.

Fitz-Adelm's son, Richard de Burgo, generally called MacWilliam by the Irish, married Una, Cathal Crovdearg's grand-daughter, and procured from Henry III. a grant of all Connaught, except five cantreds reserved for the support of the post at Athlone. From the first the position of the Anglo-Normans in Connaught differed from their position in other parts of Ireland. They were there rather as allies of the native chiefs than as conquerors, and the easy lapse of their descendants into Irish habits is the less to be wondered at. Richard de Burgo obtained a confirmation of his grant in 1226, through the favour of his kinsman, the great justiciar, Hubert, and he soon afterwards made himself master of Galway, which he fortified strongly, and made the chief place of Connaught. After his time the O'Connors never regained possession of it, and the importance of the royal tribe steadily diminished during the whole of the thirteenth century. Richard de Burgo's eldest son Walter married Maud, daughter and heiress of the younger Hugo de Lacy, who died in 1243, and he thus became Earl of Ulster as well as[Pg 62] Lord of Connaught. His son Richard, commonly called the Red Earl, advanced the power of the Anglo-Norman state to the furthest point which it ever attained.

Poverty of the colony under Henry III.

Constant war is not favourable to the production of wealth, and it seems probable that no very considerable progress was made in the arts of peace. Tallage was first imposed on Ireland in 1217, in the name of Henry III., but it seems to have yielded little, and a generation later there was equal difficulty in collecting a tithe for the Pope. Innocent IV. ordered that a sum should be so raised for the liberation of the Holy Land, and very stringent letters were sent to Ireland in 1254; but collector Lawrence Sumercote declared that the difficulties were insuperable. The Irish, he explained, never saved anything, but lived riotously and gave liberally to all, and he professed that he would 'rather be imprisoned than crucified any longer in Ireland for the business of the Cross.' The plan of drawing upon Ireland for English or Continental wars was, however, largely practised during the reign of Henry III., and it tended to sap the strength of the colony. Ready money might be scarce, but there were men, and they could be ill-spared from the work of defending their lands against a native race who were ever on the watch to take advantage of their absence or neglect.

Edward I. had not time to attend to Ireland personally.

A vast number of documents remain to show that Edward I. took great pains about Ireland. Phelim O'Connor, who died in 1265, may be regarded as the last King of Connaught. His son Hugh did indeed assume the title, and, according to the annalists, 'executed his royal depredations on the men of Offaly, where he committed many burnings and killings;' but his kingship does not appear to have been officially recognised, and the De Burgos were the true rulers. The Red Earl was supreme in the northern half of Ireland; but O'Neill was recognised as King of Tyrone, while his claim to be head of all the Irish in Ireland was denied. O'Cahan was also sometimes given the title of king. O'Donnell was treated with less respect, and a price was set upon his head, which appears to have been actually brought to Dublin in 1283. In 1281 Hugh Boy O'Neill, whom the annalists call 'royal heir of all[Pg 63] Erin, head of the hospitality and valour of the Gael,' sided with the English against Donnell Oge O'Donnell, who is called 'King of the north, the best Gael for hospitality and dignity; the general guardian of the west of Europe, and the knitting-needle of the arch sovereignty, and the rivetting hammer of every good law, and the top-nut of the Gael in valour.' A battle was fought near Dungannon, and O'Donnell, who had under him the O'Rourkes and MacMahons, and 'nearly the majority of the Irish of Connaught and Ulster,' was defeated and slain. Two years later Hugh Boy was killed by the MacMahons. The story of this contest is a good illustration of the hopeless incapacity of the natives for anything like a national combination. If Edward I. had been able to attend to Ireland personally, it is at least probable that he would have conquered the country as completely as Wales.

Frequency of quarrels among the colonists.

In 1275, Edward granted the whole of Thomond to Thomas de Clare, who took advantage of the dissensions among the O'Briens, and built the strong castle of Bunratty to dominate the district. The conquest of Thomond was, however, never completed, or nearly completed, nor did the De Clares succeed in establishing themselves like the De Burgos. They might have done so had they not come so late into the field, and their failure was certainly not owing to any exceptional power of combination shown by the Irish. It was rather due to quarrels among the colonists, whose strength was being constantly sapped by taking part in Edward's Scotch wars, and who were not recruited by any considerable immigration. In 1245, the male line of the Earl Marshal was finally extinguished, and the inheritance of Strongbow fell to five sisters, the great granddaughters of Dermod MacMurrough. Matilda, the eldest, obtained Carlow and carried the hereditary office of Earl Marshal to her husband, Hugh Bigot, Earl of Norfolk. Joan, the second, received Wexford. Isabella, the third, had Kilkenny, which her descendants sold to the Ormonde family. Sibilla, the fourth, had Kildare for her share. Eva, the youngest sister, married William De Braose; and through her daughter, who was married to Roger Mortimer, became ancestress of most of[Pg 64] the royal houses of Europe. As the five daughters of William Earl Marshal were all married, and had all children, the history of Leinster becomes very confusing. Had it remained in one strong hand the Irish would hardly have recovered their ground. But, as Giraldus points out, the 'four great pillars of the conquest, Fitz-Stephen, Hervey, Raymond, and John de Courcy, by the hidden but never unjust judgment of God, were not blessed with any legitimate offspring.' A similar fatality attended many others, including Earl Richard, to whom, and not to Fitz-Stephen, common fame, more true in this case than contemporary history, has attributed the real leadership among the Anglo-Norman invaders of Ireland.

Edward I. weakens the colony by drawing men and supplies from it.

In his great campaign of 1296 Edward had much help from Ireland. The Earl of Ulster was among those who led contingents to Scotland, and the names of Power, Butler, Fitzthomas, Wogan, Rocheford, Purcell, Cantoke, and Barry appear among the leaders. The whole force from Ireland consisted of 310 men-at-arms, 266 hobelers or horsemen with unarmoured horses, and 2,576 foot, including many archers and crossbowmen. All who went received pardons, but some refused or neglected to obey the royal summons. In 1298 Edward drew provisions from Ireland. His requisition included 8,000 quarters of wheat, chiefly fine flour in casks; 10,000 quarters of oats; much bran, bacon, salt beef, and salt fish; and 10,000 casks of wine. If so much wine could not be got in Ireland, then the Viceroy was to agree with some merchant to bring it from Gascony as quick as possible. Edward used Ireland as a base for operations, or as a recruiting ground, but he never had time to give it much of his personal care. First Wales, then Gascony, then Palestine, then Scotland engrossed his vast energies; but Ireland was left to herself. Without the means to keep order themselves, Viceroys found it necessary to preserve the colony by stirring up dissensions among the Irish. The justiciar, Robert d'Ufford, was sent for by Edward and charged with this evil policy. He answered, that to save the King's coffers, and to keep the peace, he thought it expedient to wink at one knave cutting off another. 'Whereat,' says[Pg 65] an old author, 'the King smiled, and bade him return to Ireland.'

Disorders after the death of Edward I.
John's imperfect partition of Ireland into shires was still more imperfectly carried out. At the death of Edward I. four out of his grandfather's twelve counties—namely, Meath, Wexford, Carlow, and Kilkenny—were liberties or exempt jurisdictions in the hands of what Davies calls 'absolute palatines,' claiming and exercising almost every attribute of sovereignty. The Fitzgeralds had acquired similar authority over a portion of Desmond, and the De Clares over a portion of Thomond. Connaught and Ulster were under the De Burghs, in so far as they had been reduced at all, and Roscommon was a royal castle and the head of a separate county. At Randon on Lough Ree was another royal castle, and these were almost the only strongholds of the Crown in Connaught; for Galway was quite subject to the De Burghs. Within their palatinate jurisdictions, the great nobles made barons and knights, appointed sheriffs, and executed justice. The King's writ only ran in the Church lands, and was executed by a separate sheriff. So complete was the distinction, that in the mediæval parliaments knights were separately returned for the counties and for the 'crosses,' as the ecclesiastical jurisdictions were called. The inherent weakness of such a polity was probably aggravated by the suppression of the Templars, who always kept a strong armed force. In 1308 Edward II. called for an account of their lands and revenues, and the barons of the exchequer answered that they could make no proper inquisition. 'On account,' they wrote, 'of the long distances, and of the feuds between certain of the magnates of Ireland, we do not dare to visit the places named, and jurors of the country cannot come to us for the same reason.'

Reasons why the colony declined. The Bruces invade Ireland.
Dissensions among the barons, caused by the weakness and absence of the Crown, were one great cause of the decline of the colony. Another was the policy of Edward I., which left him little time to attend to Ireland, and tempted him constantly to draw supplies of men from thence. A third was the battle of Bannockburn, which allowed victorious[Pg 66] Scotland to compete with England for the dominion of the neighbouring island; and the Irish themselves were not slow to adopt the principle that England's difficulty is Ireland's opportunity. In 1315 Edward Bruce landed near Larne with 6,000 men, including some of the best knights in Scotland. Having been joined by O'Neill and the chiefs depending on him, Bruce twice defeated the Red Earl of Ulster, occupied the strongholds of Down and Antrim, and wintered in Westmeath. In the spring

he overthrew the Viceroy, Sir Edmund Butler, at Ardscull, for the Earl of Ulster disdained to serve under the King's representative, and the English armies were therefore beaten in detail. Bruce gained another battle at Kells, wasted all northern Leinster, and then returned to Carrickfergus, where he was joined by King Robert with reinforcements. The Scots went almost where they liked, and Robert Bruce is said to have heard mass at Limerick on Palm Sunday, 1317. They did not cross the Shannon, and seem not to have gone further south than Cashel. Dublin was not attacked, though the invaders came as near as Castleknock. On Easter Thursday, 1317, Roger Mortimer landed at Youghal with 15,000 men and full viceregal powers, and the Bruces retired before him into Ulster. They had devastated the country, and lost many men from the famine which they themselves had caused.

The Bruces fail to conquer Ireland.

The Bruces were descended from Strongbow and from Dermod MacMurrough, and Robert's wife was descended from Roderic O'Connor. The true principles of hereditary succession were not fully accepted, and they might pretend some right to interfere in Ireland. They had been invited by the De Lacies of Meath, who for want of male heirs saw their territory divided between De Verdon and De Mortimer. In the first flush of his victorious advance from the south, Roger Mortimer called the De Lacies before him. They refused to appear, and were proclaimed traitors, but continued to adhere to Edward Bruce's fortunes. The invader, after his brother's departure, remained for more than a year at Carrickfergus, in hopes of being able to take the offensive again, and still retaining the title of King, which[Pg 67] he had assumed after his first successes. He had been so often victorious in battle that he despised the colonists, and, against the advice of his Irish allies, resolved to fight once more without waiting for reinforcements from Scotland. John de Bermingham, at the head of an army which greatly outnumbered the Scots, forced an engagement between Faughard and Dundalk, and Bruce and most of his officers were killed. The remnant of his army, with Walter and Hugo de Lacy, managed to escape to Scotland. The sovereignty of the English Crown in Ireland was never again seriously disputed; but the feudal organisation was shattered by Bruce's invasion, which did nothing to compose the differences already existing among the colonists. John de Bermingham received a grant of Louth with the title of earl, but his great services were soon forgotten, and eleven years after the battle of Dundalk he was murdered by the English of his own earldom.

Horrible cruelties of the Bruces.

English and Irish are agreed as to the cruelty and ferocity of the Bruces. Clyn the Franciscan records, in terse and vigorous Latin, that 'Robert Bruce, who bore himself as King of the Scots, crossed Ireland from Ulster, where he landed, almost to Limerick, burning, killing, plundering, and spoiling towns, castles, and even churches, both going and returning.' Clyn was an English partisan, but the same cannot be said of the Lough Cé annalists, who record that 'Edward Bruce, the destroyer of all Erin in general, both foreigners and Gaels, was slain by the foreigners of Erin, through the power of battle and bravery at Dundalk; and MacRory, King of the Hebrides, and MacDonnell, King of Argyll, together with the men of Scotland, were slain there along with him; and no better deed for the men of all Erin was performed since the beginning of the world, since the Formorian race was expelled from Erin, than this deed; for theft, and famine, and destruction of men occurred throughout Erin during his time for the space of three years and a half; and people used to eat one another, without doubt, throughout Erin.'

The Irish fail to give the Bruces effectual support.

There can, however, be no doubt that Edward Bruce[Pg 68] came to Ireland on the invitation of the Irish. Donnell O'Neill, claiming to be the true heir to the chief kingship, and the other chiefs, in the famous remonstrance which they addressed to John XXII., informed that Pope that they felt helpless for want of a leader, but were determined no longer to submit like women to Anglo-Norman oppression, and that they had therefore invited over 'the brother of the most illustrious Lord Robert, by the grace of God King of the Scots, and a descendant of the most noble of their own ancestors,' and that they had by letters patent constituted him king and lord. The blood of Roderic O'Connor and of Eva evidently went for something, but the chiefs also believed that Edward Bruce was 'a person of piety and prudence, of a chaste and modest disposition, of great sobriety, and altogether orderly and unassuming in his demeanour.' Scottish historians are not entirely of the same opinion. It is indeed probable that Bruce had no other idea than to carve out a kingdom with his sword, like a genuine Norman as he was. He had the memory of Earl Richard, of Fitz-Stephen, and of De Courcy to guide him; and if a more modern instance was required, there could be none better than that of his brother Robert.

[Pg 69]

MAP OF IRELAND ABOUT 1300.
CHAPTER V.

FROM THE INVASION OF THE BRUCES TO THE YEAR 1346.

The Irish never united. The O'Connors are almost destroyed by the De Burgos.

The Irish invited Bruce, but they made no regular or general effort in his favour. Their total incapacity for anything like national organisation had forbidden the idea of a native sovereign, and perhaps the majority of them thought one Norman baron no better than another. The year 1316, in which Bruce landed, witnessed the almost total destruction of the O'Connors, the tribe which had last held the chief kingship. Their relationship with the De Burgos, Berminghams, and other Anglo-Normans may be traced in great detail in the annalists. Felim O'Connor, whom the Connaught historiographers call undisputed heir presumptive to the sovereignty of Erin, formed one of those great confederacies which occur so frequently in Irish history, and which so seldom had any results. The O'Kellys, MacDermods, O'Maddens, O'Dowds, O'Haras, O'Kearneys, O'Farrells, MacMahons, and many others were represented; and the Anglo-Normans, who also mustered in great force, were commanded by the Red Earl's brother, Sir William de Burgo, and by Richard Bermingham, fourth baron of Athenry, at the gate of which town the decisive struggle took place. The Irish were defeated with the loss of something like 10,000 men. Felim O'Connor fell, and his tribe never recovered its position in Connaught. In late times we have O'Connor Don and O'Connor Roe in Roscommon, O'Connor Sligo, O'Connor Kerry near the mouth of the Shannon, and O'Connor Faly in what is now the King's County, but the De Burgos became supreme in Connaught.

The Irish recover ground under Edward II. and his successors.

In other parts of Ireland the Celts were more successful. In 1317 or 1318 the O'Carrolls gained a victory over Sir[Pg 70] Edmund Butler, but Clyn places his loss at about two hundred only. More important was the battle of Disert O'Dea, in which Richard de Clare was defeated and slain. This fight destroyed the pretensions of the De Clares, and the O'Briens remained supreme in Thomond as long as such supremacies lasted anywhere. In Leinster, too, the Irish became more and more troublesome, and Clyn unwillingly records successes of the O'Nolans and O'Tooles over the Poers and other settlers. The dissensions of the colonists were yet more fatal than the prowess of the natives. Eva's descendants were for ever fighting among themselves, and it was the Red Earl's jealousy of Sir Edmund Butler which prevented a united effort from being made against Bruce. 'After having violently expelled us,' wrote the Irish to John XXII., 'from our spacious habitations and patrimonial inheritances, they have compelled us to repair, in the hope of saving our lives, to mountains and woods, to bogs and barren wastes, and to the caves of the rocks, where, like the beasts, we have long been fain to dwell.' The close of Edward II.'s reign saw them everywhere ready to descend from their hills, and to emerge from their woods. For nearly two hundred years the history of Ireland is in the main a history of Celtic gains at the expense of Anglo-Normans and Englishmen; if, indeed, anarchy can rightly be accounted gain to any race or community of men.

The last Earl of Ulster is murdered, 1333. The De Burgos and other Anglo-Normans assume Irish names and habits.

In 1326 the Red Earl of Ulster retired into the monastery of Athassel, where he died soon afterwards. His great power descended to his grandson William, who was murdered at or near Carrickfergus in 1333 by the Mandevilles and other Ulster colonists. By his wife, Maud Plantagenet, great-grand-daughter of Henry III., he left one child, Elizabeth, who was only a few months old at the date of his murder. Twenty years afterwards she married Lionel Duke of Clarence, and became ancestress of the Tudors and Stuarts. The Earldom of Ulster thus ultimately merged in the Crown. But the Irish De Burgos refused to acknowledge a baby, who, as a royal ward, would be brought up independently of them; and they preferred to follow the sons of Sir William, the Red[Pg 71] Earl's brother. William the elder assumed the title of MacWilliam Uachtar, or the Upper, took all Galway for his portion, and became ancestor of the Clanricarde family. His brother, Sir Edmund, as MacWilliam Iochtar, or the Lower, took Mayo, and founded the family which bears that title. They threw off their allegiance to England, and became more Irish than the Irish. They reappear in the sixteenth century under the modern name of Burke. About the same time several other Anglo-Normans assumed Irish names. The Stauntons became MacAveelys; the Berminghams MacFeoris; the D'Exeters, MacJordans; the Barretts, MacAndrews, MacThomins, MacRoberts, and MacPaddins; the Nangles, MacCostelloes; the Mayo Prendergasts, MacMaurices. The De Burgos themselves had many subordinate branches, each with its peculiar Irish name, as MacDavid, MacPhilbin, MacShoneen, MacGibbon, MacWalter, and MacRaymond. Nor was the practice confined to Connaught. Some of the Leinster Fitzgeralds became MacThomases and MacBarons; and some of the same house in Munster were transfigured into MacGibbons, MacThomaisins, and MacEdmonds. Many other Anglo-Normans or English families were more or less completely transformed in the same way. It is only necessary to mention that the Wesleys or Wellesleys, who gave England its greatest captain, were sometimes called MacFabrenes; and that the Bissetts of Antrim, whose connections in Scotland gave the Tudors such trouble, may still be traced as Makeons. In the district near Dublin, which got the name of the English Pale, some Irish residents took English names, and the practice was encouraged by a statute of Edward IV. There is probably no country in Europe where the population is so thoroughly mixed as it is in Ireland.

Edward III. creates three great earldoms: Kildare, Desmond, and Ormonde.

As the Earls of Ulster disappear, other families attain prominence, and the earlier Tudor history is mainly occupied with the struggles of three earldoms, created in the first half of the fourteenth century. The name Geraldine, to which Giraldus Cambrensis gave a more extended signification, was in later times confined to the descendants of Maurice Fitzgerald, one of Nesta's many sons. One branch was firmly[Pg 72] settled in Kildare before the death of Henry II., and in the reign of Edward I. the head of it was John Fitz-Thomas, whose dissensions with William de Vesci, Lord of Kildare, ended in an appeal to the King, and a challenge to the trial by combat. Fitz-Thomas was the challenger, and on his adversary failing to appear, he received a royal grant of De Vesci's lands. In 1316 Edward II. created him Earl of Kildare, and the Duke of Leinster is descended from him. During most of the fifteenth century, and for the first third of the sixteenth, this was on the whole the most powerful family in Ireland. The Earls of Kildare commanded the whole strength of that county, and its proximity to Dublin often enabled them to control the government. Meath was too much divided for its proprietors to act as a counterpoise, and the strength of the rival house of Ormonde lay at a distance from the capital, and was exposed to attacks from another branch of the Geraldines, whose chief was created Earl of Desmond in 1329. The Desmonds first rose at the expense of the MacCarthies in Kerry. A marriage with the heiress of Fitz-Anthony brought them the western half of the county Waterford and other large estates. This lady's son married the heiress of the Cogans, and her great property in Cork was added to the rest. The Desmonds never became quite so completely Hibernicised as the De Burgos; but they attained something very like independence, and more than once proved too strong for the government. The third great earldom was founded in the person of Edmund Butler, who was created Earl of Carrick in 1315; the better known title of Ormonde being conferred on his son James in 1328. The founder of the family was Theobald Fitz-Walter, who accompanied Henry II. to Ireland, and was by him made hereditary butler with a grant of the prisage of wines. The name of office was adopted by his descendants, who derived great advantage from the grant. Ormonde is properly the northern part of Tipperary, but the earls became palatine lords of nearly all the county, and owners of vast estates in Kilkenny and Wexford. Their principal castles were Kilkenny, Gowran, Carrick-on-Suir, and Arklow. The possession of the latter place gave them[Pg 73] ready access to England, and through all turns of weal and woe they ever remained faithful to the Crown. If regard be had to the length of time that it retained eminence, or to the average ability of its chiefs, or to its comparative civilisation in rude times, the House of Ormonde must be accounted the most distinguished of the Anglo-Norman families of Ireland.

Towns in Ireland: Dublin and Drogheda.

The native Irish had no regular towns. The Anglo-Normans took possession of those founded by the Ostmen, which were all on the coast, and founded many others, of which only three or four, and those not the most important, were at a distance from navigable rivers. Athassel in Tipperary is sometimes called a town, but it never became a municipality, and can have been little more than an aggregation of poor houses about the great monastery, and there may have been other similar cases. Dublin obtained its first charter from Henry II. in 1171 or 1172, and Drogheda from Henry III. in 1229.

'Dublin and Drogheda,' says the historian of the Irish capital, 'were neither distinctly English nor Irish. Their citizens, as tax-contributing and acknowledged subjects of England, relied on her for protection against oppressive Anglo-Norman nobles and hostile natives. The Irish—unless Anglicised—had no legal part in these communities, but continuous mutual intercourse was sustained by the advantages derived from traffic.' 'In our documents,' adds the same writer, 'Scandinavians or Ostmans but rarely appear, although in 1215 the latter people were of sufficient importance to have been associated with the English of Dublin by King John as parties to an inquiry held there by his justiciary. The proportion of the various national elements cannot be absolutely determined by the forms of names;' for many names originated in personal peculiarities, many were translated from one language to another, and many Irishmen became denizens, and adopted an English patronymic. The 'Irish town' which exists outside the old bounds of Dublin, Limerick, Kilkenny, Clonmel, and other places, doubtless perpetuates the memory of a time when the natives congre[Pg 74]gated in the neighbourhood of civic communities to which they did not belong.[35]

Other towns: Limerick, Waterford, and Cork the chief.

What has been said of Dublin and Drogheda applies to the other cities and towns of Ireland. Limerick received its first charter from John in 1197, Waterford from the same prince in 1206, and Cork from Henry III. in 1242. These were the chief centres of trade and of English law in the south of Ireland. The less important municipalities owed their origin generally to some great noble, the Crown afterwards adopting them and granting fresh privileges. Kilkenny received a charter from the Earl Marshal between 1202 and 1218. New Ross, well situated at the junction of the Nore and Barrow, belonged to the same great man, and excited the jealousy of Waterford at least as early as 1215. Clonmel was included in a grant made by Henry II. to Otho de Grandison. It passed into the hands of the De Burgos, who probably incorporated it, and who received a royal grant to hold a fair there in 1225. Fethard, Callan, Gowran, and other inland towns were of less consequence, but were still distinctly English in origin and character. Youghal and Kinsale were also corporate towns. The latter received a charter from Edward III. in 1333, and the former, which had been long identified with the Desmond family, seems not to have been regularly incorporated till 1462. The Kinsale charter recites that the town was surrounded by Irish enemies and English rebels, and that the burgesses were worn out in repelling the same. The mediæval kings commonly granted the customs and tolls of loyal towns to be expended by the inhabitants in repairing their walls.

Galway.

Galway has a history of its own. The O'Connors had a fortified post there before the Anglo-Norman invasion, and it soon attracted the attention of the invaders. In 1232 it was for the first time taken by Richard de Burgo, who lost it once, but recovered it and made it the capital of his province. The building of the walls was begun about the beginning of the reign of Edward I., and murage charters[Pg 75] were granted probably by that king, and certainly by Edward III. and Richard II. A charter of incorporation was granted in 1396, but the names of certain chief magistrates, provosts, portreeves, and sovereigns, are preserved from 1274 to 1485, when the first mayor took office. Fourteen

English families, afterwards known as the tribes of Galway, engrossed civic power, and from 1485 to 1654 every mayor, with a single doubtful exception, was chosen from among them. When the De Burgos turned Irish and renounced their allegiance, the loyal citizens soon learned to treat them as enemies, and in 1518 the corporation resolved that no inhabitant should receive into his house 'at Christmas, Easter, nor no feast else, any of the Burkes, MacWilliams, the Kellys, nor no sept else, without licence of the mayor and council, on pain to forfeit 5l. that neither O nor Mac shall strut nor swagger through the streets of Galway.' Their great enemies were the O'Flaherties of Iar-Connaught, and it is said the prayer 'from the ferocious O'Flaherties, good Lord, deliver us,' was once inscribed over the west gate of the town. Athenry, which was built by the Bermingham family, was long and closely connected with Galway. It received a murage charter in 1312.[36]

Anglo-Norman families of importance.

Besides the three great earldoms, there were several Anglo-Norman families who continued to have considerable importance in Tudor times. Robert le Poer, or De Poher, received a grant from Henry II., which made his descendants, now generally called Power, supreme in the eastern half of the county Waterford. In the middle ages they were often at war with the citizens of Waterford. Their chief seat was Curraghmore, and they are represented, through a lady, by the Marquis of Waterford. The western half of the same county, which came by marriage to the Desmonds, fell to the descendants of the seventh earl's second son, known as the[Pg 76] Fitzgeralds, of Decies, and seated at Dromana. The Fitzmaurices, descended from Raymond le Gros, occupied that part of north Kerry which is still called Clanmaurice. They became Barons of Lixnaw, and are represented by the Marquis of Lansdowne. The family of the White Knight was descended from Gilbert, eldest son of John More Fitzgerald by his second wife, Honora O'Connor; his half brother by Margery Fitz-Anthony being the first Earl of Desmond. The White Knights were called Macgibbon and Fitzgibbon, and their memory is preserved by the barony of Clangibbon, in the county of Cork. From John, the second of Honora O'Connor's sons, is descended the Knight of the Valley, or of Glin on the Shannon. Maurice, the third brother, was the first Knight of Kerry. Another branch of the Fitzgeralds, known as hereditary seneschals of Imokilly, were settled in the fifteenth and sixteenth centuries at Castle Martyr. The Barrys, descendants of Nesta as well as the Geraldines, were settled in that part of the county of Cork called Barrymore; and the Roches were established soon after the first invasion about Castletown-Roche, and Fermoy. Of the families who obtained portions of De Lacy's great territory, the most important were the Nugents, Barons of Delvin, and the Flemings, Barons of Slane on the Boyne. The Plunkets, who are supposed to be of Danish origin, were in the middle ages settled chiefly in Meath; and there they are still. They became Barons of Killeen, Dunsany, and Louth. The Prestons, Viscounts of Gormanston, and the Barnewalls, Barons of Trimleston, may also be noticed; but all the families of the Pale were overshadowed by the House of Kildare.

The colony steadily declines under Edward III.

So far as the English colony in Ireland is concerned, the long reign of Edward III. must be regarded as a period of decay. The murder of the last Earl of Ulster in 1333, and the consequent secession of the De Burghs, hastened the destruction of a fabric which had always hung loosely together. The sons of Hugh Boy O'Neill, who was killed in 1283, established themselves firmly in Eastern Ulster, and undid nearly all the work of De

Courcey and his successors. They[Pg 77] gave to Antrim the name of Clan-Hugh-Boy, or Clandeboye, as it is now written. Only the Savages maintained themselves in Ardes; and the MacQuillins, a family of Welsh origin, between the Bush and the Bann, in the district afterwards called the Route. The three royal fortresses which bridled Connaught, Athlone, Roscommon, and Randon, all fell into the hands of the Irish. In Leinster also the natives rapidly gained ground. Lysaght O'More formed a confederacy of nearly all the midland tribes, and expelled the settlers from the district between the Barrow and the Shannon. His career was short, but his work was lasting. 'In 1342,' says Clyn, 'he was killed when drunk by his own servant. He was a rich and powerful man, and honoured among his own people. He expelled nearly all the English from his lands, and burned eight of their castles in one evening. He destroyed Roger Mortimer's noble fortress of Dunamase, and usurped the lordship of his own country. He was a servant, he became a lord; he was a subject, he became a prince.' Bunratty Castle in Clare was dismantled by the O'Briens and Macnamaras, and a branch of the former established themselves in Tipperary. Of William Carragh O'Brien, of Aherlow, one of the chiefs of this sept, Clyn gives a very unflattering account. 'He was,' he declares, 'a bad and perverse man who lived ill and died ill, passing all his time in waylayings, thefts, spoils, and murders.'

Dissension rife among the colonists.

The constant quarrels of the colonists, and the corruption of their officials, laid them open to the attacks of the natives, and the state of Ireland attracted so much attention that the Parliament held at Westminster in 1331 advised the King to cross the Channel himself. Edward III. never had much time to attend to Ireland, but he seems to have been aware that he had duties in the matter. In 1338 he decreed that none but Englishmen born should fill legal offices; but this did not mend matters, and the administration of justice continued to be as corrupt as ever. The new comers married in Ireland, and were as ready to job for their children as if they had been descended from the first colonists. In 1341 the King ordered that Englishmen with[Pg 78] estates in England should be preferred, but the supply of such men was necessarily limited. The main cause of the corruption prevalent was no doubt the poverty of the Crown. Officials were ill paid, or not paid at all, and they supported themselves by embezzling funds or by selling justice. An unjust proposal to increase the revenue by resuming royal grants naturally aggravated every evil, and the English by blood were arrayed against the English by birth. Sir John Morris, the deputy who was ordered to carry out the new policy, summoned a Parliament to meet at Dublin in October, 1341. But Maurice Fitz-Thomas, first Earl of Desmond, persuaded a large section of the nobility to ignore the writs, to attend a rival assembly at Kilkenny, and to draw up a remonstrance addressed to the King. The malcontents wished to be informed how a governor without military skill could rule a land where war never ceased, how an official could become quickly rich, and how it came about that the King was never the richer for Ireland? Edward abandoned the intention of resuming the grants, but subsequent events show that he did not really forgive Desmond.

D'Ufford's futile attempts to recover the Earldom of Ulster.

Ralph d'Ufford had married Maud Plantagenet, widow of the murdered Earl of Ulster, and in 1344 he was sent over as Viceroy with very large powers. One of his objects was to resume possession of Ulster for the benefit of his step-daughter, the royal ward; but he totally failed in obtaining rent out of the lands, or in ousting those who had seized them. After chastising the Irish in the neighbourhood of Dublin, d'Ufford resolved to invade Ulster with a regular army. The MacArtanes attacked him at the Moyrie Pass, and he narrowly escaped annihilation. Having cut his way through with the help of the settlers in Louth and Monaghan, he made his way into the northern province, but no permanent results followed. Desmond and others having refused to attend his Parliament, the Viceroy went to Kerry, took Castle Island, and hanged its principal defenders. He imprisoned the Earl of Kildare and seized his estates, and then took action upon a bond executed in 1333, by which twenty-six of the chief men of the colony became bound for Desmond's[Pg 79] good behaviour. Many of the sureties had aided the Viceroy, but he, nevertheless, seized their lands. The Earl of Ormonde and two more were the only exceptions. The ruin caused by this policy was out of all proportion to the good, and in the history of the English in Ireland no one has a worse name than Sir Ralph d'Ufford, except perhaps his high-born wife, whose resentments were supposed to guide him. His hand was as heavy against the Church as against the temporal nobles. The annalist Pembridge, who was a contemporary, declares that he brought bad weather to Ireland, and that it lasted all his time. 'On Palm Sunday,' says the same writer, 'which was on April 9, 1346, Ralph d'Ufford died, whose death was very much lamented by his wife and family; but the loyal subjects of Ireland rejoiced at it, and both the clergy and laity for joy celebrated a solemn feast at Easter. Upon his death the floods ceased, and the air again grew wholesome, and the common people thanked God for it.'

FOOTNOTES:

[35] The quotations are from Gilbert's Historic and Municipal Documents of Ireland, pp. xxviii. and xxx.

[36] Hardiman's History of Galway contains as much as most readers will care to know about that town. The following distich makes it possible to remember the tribes:—

Athy, Blake, Bodkin, Browne, Deane, Darcy, Lynch,
Joyce, Kirwan, Martin, Morris, Skerrett, French.
To which Ffont or Faunt must be added.

[Pg 80]

CHAPTER VI.

FROM THE YEAR 1346 TO THE ACCESSION OF HENRY VII.

Lionel, Duke of Clarence, is not more successful than D'Ufford.Lionel holds a Parliament at Kilkenny, 1367.

The Crown did nothing for Ireland. Torn by intestine quarrels, and denied a just government, the colony grew yearly weaker. Many of the settlers found their position intolerable, and, in spite of severe ordinances, absenteeism constantly increased. In 1361 Edward summoned to Westminster no less than sixty-three non-resident landowners, including the heads of several great abbeys, who derived revenues from Ireland and gave nothing in return. They were ordered to provide an army suitable for the King's son Lionel, Duke of Clarence and Earl of Ulster by marriage, who proceeded to Ireland as Viceroy. He was accompanied by his wife, but failed, as D'Ufford had done, to obtain any

54

profit from her lordship of Ulster, and was scarcely successful even against the clans near Dublin. The O'Byrnes and O'Tooles cut off many of his English soldiers, and the Duke was obliged to seek aid from the more experienced colonists. Like many governors who have come to Ireland with great pretensions, Lionel found his position most humiliating, and he spent a great part of his time in England. His authority was delegated to deputies, and the feuds between English by blood and English by birth ran higher than ever. In 1367 he returned and summoned a Parliament, whose enactments gave legal sanction to the fact that the King was no longer lord of more than a comparatively small portion of Ireland.

The statute of Kilkenny contains a great many rather heterogeneous rules. What makes it of such great importance is its formal recognition of the existence of an English Pale, and of a hostile Irish people outside it. The word[Pg 81] Pale may not have been in use for a century later, but the thing was fully established.

Composition of the Parliament of Kilkenny.
The Parliament of Kilkenny did not, however, confine its attention to the narrow limits of the 'four obedient shires.' The distinction between English and Irish land was conceded, but it was still hoped that most of the shireland would be preserved to English law. The sheriffs or seneschals of ten counties or liberties, comprising all Leinster, except the modern King's and Queen's Counties, as well as Tipperary and Waterford, were required to produce their accounts at Dublin; but those of Connaught, Kerry, Cork, and Limerick were excused on account of distance, and were required only to attend commissioners of the exchequer when they came to their bailiwicks, and to render an account to them. Ulster, the Duchess of Clarence's patrimony, is not even mentioned by her husband's Parliament. Of the composition of that assembly we have no record, but it was attended by the Archbishops of Dublin, Cashel, and Tuam, and by the Bishops of Waterford and Lismore, Killaloe, Ossory, Leighlin, and Cloyne. The Archbishops of Cashel and Tuam and the Bishop of Killaloe were Irishmen; the rest were of English race, and some of them born in England.

The Statute of Kilkenny endeavours to separate the two races.
The statute begins by reciting that for a long time after the conquest the English in Ireland spoke English, and in general behaved like Englishmen; but that of late years many had fallen away and adopted the Irish language and habits, whereby the King's authority and the English interest were depressed, and the Irish enemy 'against reason' exalted. In order to remedy this marriage, fosterage, gossipred, and even concubinage with the Irish was declared high treason. Supplying horses and armour to Irishmen at any time was visited with like penalties, and so was furnishing them with provisions in time of war. Englishmen and even Irishmen living among the English were to speak English, to bear English names only, and to ride and dress in the English fashion, on pain of forfeiture until they should submit and find security. If they had no lands they might lie in prison till security was forthcoming. Special penalties were provided for[Pg 82] offenders who had 100l. a year in land. The English born in Ireland and in England were to be in all respects equal, and were not to call each other English hobbe or Irish dog, on pain of a year's imprisonment and a fine at the King's pleasure. War with the Irish was inculcated as a solemn duty, and the practice of buying off invasions was condemned. The end aimed at was that Irish enemies should be finally destroyed, and many minute rules were made for

arming the colony properly. The rude Irish game of hurling was discountenanced, and the borderers were enjoined to make themselves fit for constant war by practising such gentlemanlike sports as archery and lance-play. Imprisonment and fine were to follow a neglect of these precepts. Provision was made to prevent the Irish from forestalling the markets by establishing fairs of their own, and from grazing their cattle in the settled districts. Very severe regulations were made against Irish hangers-on—pipers to wit, story-tellers, babblers, and rhymers, all of whom acted habitually as spies. The keeping of kerne and idlemen, armed or unarmed, at the expense of other people, was sternly forbidden, and qualified as open robbery. It became, nevertheless, the greatest and commonest of all abuses. Private war among the English was to be punished as high treason, and so was the common practice of enticing friendly Irishmen to acts of violence.

The Statute of Kilkenny respects the Church, but makes distinctions.

The rights and privileges of Holy Church were jealously guarded by the Parliament of Kilkenny. Persons excommunicated for infringing her franchises were to be imprisoned by the civil power until restitution was made. Tithes were specially protected, and the excommunicated were not to be countenanced by King or people. But the distinction between the hostile races was maintained in matters ecclesiastical. No Irishman was to be admitted by provision, collation, or presentation among the English. Such preferments were declared void, and the next presentation was to lapse to the Crown. Religious houses situated among the English were strictly forbidden to receive Irishmen, but Englishmen by birth and by blood were given equal rights. The Irish prelates present probably found no difficulty in accepting[Pg 83] these principles, for they might, and did, retaliate by refusing to receive English clerks in Irish districts. The Archbishops and Bishops assembled at Kilkenny lent a special sanction to the statute by agreeing to excommunicate all who broke it, and they declared such offenders duly excommunicated in advance.

Effects of the Statute of Kilkenny.

Sir John Davies, with less than his usual accuracy, has declared that 'the execution of these laws, together with the presence of the King's son, made a notable alteration in the state and manners of the people within the space of seven years, which was the term of this prince's lieutenancy.' Now, the Statute of Kilkenny was not passed till 1367, and Lionel died in 1368. The Act of Henry III., on which Davies chiefly founded his statement, says the land continued in prosperity and honour while the Kilkenny laws were executed, and fell to ruin and desolation upon their falling into abeyance. But the annalists tell a different story, and it is not easy to say what those fat years were. In 1370, only three years after the passing of the much vaunted statute, the Earl of Desmond and others were taken prisoners by the O'Briens and Macnamaras, and the deputy, Sir William de Windsor, was obliged to leave the O'Tooles unchastised in order to hurry to the defence of Munster. Newcastle, within a day's ride from Dublin, was taken and dismantled. The judges could not get as far as Carlow. In 1377 the O'Farrells gained a great advantage over the English of Meath. The general result of the fighting during the ten years which followed the Parliament of Kilkenny was that the Irish retained possession of at least all which they had previously won. What the statute really did was to separate the two races more completely.

Edward III. weakens the colony by drawing men from it.

Edward III. repeated his grandfather's mistake, and drew away many of the colonists to his Scotch and Continental wars. An Anglo-Irish contingent fought at Halidon Hill, and it was while making preparations for that campaign that the Earl of Ulster lost his life. Ireland was also well represented at Creçy, and many brave men fell victims to disease at Calais. The Viceroys sent over from time to time[Pg 84] seem to have been regarded as licensed oppressors, and it is recorded of many that they left Dublin without paying their debts. Sir Thomas Rokeby, who was Deputy in 1349 and 1356, is praised by the contemporary chronicler Pembridge for beating the Irish well, and for paying his way honestly. 'I will,' he said, 'use wooden cups and platters, but give gold and silver for my food and clothes, and for the men in my pay.' That this golden saying, as Davies calls it, should have been thought worth recording shows what the general practice was. The three great pestilences which ravaged England ran their course in Ireland also. It was to the first of these visitations that the annalist Clyn succumbed. 'I have,' he records, 'well weighed what I have written, as befits a man who dwells among the dead in daily expectation of death; and lest the writer should perish with the writing, and the work with the workman, I leave parchment for a continuation, if by chance any of the race of Adam should escape this plague and resume my unfinished task.' On the whole, the reign of Edward III. must be regarded as one of the most disastrous in the annals of the English in Ireland.

Richard II. determines to visit Ireland. His first visit, 1394.

The reign of Richard II. is mainly remarkable for the King's two visits to Ireland. But that step was not taken until many others had failed. James Butler, third Earl of Ormonde, was Viceroy when the old King died. He continued in office, and held a Parliament at Castle Dermot, whose deliberations were interrupted by an invasion of Leinster on the western side. The O'Briens were bought off with 100 marks, but there were only nine in the treasury, and the residue was supplied by individuals who gave horses, a bed, or moderate sums of money. Ormonde resigned an office which there was no means of supporting properly, and the Earl of Kildare refused the post. In 1380 Edmund Mortimer, Earl of March, who claimed Ulster through his wife Philippa, the daughter of Duke Lionel, agreed to accept the burden for three years. He covenanted for 20,000 marks and for absolute control over the revenue of Ireland. The Irish scarcely ventured to oppose him openly; and he recovered Athlone,[Pg 85] built a bridge at Coleraine, put down rebels in southern Leinster, and might have extended his power still further had he not died of a chill, caught in fording a river near Cork. Ormonde and Desmond refused to accept the vacant government, and the Irish continued to enlarge their borders. In 1385 Robert de Vere, Earl of Oxford, the King's favourite and grandson of Ralph d'Ufford and the Countess of Ulster, was appointed Viceroy for life, and created first Marquis of Dublin, and then Duke of Ireland. All the attributes of royalty, such as the right to coin money and issue writs in his own name, were conferred on him, and he undertook to pay the King 5,000 marks a year, which the latter agreed to remit until the conquest of Ireland was complete. De Vere did not visit Ireland; but the government was carried on in his name for some years, during which the colony grew weaker and weaker. Nor did his disgrace make any more difference than his appointment had done. Limerick and Cork could scarcely defend themselves. Waterford was harassed by the Le Poers and their Irish allies. Towns in Kildare were burned, and the English Bishop of Leighlin was unable to approach his diocese. Galway threw off its allegiance, and sought the protection of MacWilliam. In 1391 the Earl of Ormonde was again persuaded to undertake the government with a salary of 3,000 marks; but he could do little more than temporise. Payments to the Irish were frequent, and as they constantly advanced the dispossessed settlers carried the story of their woes to England. Proclamations against absentees were of small effect, and at last the King determined to go himself. He landed at Waterford on October 2, 1394, with 4,000 men at arms and 30,000 archers. As soon as Art MacMurrough, whom the Leinster Irish accepted as their king, heard of Richard's arrival, he attacked New Ross, 'burned its houses and castles, and carried away gold, silver, and hostages.'

Richard has but little success.

Richard II.'s army, augmented as it was by the forces of the colony, was the largest seen in Ireland during the middle ages, and has hardly been exceeded in modern times. William III. had about 36,000 at the Boyne. Nothing was[Pg 86] performed worthy of so great a host or of the King's presence. One division of the royal army was defeated with great loss by the O'Connors of Offaly, and another by the O'Carrolls. Richard saw that his troops were unfit for war in bogs and mountains, and could not but confess that the natives had many just causes of complaint. He adopted a conciliatory policy, and induced O'Neill, O'Connor, MacMurrough, and O'Brien, as representatives of the four royal Irish races, to do homage and to receive the honour of knighthood at his hands. These four, and a great number of other chiefs, bound themselves to the King by indenture; but no money was actually paid, and for all practical purposes Caligula's shells were quite as good a badge of conquest. The German princes had a right to say that Richard was not fit for empire, since he had been unable to subdue his rebellious subjects of Ireland. He remained nine months in the island, and left the government to Roger Mortimer, Earl of March, heir-presumptive to the Crown, and claiming to be Earl of Ulster in right of his mother, the only child of Lionel, Duke of Clarence.

The Irish grow continually stronger. Richard's second visit, 1399.

Besides the earldom of Ulster, Mortimer claimed enormous estates all over Ireland, but possession had been completely divorced from feudal ownership. He attacked the Wicklow clans, but was defeated with loss. In 1398 he made a final attempt to recover some portion of his Leinster inheritance, but was defeated and slain in Carlow by the O'Tooles, O'Nolans, and Kavanaghs. In the following year Richard again visited Ireland in person. His army was nearly as large as on the first occasion, and vast quantities of stores had been collected. The Crown jewels were carried with the King, as was a yet more precious flask of oil which had been transmitted straight from heaven to Archbishop Becket while praying at the shrine of Columba. But neither arms, nor gems, nor even the sacred chrism had any effect upon Art MacMurrough. The King again landed at Waterford, and after a few days' rest moved forward to meet the redoubtable Irishman, who was posted in a wood with 3,000 men. An open space having been secured by burning houses and villages, Richard knighted young Henry of Lancaster, the[Pg 87] future victor of Agincourt, and ordered a large number of labourers to fell the wood which sheltered the enemy. Aided by the ground, MacMurrough held the royal army in check for eleven days. The communications were cut, and the men at arms had nothing but green oats for their horses. It was early in July; but the weather was wet, and the whole army suffered from exposure and hunger. A convoy which arrived at Waterford rather added to the disaster. 'Soldiers,' says a contemporary chronicler, 'rushed into the sea as if it were straw.' Casks were broached, and more than 1,000 at a time were seen drunk with the Spanish wine. Abandoning the hope of attacking the Kavanaghs in their fastnesses, Richard made his way to Dublin, the Earl of Gloucester having failed to treat with MacMurrough.

Richard's failure.

The Leinster chieftain had married an Anglo-Norman heiress, and through her claimed the barony of Narragh in Kildare. He demanded to be put in full possession of his wife's lands, and to be left unmolested to enjoy his chiefry. Otherwise he refused to come to any terms with the King. Richard threatened, but his Irish plans were interrupted by the news that Henry of Lancaster had landed in England. He lingered for some weeks in Ireland, and that delay was fatal to him. He reached Milford only to find that he had no longer a party, and thus Art MacMurrough may be said to have crowned the House of Lancaster. The Irish chief continued irreconcilable, and defied the Government until his death in 1417.

Ireland neglected by Henry IV.

With a bad title and an insecure throne Henry IV. could not be expected to pay much attention to Ireland. The strength of the colony continued to decline during his reign. He made his second son, Thomas, Viceroy, but a child in his twelfth year was not the sort of governor required. The treasury was empty, and the young prince's council had soon to announce that he had pawned his plate, and that not another penny could be borrowed. The soldiers had deserted, the household were about to disperse, and the country was so much impoverished that relief could scarcely be hoped for. The settlement was only preserved by paying black mail to[Pg 88] the Irish. The towns defended themselves as they best could, and sometimes showed considerable martial enterprise. Thus Waterford was several times attacked by the O'Driscolls, a piratical clan in West Cork, who habitually allied themselves with the Le Poers. In 1413 the citizens assumed the offensive, and armed a ship, in which the mayor and bailiffs with a strong band sailed to Baltimore, where they arrived on Christmas Day. A messenger was sent to say that the Mayor of Waterford had brought a cargo of wine, and admission was thus gained to the chief's hall. 'The Mayor,' we are told, 'took up to dance O'Driscoll and his son, the prior of the Friary, O'Driscoll's three brethren, his uncle, and his wife, and having them in their dance, the Mayor commanded every of his men to hold fast the said persons; and so, after singing a carol, came away bringing with them aboard the said ship the said O'Driscoll and his company, saying unto them they should go with him to Waterford to sing their carol and make merry that Christmas; and they being all aboard made sail presently, and arrived at Waterford, St. Stephen's day at night, where with great joy received they were with lights.'

This exploit seems to have tamed the O'Driscolls for a time, but they invaded Waterford in 1452 and 1461. On the first occasion the citizens had the worst, but on the second they gained the victory, and took the chief with six of his sons.[37]

Henry V. makes Talbot Viceroy.

In the first year of his reign Henry V. made the famous Sir John Talbot Viceroy. He was entitled to lands in Westmeath in right of his wife, and the lordship of Wexford had devolved upon his elder brother. He adopted the plan by which Bellingham and Sidney afterwards reconquered the greater part of Ireland. The array of the counties was called out under heavy penalties, and Talbot remained six days in Leix, which he so ravaged as to bring O'More to his senses. The bridge of Athy, which had been of use to none but the[Pg 89] assailants of the Pale, was rebuilt and fortified, so that the cattle of loyal people might graze in safety, which they had not done for thirty years. Passes were cut in the woods bordering on the settled districts, and there seemed some hope for the shrunken and shattered colony. But Talbot's salary of 4,000 marks fell into arrear, and his unpaid soldiers became a worse scourge than the Irish had been. The Viceroy and his brother, the Archbishop of Dublin, were constantly at daggers drawn with the White Earl of Ormonde, and the feud continued nearly till the Earl's death in 1450. It was, however, due both to Sir John Talbot and to Ormonde, his antagonist, that the Irish were kept at bay. Shakespeare's hero was the bugbear with which French mothers quieted naughty children, and he was no less feared in Ireland. With the colonists he was not popular, because the Crown refused him the means of paying his debts, and Irish writers stigmatise him as the worst man who had appeared in the world since the time of Herod.

Drain of colonists to the English civil wars.

'France,' says Sir John Davies, 'was a fairer mark to shoot at than Ireland, and could better reward the conqueror.' The latter part of his statement is questionable, but such was the view taken by the kings of England from Henry II. to Henry VII. Thomas Butler, Prior of Kilmainham, who ought to have been engaged in the defence of the Pale, took 1,500 men to help Henry V. at the siege of Rouen in 1418. The contemporary chronicler, Robert Redman, says they did excellent service with very sharp darts and crossbows. Trained in the irregular warfare of Ireland, they easily outran the Frenchmen, to whom they showed extraordinary animosity, but were less honourably distinguished by their practice of kidnapping children and selling them as slaves to the English. James, Earl of Ormonde and Wiltshire, also raised troops in Ireland for foreign service, and it is probable that many other contingents were furnished of which no record has been preserved. These forces consisted of Anglo-Irish, or at least of Irishmen settled in obedient districts, and their absence from home must have had a constant tendency to weaken the colony.[Pg 90]

Richard of York made Lord-Lieutenant for ten years, 1449.

In 1449 Richard of York visited Ireland as Viceroy. He accepted the office for ten years, in consideration of 4,000 marks for the first, and 2,000l. for each succeeding year, and of the whole local revenue. Richard was Earl of Ulster, but he preferred conciliation to any attempt at reconquest, and was, consequently, able to command the services of many Irish clans, including Magennis, MacArtane, MacMahon, and O'Reilly. The O'Byrnes were put down with the help of the Northern chiefs, O'Neill himself sent presents to the Duke, and most of the central districts became tributary. The Anglo-Normans of Munster, who had partially degenerated, renewed their allegiance, and it was generally supposed that the task of making Ireland English would at last be accomplished. The Viceroy's son George, the 'false, fleeting, perjured Clarence,' of later years, was born in Dublin, and his sponsors were Ormonde and Desmond. But very soon the fair prospect was clouded. The stipulated salary was not paid. The Irish discovered that Richard had no greater force than his predecessors, and the MacGeohegans, who had submitted, openly defied his power. He left Ireland suddenly in the autumn of 1450, and did not return for nine years.

Richard is popular, and creates a Yorkist party. Ireland almost independent.

Richard had not done much to increase the King's power in Ireland, but he created a Yorkist party there. At the time he was accused of prompting Cade's rebellion, and Jack himself was said to be a native of Ireland. The fact that both Simnel and Warbeck afterwards found their best support among the Anglo-Irish seems to show that the Kildare and Desmond partisans were already familiar with the notion of a Yorkist pretender. It is very probable that the adherents of the White Rose saw their opportunity in the fact that the Earldom of Ulster belonged to their chief, and Cade must have had an object in calling himself Mortimer. All this is plausible conjecture; but about the significance of Richard's second viceroyalty there can be no reasonable doubt. In 1459, after Salisbury's defeat at Blore Heath, the Duke of York was forced to fly, and he took refuge in Ireland, where he seized the government in spite of the Coventry Parliament. The local independence of Ireland was now for the first time[Pg 91] seriously attempted. Richard held a Parliament, which acknowledged the English Crown while repudiating the English Legislature and the English Courts of Law. The Duke of York's person was declared inviolable, and rebellion against him was made high treason. The royal privilege of coining money was also given to him. William Overy, a squire of the Earl of Ormonde, who was already acknowledged as head of the Irish Lancastrians, attempted to arrest the Duke as an attainted traitor and rebel; but he was seized, tried before Richard himself, and hanged, drawn, and quartered. After the victory of his friends at Northampton the Duke returned to England. He took with him a considerable body of Anglo-Irish partisans, and he committed the government to the Earl of Kildare.

The Yorkist faction headed by the Earl of Kildare.

Richard of York fell at Sandal Hill, but the popularity which he had gained in Ireland descended to his son. In the bloody battle of Towton the flower of the Anglo-Irish Lancastrians fell, and their leader, the Earl of Ormonde, was taken and beheaded. His house suffered an eclipse from which it was destined to emerge with greater brilliancy than ever, and the rival family of Kildare became for a time supreme in the Pale. The native Irish everywhere advanced, and English law rapidly shrunk within the narrowest limits. A Parliament, held by the Earl of Desmond in 1465, enacted that every Irishman dwelling among the English in Dublin, Meath, Louth, and Kildare, should dress in the English fashion, shave his moustache, take the oath of allegiance within a year, and assume as a surname the name of a town, of a colour, or of a trade. In the Parliament of 1480, held by the Earl of Kildare, all trade between the Pale and the Irish was forbidden by law. The Parliament of Drogheda in 1468 had already passed an Act which declared that the castle of Ballymore Eustace, 'lying between the counties of Dublin and Kildare, among the O'Byrnes and O'Tooles, Irish enemies,' should be garrisoned by Englishmen only. The Eustaces, it was explained, had given it in charge to 'one Lawrence O'Bogan, an Irishman both by father and mother, who by nature would discover the secrets of the English.' Other[Pg 92] Acts to a similar effect might be cited, and it may be said that the main object of Edward IV.'s government in Ireland was to separate the two races more completely.

George, Duke of Clarence, twice Viceroy. Execution of Thomas, Earl of Desmond, 1467.

George, Duke of Clarence, was Viceroy from 1461 to 1470, and again from 1472 till his mysterious death in 1478. Though born in Dublin, he never visited Ireland as a man, and the government was administered by a succession of Deputies. The fate of one of these Deputies, Thomas, eighth Earl of Desmond, deserves particular mention. John Tiptoft, Earl of Worcester, whose beautiful Latinity had moved Pope Æneas Sylvius to tears, was entrusted with the government in 1467, and he assembled a Parliament in which Desmond and Kildare were attainted. Kildare escaped to England, and procured a reversal of the attainder, but Desmond was enticed to Drogheda, and there beheaded. The ostensible cause for this severity is declared by an unpublished statute to have been 'alliance, fosterage, and alterage with the King's Irish enemies, and furnishing them with horses, harness, and arms, and supporting them against the King's loyal subjects.' The Anglo-Irish tradition attributes it to the vengeance of Queen Elizabeth Woodville, whose marriage Desmond had opposed. According to Russell, he told Edward that Sir John Grey's widow was too mean a match for him, that he needed allies sorely, and that he had better cast her off and link himself with some powerful prince. By this account the Queen stole the royal signet, and transmitted a secret order for the Earl's death to Ireland. Three years later Worcester was taken and beheaded during the short Lancastrian restoration; and this quite disposes of Russell's statement that King Edward 'struck his head from his neck to make satisfaction to the angry ghost of Desmond.' What is historically important in Desmond's execution is that it gave his successors an excuse for not attending Parliaments or entering walled towns. Their claim to legal exemption was not indeed allowed, but it may have had considerable effect on their conduct.[38]

Under Edward IV. and Richard III. the House of Kildare is all-powerful. The Butlers overshadowed.

After the death of Clarence, Edward made his sons,[Pg 93] George and Richard, Viceroys, and Richard III. conferred the same office on his infant son Edward. The government was carried on by Deputies, and during the last twenty years of the Yorkist dynasty almost all real power centred in the House of Kildare. It was the seventh Earl who established the brotherhood of St. George for the defence of the Pale. The thirteen members of this fraternity were chosen from among the principal landowners of the four obedient shires, thus excluding the Butlers, who formed a small Pale of their own about Kilkenny. The brothers of St. George had rather more than 200 soldiers under them, who were paid out of the royal revenue; and that constituted the entire standing army. The cities and towns maintained a precarious existence by themselves. In the charter which Richard III. granted to Galway it was specially declared that the Clanricarde Burkes had no jurisdiction within the town which their ancestors had taken and fortified. An Act passed in 1485 declares that various benefices in the diocese of Dublin were situated among the Irish, that English clerks could not serve the churches because they could not be understood or because they refused to reside, and that it was therefore necessary to collate Irish clerks; and power was given to the Archbishop to do so for two years. The statute of Kilkenny and the Acts subsidiary to it had had their natural effect. The English, in trying to become perfectly English, had shrunk almost to nothing; and the Irish, by being held always at arm's length, had become more Irish and less civilised than ever.

FOOTNOTES:

[37] The quarrels of Waterford with the O'Driscolls are given in the Calendar of Carew MSS., Miscellaneous vol. p. 470. Smith refers to a MS. in Trinity College.

[38] Besides those in the Statute Book many Irish Acts of Edward IV.'s reign may be studied in Hardiman's Statute of Kilkenny.

[Pg 94]

CHAPTER VII.

THE IRISH PARLIAMENT.

The Irish Parliament a close copy.

The history of the Irish Parliament in the middle ages corresponds pretty closely with that of England. The idea of the three estates is plainly visible as early as 1204, when John asked an aid from the archbishops, bishops, abbots, priors, archdeacons, and clergy, the earls, barons, justices, sheriffs, knights, citizens, burgesses, and freeholders of Ireland. The Common Council of the King's faithful of Ireland is afterwards often mentioned, and in 1228 Henry III. ordered his justiciary to convoke the archbishops, bishops, abbots, priors, earls and barons, knights and freeholders, and the bailiffs of every county, and to read Magna Charta to them. 1254 has been fixed as the date at which two knights from each shire were regularly summoned to the English Parliament. In the confusion which followed, the precedent slept for a while, but in Simon de Montfort's famous Parliament in 1264 burgesses as well as knights had seats. The evidences of regular election in Ireland are scanty at this early period; but legislative enactments and pecuniary aids were more than once made by the whole community of Ireland before the close of Henry III.'s reign. The germs of a Parliamentary constitution were not planted in purely Irish districts; but it is probable that ecclesiastics attended Parliament even from them, and that the natives were thus in some degree represented. In 1254 the King called by name upon the Kings O'Donnell, O'Neill, O'Reilly, and O'Flynn, upon MacCarthy of Desmond, O'Brien of Thomond, O'Phelan of Decies, and fourteen other Celtic chiefs, to help him against the Scots. He confides in their love for him to furnish such[Pg 95] help, and promises them thanks; pointedly separating their case from that of his lieges of Ireland.[39]

Growth of representative institutions.

Accepting 1295 as the date at which English Parliamentary representation settled down into something like its modern shape, we find that the great Plantagenet was not unmindful of Ireland. In that same year the justiciary Wogan issued writs to the prelates and nobles, and also to the sheriffs of Dublin, Louth, Kildare, Waterford, Tipperary, Cork, Limerick, Kerry, Connaught, and Roscommon, and to the seneschals of the liberties of Meath, Wexford, Carlow, Kilkenny, and Ulster. The sheriffs and seneschals were ordered to proceed to the election of two good and discreet knights from each county or liberty, who were to have full power to act for their districts. It does not appear that cities and boroughs were represented on this occasion; but in 1300, Wogan being still justiciary, writs were directed to counties for the election of three or four members, and to cities and boroughs for the election of two or three. The King's principal object was to get money for his Scotch war; and, with this view, Wogan visited Drogheda and other places and extorted benevolence before the Parliament met. A certain supremacy was not denied to the English Parliament, for in 1290 a vast number of petitions were made to the King in Parliament at Westminster. Among the petitioners was the Viceroy, John Sandford, Archbishop of Dublin, who begged the King to consider the state of Ireland, of which he had already advised him through Geoffrey de Joinville, a former Viceroy, who was sitting in Parliament with others of the King's Council in Ireland. Edward I. answered that he was very busy, but that he had the matter much at heart, and that he would attend to it as soon as he could.[40]

Parliament of 1295.

Of the Parliament of 1295 a particular record has fortunately been preserved. Each sheriff was ordered to make his election in the full county court, and each seneschal in[Pg 96] the full court of the liberty, and they were to attend Parliament in their proper persons—to verify the returns no doubt. The personal attendance of the sheriffs was required in England until 1406. The magnates who were summoned to Wogan's Parliament behaved as we might expect to find them behave. The Bishops of the South and East came. The Archbishop of Armagh and his suffragans sent proctors with excuses for non-attendance. The Archbishop of Tuam and his suffragans neither came nor apologised. The absence of Hugo de Lacy, one of those elected by the county of Limerick, is particularly noted, whence we may infer that the other shires and liberties were duly represented. Richard, Earl of Ulster, was present. This Parliament principally occupied itself with making regulations as to the treatment of the Irish, and in devising means for checking their inroads upon the colonised districts. The descendants of the first conquerors were already beginning to adopt Celtic customs.[41]

Parliaments of Edward II. and Edward III.

Under Edward II. Parliaments were frequent; and writs are extant which show that he, as well as Edward III., intended them to be held annually. Cases occur of bishops, priors, and temporal peers being fined for non-attendance in this reign, and there is good reason to believe that those who were summoned to Parliament generally came. In 1311 writs for a Parliament to be held at Kilkenny were issued by the justiciary Wogan to Richard, Earl of Ulster, and eighty-seven other men of name, to the prelates and ecclesiastical magnates, and to the sheriffs. The sheriffs were ordered to summon two knights from every county, and two citizens or burgesses from every city or borough, who were to have full power to act for their several communities in conjunction with the magnates, lay and clerical. Owing probably to the shape which Bruce's invasion gave to the English colony, the Parliaments of Edward III. are more strictly confined to the districts where the King had real as well as nominal authority. The murder of the last Earl of Ulster in 1333, and the conversion of the De Burghs into Irishmen, almost completed[Pg 97] the work of destruction which Bruce had only just failed to effect. To the Parliament of 1360, the Archbishops of Dublin and Cashel, the Bishops of Meath, Kildare, Lismore, Killaloe, Limerick, Emly, Cloyne, and Ferns, and the Abbots of St. Mary's and St. Thomas's at Dublin were the only prelates summoned. The Earls of Kildare and Desmond and eight knights were called up by name. Writs for the election of two knights were issued to the sheriffs of the counties of Dublin, Carlow, Louth, Kildare, Waterford, Limerick, and Cork, and of the crosses of Meath, Kilkenny, Wexford, and Tipperary; and to the seneschals of the liberties of Kilkenny, Meath, Tipperary, and Wexford. Writs for the election of citizens and burgesses were no longer directed to the sheriffs, but the mayor and bailiffs of Dublin, Drogheda, Cork, Waterford, and Limerick, the sovereign and bailiffs of Kilkenny and Ross, and the provost and bailiffs of Clonmel and Wexford were ordered to return two members each. The sheriff of Kildare and the seneschal of the liberty of Kilkenny were told what individuals they were expected to see elected. The House of Commons was then supposed to consist of twenty-eight knights and twenty-four citizens and burgesses; but the counties of Dublin and Carlow were 'justly excused' on account of the war, and the members for Drogheda, who omitted to come, were summoned before the Council under a penalty of 40l.[42]

Parliament of Kilkenny.

The famous Parliament which Lionel, Duke of Clarence, held at Kilkenny in 1367 was probably attended by representatives from a very limited district; for there were but forty members of the House of Commons in March 1374, and of these four came from the county of Dublin. But in November 1374 the number was fifty-four; in 1377 it rose to sixty-two; and in 1380 and 1382 it was fifty-eight. We may, therefore, take the number of county and borough members at the close of the fourteenth century as about sixty. The counties generally represented were Dublin, Kildare, Carlow, Meath, Louth, Waterford, Cork, Limerick, and Wex[Pg 98]ford, the liberties of Ulster, Meath, Tipperary, Kerry, and Kilkenny, and the crosses of Ulster, Tipperary, Kilkenny, and Kerry. The cities were Dublin, Cork, Waterford, Kilkenny, and Limerick, and the towns were Drogheda, Youghal, Ross, Wexford, Galway, and Athenry. Longford was a county in 1377, but was not maintained as shire ground. Many Parliaments met during the fifteenth century, but their action was more and more confined to the district round Dublin, which about the middle of the century came to be called the Pale.[43]

Hereditary peers.

1295 will probably be accepted as the date when English barons who had once sat in Parliament claimed an hereditary right to their writs of summons. It would seem that the origin of the Irish peerage, using the word in its modern sense, must be referred to a somewhat later date; for eighty-seven persons, who were perhaps all tenants of the Crown, were summoned by name to the Kilkenny Parliament in 1311. The subject is not of great historical importance, because the period of transition coincides with that in which the encroachments of the natives reduced feudal Ireland to its lowest estate. In the sixteenth century the title of baron was still popularly given to the heads of some families who had formerly been barons by tenure, but who had lost all Parliamentary rights. As in England, the knights of the shire had become the proper representatives of the gentry, and peerage grew to be the special creation of the Crown. In the Parliament of 1560 there were twenty-three temporal peers, and of these eight had been created within the century. It will be safe to assume that the number of temporal peers sitting in the Irish Parliament at any time during the one hundred years preceding Elizabeth's accession was well under thirty.[44]

Spiritual peers.

The number of spiritual greatly exceeded the number of temporal peers. There were four archbishops from the first sending of the palls in 1151. If we take the year 1500, after some unions had been effected and before the great quarrel[Pg 99] between King and Pope, we find that there were twenty-six bishops in Ireland. Some of the more distant ones were perhaps never summoned to Parliament, and long before the close of the fifteenth century we cannot doubt that many had ceased to attend the shrunken legislature of the Pale. In 1293 John, Bishop of Clonfert, an Italian and the Pope's nuncio, was fined for non-attendance; and similar penalties were imposed on Bishops of Ferns, Ossory, Cork, Ardfert, Limerick, Down, and Emly, during the reigns of Edward II., Edward III., and Richard II. There were thirteen mitred Abbots of the Cistercian order, ten mitred Priors of Augustinian canons; and the Grand Prior of Kilmainham, who represented the wealth and importance of the proscribed Templars as well as of the Hospitallers, had always a seat in Parliament. The Prior of Kilmainham was so important a person that upon the suppression of the order of St. John, Henry VIII. made its last chief a peer. The Abbot of St. Mary's and the Prior of St. Thomas's were always summoned, but it is clear that in earlier days all the mitred heads of houses were considered real as well as nominal spiritual peers. The Prior of Athassel was fined for non-attendance in 1323, the Abbot of Owney in 1325, and the Abbot of Jerpoint in 1377. Much obscurity hangs over the mediæval House of Lords in Ireland; but it must generally have rested with the Viceroy whether the temporal or spiritual peers should be most numerous in any particular Parliament.[45]

The clergy as a separate estate. Proctors.

The existence of the clergy as a separate estate in Ireland is less clear than in England; but they had the right of taxing themselves, for in 1538 the Lords Spiritual were thanked by Henry VIII. for granting him an annual twentieth of all their promotions, benefices, and possessions. Proctors of the clergy attended the Lower House, and when Henry VIII. undertook his ecclesiastical innovations, they claimed the right to veto bills. It was, however, easily shown that their consent had not formerly been held necessary;[Pg 100] and in 1537 an Act was passed declaring the proctors to be no members of Parliament. The preamble states that two proctors from each diocese had been usually summoned to attend Parliament; but that they had neither voice nor vote, and were only 'counsellors and assistants upon such things of learning as should happen in controversy to declare their opinions, much like as the Convocation within the realm of England.' Their pretensions to a veto were formally pronounced baseless, and it was declared once for all that the assent or dissent of the proctors could have no effect on the action of Parliament.[46]

The Viceroy.

The representative of the King in Ireland was generally styled justiciar for a long time after the first invasion. His powers were analogous to that of the great officer of State in England who had the same title, and who acted as regent during the frequent absences of the kings. The title of justiciar continued to be given to the Irish viceroys long after the English justiciarship changed its character—that is, about the close of Henry III.'s reign. The first person who had the title of Lord Lieutenant, if we except the early case of John de Courcy, appears to have been Lionel, Earl of Ulster and Duke of Clarence, who was sent to Ireland in 1361. Afterwards it became a common practice to make one of the royal family Lord Lieutenant, the duties being usually performed by a deputy. But the title of Lord Lieutenant, though considered higher than any other, was not confined to princes. In time the title of Deputy was given to Governors of Ireland, even when no Lord Lieutenant intervened between them and the King. Richard of York was the last Lord Lieutenant of royal blood who actually ruled at Dublin. After his time the real government was in the hands of the Earls of Kildare, who were Lords Deputy, with but brief intervals, from 1478 to 1526. During that period the title of Lord Lieutenant, but the title only, was enjoyed by Edward, Prince of Wales, by John de la Pole, Earl of Lincoln, by Jasper, Duke of Bedford, and by Henry VIII.[Pg 101] before his accession to the Crown. In the meantime, the word justiciar, or Lord Justice, had come to mean a temporary substitute for the Deputy or Lieutenant. When a sovereign died, or when a viceroy suddenly left Ireland, it became the business of the Council to elect some one in his room. When giving leave to a governor to leave his post, the sovereign sometimes named the Lord Justice. Lord Capel, who was appointed in 1695, was the last chief governor who had the title of Deputy. Since the Revolution, the head of the Irish Government has always been a Lord Lieutenant, and during his absence one, or two, or three Lords Justices have been appointed by the Irish Privy Council.[47]

FOOTNOTES:

[39] Stubbs's Const. Hist., chap. xv.; Lynch's Feudal Dignities, chaps. iii. and xi.

[40] Sweetman's Calendar of Documents, 1289; Lynch, supra.

[41] The record is printed from the Black Book of Christ Church, in the Miscellany of the Irish Archæological Society.

[42] Lynch, ut supra.

[43] Lynch, ut supra; Lodge's Register; Hardiman's Statute of Kilkenny.

[44] The names of those summoned to the Parliament of 1311 are printed by Lynch, chap. ii.; the names of those who attended in 1560 are in Tracts Relating to Ireland, vol. ii., Appendix II.

[45] Cotton's Fasti; Alemand's Histoire Monastique; Lynch, chaps. iii. and vii.

[46] Irish Statutes, 28 Hen. VIII. cap. 12.

[47] See the list of chief governors in Harris's Ware; Borlase's Reduction of Ireland; Lodge's Patentee Officers; and Gilbert's Viceroys.

[Pg 102]

CHAPTER VIII.

THE REIGN OF HENRY VII.

Accession of Henry VII., 1485.
Ireland was destined to give the victor of Bosworth much trouble, but his accession made little immediate difference to the Anglo-Irish community. Kildare continued to act as Chief Governor, and on the nomination of Jasper, Duke of Bedford, to the Lord Lieutenancy, he was formally appointed Deputy under him. His brother Thomas was allowed to retain the Great Seal. While thus leaving the administration of the island to the Yorkist Geraldines, Henry lost no time in restoring the rival House, which had suffered in defence of the Red Rose. Sir Thomas Butler was by Act of Parliament at once restored in blood, became seventh Earl of Ormonde, and was taken into high favour. The practical

leadership of the Irish Butlers was, however, never held by him, and the disputes concerning it had no doubt great effect in consolidating Kildare's power.

The Ormonde family. Sir Piers Butler.

John, sixth Earl of Ormonde, who never lived in Ireland, appointed as his deputy his cousin, Sir Edmund Butler. Earl John dying in Palestine, his brother Thomas succeeded him, and continued Sir Edmund in the custody of the Irish estates. Sir Edmund by will granted to his son Piers the same power as he had himself held, but it does not appear that this curious bequest was acknowledged either by the Earl of Ormonde or by the people of Kilkenny and Tipperary. Sir James Ormonde, as he is called, a bastard son of the fifth Earl, became the real chief of the Butlers, and is often called Earl by Irish writers; the rules of legitimate descent being then very lightly regarded in Ireland. Sir James received a regular commission from Thomas, Earl of Ormonde, as his deputy, supervisor, 'and general and special attorney' in[Pg 103] Kilkenny. Strong in the confidence of the rightful Earl and in the estimation of the people, Sir James became Kildare's chief opponent; who to weaken him espoused the cause of Sir Piers, to whom he gave his daughter Lady Margaret in marriage. 'By that means and policy,' says the 'Book of Howth,' 'the Earl of Wormond (i.e. Sir James) was so occupied in his own country that he could not attend to do any damage to the Earl of Kildare nor any of his friends.' And the chronicler Stanihurst, a Geraldine partisan, would have us believe that the successful career of Sir Piers was wholly due to the 'singular wisdom' of his wife. An eminent modern antiquary tells us that her fame still lives among the peasantry of Kilkenny, while the Red Earl is forgotten; that she is remembered as Magheen, or little Margaret, and that she is the traditional castle-builder of the district.[48]

Kildare suspected of plots. Lambert Simnel.

It has been generally stated that Henry, before he had been a year on the throne, heard that Kildare was plotting against him. From what happened later, it is likely that such a report would not have been without foundation. Perhaps there was some evidence of his complicity in Lord Lovel's abortive insurrection, and it is highly probable that he was a party to the plot which the Duchess of Burgundy was hatching against the King of England.[49] Except on the supposition that he had already been admitted to the conspirator's confidence, it is hard to see how Kildare can have received Lambert Simnel and his promoter, a young and undistinguished priest, without hesitation or inquiry. There was no Lancastrian party in Dublin, and Henry's politic exhibition of the real Earl of Warwick had no effect upon men who were determined to accept the counterfeit. In[Pg 104] common with almost every temporal grandee, the Archbishop of Dublin and the Bishops of Meath and Kildare espoused the pretender's cause; but Octavian, Archbishop of Armagh, a Florentine, and well informed, remained firm, and was supported by the Bishop of Clogher. Henry afterwards asked the Pope to excommunicate the prelates who had favoured the pretender, and it is remarkable that he mentions the Archbishop of Armagh as one of them. Among the temporal peers, Lord Howth had the sense to see that Henry would be victorious, and he kept him well informed of all that went on in Ireland.[50]

Simnel is crowned King.

Simnel remained in Ireland, and published acts were done in his name as King until the arrival of Lincoln and Lovel, with Martin Swart, an experienced German leader, and

2,000 veterans of his nation, sent by Margaret of Burgundy. Lambert was crowned in Christ Church with a diadem borrowed for the occasion from a statue of the Virgin, and was shown to the people borne aloft on the shoulders of Darcy of Platten, the tallest man of his time—details which bespeak the poverty of the country. A coronation sermon was preached by the Bishop of Meath.[51]

Kildare ordered the citizens of Waterford to join him with all their forces, but the mayor, who was a Butler, filled the town with the vassals of the House of Ormonde, and the clans depending on it, and returned for answer that they held all as traitors who had taken any part in the mock coronation. Kildare hanged the poor groom who had brought this message, an act of barbarity with which the Archbishop was much offended, and then repeated his summons. The herald, who bore the Geraldine arms on his tabard, was refused admission to Waterford, and summoned the citizens from a boat, ordering them instantly to proclaim King Edward VI. on pain of being hanged at their own doors. With becoming[Pg 105] spirit the chief magistrate replied, that they would not give the Earl so much trouble, that they looked on all his partisans as traitors, and that they were ready to give him battle thirty miles away. Kilkenny, Clonmel, Callan, Fethard, and other towns followed the example of Waterford.[52]

Battle of Stoke, 1487.

There was some division of opinion between the partisans of Simnel as to whether England should be immediately invaded. Two reasons in favour of this course prevailed over those for establishing a separate government in Ireland. The country was too poor to support 2,000 German mercenaries, and the Irish followers of Kildare, who cared little for either rose, promised themselves much pleasure from fighting and plundering in hated England. Accordingly, just a month after the mock coronation, Lambert and his friends left Dublin and landed at Foudray in Lancashire, where they were joined by Sir Thomas Broughton and some of his tenants. 'But their snowball,' in Bacon's phrase, 'did not gather as they went,' and they advanced as far as Newark without materially increasing their force. The popularity which Henry had gained during his late stay at York, and the general pardon which he had given, went far to break up the Yorkist party in the North, 'and it was an odious thing to Englishmen to have a King brought in to them upon the shoulders of Irish and Dutch.' At Stoke, the pretender's motley host came into collision with the far more numerous royal army. The Germans fought well, and so did their few English allies; 'neither did the Irish fail in courage or fierceness, but being almost naked men, only armed with darts and skeans, it was rather an execution than a fight upon them.' At least 4,000 of the pseudo-Yorkists fell, including Martin Swart, the Earl of Lincoln, and Kildare's brother, the Irish Chancellor, Thomas Fitzgerald. Lord Lovel and Sir Thomas Broughton may have escaped for a time, but they were never heard of again. It appears from a passage in the 'Annals of Ulster,' where Henry VII. is contemptuously mentioned as 'the son of a Welshman,' that[Pg 106] the native Irish believed Simnel to be what he pretended to be—the last prince of the blood royal.[53]

Loyalty of Waterford.

The loyalty of Waterford deserved special thanks, and Henry sent a letter to the mayor and citizens, in which he expressed his hearty gratitude. To show his perfect confidence he commanded them to pursue and harass the Earl of Kildare and the citizens of Dublin, both by sea and land. The trade of the Irish capital was placed at their mercy, and they were exhorted not to desist from hostilities until 'our rebel, the Earl of Kildare,'—who was also our Deputy—and his Dublin allies were brought to due obedience. Kildare sent messengers to England to make his peace, and the citizens of Dublin did likewise. 'We were daunted,' said the latter plausibly enough, 'to see not only the chief governor, whom your Highness made ruler over us, to bend or bow to that idol whom they made us to obey, but also our Father of Dublin, and most of the clergy of the nation.' After some hesitation, Henry resolved to pardon all the Irish conspirators, and even allowed Kildare to remain in the office of Deputy. In return for their pardons the nobility were required to take the oath of allegiance; and to secure its proper administration the King resolved to send a special commissioner to Ireland. Sir Richard Edgcombe, Controller of the Household, whom he had already employed on a diplomatic mission to Scotland, was the person chosen for this delicate duty.[54]

Mission of Sir Richard Edgcombe, 1488.
Sir Richard sailed from Fowey with a squadron of four vessels containing 500 men; and having tried in vain among the Scilly Islands and in the Bristol Channel to surprise certain pirates who infested those seas, he reached Kinsale on the fifth day, where he again failed to apprehend a notable pirate. Lord Barry Oge came on board to take the oath of allegiance. Edgcombe then landed, was met by Lord Courcy and the townsmen of Kinsale, received the keys of the town, and administered the oath to all persons of import[Pg 107]ance. Having granted a royal pardon, he sailed for Waterford, where he was loyally welcomed. Hearing that he had brought a pardon for Kildare, the citizens reminded him that the Earl was their bitterest enemy, and begged to be exempted from any jurisdiction which he or any other Irish lord might claim as Deputy. Sir Richard promised to advance the interests of Waterford at Court, and then went on to Dublin. Kildare kept the royal commissioner waiting for eight days, during part of which time he was entertained at Malahide, by a lady of the Talbot family. At last the Earl came to Thomas Court with 200 horse, and sent the Bishop of Meath and the Baron of Slane to conduct Sir Richard thither. On entering the room Edgcombe made no bow to the Lord Deputy, but bluntly delivered the King's letters. Five days more were given for the rest of the lords to make an appearance, and Kildare retired to Maynooth to digest the letters and verbal messages. On the fourth day Sir Richard came by pressing invitation to Maynooth, and the Earl promised that he would do everything required of him; but he continued to interpose delays in coming to any official decision. Sharply reprimanded by the royal commissioner, the lords at last agreed to take the oath of allegiance; but refused to enter into recognisances for the forfeiture of their estates in case they should again lapse from their duty, plainly declaring that they would rather become Irishmen, every one of them. With an oath of allegiance Sir Richard was fain to be content, and he drew one in very stringent form, Henry being specially described as the 'natural and right-wise' King of England. To prevent tricks, the host, upon which the oath was taken, was consecrated by Edgcombe's own chaplain. The nobility present, and the principal ecclesiastical dignitaries about Dublin, were sworn or did homage, and particularly bound themselves to support and execute the censures of the Church, as pronounced by the Bull of Innocent VIII. upon those who should rebel against the King of England. In that instrument the Pope had declared his belief that the Crown belonged to Henry by inheritance, by conquest, and by election, independently of, and in addition to his claim in[Pg 108] right of Elizabeth of York. Among the commoners whom it was thought necessary to swear specially was Darcy of Platten, the tall man who had borne Lambert on his shoulders. The

civic authorities of Dublin, Drogheda, and Trim, having been sworn before him in their own towns, Sir Richard embarked at Dalkey on the thirty-fourth day after his arrival at Kinsale. Of all Simnel's partisans, Keating, Prior of Kilmainham, was the only one who did not receive a pardon.[55]

The Irish nobility summoned to England, 1489.

Kildare sent the Bishop of Meath to England to watch his interests, and Octavian also sent an agent to procure for him the custody of the Great Seal. The Primate complained that Kildare, despite his recent oath, had begun plotting against him before Edgcombe had reached the English shore. 'I know,' he said, 'for certain that if the said Earl of Kildare obtains the government of Ireland by royal authority, and has the Chancellor of Ireland also at his back, that I have no hope of quiet in Ireland.' Henry did not give the seal to the Archbishop, but he summoned all the Irish nobility to Court; and all obeyed except Desmond and Fitzmaurice of Kerry. 'My masters of Ireland,' said the King, when giving them audience, 'you will crown apes at length.' Afterwards at dinner he gave point to this remark by ordering Lambert Simnel to hand wine to those who had so lately crowned him King. 'None would have taken the cup out of his hand, but bade the great devil of hell him take, before that ever they saw him.' 'Bring me the cup if the wine be good,' said the Lord of Howth, being a merry gentleman, 'and I shall drink it off for the wine's sake, and mine own sake also, and for thee, as thou art, so I leave thee, a poor innocent.' Henry kept the lords at Court long enough for them to feel the expense burdensome, and then despatched them, making Lord Howth, who had alone remained loyal, a present of 300l. in gold, and the robe which he wore at the reception. Some of the others had expected little less than the axe for their reward.[56]

[Pg 109]

Kildare Deputy till 1492. Butlers and Geraldines.

The influence of Kildare was not much shaken by his complicity in Simnel's adventure, and it was not till 1492 that he was deprived of the office of Deputy. It was conferred on Walter Fitz-Simons, Archbishop of Dublin. About the same time Rowland Fitz-Eustace, Baron of Portlester, the Earl's uncle, who had been Lord Treasurer for thirty-eight years, was suddenly removed and threatened with a hostile inquiry into his accounts during the whole period. Sir James Ormonde, knighted by Henry in person, for his services against Lambert, was appointed in his room, and another Butler was made Master of the Rolls. The quarrel between the two Houses blazed up fiercely; and Kildare, to reassert his influence, summoned a great meeting of citizens on Oxmantown Green.

The two factions came to blows, some lives were lost, and Kildare attempted to seize the city by a sudden movement. The gates were, however, shut in time; but Ship Street, then outside the walls, was burned. The Geraldines wasted the Butler territory, and the Butlers in their turn ravaged Kildare and encamped in great force on the southern side of Dublin. A meeting of the two chiefs in St. Patrick's Cathedral was then arranged. A riot took place in the church, a flight of arrows was discharged, and Sir James, suspecting treason, barred himself into the Chapter-house. The Earl came to the door with offers of peace, and a hole was cut in the timber through which the rivals might shake hands. Sir James hesitated to risk his hand, but Kildare settled the question by putting in his own. The door was then opened, they embraced each other, and peace followed for a time. To make amends for the desecration of the church, the Pope ordered that the mayor should go barefoot through the city on Corpus Christi day, and this practice was continued till the Reformation. The door with the hole in it is still preserved, or was so until very lately.[57]

Perkin Warbeck lands 1491, but leaves the next year.

'Ireland at this time,' says Ware, 'was as it were a theatre or stage on which masked princes entered, though[Pg 110] soon after, their visors being taken off, they were expulsed the stage.' Perkin Warbeck landed at Cork late in 1491, or early in 1492, and was entertained by John Walters, an eminent merchant and future mayor. The citizens from the beginning insisted on regarding him as a royal personage, first as a son of Clarence, afterwards as a bastard of Richard III., and finally as Richard, Duke of York, Edward IV.'s younger son. Having adopted the latter character, Perkin wrote letters, extant in Ware's time, in which he sought help from the Earls of Desmond and Kildare. The former at once espoused his cause; the latter, according to his own account, would have nothing to do with 'the French lad.' Desmond joined Perkin in soliciting the aid of James IV. of Scotland, and he remained for about a year at Cork, learning English, but apparently without exciting any anxiety in England. Towards the close of 1492 he withdrew to France, where Charles VIII. received him as a prince, and where he was joined by disaffected Yorkists. Henry having made a successful campaign in France, Perkin was dismissed and went to Flanders, where Margaret of Burgundy acknowledged him as her nephew, and no doubt instructed him how to fill the part.[58]

Parliament of 1493.

In 1493 the Archbishop of Dublin held a Parliament, where many things were done unfavourable to the Geraldine faction; and on August 12, John Walters and other accomplices of the pretender were summoned to surrender. The Archbishop shortly went over to England, where he made Henry clearly acquainted with the state of affairs in Ireland, and was followed by Kildare, who had an opportunity of telling his own story. In consequence of what he had learned, the King resolved to appoint a Deputy unconnected with any Irish party; and fixed upon Sir Edward Poynings, whom he had already employed as envoy to the Archduke Philip, when remonstrating against the countenance given to Perkin in Flanders. While Archbishop Fitz-Simons was in England, Viscount Gormanston filled the office of Deputy,[Pg 111] and even ventured to summons a Parliament; but the Duke of Bedford having in the meantime resigned the lieutenancy, his substitute's action was afterwards declared null and void.

Sir Edward Poynings Deputy, 1494.

Poynings landed at Howth on October 13, 1494, with 1,000 men. He was accompanied by Henry Dean, Bishop of Bangor and afterwards Archbishop of Canterbury, as Chancellor, by Sir Hugh Conway as Treasurer, and by three other Englishmen appointed to the chief places in the three common law courts. Joining his forces with those of Kildare and of Sir James Ormonde, Poynings immediately undertook an expedition to Ulster, with a view of chastising O'Donnell, who had lately been honourably received in Scotland, and was probably implicated in Perkin's project. When the army reached O'Hanlon's county, Sir James Ormonde persuaded the Deputy that Kildare was plotting with the Irish against his life, and some colour was given to the charge by the conduct of the Earl's brother James, who seized Carlow Castle, mounted the Geraldine banner, and refused to surrender when summoned in the King's name. Having with difficulty reduced Carlow, Poynings repaired to Drogheda, where he held a Parliament, whose legislation was destined to have a momentous effect on Irish history. The invasion of Ulster was abandoned, and Bacon, with the experience of the next century, summarily disposes of it as 'a wild chase on the wild Irish.'

Parliament of Drogheda, 1494.

The Acts of this Parliament of 1494 are numerous, many of them being intended to make the administration more directly dependent on the Crown. Thus, the judges and other high officials were made to hold at the King's pleasure, instead of by patent as had been customary heretofore. It was made illegal for great men to retain free citizens and burgesses in their pay, or for anyone to make war without the governor's licence, or for anyone to stir up the Irish against the English. It was made unlawful to keep firearms without the Deputy's licence. The Statutes of Kilkenny were confirmed or re-enacted, with the exception of those against using the Irish language and those obliging every subject to ride in a saddle. Family war cries, such as[Pg 112] 'Butleraboo' and 'Cromaboo,' were strictly prohibited. Coyne and livery were visited with severe penalties; but advantageous terms were fixed, upon which the King might obtain provisions for his soldiers. All Acts against papal provisions theretofore made, either in England or Ireland, were declared to be in full force, though the Government had no means whatever of preventing them, or of making other arrangements for the vast majority of Irish benefices.[59]

Poynings' Acts.

The statutes known in after days as Poynings' Acts were two in number. By the first it was enacted that no future Parliaments should be held in Ireland, 'but at such season as the King's Lieutenant and Council there first do certify the King under the great seal of that land (Ireland), the causes and considerations, and all such acts as them seemeth should pass in the same Parliament.' Should the King in Council approve them, then the Irish Parliament should be summoned under the great seal of England, and not otherwise. By the second Act it was provided that all public statutes 'late made within the said realm of England' should be in force in Ireland. The lawyers decided that this applied to all English Acts prior to the tenth year of Henry VII. And thus the dependence of the Irish Parliament on that of England was established in the fullest degree.[60]

Attainder of Kildare.

Kildare was attainted by the Drogheda Parliament, the Act stating that he had provoked Irish enemies and English rebels to levy war against the King, that he had conspired with O'Hanlon to kill the Deputy, that he had caused his brother James to seize Carlow and hold it against the King, that he had used coyne and livery, and that he had conspired with the King of Scots and the Earl of Desmond for an invasion of Ireland. The Earl was arrested and sent to England, there to await Henry's own judgment on these and other matters. The chief of the southern Geraldines had in the meantime again given his adhesion to the cause of Perkin Warbeck.[61]

[Pg 113]

Second visit of Perkin Warbeck. Siege of Waterford, 1495.

Less than three weeks after his disgraceful failure in Kent, Perkin was with Desmond in Munster. Eleven ships, of which some were Scotch, attacked Waterford from the river, while Desmond and his Irish allies with 2,400 men threatened the city from the southern side. Poynings marched against the invaders in person; but the real work was done by the mayor and citizens, who dammed the stream called John's River, so as to prevent Desmond from joining Perkin: while they battered the fleet with cannon planted on Reginald's Tower. They made several sallies, killed their prisoners, and stuck their heads on stakes in the market-place. When the siege had lasted eleven days one of Perkin's ships was sunk by the fire from the town, and the adventurer then fled precipitately. At least three vessels fell into the hands of the besieged or their allies, and the citizens followed Perkin to Cork, where his friends protected him. Afterwards he made his way to Scotland, where James IV. received him with the honours due to a prince, and gave him the hand of his cousin, Lady Catherine Gordon. James, who was of an ambitious and visionary turn of mind, may perhaps have thought it possible to restore the days of Bruce, and to conquer some part of Ireland for himself. Two successive O'Donnells acknowledged themselves his subjects, and with their help and that of sailors like the Bartons, Scotland might have disputed with England the possession of Northern Ireland at least. The elder Hugh O'Donnell, who died in 1505, was a man of considerable ability, the annalists, with their usual magniloquence, styling him the 'Augustus of the North of Europe;' and with more truth asserting that he was the most powerful person in the North of Ireland.[62]

Poynings leaves Ireland, 1496.

Poynings quitted Ireland in January 1496, leaving the government in the Bishop of Bangor's hands. Important as was the recent legislation, it cannot be said that Henry had made any real change in the system of government. His[Pg 114] great idea, like that of his descendants, was to make Ireland pay her own expenses, and for that purpose he sent over two able officers, with instructions to overhaul the entire system of government. Plenty of zeal seems to have been shown, but the result was not encouraging. No year passed in Ireland without some small war, and the established custom of hiring native mercenaries tended to prevent any improvement. Sir James Ormonde and other leaders found their account in constant disturbance, and expense always more than kept pace with revenue.[63]

Friars employed by the Government.

The accounts of Vice-Treasurer Hattecliffe, to whom Henry committed the control of Irish finance, seem to show that Poynings and others found a difficulty in obtaining the aid of subordinate officers. They had, however, a resource which Elizabeth lacked, in the power of employing priests and friars. Thus we find a Franciscan of Dublin sent to spy out the manners of the people inhabiting the marches of the Pale, and again acting as a messenger between the Council in Dublin and the Deputy in the field. A canon named John Staunton was sent to act as a spy 'in Munster and elsewhere about the Earl of Desmond, Perkin Warbeck, and other rebels.' On another occasion a Carmelite was the means of communication between the Government and Sir James Ormonde, and it is probable that many more of the messengers were clergymen, though the fact is not so mentioned.[64]

Turbulence of the Geraldines. Restoration of Kildare, 1496.

That there was no peace, and consequently no diminution of expense, is not to be altogether attributed to the rapacity of Sir James Ormonde and other leaders of kerne and gallowglasses. The Geraldines took care that the country should be disturbed during the Earl's absence, as we find by the following significant entry:—'Two shillings to Philip Messanger for carrying the Lord Justice's letters directed to Richard Paynteneye of Carbury, Edward Dowdall of Slane, to the sovereign of Athboy, and others, ordering them to have sundry fires made on sundry mountains—viz. the mountains of Tara,[Pg 115] Lyons, Athboy, and Slane, to warn the King's lieges in case James, the Earl's son, and others the King's Irish enemies, should bring a power to invade the English districts.' Several other payments were made to the same messenger for services in connection with these Geraldine inroads, and Henry came gradually to think that Kildare did more harm as a prisoner than he could possibly do if he were at liberty. Whether the account of the Earl's behaviour at Court, which has been copied from the 'Book of Howth' into most histories, be true or not, there can be little doubt that Henry thought it better that he should rule all Ireland, than that he should have further opportunities of showing that all Ireland could not rule him. The gravest charge against him was that of conspiring with O'Hanlon to murder Poynings, and this was disposed of by the evidence of O'Hanlon. Prince Henry became titular Lord-Lieutenant, the attainder was reversed by the English Parliament, and Kildare received a commission as Lord Deputy under the King's son. His first wife, Alison Eustace, is said to have died through the agitation caused by his imprisonment, and he now added to his influence by marrying Elizabeth St. John, the King's first cousin. Leaving his son Gerald as a hostage at the English Court, he returned to Dublin as soon as possible, received the sword from Deane, successfully invaded the O'Briens and Macnamaras, and was fully reconciled to the Archbishop of Armagh. The Great Seal was given to Fitzsimons, Archbishop of Dublin, a prelate who had the courage to tell Henry that a certain courtly orator flattered him too much. 'Our father of Dublin,' replied the King, 'we minded to find the same fault ourselves.'[65]

Warbeck's third visit, 1497.

On July 20, 1497, Perkin Warbeck again made his appearance at Cork. He got no help this time from Desmond, who had been pardoned, and who had perhaps made up his mind that the adventurer was an impostor. Sir James Ormonde was accused of favouring him. The citizens of Waterford at once gave Henry notice, and with four ships fitted out by themselves gave chase to Perkin, who found no encouragement[Pg 116] in Ireland, and lost no time in going to join the Cornish malcontents. Narrowly escaping capture at sea, he managed to raise a force of 6,000 or 7,000 men, besieged Exeter and Taunton unsuccessfully, and then ran away without striking a blow, and took sanctuary at Beaulieu in Hampshire. The inglorious close of his career is unconnected with Ireland, and he seems on this last occasion to have had no Irish allies. The citizens of Waterford received from the King a cap of maintenance to be borne on certain occasions before the mayor, and the title of Urbs intacta, in which the city still glories. The sum of 1,000 marks which he had promised for the capture of Perkin was not, strictly speaking, earned by the Waterford men; and their loyal and, doubtless, very costly exertions, received no money recompense from the frugal King.[66]

Considerations as to Simnel and Warbeck.

The modern historian, whose fortune it has been to clear up all doubts about Perkin Warbeck, takes Lord Bacon to task for overrating the excellence of the pretender's acting.

But Bernard Andreas, the principal if not the only contemporary writer, certainly gives one to understand that he played his part very plausibly.

'Carried to Ireland by a fair wind he suborned with his very cunning temptations a great part of the barbarians of that island. For he unfolded and retold from his ready memory all the times of Edward IV., and without book repeated the names of all his familiars and servants as he had been taught them from a boy. He habitually added circumstances of time, place, and person, with which he very easily persuaded the levity of those men. And with the help of such figments the matter grew so important, that men of prudence and high nobility were induced to believe the same. What followed? Certain prophecies concerning him were scattered far and wide by false prophets, which completely blinded the mental perceptions of the common people.'

It must be admitted that Lord Bacon did not speak with[Pg 117]out considerable authority. A contemporary French poem, which was probably also written by Bernard Andreas, gives a very unflattering account of Ireland as a cave of robbers, 'where is neither peace, love, nor concord, but only treasons and the foulest deeds.' Such material help as the pretender received was entirely among the Anglo-Irish. The native annalists do not mention him, whereas Simnel is, at least by one writer, spoken of as an undoubted prince of the blood royal.[67]

Sir Piers Butler kills Sir James Ormonde, 1497.

Sir James Ormonde, whose mother was an O'Brien, used the help of his Irish connections to oppress Sir Piers Butler, whom he imprisoned, but afterwards released at Desmond's request, 'upon trust that he should have married the Earl's daughter.' One of Kildare's first acts after his restoration was to summon Sir James to Dublin, and to proclaim him outlaw on his refusal. But this scarcely lessened his power in the Butler country, and did not even prevent him from assuming the title of Earl of Ormonde. Driven to great straits, Sir Piers asserted that his rival had imprisoned him 'contrary to his oath and promise made upon the holy cross and other great relics ... and that the same Sir James, not pondering his said oath and promise, showed openly that wheresoever he would find me he would kill me.' After this Sir James, for the second time, refused to appear before the King. The two Butlers met accidentally in the open field between Dunmore and Kilkenny, and after a short struggle Sir James was slain.[68]

Consequent peace between Butlers and Geraldines.

According to some accounts this encounter or murder, whichever it may be thought, was caused by Lady Margaret Butler's complaint that she could get no wine, though in delicate health. 'Truly, Margaret,' he answered, 'thou shalt have store of wine within this four and twenty hours, or else thou shalt feed alone on milk for me.' One writer says that there were desperate odds against Sir Piers; and if this be[Pg 118] true, and considering the then state of Ireland, the guilt of murder can hardly attach to him. The death of Sir James was decidedly beneficial to Ireland, for it made peace between the Houses of Kildare and Ormonde.[69]

Parliament of 1498.

In 1498 Kildare received a commission to hold a Parliament which was not to last for more than six months. The first Act of this Parliament was to confirm the reversal of the Lord Deputy's attainder, who by a singular anomaly thus exercised viceregal authority, notwithstanding the corruption of his own blood; the last to attaint Lord Barrymore and John Waters for their dealings with Perkin Warbeck. Waters was caught, found guilty by a Westminster jury, and hanged at Tyburn, alongside of the pretender. Lord Barrymore escaped arrest, but was murdered by his brother, the Archdeacon of Cork. Kildare visited and garrisoned Cork, forcing the chief inhabitants to take the oath of allegiance to Henry, and to give bonds for future good behaviour. Of the other Acts passed, the most important was one for the discouragement of Irish habits and weapons. Henceforth dwellers within the Pale were enjoined to wear only English dress, and to wield only 'English artillery,' such as swords, bucklers, pavesses, bows, arrows, bills, crossbows, guns, or such hand weapons—darts and spears being prohibited; and they were to ride in saddles in the English fashion.[70]

Kildare's wars in Ulster. Cannon are used.

It was Kildare's fortune not only to give trouble himself, but to be the progenitor of those who were to give trouble in future. The rebellion of his grandson Thomas Fitzgerald was to cause the eclipse of his house. The descendants of his daughter Alice were to be the chief disturbers of the Elizabethan monarchy in Ireland. She had married Con More O'Neill, who was naturalised by Act of Parliament, and this gave her father a fair excuse for interfering in the affairs of Ulster. Con More had been treacherously killed by his brother Henry in 1493, and the murderer fought for[Pg 119] supremacy with his brother Donnell. Henry was at first successful, and Donnell, whom Lady Alice appears to have favoured, could only keep up a desultory opposition. In 1497 a peace or truce was made, but in the following year Tirlough and Con, Lady Alice's two young sons, killed Henry in revenge for their father's death, and invited Kildare to come himself into Ulster. Besides his grandsons, the Lord Deputy had the help of Donnell O'Neill, of Maguire, of O'Donnell, and of most of the neighbouring clans against Henry O'Neill's sons and partisans. Cannon were brought against Dungannon, which soon surrendered. Omagh was afterwards taken, and Donnell was established as chief of Tyrone. Firearms were perhaps first brought to Ireland in 1483, when six muskets, considered a great rarity, were sent from Germany as a present to Kildare, and were borne by his guards more for show than for use. In 1487 an O'Donnell was killed by a cannon or musket shot in a local broil, and in the following year Kildare brought ordnance against Balrath Castle. In 1495, as we have seen, heavy guns were successfully used for the defence of Waterford, and the mention of firearms in the Act of 1498 shows that their importance was quickly recognised. Cannon came in time to be the peculiar weapons of the King, their great expense putting them out of the reach of private combatants, and no doubt it was gunpowder that caused the downfall both of the feudal and of the tribal systems.[71]

Kildare's wars in Connaught and Ulster.

In 1499 the Lord Deputy, who acted pretty much as if there were no King in England, made an excursion into Connaught, and garrisoned certain castles. About the same time Piers Butler was defeated in battle by the O'Briens, but the causes of neither quarrel have been handed down to us. It was the policy of the Anglo-Norman nobles in Ireland to make themselves allies among the Irish, and in pursuance of this idea the Earl gave up his son Henry to be fostered by his late ally, Hugh Roe O'Donnell, who came to visit him in the Pale. Kildare afterwards held a Parliament at Castle[Pg 120] Dermot; but its acts had no political significance, unless the punishment of certain nobles for not wearing Parliament-robes, and for not using saddles, be considered an exception.

Donnell O'Neill and his nephews did not long remain at peace, and O'Donnell, siding with the latter, expelled Donnell from Dungannon. Kildare again invaded Tyrone, in conjunction with O'Donnell, and took Kinard Castle, which he handed over to his grandson Tirlough; but six weeks later it was retaken by Donnell O'Neill. For more than two years after this no event of any importance is recorded; there were ceaseless wars among the Irish, but the Lord Deputy does not seem to have interfered with them.

Kildare in England, 1503.
In 1503 Kildare visited England by the King's orders, and remained there three months. Having licence from Henry to appoint a substitute, he selected his old antagonist the Archbishop of Dublin to act as Lord Justice in his absence. The Earl remained three months in England, and was allowed to bring back his son Gerald, who had been a hostage for eight years. Gerald, who was accompanied by his bride, Elizabeth Zouche, received his appointment as Lord Treasurer of Ireland a few months later.[72]

Battle of Knocktoe, 1504.
In 1504 a quarrel arose between Kildare and Ulick MacWilliam Burke, Lord of Clanricarde, who had married his daughter, Lady Eustacia. The only cause assigned by any of the authorities is, that MacWilliam ill-treated his wife. He had, however, seized the town of Galway, and that might be provocation enough for a Lord Deputy. Two great armies were collected—MacWilliam having the O'Briens and Macnamaras, the Connaught O'Connors, and the MacBriens, O'Kennedys, and O'Carrolls on his side. With the Deputy were a portion at least of the O'Neills, O'Donnell, MacDermot, Magennis, O'Connor Faly, O'Ferrall, MacMahon, O'Reilly, O'Hanlon, and some of the Mayo Burkes, the Mayor of Dublin, the Earl of Desmond, and the Lords Gormanston, Slane, Delvin, Killeen, Dunsany, Trimleston, and Howth. Notwithstanding this formidable array of names,[Pg 121] Kildare's army was far inferior to MacWilliam's in point of numbers. Both bishops and lawyers appeared at the council of war which preceded the battle: Art O'Neill objecting to the former and O'Connor Faly to the other. The one declared that the bishops' duty was 'to pray, to preach, and to make fair weather, and not to be privy to manslaughter;' and the other expressed great contempt for pen and ink and for 'the weak and doubtful stomachs of learned men.' 'I never,' he said, 'saw those that were learned ever give good counsel in matters of war, for they were always doubting, and staying, and persuading, more in frivolous and uncertain words than Ector or Launcelot's doings.' Lord Gormanston was unwilling to risk so much without first knowing the King's pleasure; but Lord Howth, as represented by the family chronicler, saw that good advice might come too late, and that being in the field they must fight. He proposed that they should conquer or die, having first placed their sons in safety, so as to secure vengeance in case of defeat. This plan was frustrated by young Gerald's refusal to retire. MacWilliam's army made certain of victory, and spent the night drinking, playing cards, and arranging about the custody of prisoners. The battle took place at Knocktuagh or Knocktoe, now generally written Knockdoe, a hill near Clare Galway. Kildare is said to have reminded his followers that the enemy, though very numerous, were ill-armed, many with one spear only and a knife, and 'without wisdom or good order, marching to battle as drunken as swine to a trough.' When the fighting began 'Great Darcy'—the man who

had borne Lambert Simnel on his shoulders—appeared as one of the chief champions on the Deputy's side. Kildare gained a complete victory. The 'Book of Howth' represents the gentry of the Pale as sustaining the brunt of the battle, while the 'Four Masters' tell the story as if both armies consisted of aboriginal Irishmen only. According to the former authority, Lord Gormanston made the following speech to the Lord Deputy:—'We have done one good work, and if we do the other we shall do well. We have for the most number killed our enemies, and if we do the like[Pg 122] with all the Irishmen that we have with us, it were a good deed.'

Galway and Athenry were occupied without difficulty after the battle, and the Lord Deputy's Irish allies withdrew to their own countries. The arduous task remained of persuading Henry VII. that all had been done in his interest. Kildare sent his old antagonist the Archbishop of Dublin to Court, who performed his mission so well that the King professed himself quite satisfied, and soon afterwards made his Deputy a Knight of the Garter. Perhaps Henry was not really deceived, but thought it good policy to make his great subject's victories his own. Sixty years afterwards, when Sir Henry Sidney solicited a garter for another Earl of Kildare, he urged his suit in these words:—'King Henry VII. made his grandfather, and wist full what he did when he did so; he enlarged the Pale, and enriched the same more than 10,000l. worth.'[73]

Parliament of 1508.
Of the remaining years of Henry VII.'s reign but little seems to be recorded, except that the chronic war among the native tribes did not cease. Kildare held a Parliament in 1508, in which a subsidy of 13s. 4d. was granted out of every ploughland, whether lay or clerical. About the same time a party of the O'Neills took Carrickfergus Castle, and carried off the mayor. In 1509 Kildare again invaded Tyrone in the interests of his grandsons, and demolished Omagh. When the King died he was in full possession of the government, and without a rival in those parts of Ireland which were in any real sense subject to the English Crown.[74]

Henry endeavoured to separate the two races.
It was the decided policy of Henry VII. to act in the spirit of the Statute of Kilkenny, and to separate the English[Pg 123] and Irish districts. The well-known name of the Pale, or the English Pale, seems to have come into general use about the close of the fifteenth century. A great number of ordinances remain to prove how necessary it was for the Englishry to bear arms, and the practice of fortifying the home district against the Irish became a subject of legal enactment at least as early as 1429. An Act of the Parliament of 1475 declares that a dyke had been made and kept up from Tallaght to Tassagard, at the sole cost of four baronies—Coolock, Balrothery, Castleknock, and Newcastle—and provision was made by statute for its future maintenance. This was an inner line for the defence of Dublin only, but the Parliament of Drogheda made a similar provision for the whole Pale. It was enacted that every inhabitant of the marches or inland borders of Dublin, Meath, Kildare, and Louth, should, under a penalty of 40s., make and maintain 'a double ditch of six feet above ground, at one side, which meareth next unto Irishmen,' the landlord forgiving a year's rent in consideration of this work. The legal provision was afterwards enforced by writs addressed to the sheriffs and justices, and the name of Pale was perhaps first given to the district so enclosed. The building of this

Mahratta ditch may be considered to mark the lowest point reached by the English power in Ireland.[75]

FOOTNOTES:

[48] History of St. Canice, by Graves and Prim, especially pp. 187 and 193; also Mr. Graves's Presentments, p. 79; Archdall's Lodge's Peerage, art. 'Mount Garrett.'

[49] It is hard to say whether the instructions for John Estrete, attributed by Mr. Gairdner to the very beginning of Henry's reign, are by him or by Richard III. Henry would hardly have promised to make Kildare Deputy for ten years on condition of his going to Court, and the allusions to Edward IV. are more likely to have been made by Richard.—Letters of Richard III. and Henry VII., vol. i. p. 91. The three letters in the Appendix cannot be earlier than 1488.

[50] Writing to Morton or Fox, Octavian says, 'Profano coronationis pueri in Hiberniâ sceleri, me solo excepto, nullus obstitit manifeste.' This hardly gives due credit to the Bishop of Clogher.—Letters of Richard III. and Henry VII., vol. i. p. 383. Henry's letter to Pius II. is at p. 94. 'Armachanensis' must be a mistake on the King's part.

[51] Lambert was crowned May 2, 1487.

[52] Book of Howth, and an account in Carew (followed by Smith), iv. p. 473.

[53] Bacon; Book of Howth; O'Donovan's Four Masters, ad ann. 1485. The battle of Stoke was fought June 16, 1487.

[54] Henry's letter to Waterford is in Smith's Waterford; the letter of the Dublin people in Ware's Annals.

[55] Sir Richard Edgcombe's voyage, in Harris's Hibernica.

[56] Book of Howth; Letters of Richard III. and Henry VII., vol. i. p. 384.

[57] The Earls of Kildare; Harris's Dublin; Four Masters, ad ann. 1492.

[58] Ware; Gairdner's Life of Richard III.; Letters of Richard III. and Henry VII., ii. 55.

[59] Irish Statutes, 10 Henry VII., Dec. 1, 1494.

[60] Ibid., chaps. iv. and xxii.

[61] Gilbert's Viceroys, p. 454, and Ware. The Act is not in the printed statutes.

[62] Letters of Richard III. and Henry VII., vol. ii. pp. lxxvi. 237, 242, 299; Histories of Waterford, by Smith and Rylands; Four Masters and Annals of Lough Cé ad ann. 1505.

[63] Letters of Richard III. and Henry VII., vol. ii. pp. 64 and 67.

[64] Hattecliffe's accounts in Letters of Richard III. and Henry VII., vol. ii. pp. 297-318.

[65] Ware; Hattecliffe's Accounts; Earls of Kildare.

[66] Gairdner's Richard III.; Smith's Waterford, where is given the correspondence between Henry and the city; Carew, vol. v. p. 472, where the events of 1487, 1495, and 1497 are mixed up; Sir Piers Butler to the Earl of Ormonde, in Graves's St. Canice, p. 193.

[67] Four Masters, with O'Donovan's notes, under 1485. The 'Annals' of Andreas and the 'Douze triomphes de Henri VII.,' are in Memorials of Henry VII., ed. Gairdner.

[68] Sir Piers Butler to the Earl of Ormonde, in Graves's St. Canice, p. 193. Stanihurst says Sir Piers waylaid his enemy.

[69] All the authorities bearing on this event are collected in Graves's St. Canice, pp. 193-198.

[70] The Acts of this Parliament (supposed lost) are printed by Mr. Gilbert in his Facsimiles of Irish National MSS., vol. iii., from the English Patent Rolls. Ware; Four Masters.

[71] Four Masters and O'Donovan's notes, under 1487, 1488, and 1498.

[72] Ware; Four Masters.

[73] Sidney to Leicester, March 1, 1566, in the Irish State Papers. The account of the battle of Knocktoe is made up from Ware, Stanihurst, the Four Masters, and the Book of Howth. The Four Masters seem to have thought that the forces of the Pale were not engaged, and O'Donovan rather countenances them, but the Annals of Lough Cé say Kildare mustered 'all the foreigners and Irish of Leinster and of Northern Ireland.' (Ad ann. 1504.) The details in the Book of Howth may not be all correct, though there is nothing antecedently improbable in Lord Gormanston's truculent speech.

[74] Irish Statutes, 24 Hen. VII.; Letters and Papers of Henry VIII., Oct. 7, 1515.

[75] The statutes referred to are printed in Hardiman's Statute of Kilkenny. See Gilbert's Viceroys, p. 459.

[Pg 124]

MAP OF IRELAND ABOUT 1500.
CHAPTER IX.

FROM THE ACCESSION OF HENRY VIII. TO THE YEAR 1534.

Accession of Henry VIII., 1509. Kildare remains in power.

Henry VIII. was proclaimed without opposition, and amid great rejoicings in all the principal towns, but his accession made no immediate difference to Ireland. Kildare prepared to go to the new King, but the Council, who felt their helplessness without him, chose him Lord Justice, and constrained him to stay. His patent as Lord Deputy was not long withheld, and other official men were for the time continued in authority. The Earl was summoned to Court, but excused himself on the grounds that he could not be spared, and, as the Council sustained him, the King made no objection. Attended by the chief men of the Pale he invaded Munster, and, being joined by O'Donnell, penetrated into Desmond and took Castlemaine, as well as the so-called palace of the MacCarthies near Killarney. He met with scarcely any resistance, and seems to have had no higher object than plunder. Near Limerick, Kildare was joined by Desmond's eldest son with the main force of the southern Geraldines and the MacCarthies of Carbery and Muskerry. The Lord Deputy passed into Clare by a wooden bridge which the O'Briens had erected near Castleconnell, and which he broke down behind him. Here he was met by Tirlough O'Brien, the chief's son, accompanied by the Macnamaras and the Clanricarde Burkes. The hostile armies bivouacked at such close quarters that they could hear each other talking at night. At daybreak Kildare retired along the right bank of the Shannon, and reached Limerick in safety with the bulk of his plunder. The Munster Geraldines, with their Irish auxiliaries, marched in the van as[Pg 125] not being over trustworthy. In the rear, the post of honour in a retreat, were the O'Donnells and the men of the Pale. Such was the settlement of differences between Geraldines and De Burgos, which the chief governor had alleged as the main obstacle to his attendance upon his sovereign. It was indeed his interest to be always at war, for he had obtained a grant in tail of all such possessions as he could recover from any rebel in Ireland.[76] This method of paying a viceroy with letters of marque cost the Crown nothing, but the greatest ingenuity could hardly have devised a plan more fatal to an unfortunate dependency.

Activity of Kildare, 1512, 1513.

During the next year Kildare kept pretty quiet, but was soon again in the field. Crossing the Shannon at Athlone he plundered and burned all before him to Roscommon, where he placed a garrison, and then prolonged his destroying course to Boyle. Here he met O'Donnell, who came to him over the Curlew Mountains. This chief had lately made a pilgrimage to Rome, and spent four months in London going and as many more on his return. He was well received by Henry VIII., but we have unfortunately no details. In this same year Kildare invaded Ulster, took the castle of Belfast, and spoiled the land far and wide. In the following summer he marched against Ely O'Carroll, but while watering his horse in a stream near his own castle of Kilkea he was shot by one of the O'Mores, and died soon afterwards.[77] His son Gerald was at once chosen Lord Justice by the Council, and the King continued him in authority[78] on the same terms, and with a similar grant of all lands he could recover from the rebels.

The Earldom of Ormonde in abeyance.

The rival house of Ormonde was at this time depressed by the loss of its head without male issue. Early in 1515 died Thomas, the seventh Earl, the only Irish peer whom Henry VII. or Henry VIII. called to the English House of Lords, who was reputed the richest subject of the Crown, and[Pg 126] is said to have left the enormous sum of

40,000l. in money, besides jewels. He had two daughters, who inherited his personal property and seventy-two manors in England. Ann, the eldest, was married to Sir James St. Leger, Margaret, the younger, to Sir William Boleyn, by whom she had Sir Thomas, who became grandfather to Queen Elizabeth. Sir Piers Butler, a descendant of the third Earl, was heir male to the title and to the settled Irish estates, which at once became matters of dispute between him and the ladies St. Leger and Boleyn. With the full approval of the Irish Butlers, Sir Piers at once assumed the title of Earl. He had married Lady Margaret Fitzgerald, sister of the new Lord Deputy Kildare, a woman of lofty character and stature, to whom Irish tradition, with an endearing irony, has given the name of Magheen or Little Margaret. In compliance with letters from the King, Sir Piers was ordered to appear before his brother-in-law and the Irish Council; but he sent his wife instead, to urge that he was busy fighting. The lady, who must have had a delicate task between her husband and her brother, procured an adjournment, and it was stipulated that no rents should be paid in the meantime. The late Earl's daughters appeared by counsel in due course, and it is evident that Henry leaned strongly to their side. They offered evidence of title, but Sir Piers staid away and left all to his wife and his lawyers. The latter contented themselves with practically demurring to the jurisdiction, and prayed to have the case tried at common law; which would probably have secured a decision for their client. The Lord Deputy referred all back to the King, and the tenants continued to pay no rent. Kildare wished to command Sir Piers on his allegiance to appear before the King in England on a certain day; but he was overruled by the Council, who believed that this would drive Butler into rebellion; and as its acknowledged chief, he could command all the forces of his family. He chanced, moreover, to be at peace with the reigning Desmond, and he had strengthened himself by alliances among the Irish. These considerations prevailed with the King or with Wolsey, and the case remained in[Pg 127] abeyance; but it had gone far enough to cause an irreparable breach between Kildare and the rival chief.[79]

Kildare visits England in 1515. His restless policy.

Meanwhile, the Lord Deputy trod in his father's footsteps. He made successful raids on the O'Mores and O'Reillys, and for slaying many of the latter had a grant of the customs of Strangford and other places in Down. A visit to England in 1515 resulted in permission to hold a Parliament in the following year, but it produced no legislation of importance. He took and dismantled Leap Castle, the stronghold of the O'Carrolls, which his father had failed to gain, and he surprised Clonmel by a sudden march, though we know not what offence that town had given him. When he was busy in the north, where he destroyed O'Neill's castle at Dungannon and stormed Dundrum, which was defended by Magennis, the O'Carrolls rose again and invaded Meath. Again Kildare visited Ely and destroyed another castle. The history of two viceroyalties may indeed be told in a single sentence. Every year or two the Earl of Kildare harried some Irish country, and then reported such and such execution done upon the King's enemies. There was no attempt to keep the peace among the natives, the highest policy being the setting of one chief against another. The O'Neills and O'Donnells continued their everlasting feuds, and nearly every tribe was constantly at war. Occasionally they made foreign alliances, as in the case of O'Donnell, who was a travelled man. A French knight coming on a visit to St. Patrick's Purgatory was hospitably received by the chief, and offered to recover Sligo from the O'Connors. The offer was accepted, and in due course an armed vessel appeared in Killybegs Harbour. Sligo was battered from the sea, the O'Donnells co-operating by land, and the castle surrendered. We hear no more of the mysterious Frenchman.[80] Ware says that Ireland was peaceable during the year 1518, but the Irish annalists tell a very different story.[81]

Miserable state of the country.

The chiefs of English race were almost as restless as the[Pg 128] Celts whom they affected to despise, and the state of the Pale was as bad as bad could be. John Kite, a Londoner, who had been promoted to the throne of Armagh by Wolsey's influence, informed his patron that he tried to comfort the people by promising that the King would soon come to reform the land. He insisted very reasonably that the King was as much bound to maintain order and justice in Ireland as in England herself. The sea was no safer than the land, and the ship which brought the Archbishop from Chester had been attacked by two pirates; but the men of Drogheda—no thanks to the Government—had captured the rovers. Even the Countess Dowager of Kildare, who was the daughter of an English knight, complained that her stepson allowed O'Neill to levy tribute on her lands, and that her property and that of her dependents was laid waste. Portions that had escaped the Irish were seized by the Earl's own steward. Kildare had many other accusers, and was at length summoned over to give an account. He was allowed to appoint a Deputy, and nominated his cousin, Maurice Fitzgerald of Lackagh, who was soon afterwards killed by the O'Mores. But the cry of the land had been heard at last, and Henry resolved to send over a governor whom he could trust. The lot fell upon Thomas, Earl of Surrey, the son and companion in arms of the victor of Flodden, whose influence at Court probably made his absence desirable to Wolsey.[82]

Thomas Earl of Surrey, Lord-Lieutenant, 1520. Anarchy.

The first thirty pages of the printed State Papers are taken up with a report to the King on the state of Ireland, founded on an earlier document, but corrected and brought down nearly to the date of Surrey's appointment. It discloses a state of things calculated to try the ablest governor. In Ulster and Connaught, in the counties of Waterford, Cork, Kilkenny, Limerick, Kerry, Carlow, Westmeath, and Wicklow, and in parts of Kildare and Wexford, there was neither magistrate nor sheriff. Districts wholly or partially[Pg 129] peopled by men of English race were under black-rent to the native chiefs. This odious tax was paid by the Savages of Lecale in Down to the O'Neills of Clandeboye. The great chief of Tyrone levied his dues in Louth. Meath and Kildare were tributary to O'Connor Faly, Wexford to the Kavanaghs, Kilkenny and Tipperary to O'Carroll, Limerick to the O'Briens, and Cork to the MacCarthies. MacMurrough Kavanagh, who in the eyes of the natives represented the ancient royalty of Leinster, actually received eighty marks out of an almost empty exchequer. The sum of the several black-rents amounted to 740l., and this was at a time when a soldier received fourpence a day. Dublin was in constant danger, and one of Henry's first acts was to grant 20l., a year to the citizens for repairing their walls, which had crumbled through decrease of population, pestilence, and Irish violence. A line drawn from Dundalk to Kells, from Kells to Kilcullen Bridge, and thence by Ballymore Eustace, and Tallaght to Dalkey, enclosed the whole actual Pale, upon which fell all the expenses of an establishment intended to meet the wants of all Ireland. The King's taxes had to be paid, coyne and livery were extorted, horses and carriages were requisitioned for the public service; and with all this the Government could give no protection, no judge went circuit, and black-rent was perforce paid in addition. 'The King's army in England,' said Henry's informant, 'is the commons, the King's army in

Ireland is such as oppress the commons.' The nobility and gentry copied the Government, and it was more than suspected that they dreaded any reform which would force them to obey the law; 'for there is no land in all this world that has more liberty in vices than Ireland, and less liberty in virtue.' The Church showed no better example than the lay magnates; 'for there is no archbishop nor bishop, abbot nor prior, parson nor vicar, nor any other person of the Church, high or low, great or small, that useth to preach the Word of God, saving the poor friars' beggars.' Some Irish chiefs kept better order than the Government; 'but not to the intent that his subjects should escape harmless,[Pg 130] but to the intent to devour them by himself, like as a greedy hound delivereth the sheep from the wolf.'

Remedies suggested.

Ireland has never lacked physicians, though she has often been nothing bettered by them. The most obvious means to strengthen the English power was to make the men of the Pale keep arms and practice their use; and this had been the constant cry of governors and legislators for many generations. Henry had directed Kildare to get an Act passed obliging every merchant trading from England to Ireland to bring a pound's worth of bows and arrows for every 20l. of wares, so as to prevent the King's subjects from applying themselves to Irish archery. Patrick Finglas, Baron of the Exchequer, was less sanguine than the writer of the State Paper which has been so largely quoted. That reformer ventured to prophesy that if his advice were taken the war of Ireland would cease for ever, the King would recover Constantinople and die Emperor of Rome, and Ireland once reduced to order would be 'none other than a very paradise, delicious of all pleasance.' But Finglas admitted that reform must necessarily be gradual, and advised the King to confine himself at first to the reclamation of Leinster. He recommended that the chief abbeys and castles should be entrusted to Englishmen, from Bray Head round the coast to Dunbrody on the Suir, and inland from Baltinglass and Carlow along the Barrow to Ross. The Wicklow Highlanders would be thus bridled and unable to attack Kildare. Athy and other places were to be held against the O'Connors and O'Mores. The Butlers seem to have been thought able to take care of themselves. It would not do to give up the castles to men who had great possessions in England, and who would never encourage English farmers to become their tenants. At first settlers would have to be protected, but in time would take care of themselves. There would be no difficulty about tilling the soil, 'for there be no better labourers than the poor commons of Ireland, nor sooner will be brought to good frame, if they be kept under a law.'[83]

Irish exactions.

Besides the payment of black-rent, the commons of Ire[Pg 131]land were oppressed by innumerable exactions, of which the principal may be described once for all. Bonaght was a tax imposed by a chief for the support of his mercenary horsemen, gallowglasses, and kerne. The name was often transferred from the tax to those who were maintained by it, and Bonaght, or Bony, became the generic name for an Irish mercenary or for one from the Scotch isles. Sorohen was an obligation on certain lands to support the chief with his train for twenty-four hours once a quarter, or, according to another account, as often as once a fortnight. Coshery was the chief's right to sponge upon his vassals with as many followers as he pleased. Cuddies, or night-suppers, were due by certain lands upon which the chief might quarter himself and his train for four days four times a year. Shragh and mart were yearly exactions in money and kine respectively, apparently imposed at the will of the chief. Worse than any of these was coyne and livery—that is, the taking of horse-meat and man-meat from everyone at the will of the chief; in other words, the right of the strongest to take what he liked. Coyne and livery were not the invention of an Irish chief, but of one of those Anglo-Normans who knew how to better native instruction. Maurice Fitz-Thomas, Earl of Desmond, is said to have begun it under Edward II. as the only available means of coping with Edward Bruce. Originally a contrivance for carrying on war at the enemy's expense, it came to be used by all great men at all seasons. James, the ninth Earl of Desmond, has the credit of first imposing it on loyal subjects, but the Crown was primarily to blame for neglecting to keep order. Lords Deputies showed no better example than private oppressors.[84]

Surrey finds all in confusion.

Surrey landed with his family at Dublin on May 23, bringing 100 men of the royal guard as a peculiar mark of favour. He found the country in rather more than its usual confusion. He sent Archbishop Rokeby to Waterford, who[Pg 132] succeeded in preventing Sir Piers Butler from fighting with Desmond, and he himself marched into Leix with his English soldiers, 120 Irish mercenaries, and 300 kerne. The English of the Pale, who, from love or fear of Kildare, usually mustered so strong on these occasions, contributed only forty-eight horse and 120 foot. Surrey made war in the usual Irish fashion, and burned Connell O'More's country. He was joined by Sir Piers Butler, who brought a strong contingent, including Mulrony O'Carroll, whom he induced to take the oath of allegiance. O'Carroll had latterly done great harm in the Pale, and he was considered the best leader among the Irish. He refused to take the oath until Surrey rashly promised that Kildare should never be Deputy again. On being pressed about a letter which the Earl was said to have written to him, he at first said that he would not inform even were he to receive the viceregal pavilion full of gold; but in spite of all this bravado he allowed his brothers to be examined, and they both swore that they had stood by and heard the letter read. Surrey never saw the document itself, nor has it been preserved. According to the report which we have, Kildare had directed O'Carroll to keep the peace till the arrival of an English Deputy, and then to make war on all Englishmen except the writer's friends. The object was to make all government but his own impossible.[85]

O'Donnell is friendly.

On his return to Dublin, Surrey found O'Donnell waiting for him. That chief had probably pleasant recollections of his visit to the English Court, and was not unwilling to strengthen himself against his rival O'Neill. He told Surrey that his powerful neighbour had urged him to make war on the Pale, and had declared his own intention of doing so, in compliance with Kildare's directions. O'Donnell promised to invade Tyrone if the Lord-Lieutenant would do likewise from the opposite quarter, and remarked emphatically that if the King ever set Kildare in authority again he might as well convey Ireland to him and his heirs for ever.

[Pg 133]

O'Neill temporises.

Early in August, Surrey, accompanied by Sir Piers Butler and his forces, entered Farney and punished MacMahon for the assistance given to O'Neill in his attacks on the Pale. O'Neill made some sort of verbal submission, and the Lord-Lieutenant returned to

Dublin, where he detected a conspiracy among his soldiers, some of whom found life intolerable in Ireland. Their plan was to seize a small vessel in the river, and by her means a larger one on the high seas, and so to become rovers. The Irish lawyers held that the Viceroy could not hang them; for they had committed no overt act, and his patent did not authorise him to proceed by martial law. It is clear that the Crown was held capable of dispensing with the common law, at least in the case of soldiers.[86]

Desmonds and MacCarthies.

In September an important private war was waged in Munster. James, Earl of Desmond, according to the usual practice of his family, made a perfectly unprovoked attack upon Cormac Oge MacCarthy, the chief of Muskerry. Having secured the assistance of Sir Thomas Fitzgerald, the Earl's uncle and his own sister's husband, and of his kinsman MacCarthy Reagh, Cormac Oge defeated Desmond in a pitched battle near Mourne Abbey, to the south of Mallow. The messenger who brought the news to Dublin reported that the Earl had lost 1,500 foot and 500 horse. The Lord-Lieutenant was not sorry, for he had straitly charged Desmond to leave the MacCarthies alone. The fate of the Desmonds has excited much not very well directed sympathy: it would better become Irishmen to remember that they were the worst oppressors of their Celtic neighbours.

When Surrey visited Munster soon after, Desmond met him at Clonmel, and was as loyal in words as Sir Piers Butler had been in deeds. At Waterford he met MacCarthy Reagh and Cormac Oge, who were adherents of Sir Piers, and who had come on his invitation. They spoke fairly, bound themselves to keep the peace and professed themselves loyal, so that they might be protected. Surrey wished to make[Pg 134] Cormac Oge a Privy Councillor and a Baron of Parliament, and he calls him a 'sad wise man.' Cormac produced a charter under the Great Seal, a copy of which was sent to England with an assurance that it comprised no lands to which the King was entitled.[87]

Henry speaks boldly to the Irish.

It was probably to Cormac Oge that Henry wrote a remarkable letter, which shows his intentions at this time. The Irishman, whether Cormac Oge or another, was willing to surrender his lands and take an estate tail from the Crown at a fair rent. It was the interest of native chieftains to do this, because it secured them as against the Government, while it enabled them to transmit to their children a property which was not theirs at all, but held in trust for the clan at the election of the clansmen. The one fear of Henry's correspondent was that he should after all be abandoned to Kildare's vengeance, and he counselled the employment of a large army. To this the King answered that he had no intention whatever of giving up his plans for the reduction of Ireland, that he would not remove Surrey, and that he would not reinstate Kildare in the government. When peaceful means failed it would be time to put forth his strength. In language which reminds us of the royal speech in the ballad of 'Chevy Chase,' he remarked that this Irish enterprise was a trifle compared with those which he had in hand against France and Scotland. This was politic language in dealing with a half-civilised MacCarthy, but Henry spoke very differently to his own servants. There was talk of an alliance between Argyll and O'Neill, and of a Scotch descent upon Ireland. The Continent was disturbed, and the burden of three armies would be intolerable. And yet he would try to do justice to Ireland. He was an absolute monarch and above legal trammels, but might even condescend to consider himself bound, if by so doing he could induce Irish chiefs to live by law. If that of

England proved too strong for weak stomachs, they might even retain some[Pg 135] of their native customs. The Earldom of Ulster was legally his own, but he would not willingly take it by force. If clemency failed, in the last resort he would try the strength of his hand, for realms without justice were but tyrannies, communities of beasts rather than reasoning men. Brave words! but woefully belied in action.[88]

Surrey is not sanguine.

Surrey was not to be deceived, and steadily refused to prophesy smooth things. He believed that Ireland could only be reduced by conquest, and that the easiest method was to master one district at a time, gradually pushing forward the frontier until the whole country was obedient. A permanent army of 500 men might perhaps effect this, while at least 6,000 would be required for a rapid conquest. Edward I. had taken ten years to subdue Wales, and that great king had given almost constant personal attention to the work. Yet Wales was unprotected by the sea, and was not a fifth part the size of Ireland. All artillery and munitions of war would have to be brought from England, and fortresses must be built to bridle each tract of country successively occupied. Nor could a military occupation endure unless accompanied by a large plan of colonisation. Thus only could the natives be brought to labour and settled order. We can see, though Henry VIII. could not, how justly Surrey estimated the magnitude of England's task in Ireland.[89]

Activity of Surrey.

In July 1521 the Irish bordering on the Pale took their usual advantage of the season. O'Connor, O'More, and O'Carroll, the latter all unmindful of his last year's oath and of more recent promises, collected a great host and prepared to attack the Pale. Surrey, who had lately prorogued his Parliament after a ten days' session, was in Dublin, and by his promptitude averted the danger. O'Connor's castle, near Edenderry, was soon in his hands, being unable to resist the[Pg 136] fire of three pieces of heavy ordnance for a single day. It became an axiom in Irish warfare that the Government could always make its way with artillery. Surrey proposed to hold O'Connor's stronghold permanently, and to use it against the Irishry as Berwick was used against the Scots. He destroyed all the corn far and wide, the people with their cattle flying before him, while Sir Piers Butler played the like part in Ely O'Carroll. The vigour shown by the Lord-Lieutenant had the effect which vigour generally has in Ireland, and the confederacy gave him little further trouble. Meanwhile, the North was in a blaze. O'Donnell professed loyalty, but was not trusted by Surrey, who, however, thought it wise to humour him. O'Neill was willing to be on good terms with the Government, and was on his way to Dundalk accompanied by Magennis and a large force, when the O'Donnells attacked him in the rear. Fifteen hundred cows were driven off and seventeen of the Magennis' villages burned, so that the allies were forced to retrace their steps. The chief of Tyrconnell feared that if his great neighbour were once at peace with the Pale he would be too strong for him in the everlasting private war of Northern Ulster.[90]

Uncertainty of English policy.

It is not the least of Ireland's misfortunes that her rulers have ever been subject to hot and cold fits. In the autumn of 1521 Henry suddenly changed his mind. Disgusted at the apparently almost fruitless expense, he not only relieved Surrey at his own earnest request, but also abandoned his policy. War broke out between Charles and Francis, and the reformation of Ireland, which had but lately seemed so necessary a work for a

Christian king, was lightly postponed to a more convenient season. Surrey is the first of a long series of able men whose efforts, generally very ill seconded at home, in the end brought Ireland under the English sceptre. His means were inconsiderable. In the expedition against O'More, which he undertook very soon after landing, his whole force seems not to have exceeded 700. He[Pg 137] then asked the King for eighty horsemen from the North of England, and for leave to discharge as many of the guardsmen as he might think fit. Many of these were well-to-do householders, and liked Ireland so little that they were content to leave it on receiving twopence, or even a penny, a day. One hundred horsemen were accordingly sent, under the command of Sir John Bulmer, who was Surrey's personal friend, and fifty more were added from Wales. The captain received half-a-crown and the lieutenant eighteenpence a day. On their arrival 117 guardsmen were discharged upon a penny a day. Fourpence appears to have been a soldier's ordinary pay in Ireland, and Surrey maintained that this was not enough. Neither Welshmen nor Northumbrians proved to his taste, most of them being mounted archers and not spearmen. He thought better men might be had in the country, and Henry was willing to give him much latitude, though he cautioned him against employing too many Irishmen, lest the sword should hurt his hand. The King gave his Viceroy the power of life and death, reserving noble personages, and the right of making knights. A golden collar was sent for O'Neill, and it was supposed that such cheap defences would avail against a chief who could easily raise 1,600 men. Of two evils Surrey chose the less; he discharged most of Bulmer's men, whom he pronounced ill-looking, worthless rascals, and took Englishmen of the Pale in their places. The difficulty of buying forage was thus obviated, as native horsemen could find it for themselves.[91]

Parliament of 1521.
A Parliament sat in Dublin for ten days in June 1521, and after many prorogations was not finally dissolved till March 1522, when Surrey had left Ireland. There appears to be no record of the peers who attended, or of the places represented, and so little mention is afterwards made of this Parliament that the interest attaching to it was probably slight. Acts were passed making arson treason, forbidding[Pg 138] the exportation of wool as the cause of a 'dearth of cloth and idleness of many folks,' and providing against the failure of justice through lack of jurors.[92]

Want of money.
The Irish Government had no command of money, the judicious employment of which might enable them to dispense with troops. Surrey's expedition to Munster was near failing for want of means to pay his men. Before the end of August the exchequer was habitually empty; no taxes were due till Michaelmas, nor leviable till Christmas; and nothing was to be had except for ready money.[93] The King sent 4,000l., but would not face the necessities of the case. It seemed to him monstrous to have to spend 1,600l. or 1,700l. a year merely for the defence of the Pale. His remittances were mere palliatives, and Surrey was in difficulties during his whole term of office.

Surrey recalled at his own request, 1521.
Surrey had to cope with disease as well as poverty. It was scarcely possible to find healthy quarters for soldiers, and the people fled everywhere into the fields, leaving unburied bodies behind them. No place in Ireland was safe, and the Lord-Lieutenant, who lost three of his servants, was anxious about his wife and children. Sir John Bulmer

never had a day of health in Ireland, and was glad to get home safe without having seen any service. In the second year of his government, Surrey himself was affected with the fever and diarrhœa which have often been fatal to the English in Ireland, but his prayers were heard at last, and he was recalled in time to save his life. He was much regretted by the inhabitants of the Pale, who recognised his good nature, integrity, and ability. Those who best knew the subject believed that he really saw how the country might be reduced to order, and it was hoped that he would return with sufficient means. Meanwhile, the Irish Council entreated Wolsey to be guided by his advice.[94]

[Pg 139]

He leaves a great reputation.

Beloved by the King's subjects and feared by rebels, Surrey left one of the fairest names among those who have ruled Ireland. He paid in full for everything, so that the market followed him wherever he went, and he declared that he would rather eat grass than feast with the curses of the poor. His retinue had orders to behave in Ireland as they would at home. So generous was he that the common people thought him the King's son. Nor was he less just, for he gave full notice of his intended departure, and discharged all debts due by him or his. It was thought that he never offended within the compass of the seven deadly sins during his stay in Ireland; tradition, with a fine contempt for facts, adds that 'in his time was corn, cattle, fish, health, and fair weather, that the like was not seen many years before.' We know from his own letters that corn was dear and sickness prevalent, and we may be very sure that the weather was not always fair.[95]

Sir Piers Butler is made Lord Deputy, 1522.

Henry had too much respect for Surrey's opinion to hand back Ireland at once to Kildare; but he had resolved to reduce expenses, and was therefore obliged to place the government in the hands of someone who had the strength to make authority respected. No one satisfied this condition except Sir Piers Butler, and Surrey was allowed to appoint him Deputy, retaining the office of Lord-Lieutenant himself. There were objections to Sir Piers, as to every Irish governor. The Butlers would not take the field except under him or his eldest son, and he was generally laid up with gout all the winter. Lord James, as the heir was called, was active enough, but young and inexperienced. The choice, however, lay between Ormonde and Kildare, and Sir Piers was so cautiously handled, that he abstained from driving a hard bargain.

The experiment is not successful. O'Neills and O'Donnells.

The experiment was not very successful; for the Geraldines were all-powerful in the Pale, and the new Lord Deputy, when in Dublin, was separated from his own country[Pg 140] by his rival's dominions. He took the oath on March 26, 1522, but the O'Mores, who had heard that Kildare was on his way to restore the good old times, soon began to threaten the Pale. In the North a war broke out on such an unusually large scale as to make it probable that O'Neill had promised Kildare to give the new Deputy as much trouble as possible. Indeed, when Kildare did actually return, he at once went to O'Neill's aid. The chief of Tyrone may have required little persuasion to attack his hereditary foes, but the number of his allies was very uncommon. MacWilliam of Clanricarde, Tirlough O'Brien, Bishop of Killaloe, with many of his clansmen, O'Connor Don and O'Connor Roe, MacWilliam of Mayo, and MacDermot of Moylurg, all agreed to assemble on the southern border of Donegal. O'Neill brought to the trysting place Magennis, O'Rourke, and MacMahon, and many Scottish mercenaries in the hereditary service of his family. 'Great numbers,' we are told, 'of the English of Meath, and the gallowglasses of the province of Leinster, of the Clan-Donnell and Clan-Sheehy, also came thither, from their attachment to the daughter of the Earl of Kildare, who was O'Neill's mother.' To oppose this vast host, O'Donnell had only the clans immediately subject to him, O'Boyle, O'Gallagher, O'Dogherty, and the three septs of MacSwiney, hereditary gallowglasses of Tyrconnell. He mustered his forces near Trim, on the Tyrone side of the Finn, and there awaited the onset. But O'Neill adopted tactics very usual in Irish warfare, passed by the northern shore of Lough Erne, reached Ballyshannon without fighting, and slaughtered the garrison of MacSwineys there. O'Donnell retaliated by sending his son Manus to ravage the nearest districts of Tyrone, and himself hurried in pursuit of O'Neill across the pass now called Barnesmore Gap. Again declining battle, O'Neill turned back, spoiled the country between Donegal and Letterkenny, and encamped on the hill which overlooks Strabane. O'Donnell returned very quickly over Barnesmore, and, having been rejoined by his son, faced the enemy near Lifford. There he held a council of war, and his followers in desperation re[Pg 141]solved on an immediate fight. Leaving their horses behind, the O'Donnells crept up unperceived, drove in the outposts, and entered the camp pell-mell. In the darkness and confusion faces could not be distinguished, and many O'Neills fell by the hands of their brethren. Nine hundred dead bodies were counted in the morning, including many of the Leinster men who had come for the love of Kildare. Celtic war always presents the same features, and the victorious O'Donnells quickly disbanded with the horses and armour, the strong liquors and the rich drinking vessels of the vanquished.[96]

O'Donnell is stronger than O'Neill.

When he had again collected his men, O'Donnell recrossed Barnesmore, passed between Lough Melvin and the sea, and encamped at the foot of Benbulben, the bold hill which tourists admire from Sligo. The Connaught men were besieging that place when they heard of O'Donnell's victory, and of his near approach. They offered to negotiate, and, having thus gained time, they broke up from Sligo and retreated rapidly to the Curlew mountains, where they separated. The panegyrists of the O'Donnells sing pæans over two victories obtained without the help of English or Scotch allies, and remarkable in Irish warfare, the one for its slaughter, the other for its bloodlessness. Next year O'Donnell carried the war into Tyrone, which he ravaged as far as Dungannon. At Knockinlossy he destroyed a beautiful herb-garden, which must have been a rare thing in those days, and from Tullahogue, where he established a temporary camp, he spoiled the land far and wide. All the plunder was carried off safely, and the invaders then returned for more; but peace was made instead, and they turned their arms against O'Rourke. Fermanagh was wasted as Tyrone had been, and we cannot be surprised that chiefs who thus preyed on each other should fail to make head against the English Government.[97]

Sir Piers Butler is thwarted by the Geraldines.

During his short tenure of office, Sir Piers Butler undertook but one warlike expedition. He chastised the O'Briens,[Pg 142] and killed one of their leaders at the ford of Camus on the Suir. But Kildare had returned to Ireland, and was active in the field, acting at first in apparent unison with the Lord Deputy. Supported by O'Neill, to whose arbitration differences were submitted, he reduced to quiet the clans on the border of the

Pale. With both Butlers and Geraldines, the main object was to enlarge and secure their hereditary territories; but the former sought support in England, the latter among the wild tribes of Ulster. Lady Kildare, a daughter of Grey, Marquis of Dorset, whom the Earl had married during his late visit to England, complained bitterly to Wolsey that Sir Piers oppressed her husband, spoiled his tenants and friends, and made alliances with the wild Irish. She attributed this to Kildare's refusal to act partially in the dispute with the Boleyn family. Sir Piers Butler had married Kildare's sister, and he might not unreasonably count upon his brother-in-law's assistance; but throughout the contests of this century personal considerations were of little power compared with those of clanship and family pride. Kildare's brother James killed Robert Talbot of Belgard, on his way to Kilkenny, and it seems that the Geraldines regarded all gentlemen of the Pale who opposed them as no better than spies. But Sir Piers was naturally incensed at the outrage on his friend and visitor.[98]

Kildare in Ulster.

The general lawlessness is well shown by an expedition which Kildare undertook against O'Neill of Clandeboye, partly, as he owned, in revenge of the damage done to his property there, and partly, as he told the King, to punish attacks upon English merchants. At Carrickfergus he found a Breton ship which had just landed a cargo of Gascon wine. England and France were at peace, but the foreigners were fain to avoid capture by putting to sea without having been paid for their goods. The taste for claret was early developed in Ireland, and this relief from payment may have had a charm like the exemption from legal duties in more modern times. A Scotch vessel laden with provisions, which lay out[Pg 143] in Belfast Lough, was attacked by the Geraldines in boats and forced ashore. Hugh O'Neill, who had 1,500 Scots with him, rescued the crew, and in revenge Kildare destroyed Belfast and two other castles, and burned the country for twenty-four miles round. The Mayor of Carrickfergus and three of the chief townsmen were sent prisoners to England for trading with the French and Scots. If we are to believe Kildare's account, the Lord Deputy took the opportunity of handing over his castles to the O'Connors, of making a league with O'Carroll, and of carrying off 500 stud mares and colts from the county of Kildare.[99]

Kildare is restored.

It became evident at last that Sir Piers Butler was not strong enough to govern without Kildare's help, and Henry reverted to his father's policy of entrusting all Ireland to the man whom all Ireland could not govern. One more effort was made to reconcile the rivals by sending over royal commissioners, who prevailed upon them to make an agreement under seal as the basis of mutual concession. Kildare's stud mares had been taken by a namesake of his own, but Sir Piers covenanted to give them up if they came within his power. The subsidy payable by Tipperary to Kildare when he was Deputy was forgiven, as was half the subsidy paid by the county of Kildare to Butler during his tenure of office. In general, everyone was to behave well, to keep the peace, and not to make friends with Irish rebels.[100]

Arrangements for local government.

Butler and Kildare, and the principal gentlemen living on the marches of the Pale, were bound at this time to adopt a certain order in their countries, the two greater chiefs under penalties of 1,000 marks each, and the others in sums varying from 200 marks to

401. They made themselves liable in general for their own acts and for those of their sons and brethren, covenanting not to use the Brehon law nor those Irish exactions which usually accompanied it, and to repress crime as far as their power reached. Kildare, on his appoint[Pg 144]ment as Deputy, covenanted with the King not to make war or peace with Irishmen at the public charge without consent of the Council. This was intended to prevent another Knocktoe. Coyne and livery for the public service were to be reduced to fixed rules. Householders were to be allowed to compound by paying twopence a meal for a footman, and threehalfpence for a horseman or groom; twelve sheaves of oats for a trooper, and eight for a draught horse was to be the allowance, and not more than one boy was to accompany each horse. If the Earl travelled on private business, or on his way to attend Parliament, he was not to take coyne and livery save from his own tenants; and in no case except for the actual use of soldiers, nor for more than one night in one place, nor for successive nights within a distance of nine miles. It had been the custom to charge the farmers for 'black men,' that is, for soldiers who only existed in name and as a means of extortion. Treaties with Irishmen were not to be made to prejudice the Crown, nor were pardons to be given without the consent of the Council. The King's castles were to be kept in repair, and the Earl was to do his best to make the people of the Pale speak, dress, and shave like Englishmen. The salaries of the judges were to be paid; and Kildare promised if possible to have sheriffs, escheators, and coroners appointed in Meath, Dublin, Louth, Wexford, Kilkenny, Tipperary, and Waterford, and to provide for the holding of Quarter Sessions in due course.[101] It is noteworthy that the counties of Kildare and Cork are not mentioned, and that Tipperary is; the probability being that the two former were purposely excluded as being under Geraldine influence. As to the Butler Palatinate of Tipperary, it is possible that only the ecclesiastical portion or cross was intended, but it is likely that Kildare purposely placed his rival's district in a worse position than his own or those of Desmond. On the other hand, he promised not to go to war with the Butlers, or with their allies the Darcys and Nugents, without the consent of the Council. The new Lord Deputy promised not to purchase during his tenure of office any lands of which the title[Pg 145] was in dispute. James Fitzgerald was carried to England to answer for the death of Talbot, and led through the streets of London with a halter round his neck; but was pardoned in defiance of Wolsey's opinion at the intercession of Denton, Dean of Lichfield, who had been one of the commissioners lately sent to Ireland.[102]

The Butlers and Geraldines still quarrel.

In spite of all precautions, the perennial quarrel of Butlers and Geraldines was not stopped by the appointment of Kildare. Sir Piers sent his son James to London to watch the family interests there, in which task he was to be guided by Robert Cowley. Kildare even asserted that Sir Piers had given a signet to his trusty adherent, with the aid of which he might attest any written statement he chose to make. James Butler was either really too much occupied with the pleasure of the Court, or was crafty enough to appear so, while waiting for an opportunity. 'Surely,' his father wrote, 'unless I see your time better employed in attendance of my great business, than ye have done hither, I will be well advised or I do send you any more, to your costs.' A chief part of the business was the prisage of wines, especially at Waterford, which had always formed an important part of the Butler revenue. Kildare, as Lord Deputy, had insisted that an account should be given into the Exchequer, and Sir Piers argued that this was done merely to annoy him, and not at all out of regard to the King's revenue. He declared that the indentures which the new

Deputy had executed were 'in no point observed,' and, in particular, that coyne and livery were ruthlessly exacted, two villages in Kilkenny having to maintain no less than 420 gallowglasses. The Butler tenants were so impoverished that they could pay no rent and, moreover, the Deputy had not paid the half-subsidy of 800l. as he had bound himself to do. The King peremptorily ordered payment, but the claim was still disputed, and it does not appear that the money was ever handed over. Meanwhile, Lord Leonard Grey, the Deputy's brother-in-law, pressed many grave complaints upon the royal attention. Sir Piers[Pg 146] was accused of levying coyne and livery for craftsmen as well as soldiers, and for his hunting establishment. There were separate packs for hare, stag, and martin, and no less than sixty greyhounds; the whole charge on Kilkenny and Tipperary amounting to 2,000 marks.[103]

Recriminations. Great disorders.

Sir Piers was further accused of illegally occupying Callan and other royal manors in Kilkenny and Tipperary, but these lands were soon afterwards specially granted to him and his wife, and to their heirs male. Kildare charged his rival with helping O'Carroll and lending him cannon to defend Leap Castle against him. The fact was hardly disputed, but it had occurred as far back as 1516, and it was alleged in answer that the attack on O'Carroll was wanton and unprovoked. There were also accusations of intriguing with the O'Mores, of spoiling a village in Kildare and slaughtering the people even at the altar, of using the Castle of Arklow to rob the lieges by land and sea, of levying illegal taxes, and, in short, of behaving as Anglo-Irish noblemen generally did. A far graver charge against Sir Piers was the not having punished certain of his servants who were present at the barbarous murder of Maurice Doran, Bishop of Leighlin. The murderer was Maurice Kavanagh, his own Archdeacon, whom the Bishop had reproved for his crimes. It was said, moreover, that the churches in Tipperary and Kilkenny were ruinous, and that Sir Piers was in all things under the influence of his wife, the Lord Deputy's sister. It is satisfactory to know that the Bishop's tonsured assassin did not escape, for Kildare had him hanged and disembowelled at the scene of the murder: he was a near relation of Sir Piers Butler, which may account for the Lord Deputy's anxiety to do justice in this particular case.[104]

Kildare again in Ulster, 1524.

Kildare never ceased to harass such Irish chiefs as he[Pg 147] chose to consider his enemies. In the autumn of 1524 he led an army to help his kinsman O'Neill against O'Donnell, and encamped near Strabane. Manus O'Donnell, who had just returned from Scotland, wished to attack at once with his strong force of Macdonnells; but he was overruled by his father, who feared the Deputy's artillery. Flights of arrows were directed against the intrenchments all night, and in the morning Kildare thought it prudent to make peace and to depart without fighting. His old enemy Hugh O'Neill attempted to intercept him, but was killed in the skirmish which ensued. After this Kildare seems to have kept quiet for some months, and to have endeavoured to make peace among the Ulster clans. O'Neill and O'Donnell, or O'Donnell's son Manus, visited Dublin; but all efforts to reconcile them were ineffectual, 'so that they returned to their homes in strife, and the war continued as before.'[105]

Butler goes to England, 1526. Kildare sent for the next year.

In September 1526 Sir Piers Butler went to England to press his various suits, and to complain of Kildare's conduct. At Bristol he was in great danger of his life, the citizens having quarrelled with his retinue, who were probably for the most part Irish in speech and habits. According to Sir Piers the townsmen were the aggressors, and no provocation was given to the 600 men who surrounded his lodgings and threatened to set the house on fire. In spite of the interposition of the mayor and of some of the King's officers, Sir Piers was obliged to surrender certain of his men and to find securities for the rest. A grant of considerable possessions in Ireland rewarded him for the troubles and dangers of the journey to Court. He accused Kildare of conspiring with Irish enemies to help Desmond in the foreign intrigues which he was undoubtedly carrying on, and of neglecting to arrest him when ordered to do so by special letters from the King. It was said that he entered Munster for the ostensible purpose of effecting this arrest, but sent private word to Desmond to avoid him, and to plead his privilege not to attend Parliament or enter walled towns. It was scarcely fair to expect that the head of one branch[Pg 148] of the Geraldines should willingly imprison the head of the other; but Kildare was also accused of employing Irish enemies to oppress the Butlers, was summoned to London, and was at once committed to the Tower. He was soon brought before the Council, and Wolsey is said to have assailed him in a violent speech, calling him King of Ireland, a king who was able to bring back his own from the furthest edge of Ulster, but who would do nothing against a rebellious lord who had defied the Crown of England. After a time Kildare interrupted the Cardinal, saying that he was no orator, and that if he did not answer each charge in detail as it was uttered, his memory would fail him and his case would thus be prejudiced. This was considered reasonable, and the Earl hastened to ridicule the notion that Desmond's liberty depended on him. 'Cannot,' he asked, 'the Earl of Desmond shift, but I must be of counsel? Cannot he hide him except I wink?' Then he turned round upon Wolsey, whom he averred to be quite as much king in England as he was in Ireland. Indeed, he would willingly change places for one month, and would engage to pick up more crumbs in that time than could be bought with all the revenues of his Irish earldom. 'I slumber,' he continued, 'in a hard cabin, when you sleep in a soft bed of down; I serve under the King his cope of heaven, when you are served under a canopy; I drink water out of my skull, when you drink wine out of golden cups; my courser is trained to the field, when your genet is taught to amble; when you are begraced and belorded, and crouched and kneeled unto, then find I small grace with our Irish borderers, except I cut them off by the knees.' Wolsey broke up the Council in high dudgeon, and sent the Earl back to the Tower until further evidence should arrive from Ireland. Before leaving Dublin, Kildare had taken the precaution of seeing each Councillor separately and binding him by oath to write in his favour.[106]

Wolsey accused of plotting Kildare's death.

Wolsey is said to have taken it upon himself to send a death-warrant to the Governor of the Tower, which arrived[Pg 149] while that officer was playing shovel-board with his prisoner. On reading it the Lieutenant sighed, and Kildare remarked, 'By St. Bride, there is some mad game in that scroll, but fall how it will this throw is for a huddle.' On learning the contents of the paper he begged his gaoler to go straight to the King and ask his real pleasure. Unwilling to offend Wolsey, but still more unwilling to obey him, the Lieutenant repaired to Whitehall and was at once admitted, though it was ten o'clock at night. The King immediately respited the execution, and is said to have used strong language, calling Wolsey a saucy, over-officious priest, and threatening him with unpleasant consequences.[107]

But the Cardinal has perhaps been misrepresented.

Such is the received story. Yet Wolsey, who is represented as thirsting for Kildare's blood, was not even disposed to remove him from the viceroyalty. This forbearance arose from no love for the troublesome Earl, but it was thought that if he were detained in England and treated with some show of favour, his Irish adherents would be afraid to move. In case the King should nevertheless resolve to remove Kildare, then Wolsey advised that Sir Piers should again be made Deputy, the real government being in the hands of his son. Henry, however, thought that James Butler was too young for so great a charge, and that the noblemen of Ireland would disdain to be led by one who was junior to them all.[108]

The Earldom of Ormonde.

While Kildare's fortunes were thus clouded, his rival was at Court looking after his own interests. The Earldom of Ormonde, to which he was the true heir male, had been conferred, together with that of Wiltshire, on Sir Thomas Boleyn, grandson, through his mother, of the late Earl. Sir Piers, who was too prudent to oppose the father of Anne and Mary Boleyn, and who perhaps thought one earldom nearly as good as another, was content to accept the title of Ossory. Five years before, Henry had thought to reconcile the rival claimants by marrying James Butler to Anne Boleyn, but[Pg 150] the negotiation had come to nothing, and the King now destined the lady for himself.[109]

Sir Piers Butler is created Earl of Ossory.

The new creation was made at Windsor with great pomp. Arriving late in the evening from London, Sir Piers, who was in delicate health, lay at his own lodgings in the town, as being warmer and more comfortable than the rooms of the Lord Chamberlain, with whom he breakfasted next morning. We are particularly told that good fires were lit after mass. The Marquis of Exeter and the Earl of Oxford led the new peer into the presence chamber, the Earl of Rutland bearing the sword. The grandees dined together at the King's expense after the investiture, and then, having changed his dress, the Earl was again conducted into the royal presence by the Marquis of Exeter. Having taken leave of Henry and of the Queen and Princess, and having duly feed the waiters, Ossory returned to London, where he paid a parting visit to Wolsey, and then returned into his own country.[110]

The Vice-Deputy Delvin is captured by the O'Connors, 1528.

Leaving Kildare in the Tower, we must now go back to Ireland, where Richard Nugent, seventh Baron of Delvin, had been acting as Vice-Deputy, Sir James Fitzgerald, whom Kildare had left in charge, having been superseded by the Irish Council. When Archbishop Inge and Chief Justice Bermingham heard of Kildare's imprisonment, they wrote to Wolsey regretting the Earl's absence, and expressing their doubts as to whether he was guilty of any such practices as were charged against him. They considered Delvin incompetent, for he had no great fortune of his own to eke out the scanty revenue of Ireland. The people were more heavily taxed than ever, and they were not defended; for the armed bands which were always at Kildare's beck and call would serve no one else. As the Pale was desolated by the absence of one Earl, so were Tipperary and Kilkenny by the absence of another; and the worst was to be feared unless they both speedily returned. These gloomy forebodings were soon fulfilled; for Delvin, against the advice of the[Pg 151] Council, withheld the black-rent which O'Connor, Kildare's son-in-law, had been used to receive from Meath. The aggrieved chief surprised the Vice-Deputy on the march, killed most of his men, and took him prisoner. Lord Butler, who was present, had prudently provided himself with a safe-conduct; he lodged that night with the victorious O'Connor, and was allowed to have an interview with his distinguished prisoner. The chief and his brothers were present, and the two noblemen were not allowed to speak English nor to confer in private. Speaking in Irish, O'Connor insisted on having his black-rent again, or being paid a ransom for the Vice-Deputy, and on receiving a distinct promise that the men of the Pale should not avenge his overthrow. But Butler's diplomacy was not yet exhausted. By the advice of a Mr. White, who was among O'Connor's guests, he sought a private interview with Cahir, the chief's brother, who of course had a party of his own among the clansmen. Cahir readily agreed to escort Lord Butler out of his brother's country, and was afterwards persuaded to visit Lord Ossory at Kilkenny. He professed loyalty and was ready to prove it by his actions, if only he could be sure that Kildare would not sooner or later return and have his revenge—that was his only fear.[111]

The Geraldines still in the ascendant.

While his son was thus by policy undermining the Irish enemies of his house, Ossory was busy looking about for Irish allies. Hard pressed by the Desmonds and O'Briens, he wished to avoid a rupture with the O'Connors, and tried the efficacy of smooth speeches. As the price of an alliance against this possible foe O'Carroll demanded 40l., besides anything that the King or Deputy might give. O'More claimed the help of the Butlers against Kildare, and a money reward also. MacGilpatrick stipulated that Ossory should release him from debts amounting to 400 marks. The Earl agreed to these terms; but his immediate object was not attained, for Delvin remained a prisoner until early in the following year. In the meanwhile Sir Thomas Fitzgerald,[Pg 152] Kildare's brother, acted as Deputy, and the Geraldine policy was practically successful.[112]

Kildare is accused by Cowley and others, 1528.

The late Lord-Lieutenant, now Duke of Norfolk, attributed all the woes of Ireland to the quarrel between Butlers and Geraldines, and he was on the whole in favour of maintaining the latter faction in power. Ossory and his son were loyal enough, but they could scarcely hold their own against the Desmonds and O'Briens, and could do nothing in the Pale, where they had no natural authority and where public opinion was against them. They would be entirely dependent on their own followers, who would eat more than their services were worth. On the other hand, Robert Cowley, Ossory's faithful agent, was always at hand to prevent Henry and Wolsey from yielding too completely to Norfolk's advice. It is said that on one occasion he complained of Kildare to the Council, and that he shed tears in the course of his speech 'for pity,' as he said, 'upon his father's son.' 'He is,' retorted the Earl, 'like the plover taken in setting his snares, and waiting for his desired purpose, his eyes being against the wind and the water dropping out. So many plovers as he taketh he knocketh their brains out with his thumb, notwithstanding his watery tears of contemplation. Even like doth Mr. Cowley with me; his tears cometh down; he layeth shrewd matters or articles to my charge.'[113]

The Duke of Richmond Lord-Lieutenant, 1529. His Deputy, Sir William Skeffington.

If this story be true we must assign it to the autumn of 1528, when Cowley was certainly in London. O'Connor had just invaded the Pale, and evidence afterwards came to light which connected Kildare with his son-in-law's proceedings. Early in August, Kildare's daughter Alice, the wife of Lord Slane, came to Ireland and went straight to O'Connor's house. Sir Gerald MacShane Fitzgerald afterwards swore before the Irish Council that Melour Faye had revealed to him a secret agreement between himself and Kildare, and[Pg 153] that Lady Slane's arrival was the preconcerted signal that her father was detained in England. Ossory was at war with Desmond when O'Connor made his attack, but abandoned his expedition and hurried off to defend the Pale. He took occasion to remind Wolsey of the hereditary policy of the house of Kildare. By stirring up rebellion in Ireland when he was detained at Court the late Earl had made himself chief governor for life; his son had followed suit, and the Pale had practically transferred its allegiance from the King of England to the Earl of Kildare. Henry thought it prudent to give the Earl his liberty, but resolved to have a Viceroy who should hold Ireland for the Crown only. He made his son, the Duke of Richmond, Lord-Lieutenant, thereby giving the Emperor great offence, and assigned him as Deputy Sir William Skeffington, a Leicestershire man, who had been long in the public service. Meanwhile the sovereign had frowned. In the month following that in which Skeffington was appointed, Wolsey saw Henry at Grafton for the last time, and three weeks later he was indicted in the King's Bench. Kildare remained in London, for he was one of those who signed the famous letter to Clement VII., in which the English notables reproached the Pope for his partiality, and laid upon him the responsibility of a disputed succession, with all its terrors and troubles.[114]

Skeffington's instructions.

Skeffington had long served as Master of the Ordnance, whence the Irish, who may have been offended at the appointment of a commoner, gave him the name of 'the gunner.' He was accompanied by Edward Staples, a Lincolnshire man, whom the King had appointed Bishop of Meath, and brought with him 200 horse and a sum of money. He was instructed in the first place to reconcile, if possible, the conflicting interests of the Earls of Kildare, Ossory, and Desmond. He was not to make any serious attack on the wild Irish without the consent of the majority of the Council,[Pg 154] especially when it would involve charging the country with the support of an army. The established custom of taking provisions for the ordinary movements of troops was, however, allowed. Skeffington was to hold a Parliament, but was to get all the money he could by way of subsidy before it met, and to pay the gross levy into the Vice-Treasurer's hands. Kildare's loyal promises were to be taken as sincere, and the Deputy was enjoined to help him in his enterprises as if they were undertaken in the King's name. The Earl might retain half the proceeds, provided the remainder were handed over to the Vice-Treasurer.[115]

The O'Tooles chastised, 1530. Ulster invaded, 1531. Submission of O'Donnell.

Kildare returned to Ireland some months after Skeffington's arrival, and his first exploit was to chastise the O'Tooles, with the help of 200 archers supplied by the city of Dublin. Next year Ulster was invaded. A treaty had already been concluded at Drogheda, by which O'Donnell promised the King allegiance, and bound himself to assist Skeffington against all his Majesty's enemies. He covenanted for O'Reilly, Maguire, and

MacQuillin, as well as for himself, and Skeffington bound himself to give them such help and protection as was due to the King's subjects. In pursuance of this agreement Skeffington, accompanied by Kildare and Ossory, ravaged Tyrone on both sides of the Blackwater, from Clogher to Caledon, and penetrated to Monaghan, which was undefended. There O'Donnell and some malcontent O'Neills met them, but they did not venture to meet the tyrant of the North in the field, a measure of the weakness of government at that time.[116]

Skeffington is overshadowed by Kildare.

It clearly appeared that the Lord Deputy was in a false position as regards Kildare. When the Butlers were out on a foray, the Geraldines attacked their camp, killed the officer on guard, and carried off horses, arms, and provisions. It[Pg 155] was even said that the Earl of Kildare displayed his banner openly, and led his men to the attack. With great difficulty and at Skeffington's earnest request, Ossory prevented his followers from retaliating, but he poured complaints into Cromwell's attentive ears. Kildare allowed his adherents to seize the titular Baron of Burntchurch in Kilkenny, while passing through Castledermot, on his way to attend Parliament. The Baron was a Fitzgerald, but on friendly terms with Ossory, who would have rescued him in spite of Kildare but for the Lord Deputy's express prohibition; as it was, the poor man lost his horse, money, and apparel without redress. 'This,' said Ossory, 'is a good encouragement to malefactors to commit spoils, having the advantage thereof without punishment or restitution.' It was not the first nor the last time in Ireland that the friends of law and order have been less safe than its enemies, and that the Government has hampered those whom it could not protect. Indeed, the Kilkenny borough members fared no better than their neighbours, for they were seized at the gate of Athy by Murtagh MacOwney, who wished that he had the King in the end of a handlock, and the Deputy in the other end, as surely as he had the worthy burgesses. In fact, Skeffington had scarcely any power. Kildare detained the hostages of the natives, in spite of direct orders to send them to Dublin, and thus let it be clearly seen that the King's representative was a mere instrument in his hands.[117]

Kildare goes to England, 1532, and regains favour.

It was commonly said in Ireland that all the parchment and wax in England would not bring the Earl of Kildare thither again; but this saying turned out not to be true. So well had the Earl managed his affairs, that he ventured across the Channel early in 1532, and, after a six months' residence at Court, returned with the legal as well as the real power of a Chief Governor. Sir John Rawson, Prior of Kilmainham, and Chief Justice Bermingham, supported Kildare's counter-charges against Ossory, and accused Skeffington of partiality in his favour. There was an attempt to show that Ossory's[Pg 156] hostility arose from the fear that Kildare would support Wiltshire's claims upon the Ormonde estates. But Ossory maintained that he had long since compromised all claims against his property, that Kildare's advocacy of Wiltshire's pretensions was collusive and fraudulent, and the King would be the real loser of the possession, if such castles as Arklow and Tullow were given to the too powerful Geraldine under colour of another man's sham title. Anne Boleyn's star was now at its zenith; her father was fond of money, and perhaps saw a chance of extorting it from opposite quarters. It is clear that any claim of his was likely at this time to be favourably regarded, and it may be in this way that the lately waning influence of Kildare was restored.

Kildare again Deputy.

Having secured the much-coveted patent, Kildare hastened to Dublin and relieved Skeffington, who, having arrears of business to transact, was allowed to dance attendance among other suitors in his successor's ante-chamber. On the very day of his arrival, the new Lord Deputy took the Great Seal from his enemy Archbishop Alen, and gave it to the Primate Cromer. As a sop to the opposite faction, Lord Butler was made Lord Treasurer by the King; but the Deputy was supreme in the Council, and those who were not his friends thought only of saving themselves from his anger. Thus relieved from all restraint, and perhaps thinking himself indispensable, as indeed he well might, the Earl turned upon his hereditary enemy. While his brother Sir John Fitzgerald was helping O'Neill to ravage Louth, the lawful guardian of the Pale devastated Kilkenny; his men were allowed to plunder the peaceable folk resorting to Castledermot Fair, and to murder a due proportion. He used the sword which the King had committed to him 'utterly to extinguish the fame and honour of any other noble man within that land ... shadowed with that authority, so that, whatever he did, it should not be repugned at.'[118]

The O'Carrolls.

There was at this time a fierce dispute as to who should succeed Mulrony O'Carroll, who among southern chiefs in his[Pg 157] time 'destroyed most in regard to foreigners and improved most in regard to Gaedhill.' A brother would in the usual course have succeeded to these glories; but there was always a strong tendency to substitute the hereditary for the elective principle, and a claim was advanced on behalf of Mulrony's son Fergananim, to whom Kildare, choosing his time, had just given his daughter. Ossory of course espoused the cause of the brothers, but was defeated with the loss of several small pieces of cannon. On the same day the old chief died, and, as he favoured his son's pretensions, this was numbered among his victories. Having been a man of blood, and having lavished some of his plunder upon the clergy, he was rewarded after death with hyperbolical praises. 'He was,' the 'Four Masters' inform us, 'a protecting hero to all; the guiding firm helm of his tribe; a triumphant traverser of tribes; a jocund and majestic Munster champion; a precious stone; a carbuncle gem; the anvil of the solidity, and the golden pillar of the Elyans.' Fergananim was at first acknowledged as chief, but his uncle soon occupied Birr and other castles, and ravaged the country from thence. The Lord Deputy came in person before Birr, and received a bullet wound in the side. As he groaned with the pain, a kerne is reported to have encouraged him by saying that he himself had three bullets in him, and felt none the worse. 'I wish,' replied the Earl, 'you had this one along with the others.'[119] He was less fortunate than his follower, for the bullet, which came out of itself some months later, lamed him for life, and affected his speech. Birr Castle was, however, taken.[120]

Parliament of 1533. Miserable state of the country.

Kildare held a Parliament in Dublin in 1533, but we know nearly as little about it as about that held by Surrey. The most important law passed appears to have been one for the punishment of those who stole corn under colour of taking wages for harvest work in kind. This meeting of Parliament[Pg 158] gave rise to a renewal of the old dispute about precedency between Armagh and Dublin. Alen could no longer rely upon the patronage of Wolsey, and it is certain that Kildare's influence would be exerted against him. But the Deputy had been making so many enemies, that the increased hostility of Alen would not count for much. A heavy reckoning had been scored up; and John Dethyke, or Derrick, a prebendary of St. Patrick, gave voice to the prevailing discontent. With bitter irony he assured Cromwell that the people were excellently disposed and full of abstinence. Their accustomed ceremony was to abstain from flesh on Wednesday, but their devotion had so much increased that they now abstained likewise on Sunday, Monday, Tuesday, and Thursday. 'I trust to Jesu,' he continued. 'Ye shall hear that there shall be many saints among them; but they play the fox's part, shy of hens when he could not reach them.' All the butchers in Dublin had not as much meat between them as would make a mess of broth, and those who owned no cattle were driven to dry bread. Marauders entered the suburbs of Dublin, and one butcher had lost 220 beasts. No one could safely ride a mile out of town, and it was useless to complain; for the Deputy was visited with that distressing form of deafness which affects those who do not wish to hear. The poor butchers had accordingly shut up their shops, and taken to making leather breeches, as if it were perpetual Lent. And not only did the Viceroy do nothing, but he took the opportunity of removing the King's artillery from Dublin to his own castles. Meanwhile, the O'Byrnes actually entered Dublin Castle, and carried off prisoners and cattle, 'insomuch as nightly since great watch is in the city of Dublin, fearing that the same should be pilfered, prostrate, and destroyed, whereof they never dreaded so much.' Even Sir James Fitzgerald complained that his brother oppressed him cruelly for having done good service under Skeffington, and Norfolk's tenants in Carlow were in no better plight.[121]

[Pg 159]

Charges accumulate against Kildare.
The Council did not directly attack Kildare; but they sent over Sir John Alen, the Master of the Rolls, to enlighten Henry upon the true state of affairs. They directed Alen to report that English laws and customs were unknown except within twenty miles of Dublin, and that unless something were done they would soon be driven even from that contracted area. Various errors of policy, such as the practice of entrusting viceregal power to Irish lords and of giving away Crown lands, had so strengthened the Irishry and weakened the Pale, that the King would soon not have revenue enough to maintain a Deputy. Two archbishops, two bishops, four of the great regular ecclesiastics, two temporal peers, and three judges signed the document embodying these severe strictures, and they reminded Henry that unless he looked the better to it, Ireland might be used against him by any enterprising foreign enemy. Even more outspoken was a native of Ireland, closely associated with the Master of the Rolls, who declared that loyal subjects had been ill requited, and that people had come to look upon the viceroyalty as part of Kildare's inheritance. Everyone who opposed him suffered for it, and all his offences were passed over. 'Always after the malice of the Geraldines was resisted and the land staid, the King withdrew his aid from thence, putting the malefactors in his authority; whereas, if he had continued the same there, and suppressed the others, undoubtedly a marvellous profit and commodity should have issued thereby.... What subjects under any prince in the world would love, obey, or defend the right of that prince, which (notwithstanding their true hearts and service toward him) would afterwards put them under the governance of such as should daily practise to prosecute and destroy them for the same?' The question has often been asked in Ireland since then.[122]

The Geraldines become intolerable.

The confusion between the Earl of Kildare, in his own character, and in that of Lord Deputy, was not at all conducive to good government. Private opposition to the subject[Pg 160] was easily represented as treason to the King in his representative's person, and was indeed likely enough to grow into it. It was believed that the recent murder of Ossory's son Thomas by Dermot Fitzpatrick was not altogether the work of Irishry. Kildare and his sons and brothers provoked attacks on every side. The moral effect of O'Byrne's raid had of course been disastrous, and no one felt himself safe. The principal remedies suggested were the appointment of a Deputy for a long term, Norfolk being preferred, and after him Skeffington, the abolition of Irish customs, and the education of young noblemen and chiefs' sons at the English Court. Local presidencies were also recommended, but the first thing was to get rid of Kildare. The Geraldines indeed did not conceal that their interests were not those of the Crown. 'Thou fool,' said Sir Gerald MacShane to the Earl's brother Thomas, who had some legal scruples, 'thou shalt be the more esteemed in Ireland to take part against the King; for what hadst thou been if thy father had not done so? What was he set by until he crowned a King here; took Garth, the King's captain, prisoner; hanged his son; resisted Poynings and all Deputies; killed them of Dublin upon Oxmantown Green; would suffer no man to rule here for the King, but himself? Then the King regarded him, made him Deputy and married thy mother to him; or else thou shouldst never have had foot of land, where now thou mayst dispend 400 marks by year, or above.'[123]

Kildare is forced to go to England, 1534.
As the result of Alen's efforts, Kildare was summoned to Court. The Earl doubtless felt that his chances would be small if once the Tower gates closed upon him, and he sent his wife over to get the order revoked, on the old ground that he could not be spared. Lady Kildare's diplomacy failed, and her husband was summoned a second time; but was allowed to appoint a Vice-Deputy. This may, or may not, have been a bait to induce him to go quietly, for nothing less than an army could have taken him by force. Skeffington had been working hard against his enemy, and was in[Pg 161] constant communication with Cromwell, watching the port of Chester, so as to be in London as soon or sooner than the Earl. He reported that Lady Kildare's servants delayed the King's letters purposely, and that he was most anxious for the moment when he should at last be able to prove his charges against the Lord-Deputy.[124]

His eldest son remains as Deputy.
Kildare had now no choice but between obedience and open rebellion. Before embarking at Drogheda he delivered the sword to his eldest son in the presence of several members of Council. Thomas Lord Offaly, better known as Lord Thomas and Silken Thomas, was about twenty years old, and his father advised him to be guided in all things by his uncle, Sir James Fitzgerald; his cousin, Sir Thomas Eustace; his great-aunt, Lady Janet Eustace, and her husband and son, Walter and James Delahide. It is impossible to pronounce on the genuineness of the speech which the chronicler puts into Kildare's mouth, but the advice contained in it would have been well suited to the occasion. He told his son that his youth should be guided by age; his ignorance by experience. He was, he said, putting a naked sword into a young man's hand, and urged him to defer to the Council, 'for albeit in authority you rule them, yet in counsel they must rule you.'[125]

FOOTNOTES:

[76] See his patent of Nov. 8, 1510. Council of Ireland to the King, June 8, 1509, in Brewer; Four Masters; Annals of Lough Cé.

[77] Earls of Kildare, p. 69; Ware; Four Masters. Kildare died Sept. 3, 1513.

[78] See the grant in Brewer, Dec. 2, 1513, and again, March 24, 1516.

[79] Kildare to the King, Dec. 1, and Archbishop Rokeby to Wolsey, Dec. 12, 1515, both in Brewer.

[80] Four Masters, 1516.

[81] Ibid.

[82] Kite to Wolsey, May 1 and June 7, 1514, R.O.; Lady Kildare's Articles of Complaint, 1515, R.O.; Ware's Annals.

[83] The tract by Finglas is in Carew, under 1515.

[84] For further details of Irish exactions see Ware's Antiquities, and Presentments of Irish Grand Juries in the Sixteenth Century, ed. Hore and Graves, p. 266, sqq. Articles by Sir William Darcy, June 24, 1515, in Carew.

[85] The paper printed by Leland, ii. 132, contains only Donogh O'Carroll's recollections. Surrey to Wolsey, September 6, 1520.

[86] The Lord-Lieutenant and Council to the King, August 25; Surrey to Wolsey, August 27; Surrey to the King, July 29, 1521.

[87] The Lord-Lieutenant and Council to the King, October 6; Surrey to Wolsey, November 3; Surrey to Wolsey, April 27, 1521.

[88] The King to Surrey, No. 12 of the printed State Papers; the King to an Irishman, No. 14 of the same; Instructions for Sir John Petchie, No. 18 of the same.

[89] Surrey to the King, July 31, 1521.

[90] Stile to Wolsey, July 30, 1571; Surrey to the King, July 29 and September 14; Ware.

[91] The King to Surrey, May 1520; Surrey to Wolsey, September 6 and 25; the King to Surrey, S.P. No. 12; Surrey to Wolsey, November 3; Surrey to the King, September 14, 1521.

[92] Irish Statutes, 13 Henry VIII.

[93] The Lord-Lieutenant and Council to the King, August 25, 1520. The King to Surrey, Nos. 12 and 19 in the printed S.P.

[94] Surrey to the King, September 16, 1521; to Pace, December 2. The latter letter was written in bed. Surrey to Wolsey, August 2 and November 3, 1520.

[95] The Council of Ireland to Wolsey, December 21 and February 28, 1522; Dowling's Annals, 1519; Sir John Davies' Discovery; the Book of Howth.

[96] Four Masters; Annals of Lough Cé, 1522. Stile to Wolsey, April 25, 1522.

[97] Four Masters, 1522; Annals of Lough Cé.

[98] Ware; Lady Kildare to Wolsey, May 25, 1523.

[99] Kildare to the King, May 24, 1523.

[100] Indentures between Kildare, Ormond (sic), the King's Commissioners, and others, July 28, 1524. The Commissioners were Sir A. Fitzherbert, Ralph Egerton, and James Denton, Dean of Lichfield. Kildare to the King, May 24, 1523.

[101] Indentures as above; Recognisances for the Marchers, July 12, 1524.

[102] Indentures between Kildare and the King, August 4, 1524. Recognisances for the Marchers, July 12, 1574. Ware.

[103] The King to Kildare, May 20, 1525; Articles on behalf of Kildare, No. 42 in printed State Papers; Presentments of the County and City of Kilkenny, 1537, ed. Hore and Graves; Sir Piers Butler to his son, April 22, 1524.

[104] Articles on behalf of Kildare, No. 42 in the printed State Papers; Dowling's Annals, 1522-1524; Hibernia Dominicana. Bishop Doran, 'eloquentissimus prædicator,' was killed in 1525.

[105] Four Masters, 1525 and 1526; Ware, 1526.

[106] Stanihurst; Lord James Butler to his father, Dec. 27, 1527, in Brewer; Ware; Russell.

[107] Stanihurst; Russell.

[108] Consideration by Vannes and Uvedale, No. 52 in the printed State Papers.

[109] See Brewer, introduction to vol. iv., p. 238, where there is a confusion between Sir Piers and his son.

[110] Carew, Feb. 22, 1528.

[111] Inge and Bermingham to Wolsey, Feb. 23, 1528; to Norfolk, May 15; the Council of Ireland to Wolsey, same date; Lord Butler to Inge, May 20.

[112] The Council of Ireland to Wolsey, May 15; Ossory to Inge, May 21; to the King, June 10.

[113] Cowley had been in the service of the late Earl of Kildare. Book of Howth.

[114] Instructions for the Lord Cardinal, No. 56 in the printed State Papers; Ossory to Wolsey, Oct. 14, 1528; Instructions by Charles V. to Gonzalo Fernandez in Carew, Feb. 24, 1530 (should be 1529). The letter to the Pope was July 30, 1530.

[115] Instructions to Skeffington, No. 57 in the printed State Papers. He landed near Dublin, August 2, 1529.

[116] Submission of O'Donnell, May 6, 1531. O'Donnell 'publice proposuit et fatebatur dominum suum fuisse et esse fidelem et ligeum subditum Domini Regis;' Four Masters, 1531. In his Instructions for Cromwell, Jan. 2, 1532, Ossory notes that his contingent was better than Kildare's, and that he bore the whole cost himself.

[117] Ossory to Cromwell, January 2, 1532.

[118] Report to Cromwell, No. 64 of the printed State Papers; Lodge's Peerage by Archdall, art. 'Duke of Leinster.' Ware; Stanihurst.

[119] 'Cui quidam turbarius jocose dixerat, "Domine, cur gemis tam dire, cum ego semel habui iii bulletos in me, et vides, domine, quam sanus sum ad præsens?" Cui comes mite respondit (in agonia) quod hunc etiam bulletum vellet ipsum in se una cum cæteris habuisse.'—Dowling's Annals, wrongly placed at 1528.

[120] Four Masters, 1532. Annals of Lough Cé.

[121] Jus Primatiale Armachanum, Part I. No. 361; Dethyke to Cromwell, Sept. 3, 1533; Report to Cromwell, No. 64 of the printed State Papers; Sir James Fitzgerald to the King, August 31.

[122] Report to Cromwell, printed State Papers, vol. ii. p. 174. Instructions to Sir John Alen, No. 63 in same.

[123] Report to Cromwell, quoted above.

[124] Skeffington to Cromwell, October 25 and November 4, 1533.

[125] Stanihurst.

[Pg 162]

CHAPTER X.

THE GERALDINE REBELLION—SKEFFINGTON'S ADMINISTRATION, 1534-1535.

Kildare is sent to the Tower.

Among the letters which Alen brought with him from England was one of thanks for past services to Connor Maguire, chief of Fermanagh. Maguire belonged to the party in Ulster which opposed O'Neill, and consequently Kildare; and he seems to have been in some degree under Alen's influence. He now wrote to the King, adding to the already overwhelming case against Kildare, and praying for the appointment of Skeffington. This despatch probably reached London about the same time as the Earl, who was examined by the Council and at once sent to the Tower. The heaviest charge against him was that of fortifying his own castles with the King's artillery; and it was in fact this which enabled his son to make head for a time against the Crown. He could only answer that he had intended to defend the Pale against the Irish: perhaps the hesitation caused by his wound was taken for the confession of guilt. He was no longer the man who had bearded Wolsey in his pride; and, unfortunately, his old power of repartee had descended to his son, who annoyed with his taunts those whom he should most have conciliated. The young Vice-Deputy made no secret of his dislike to the King's policy, sought alliances with O'Brien and Desmond, and gave the enemies of his House plausible grounds for stigmatising him as a traitor from the very first.[126]

His death prematurely reported.

Early in the summer of 1534 a report reached Ireland that Kildare was to be beheaded, and his son and brother[Pg 163] arrested. A poor retainer of his house living near Kilcullen is said to have brought to Lord Offaly from London a little silver-gilt heart and a pair of black dice, with a verbal message from his father bidding him not to trust the Irish Council, but to keep out of the way lest he should lose life and liberty. About the same time a private letter from Thomas Cannon, who had been in Skeffington's service, confirmed the sinister rumours already afloat. In days when there were no newspapers such letters were handed about freely, and this one fell into the hands of a priest who read English with difficulty, and who put it aside until he had time to spell out its meaning. A retainer of Offaly's, who chanced to stay the night in the priest's house, used the letter as a shoe-horn, and forgot to withdraw it. Undressing in the evening he found the paper, read it out of curiosity, and found to his dismay that it announced Kildare's death. He at once took the fatal missive to James Delahide, who carried it to the Vice-Deputy. Delahide was one of those whose advice Kildare had directed his son to take: he now counselled him to rebel and to avenge his father's death.[127]

His son rebels.

Though his death was at hand Kildare still lived, and there is no reason to suspect foul play: he was old and suffering from wounds, and confinement or anxiety may well have hastened his end. But his impetuous son assumed the worst, and at once prepared for war. His Irish connections O'Neill and O'Connor approved his resolution; but the Earl of Desmond, Sir Thomas Eustace of Baltinglass, Fitzmaurice of Kerry, Fleming, Lord of Slane, and most of the Anglo-Irish well-wishers of his House, counselled prudence. Lord Chancellor Cromer, a grave and learned divine, gave similar advice. But Rehoboam would not be persuaded. On St. Barnabas' Day he rode through Dublin with

140 armed retainers, each wearing a silken fringe on his helmet, a mode of decoration which gave Offaly the name by which he is best remembered. Passing through Dame's Gate the Geraldines forded the Liffey and rode to St. Mary's Abbey, where he had summoned a[Pg 164] meeting of the Council. No sooner had the Deputy taken the chair than his armed followers invaded the council-chamber, and waited with ill-concealed impatience while their leader made a speech, in which he declared himself no longer King Henry's officer, and called on all who hated cruelty and tyranny to join him in open war. He then tendered the sword of state to the Primate, who besought him with tears in his eyes not to do so mad and wicked an act. 'They are not yet born,' he said, 'that shall hereafter feel the smart of this uproar.' The Chancellor's speech was probably unintelligible to most of the intruders; and the effect of it was at once dispelled by an Irish bard named Nelan, who recited a long heroic poem in honour of Silken Thomas, and upbraided him with lingering too long. Stung by this taunt, Offaly replied that he was much obliged to the Archbishop for his advice, but that he came to announce his own intention and not to seek counsel: he then threw down the sword and left the room. He was now a subject, and the Council at once ordered his arrest; but the Mayor had no force at his command, and the rebel was allowed to rejoin his forces on Oxmantown Green. Archbishop Alen, who had good reasons for fear, took refuge in the castle, and the Chief Baron, who accompanied him, wrote to Cromwell for help.[128]

    The Butlers remain loyal.

    It was rumoured that Offaly would destroy everything in the Pale, so that no support might remain for a royal army: he gave out that he would kill or banish everyone born in England, and declared forfeit the goods of all who remained loyal. He wrote to his cousin Lord Butler, offering to divide Ireland with him if he would help to conquer it; but Butler, one of the ablest of his race, declined with proper indignation. He refused to barter his truth for a piece of Ireland, and was not at all disposed to hang for good fellowship. 'Were it so,' he wrote '(as it cannot be), that the chickens you reckon were both hatched and feathered; yet be thou sure, I had rather in this quarrel die thine enemy than live thy partner.' Ossory had left the King but a few days before,[Pg 165] having undertaken for himself and his son to assist to their utmost power the due course of law, and above all strenuously to resist the usurped jurisdiction of the Bishop of Rome. Skeffington was again Deputy, and Ossory promised to maintain his authority. The Government was in fact placed to a great extent under the protection of the House of Ormonde. In return for these promises, and in consideration of the singular confidence and trust which the King had conceived in the Earl and his son, and in respect of the truth which always had continued in them and their blood to the Crown of England, and as a token of confidence in their ability, the Government of Tipperary and Kilkenny, and of other districts at the Deputy's discretion, were granted to Ossory and his son. They were not the men to renounce such solid advantage for the shadowy realm which their rash kinsman offered.[129]

    Murder of Archbishop Alen.

    It would have been well for Archbishop Alen had he adhered to his first resolution of remaining inside the castle walls, which, as it turned out, were quite able to protect him. Six weeks after the first outbreak, and while the rebels were threatening Dublin, he put himself under the guidance of Bartholomew Fitzgerald, a confidential servant, who brought a small boat to Dame's Gate. The Archbishop embarked, but the wind was contrary and perhaps the boatmen hostile; at all events, the boat stuck fast on the sands at Clontarf. The fugitive took refuge in a gentleman's house at Artane; but Offaly appeared at the door next morning and ordered two of his followers, John Teeling and Nicholas Wafer, to bring out the Archbishop. They dragged the old man out of bed, and brought him before their leader. Alen begged for mercy, acknowledging that his captor had no reason to wish him well, but claiming regard for his office if not for his person. Offaly turned away contemptuously, and, speaking in Irish, ordered his men to 'take away the churl.' Teeling and Wafer immediately dashed out the Archbishop's brains. Robert Reyley, who, if not actually an eye-witness, must have been[Pg 166] close at hand, was at once sent off to Maynooth with a casket which was found on Alen's person, and he afterwards swore that he did not know whether Offaly ordered the murder or not. The rebel chief always maintained that his intention was to detain and not to kill; but he thought it necessary to send his chaplain to Rome to seek absolution.[130]

Dublin is threatened.

The sword of state which should have protected them having been exchanged for a rod to scourge them, the citizens of Dublin were left to their own slender resources. Instigated by Offaly, and assisted by John Burnell of Balgriffin, a gentleman of the Pale, the O'Tooles descended from their mountains and ravaged the flat country to the north of the city. In an attempt to intercept the raiders on their return, the citizens were defeated with great loss near Kilmainham. Assuming that they were at his mercy, Offaly offered the citizens their lives if they would let him enter to besiege the castle. John White, the Constable, who was afterwards knighted for his services, made no objection provided he were allowed time to victual. A spirited Alderman, John Fitzsimons, furnished a great part of the provisions[131] at his own expense, and also employed a smith in his own house to forge a chain for the drawbridge. To such a state of destitution had Geraldine ascendency brought the principal royal fortress in Ireland. Another Alderman, Francis Herbert, was sent off to beg help from the King.[132]

Defence of Dublin.

White having announced himself ready, the citizens admitted about 100 of the rebels under the command of James Field of Lusk, who had with him Teeling and Wafer, the Archbishop's murderers, and three noted pirates, named Brode, Rookes, and Purcell. The ordnance at Field's command, part of that which had been entrusted to the late Earl of Kildare for the defence of the realm, was too light to make[Pg 167] any great impression on the castle, upon whose walls it ought to have been mounted; and in the meantime Ossory was sweeping away the cattle from Kildare. The temptation to retaliate was too strong for Offaly, or perhaps for his men, and he turned aside from Dublin to punish the Butlers. Tullow Castle delayed him for five precious days, after which he had the satisfaction of slaughtering the garrison, and five more days were spent in inaction on the Barrow. Again did Offaly offer to divide Ireland, including even his own inheritance, with Ossory; but the Earl refused as his son had done, and only consented to a truce which would leave him free to defend Tipperary against a threatened attack from Desmond. The Butler forces being thus divided, and help having come from O'Neill, Offaly broke the truce and began to plunder Kilkenny. At Thomastown Lord Butler was wounded in a skirmish, and had to retire to Dunmore until cured; while Offaly, who had possession of Athy, Kilkea, Carlow, and Castledermot, collected a great host of O'Mores, O'Connors, Kavanaghs, and O'Byrnes. But these auxiliaries do not seem to have been of much use;

for Ossory had still men enough to burn and spoil the northern part of Carlow, though not to attempt the relief of Dublin.[133]

The rebels are beaten off.

Francis Herbert returned very speedily from the King, bringing letters in which Henry promised immediate succour. Despairing of success, Field anticipated the action of Rosen at Londonderry, and threatened to expose the citizens' children on the trenches, so as to prevent the garrison from using their guns. Indignant at this breach of faith, and encouraged by the near prospect of relief, the citizens shut their gates and seized most of those who were besieging the castle. A few escaped across the river, and brought the news to Offaly, who returned to Dublin only to find it bent upon the most desperate resistance. Having summoned the city in vain, he cut the leaden pipes which supplied it with water; but there must have been wells also, for no effects followed. He then besieged the castle from Ship Street, where there was cover for his men,[Pg 168] but White had some fireworks, which enabled him to burn down the thatched houses of the suburb and give his guns full play. Herbert distinguished himself by shooting twenty-four of the enemy, including one of their chief leaders. Being thus driven from the castle, Offaly attempted the city wall from Thomas Street, demolishing the party walls of the houses so as to make two covered galleries leading up to the New Gate. One of his shots pierced the gate and killed a man who was trying to get water at a pipe in the middle of the Corn Market. A remarkable feat is recorded of Staunton, the gaoler or warder of New Gate. Having galled the rebels by his sharp-shooting, he had become a particular mark for their fire, and he saw a musketeer trying to cover him. He not only shot him in the forehead, but, notwithstanding the hail of bullets issued from the gate, stripped the dead man, and brought his gun and clothes into the town. The Geraldines then tried to burn the gate; but a sally of the besieged through the smoke and flame made them suppose that the city had been relieved, and they withdrew precipitately, leaving a piece of artillery and 100 dead behind them. Offaly lingered for the night in the precincts of the Grey Friary, from which Francis Street takes its name, and next day rejoined his men, who had believed him dead. He made no attempt to renew the siege.[134]

The citizens refuse to help the rebels.

In this, as in so many other Irish insurrections, there was no want of double traitors; of men who had neither the constancy to remain loyal nor the courage to persevere in rebellion. Many of the arrows shot over the walls were headless, and some bore letters which revealed to the garrison every plan of the besiegers. The children of the citizens, whom he had hitherto detained as hostages, could now be of no use to Offaly, and he exchanged them for some of his own men who had been captured. He tried to get money, ammunition, and other help from the citizens in return for raising the siege; but the men of Dublin knew their advantage, and answered that they had no money to spare. They argued that if his intentions were loyal he had no need of warlike stores, and that to supply him might be to make a rod for[Pg 169] their own backs. They were, however, willing to supply him with enough parchment to engross his pardon upon, and to join him in begging humbly for it. Having neither powder nor shot, Offaly could not retort to any purpose, and he withdrew to put his ancestral castle of Maynooth in a posture of defence.[135]

Reinforcements arrive from England.

Besides retaining some of the citizens' children, the rebels had captured Chief Justice Luttrell and Lord Howth. A truce was therefore concluded for six weeks, but Offaly broke it within twenty-four hours by burning corn belonging to the Prior of Kilmainham. Meanwhile Skeffington had sailed from North Wales. The bulk of his fleet and army were intended for Waterford, but Sir William Brereton and Captain Salisbury were detached with 400 men for the relief of Dublin. Brereton took command of the city, and saw that proper watch was kept. Shortly afterwards eighty Northern spearmen under Musgrave and Hamerton landed or were driven ashore at Clontarf, where the rebels met them in great force. They were perhaps picked men, for their white coats and red crosses are particularly mentioned: at all events, they made a gallant resistance, and Offaly was wounded. Musgrave and Hamerton were both killed, and the rebel chief is said to have mourned deeply for the former, who was his cousin. The main force of the insurgents hung about the Hill of Howth in hope of preventing other English troops from landing, and Brode, Purcell, and Rookes cruised in the offing with their piratical vessels.[136]

Arrival of Skeffington.
Although the wind served well for Ireland, Skeffington, who was old and delicate, delayed long at Beaumaris. The North-countrymen, on whom he placed his chief reliance, chafed at the delay; and many of their horses, which were perhaps not very well stowed, died from being cooped up on board ship for three weeks. At last, on the very day on which the siege of Dublin was raised, the Lord-Deputy[Pg 170] sailed. The fleet was driven by a gale under Lambay, where a report reached it that Dublin had fallen. The news was not believed, but Brereton and Salisbury were detached. They reached the Liffey without any difficulty; and there was no reason why Skeffington should not have done so, but that he had made up his mind to go to Waterford. As it was, he was able to lie close to Skerries and to send in his boats, which burned four Geraldine vessels at anchor in the roads. The fleet then made sail again, and was again driven under Lambay, whence two ships made chase after Brode, the pirate, and drove him ashore near Drogheda. At last the Lord Deputy was persuaded to take the obvious course, and landed safely at Dublin more than a week after Brereton. Other troops from Bristol, under Sir John St. Loo, reached Waterford about the same time. Messengers were at once sent to Drogheda, and Brode and his crew were brought by sea to Dublin.[137]

Offaly is proclaimed a traitor.
Driven from Dublin, Offaly threatened Drogheda with some 400 horse, but Skeffington, with unwonted energy, marched the whole distance in one day, and the rebels did not venture to attack him. The Geraldine chief was proclaimed traitor at the market-cross, and the gentlemen of Louth and Meath, finding that there was again something in the shape of a government, came in fast to the Lord-Deputy. Meanwhile Ossory and St. Loo were at work in the south, and agreed to meet Skeffington at Kildare's castle of Kilkea. The Earl and the English knight kept their appointment, but the Deputy was again ill, and without artillery nothing could be done. Ossory had enough to do to keep the O'Mores and Kavanaghs in check, but he gained one important ally in the person of Sir Thomas Eustace, of Baltinglass, who brought forty of his kinsmen and left hostages in the Earl's hands. Eustace kept his word, and received a peerage for his services, an honour forfeited in Elizabeth's time for a[Pg 171] rebellion, which, if one of the most foolish, was also one of the least selfish of the many recorded in Irish annals.[138]

The rebellion continues.

During the greater part of the winter Offaly ranged up and down the Pale, not sparing the Kildare estates, which he was not likely ever to enjoy in peace. On one occasion he came into collision with Brereton near Trim, and lost 150 men; but when a garrison of forty men were left in the town he had no difficulty in recapturing it, and a garrison of twenty men failed to hold Kildare against him. His following was reduced to 100 horse and 300 kerne, who had scarcely a dozen muskets among them; but with this band he wandered where he pleased, even to the walls of Dublin. Skeffington again fell sick, and the army was detained doing nothing in Dublin; he could not, according to Sir John Alen, do anything himself, and he would not let anyone else have the credit. A truce for three weeks was concluded with the rebel, and after the New Year some of the troops were allowed to leave the capital. Sir Rice Maunsell with 500 men occupied Trim— Brereton and Salisbury lay at Newcastle; and preparations were made for assuming the offensive as soon as the Lord-Deputy should be able to mount a horse. But there was great want of money, and the ill-paid soldiers took little interest in any service which did not bring them profit. They took it on themselves to find men guilty of treason and to seize their goods, 'whereas,' as Alen grimly suggested, 'the King might have them by another mean.' Munitions of war were as scarce as money, and the bows which were sent from Ludlow Castle snapped when the archers tried to bend them.[139]

The Archbishop's murderers are excommunicated. Death of Kildare.

In the meantime the ecclesiastics who administered the vacant see of Dublin pronounced sentence of excommunication in its most tremendous form against the murderers of the Archbishop. Offaly himself, his uncles John and Oliver,[Pg 172] Captain Rookes, James Delahide, and Teeling and Wafer, who seem to have been the actual murderers, were mentioned by name. Leprosy and madness, hunger and thirst were invoked upon them in this life, and eternal damnation in the life to come. No house was to shelter them, no church to give them sanctuary, no kind Christian to bestow on them a morsel of bread when starving, nor a cup of cold water when dying of thirst, on pain of being considered accessories to their crime and accursed like them. They were to be partakers with Pharaoh and Nero, Herod and Judas, Dathan and Abiram; and stones were cast towards their dwellings, as by Moses when he called down Divine wrath upon the last named. It is said that a copy of this curse was cruelly shown to the old Earl in the Tower, and that the shock snapped the enfeebled thread which still bound him to life. The fate of the seven excommunicated persons was nearly as bad as the most vindictive priest could wish. The three Geraldines were hanged at Tyburn, Rookes was hanged at Dublin, Teeling and Wafer died at Maynooth of a horrible disease, James Delahide escaped to Spain and gave the Government some further trouble, but he died an exile in Scotland.[140]

The new Earl seeks help from Emperor and Pope,

The new Earl—for Earl he was in spite of Stanihurst's statement to the contrary— took advantage of the breathing space allowed him by the Deputy's inaction to cast about for allies. He sent Dominick Power to the Emperor, armed with gifts, and with documents going to prove that Ireland was a fief of the Holy See and that it was forfeited on account of Henry's heresy. Kildare was ready to hold the country of Pope or Emperor and to pay tribute, in consideration of being protected against the English schismatics.

Twelve hawks and fourteen hobbies, or Irish palfreys, were thought suitable presents for the second Charlemagne.[141]

and from the Irish.

More immediate help was sought from the O'Briens of Clare and the O'Kellies. The latter were induced to threaten[Pg 173] Westmeath, and Con O'Brien, chief of Thomond, was already in communication with Charles V., but Con's son Donogh had married Lady Ellen Butler, and Ossory had enough influence with his son-in-law to keep him to his allegiance. Donogh, as was usual with the sons of Irish chiefs, had a strong party of his own, and prevented the clan from stirring. Ossory contrived to make the Burkes threaten the O'Kellies, and they also were neutralised.[142]

Many rebels executed.

Skeffington, having awoke to the fact that Ireland could not be subdued by an army which never left Dublin, allowed Maunsell and Brereton to divide their forces and to burn most of the Geraldine villages, including Maynooth. While gaining strength himself he had the satisfaction of ordering several executions in Dublin. Brode, who was called the traitor's admiral; Rookes, who was captured near Wexford with some of the royal ordnance in his possession; a third rover named Purcell, who had been bold enough to cut a vessel out of the Thames; and Travers, Chancellor of St. Patrick's, who had been an agent in the attempted reduction of Dublin, were all duly hanged, drawn, and quartered on Oxmantown Green.[143]

Maynooth Castle summoned. The siege.

Brereton summoned Maynooth Castle, proposing to let the garrison depart with bag and baggage, and offering pardons and rewards. But they trusted in their walls, and answered only with taunts and jeers. At last Skeffington left Dublin and encamped before the castle, which he invested closely the next day. He pronounced it to be the strongest fortress which had ever been in Ireland since the English first set foot there. No detailed account of the armament has been preserved, but there were several pieces of cannon and a garrison of over 100, of whom about one-half were gunners. Christopher Paris, the Earl's foster-brother, commanded within the castle. Skeffington's batteries opened on the third day after his arrival, and soon silenced the guns on the north-west side of the keep. The guns were then pointed against a new work on the northern side, and after[Pg 174] five days' bombardment the breach was pronounced practicable. Paris, who probably despaired of maintaining his post, now thought it time to make separate terms for himself, and shot out a letter in which he offered to sell his post for money. The garrison were accordingly allowed to sally forth and to capture a small piece of artillery. Paris pretended great satisfaction, and served out abundant liquor to his men, who proceeded to celebrate their triumph by getting drunk. In the first grey light of morning the outwork was occupied almost without resistance, and the warders were aroused from their slumbers by shouts of 'St. George! St. George!' Ladders were quickly planted against the walls of the keep, and the storming party began to ascend. Captain Holland, who was one of the first to reach the parapet, jumped down into a tub of feathers, but Brereton's company had scaled the walls at another place, and the Geraldines, completely surprised and only half sober, made but a short stand. An arrow was discharged at Holland, the weight of whose armour kept him fast in the feathers, but it missed him, and he was released in time to take an active part in the final struggle. Brereton himself ran up to the highest turret and hoisted a flag, which told the Lord-Deputy that all was over.[144]

Maynooth taken. Story of Paris.

When Skeffington entered in the evening two singing-men of the Earl's chapel prostrated themselves before him, plaintively chanting a hymn or song called 'Dulcis amica,' which affected the victors as the verses of Euripides affected the Dorians at Syracuse. They were pardoned, and Paris then came forward to claim his reward. Skeffington allowed that he had been useful, and promised that the King would not let him starve; he then asked what confidence the Earl of Kildare placed in his foster-brother, and Paris enumerated the benefits which he had received from the fallen family. 'Couldst thou,' said the Deputy sternly, 'find in thine heart to betray his castle who has been so good to thee? Truly, thou that art so hollow to him wilt never be true to us.' Then turning to his officers he ordered them to pay down the[Pg 175] stipulated price, and to execute the traitor forthwith. 'My lord,' said the wretched man, 'had I wist you would have dealt so straitly with me, your lordship should not have won this fort with so little bloodshed as you did.' Among the bystanders was James Boys, formerly Constable of Maynooth, who had resigned his office at the breaking out of the rebellion, but who may have sympathised with his old employers, and who muttered 'too late' in Irish, a saying which became proverbial for an ineffectual repentance. Paris was executed, and it does not appear that he had been promised pardon, but Skeffington's action was neither honest nor politic. He had profited by the treason, and to kill the traitor could only tend to make other rebels desperate. About forty other prisoners were taken, of whom twenty-five were executed, including the Dean of Kildare and another priest named Walsh. It appeared from the depositions of one prisoner, a priest, that there had been negotiations with the Emperor, who held out hopes of 10,000 men, and also with the King of Scots. The 'pardon of Maynooth' became a proverbial expression for the gallows.[145]

The Irish fall away from Kildare.

Kildare had in the meantime succeeded in raising an army of 7,000 men among the O'Connors of Offaly and in Connaught, but the news that Maynooth had fallen almost dispersed it. With the men who remained he advanced to Clane, where he came into collision with Skeffington, who took 140 prisoners and put them to the sword, on a renewal of the fight being threatened. Kildare then went into Thomond, intending to sail for Spain, but sent James Delahide and Robert Walsh, the parish priest of Loughseedy, in his stead. These messengers joined Power at Cadiz, but did not obtain an interview with Charles until after their chief's execution. Power was pardoned at the Emperor's request, but the others were attainted by name. Kildare's allies now gradually dropped away. O'More and MacMurrough gave[Pg 176] security to Ossory, and the Earl's followers dwindled daily, though he continued to roam about in the neighbourhood of his ancestral estates. Maynooth was too strong to attempt, but he twice took Rathangan, so that no Englishman would take charge of it; and Skeffington was forced to entrust it to Sir James Fitzgerald. After this, Kildare drove a herd of cattle under the walls, and by the hope of booty drew out a great part of the garrison, whom he cut to pieces. On one occasion, he destroyed part of the garrison of Trim by putting forward some English troopers, who pretended to be Salisbury's men; and on another, he almost succeeded in capturing a large convoy near Naas. But such stratagems could not long delay the end, and the Irish saw that the game was up. O'Neill came to Skeffington at Drogheda, and took the oath of allegiance. It was agreed among other things that any O'Neill who did wrong within the obedient districts might be tried by English law, and that homicides should not be compounded by money payments;[146] but the King's subjects taken in O'Neill's country were to be reserved for the royal consideration, and not punished capitally by the chief. O'Neill was to receive his customary black-rent, but none of his clans were to levy Irish exactions,[147] or to graze cattle in the English districts. All Englishmen were to enjoy free trade with Tyrone, and O'Neill undertook to help Skeffington in his hostings in as ample a manner as any of his predecessors had helped any previous Lord-Deputy or Lord-Lieutenant.[148]

But Skeffington makes little progress.

O'More, an able man, who was anxious to deserve well of his new friends, accompanied Brabazon into the wastes of Allen, where Kildare was lurking. After the usual plundering, he advised the Englishmen to turn as if in full retreat, but, in reality, to occupy all the passes, while the O'Mores engaged the Earl's party in the plain. But the Northumberland moss-troopers under Dacre and Musgrave had not forgotten their old habits, and made off with the booty,[Pg 177] leaving an unguarded pass, through which the Geraldines escaped.[149] The O'Mores would not kill Kildare's men, but were very active against the O'Connors; indeed, the Earl was believed to have been in O'More's hands for a time, and to have been purposely released. But Brabazon took Burnell of Balgriffin, one of the original advisers of the rebellion, and William Keatinge, captain of the Keatinge kerne, who had hitherto been the rebels' chief strength. The latter was released on giving security, but Burnell was reserved for the scaffold. The remarkable unfitness of Skeffington for the post in which Henry maintained him was strikingly shown at this time. He was unable to stir from Maynooth, and seemed half dead if he rose before ten or eleven o'clock. Marauding bands came with impunity to the castle gates, and stole the Deputy's horses; and he allowed the army to lie in the open country without orders, and to consume provisions instead of fighting. The sick man was jealous of Lord Leonard Grey, the marshal of the army, whom rumour had designated as his successor; he was himself incapable of action, and was unwilling to let others act in his stead.[150]

Surrender of Kildare.

Before his release Keatinge undertook to drive the Geraldine chief out of Kildare. The wretched peasants crept back to their fields to save what was left of the harvest; and Cahir O'Connor, who saw how things were likely to end, came to Grey and Brabazon, and took an oath to defend the King's interests against Kildare, and against his own brother. The Earl had a stronghold in a boggy wood near Rathangan, fortified with earthworks and wet ditches, and almost impregnable had it been well manned and armed. Not being defended it was easily taken, and whatever would burn was burned. At last Skeffington felt well enough to take the field, and advanced with Grey and Butler to the borders of Offaly. Despairing of the cause, and anxious to save his harvest, O'Connor came in and submitted to the Lord Deputy at Castle Jordan; and Kildare, finding himself alone, then[Pg 178] surrendered to Butler and Grey in the presence of three witnesses. Skeffington positively asserts that no condition was made, 'either of pardon, life, land, or goods;' and this is confirmed by a despatch from the Council sent three days later and signed by Lords Butler and Delvin, Rawson, Prior of Kilmainham, Saintloo, Brabazon, Aylmer, Salisbury, and Sir Rice Maunsell, the last two having been present at the surrender. But the councillors admitted that 'comfortable words were spoken to Thomas to allure him to yield,' and begged the King to spare his life according to the comfort of those words.[151]

The surrender was unconditional.

A great effort was made to cause a belief in England that the surrender was conditional, but it does not appear that the prisoner himself made any such assertion. He wrote to his connection Grey, confessing himself a rebel, but urging that he had done all by the advice of Thomas Eustace and Sir Gerald MacShane. He begged intercession for his life and lands: failing the efficacy of such aid, he had, he said, only to shift for himself as he best could. Writers favourable to the Geraldines have nevertheless stated that he was promised his life, and this has been copied into a long succession of popular manuals. Even at the time, the legal mind of Lord Chancellor Audeley refused to believe that the Irish Council had so dealt 'with so errant and cankered a traitor.' 'If this,' he added, 'be intended that he should have mercy, I marvel much that divers of the King's Council in Ireland have so largely told the King, afore this time, that there should never be good peace or order in Ireland till the blood of the Garrolds were wholly extinct. And it was also said that the Irishmen spared their effectual diligence in the persecution of him, because they heard that he should have pardon, and then he would revenge; and now it seemeth they would procure him mercy. They be people of a strange nature and much inconstancy.'[152]

Kildare is sent to England;

In writing his thanks to Skeffington the King regrets[Pg 179] that Kildare's capture had not been 'after such a sort as was convenable to his deservings'—alluding to the report that conditions had been made with him. The letter is worthy of Elizabeth at her best, and very creditable to Henry, who declares his unabated confidence in Skeffington, and promises to make every allowance for his age and infirmities. As to the disposal of the prisoner, not only Audeley but Norfolk, who spoke from the fulness of his Irish experience, thought he should be sent to the Tower and executed in due course, 'except it should appear that by his keeping alive there should grow any knowledge of treasons, or other commodity to the King's grace.' The Duke advised a long respite, lest Lord Butler and Lord Leonard Grey should lose all their credit in Ireland. The Chancellor wished to proceed in the King's Bench under the new Statute of Treasons, by which he considered that such offences, though committed in Ireland, might be tried in an English shire. Had this opinion finally prevailed, modern Ireland might be easier to govern than it ever seems likely to be. Both Norfolk and Audeley allude to the report that Kildare had been promised his life, but neither they nor the King confirm it.[153]

and harshly treated in the Tower.

An account is extant showing that twenty shillings a week were allowed for Kildare's maintenance in the Tower, but intercepted letters tell of great harshness. His object in writing was to borrow 20l. from O'Brien, who had his plate, and he urged that chief to help the Deputy as the best means of helping him. 'I never,' he wrote to a trusty servant, 'had any money since I came into prison but a noble, nor I have had neither hosen, doublet, nor shoes, nor shirt but one; nor any other garments, but a single frieze gown, for a velvet furred with budge, and so I have gone woolward, and barefoot and barelegged, divers times (when it hath not been very warm), and so I should have done still, and now, but that poor prisoners, of their gentleness, hath sometimes given me old hosen, and shoes, and old shirts.' For sixteen months the rash young man endured this misery, and then, an Irish[Pg 180] Act of attainder having passed in the meantime, he and his five uncles were carried to Tyburn and there duly hanged, drawn, and quartered.[154]

The Desmonds and MacCarthies.

Having followed the fortunes of the House of Kildare until their great eclipse, we may now turn to the southern Geraldines, who had also entered upon the slippery paths of rebellion. The dispute between Desmond and Ormonde was of old standing, the real cause of it being the fact that Munster was not large enough to hold two such families. In 1520 Surrey brought about a meeting at Waterford between James, the eleventh Earl of Desmond, and Sir Piers Butler. They were solemnly sworn to keep the peace and to help each other on lawful occasions. Cormac Oge MacCarthy, Lord of Muskerry, and MacCarthy Reagh, who had allied themselves with the Butlers as a defence against their great neighbours' oppressions, were parties to this agreement. Surrey took hostages from them, and reported that they were wise men and more conformable than some Englishmen. If the King would undertake to protect them, he thought that they and many other Irishmen would be content to hold their lands of him. The peace was short; for Desmond no sooner got back to his own country than he proceeded to waste Muskerry with fire and sword. The two MacCarthies joined their forces, and a pitched battle was fought at Mourne Abbey, near Mallow. Cormac Oge placed the cavalry under the command of his sister's husband, Thomas Moyle Fitzgerald, who was Desmond's uncle and heir presumptive; and to his charge the Geraldine partisans of course attribute the result. The Earl was totally defeated: 'and of this overthrow,' wrote the family historian more than a century later, 'the Irish to this day do brag, not remembering how often both before and after they received the like measure from the Geraldines.'[155]

Desmond intrigues with Francis I., 1523.

Two years after the fight at Mourne Abbey Desmond was[Pg 181] in secret communication with Francis I., the Constable Bourbon having at the same time similar relations with Henry VIII. The French King sent two agents to Ireland—Francis de Candolle, Lord of Oisy, who afterwards appears as having a relationship or connection with Desmond, and Francis de Bergagni. They met the Earl at Askeaton, and made a convention with him. Desmond agreed to make war on the King, provided that his father-in-law Tirlough O'Brien and others of that clan should be included in any peace made between England and France. Francis rather oddly undertook to send ships to help Desmond in collecting tribute from his subjects. The Earl and his seneschal David MacMorris were promised French pensions, and both Geraldines and O'Briens were encouraged to expect French help in any emergency. Richard de la Pole, Edward IV.'s exiled nephew, was to be set up against Henry, and Desmond undertook to support the Pretender with 400 horse and 10,000 foot, which were to remain under his command. If he succeeded in raising 15,000 foot Francis agreed to pay two angelots a month for every fully armed man, and one angelot for every kerne. Kinsale, Cork, or Youghal was to be held by the French, and Desmond promised to use his exertions in providing them with horses. The convention was ratified at St. Germain-en-Laye, but nothing whatever came of it. Had there been any good understanding between Desmond and the Scots who were threatening Ulster, a powerful diversion might have been effected; but the Earl seems to have had no higher object than the enhancement of his own local authority. Some years later a bill was prepared for the attainder of Desmond in the Irish Parliament, which recited his treason in giving aid and comfort to Frenchmen while France and England were at war. But no Parliament was then held, and Desmond died unattainted.[156]

The Butlers and the Desmond Geraldines.

During his short administration after Surrey's departure[Pg 182] Sir Piers Butler, who had heard of Desmond's dealings with France, invaded his country with the consent of many loyal Geraldines. The port towns closed their gates to the rebellious Earl, who turned upon Tipperary, and occupied the strong castle of Cahir, the same which afterwards delayed Essex and thus contributed to his fall. The Deputy hastened to the spot, and seized the bridge leading to the fortified island; but the bridge on the other side remained open and Desmond escaped. After this the O'Briens, whom many supposed to be instigated by Kildare, laid a trap for Sir Piers very like that in which his famous grandson was long afterwards caught. A parley was proposed at the ford of Camus on the Suir, and thither, according to his own account, Butler repaired with a slender escort and the most pacific intentions. The O'Briens, who were hidden in a wood, suddenly rushed out and attacked him, but his men fought bravely and killed Teig O'Brien, the chief's son, 'of all men of his age the most dreaded by his enemies.' The Ormonde district at this time lay open on account of a bridge which the O'Briens had lately built over the Shannon, and one of the complaints against Kildare was that he had not helped Sir Piers to destroy this bridge.[157]

Their disputes about Dungarvan.

A war without much plan or apparent purpose continued to rage for years between the Butlers and the southern Geraldines. In 1527 James Butler wrote to his father, who was then in England, giving him an account of certain intrigues and disturbances, and telling him plainly that it was folly trying to look after Irish affairs in London. He who would do the King service must do it on the spot. Sir John Fitzgerald of Decies, who had taken part against the head of his house, and had in consequence lost much cattle and seen many farm-houses in flames, watched his opportunity, and shut up Desmond in Dungarvan. Here he was joined by Butler, and by the Earl's cousin, Thomas Fitzgerald of Decies; but the castle defied anything short of a regular siege. Butler had a horse shot under him, but a sally was unsuccessful, and Des[Pg 183]mond thought it prudent to take the sea with forty men. He sailed into Youghal upon the flood-tide, and Dungarvan then offered to surrender to Sir Thomas Fitzgerald. Butler refused to allow this, and Sir Thomas then joined his cousin, who had begun to ravage his lands about Youghal. The prey having escaped, Dungarvan was not thought worth any further immediate trouble; but a grant of the offices of governor, constable, and steward of the place was soon afterwards passed to Sir Piers Butler on his being created Earl of Ossory. The condition was imposed that the new Earl should seek to recover Dungarvan out of Desmond's possession.[158]

Desmond immigration into Wales.

The rebel seems to have been a man of large ideas. He had the Archbishop of Cashel, a natural son of Ossory, to watch over his interests at Court, and something amounting almost to an Irish invasion of England took place under his auspices. In twelve months the almost incredible number of 20,000 Irishmen are said to have landed in Pembrokeshire—that little England beyond Wales whence the ancestors of the Geraldines had first sailed to Ireland. They spread themselves over the country about

Milford Haven and between St. David's and Tenby, and the very corporation of the latter town came under Irish influence. A townsman had two large heavily armed ships manned by Irishmen: he was himself Welsh, but he would have neither Welshman nor Englishman on board. Throughout the country side Irishmen outnumbered the natives in the proportion of four to one, and many Irish vessels frequented the coast, and were employed in trade or piracy, or in a mixture of both. Nearly all the men they brought were from Desmond's country, and it is probable that he had a share of the profits, and that he was thus enabled to keep up the contest on land.[159]

Desmond intrigues with Charles V.

The adventurous Earl had gained nothing by his alliance with France; but he did not abandon the hope of foreign[Pg 184] intervention in Ireland, and sent a present of Irish hawks and wolf-hounds to Charles V. The gifts were in charge of a trusty messenger, who landed at St. Sebastian and hastened to the Imperial Court at Toledo. Wolsey's emissaries were accurately informed of these movements, and one who lived at Renteria recommended that a royal cruiser should be sent to intercept the ambassador on his return. The man himself lacked discretion, for he showed his despatches to the papal collector at Valladolid, and their contents thus became known to the English agents. Desmond's great wish was for artillery, which would have placed nearly every castle in Munster at his mercy. Glad to find any means of annoying a King who desired to repudiate his aunt, Charles sent a gold cup to Desmond, and soon afterwards despatched his chaplain Gonzalo Fernandez to Ireland. Fernandez, who spoke very good English, was instructed to make himself thoroughly acquainted with Desmond's resources, and to offer help if he thought it advisable. He was authorised to promise that the Earl should be included in any treaties which might be made between the Emperor and Henry VIII., and to explain that his master had always been most anxious for the English King's friendship. Notwithstanding his former good offices Henry had made an alliance with France, and now sought to divorce his Queen and to give the Duchy of Ireland to his bastard in disparagement of the Princess Mary. Such proceedings Charles was determined firmly to resist.[160]

Mission of Gonzalo Fernandez to Ireland, 1529.

Fernandez left Toledo on March 3, the Spanish Government giving out that he had gone to England to recover debts due to the Emperor. He had returned by April 28. On his way out he touched at Cork, where many persons visited his ship, and he gathered from their conversation that Desmond was not popular there. After this he was driven into Berehaven, whence he wrote to the Earl; and in four days he received an answer directed to him as chaplain[Pg 185] to 'our sovereign lord the Emperor,' Desmond striving to assume the position of an Imperial feudatory, instead of that of an English subject. Fernandez then sailed to Dingle, and before he could land Desmond sent six gentlemen on board to ask his help in capturing certain English and French vessels which lay near, probably at Ventry or Smerwick. Desmond had already sent his galleys, and was going with 500 men to support them by land. The Spaniard, with a more exact idea of an ambassador's duties than the potentate to whom he was accredited, prudently excused himself. Desmond evidently did not wish Fernandez to visit any of his castles, and preferred to meet him at the water's edge. Anxious to appear a powerful independent prince, he was probably unwilling that the Spaniards should see the nakedness of the land

and his own rude way of life; and perhaps he shrunk from accumulating evidence against himself in case submission to his lawful sovereign should after all become expedient.[161]

Fernandez in Munster with Desmond.

On April 21 Fernandez disembarked. He was well received by the inhabitants and by Desmond himself, who had 500 horse and as many gallowglasses with him. The Earl asked after the Emperor's health, and again called him his sovereign lord. Fernandez read his commission first in English. Desmond then requested that it might be repeated in Latin for the benefit of his Council, and when it was finished he took off his cap and thanked the Emperor for his gracious condescension, adding the reflection that his Majesty was placed on earth to prevent one prince from injuring another. His evident design was to acknowledge the supremacy of the Empire over all the kingdoms of the world, and at the same time to place himself on a level with the King of England, from whom he held his lands, his title, and his jurisdiction. Desmond then discharged the congenial duty of magnifying himself and his ancestors. He was, he said, descended from[Pg 186] Brito, who lawfully conquered the great and the small Britain, and reduced Ireland and Scotland under his yoke. It had been prophesied that an Earl of Desmond should conquer England, and this kept the English in a constant state of tremor. The fear of its fulfilment had caused the beheading of Earl Thomas by Lord Deputy Tiptoft, and Richard, 'son of the King of England,' had invaded Ireland on account of his father's enmity with the reigning King. Afterwards that Earl had conquered all Ireland, 'some few towns only excepted.' The King of England caused the Earl of Kildare to be destroyed in prison, until his kinsman of Desmond forcibly liberated him and made him Viceroy of Ireland. In twenty-four years, during which he had been stirring up both English and Irish, first to kill Desmond's father and afterwards to make war on himself, the King of England had gained no advantage. The Earl's servants trading in France and Flanders had been imprisoned and despoiled of 9,000l. by the English King's orders. Fernandez prudently demanded that this extraordinary farrago should be written down. It is very fortunate that he was unable to retain it in his memory, for no amount of mere English evidence could give us such a measure of a Desmond's pride, or of the nonsense which rhymers or Brehons could venture to put into a Desmond's head.[162]

Desmond's proposals to the Emperor.

The Geraldine addressed Charles V. as most invincible and most sacred Cæsar, ever august; and described himself as Earl of Desmond, Lord of Decies, of O'Gunnell, and of the liberty of Kerry. He first asked for four vessels of 200 tons each, and six smaller ones, all well armed, and for 500 Flemings to work them. Fernandez objected that no consideration was offered for so great a gift, and that Desmond could give no security out of Ireland; but ultimately an article was made out in which the Earl avowed himself the Emperor's subject, and promised to help him in all his enter[Pg 187]prises. Knowing that no guarantee could be given, the Spaniard wisely asked for none but his host's word of honour. The Earl declared his fixed intention—and here at least he spoke quite sincerely—to use all his strength and that of his friends in prosecuting the war against Piers Butler, the King's Deputy, and against the cities of Limerick, Waterford, and Dublin. He begged the Emperor's help, and renewed his request for cannon; as for men, he could bring 16,500 foot and 1,500 horse into the field, and his allies could furnish 9,000 additional foot and 300 additional horse. In enumerating his allies Desmond again drew upon his imagination, for he included O'Donnell, Prince of Ulster, with his 4,000 foot and 800 horse, Maguire and Magennis in the distant north, as well as the MacCarthies with whom he was at war, and who, about this time, defeated him in a pitched battle. He also represented himself as firmly allied and frequently communicating with the King of Scotland.[163]

Fernandez is unfavourable to Desmond.

Fernandez told his master that Desmond had treated him well, and supplied his ship with fresh beef and venison. He had found him full of animosity against Wolsey, and quite ready to forget his French connections and his former compact with Francis. But the Earl acknowledged that Dublin was the chief town of Ireland, and that he had no interest there, and that his kinsman of Kildare, whom he called the ruler of the capital, had been imprisoned in the Tower. That he had been arrested partly on Desmond's account was obviously of less importance than the fact that he could be arrested at all. As to Cork, Limerick, and Waterford, Desmond had some friends there, but many more enemies. On the other hand, the Earl certainly had ten castles, and Fernandez was made to believe that the King of England had lately failed to take Dungarvan—a version of the facts which strained them considerably. The Spaniard could not doubt that Desmond had many tributary knights, and much influence among the wild Irish; but he did not form a high[Pg 188] opinion of the Earl's soldiers, among whom executions for theft and murder were very frequent. They performed wonderful feats of horsemanship without saddle or stirrups, but they had no military skill. There were some gallowglasses with halberts, but the great mass had only bows and arrows. Fernandez allows that the Earl kept good justice, but it is clear that his general impression was unfavourable.

Desmond sends messengers to Spain. The English agents are well informed.

Desmond sent John Aslaby, Archdeacon of Cloyne, and another messenger with Fernandez, and they found their way to Spain. The English agents there continued to be well informed, and they learned from one Gwyn, living at Ballinskellig, in Kerry, and trading to St. Sebastian, that Desmond had sent for 4,000 men to teach the Irish war. Gwyn truly reported that Cormac Oge was warring against the Earl, but that he would probably soon acknowledge himself beaten. There is reason to believe that a Spanish expedition to Ireland was really contemplated, but that the Biscayans intended for the service refused to go, alleging, with a fine perception of the realities of Celtic diplomacy, that the Irish would be sure to deceive the Emperor. At all events nothing was done, and Spanish intervention in Ireland was put off for half a century. Desmond was proclaimed a traitor, but he died soon afterwards, and his successor followed him in a few months, leaving his heritage in dispute. The mission of Fernandez had no direct effect upon Ireland, but it may have had a good deal to do with Wolsey's fate, and with the crooked diplomacy of the divorce question. He was heir to De Puebla, who had negotiated Catherine of Arragon's marriages, and probably knew more than any one about the brief which Julius II. was said to have sent to Ferdinand the Catholic, and which, if genuine, would have precluded Clement VII. from granting a divorce on the ground of affinity. If the brief was forged, its spuriousness could not be proved in the absence of Fernandez, and the delay was fatal to the English Cardinal.[164]

[Pg 189]

Stephen Parry's tour in the south of Ireland. Siege of Dungarvan.

Lord Leonard Grey was sent to England in charge of Kildare, but he left his company of 100 men, under a Welsh officer named Parry, with orders to attach himself to Lord Butler. Parry's despatch to Cromwell is one of the very few contemporary documents which throw light on the state of the country. He and his men entered Ossory's district at Leighlin Bridge, where the people were glad to see them, and went on to Callan, where they found English fashions generally followed. They were so well received at Callan that they stayed there nine days, and they made a further halt of three days at Clonmel, which also entertained them hospitably. Thomas Butler, a man of great local influence, who had married Ossory's daughter, and was afterwards created Lord Cahir, met the troops at Clonmel and led them over the mountains to Dungarvan. He spoke very good English, and made himself most agreeable. Gerald MacShane Fitzgerald of Decies, who was also Ossory's son-in-law, joined them on the road. This gentleman could not speak a word of English, but he was very civil, professed great loyalty, and bound himself by hostages to act under the advice of the Council. Reaching Dungarvan about the middle of September, they met Skeffington, who had made up his mind to take the place, and who brought the artillery which was henceforth to play so great a part in Irish politics. The accidental presence of a Devonshire fishing fleet enabled the Lord Deputy to invest the castle completely. On being summoned the commandant answered boldly that he held the place for his master, and that he would do the best for him, as he was sure Skeffington would in like case do for his master. Two days were spent in preparing the battery, and at five o'clock on the morning of the third the cannonade began. A breach was made by eleven, and Sir John Saintloo wished to storm it at once, but Skeffington's practised eye detected an inner barricade. Lord Butler, who was a suitor for the castle, and had no mind to be at the expense of rebuilding it, here interfered to prevent a renewal of the fire. He sent in two of his men as hostages for the constable's safety, and the latter then came out. Partly by coaxing and partly by bullying, Butler[Pg 190] persuaded him to surrender, and he and his men took the oath of allegiance and swore to maintain the succession of Anne Boleyn's child. The castle was handed over to Ossory's men.[165]

Desmond dies in 1529. Disputed succession. Parry's journey.

The Earl of Desmond whom Gonzalo Fernandez visited died in 1529, leaving no male issue, and his uncle and successor Thomas Moyle soon followed him. Thomas Moyle's son Maurice died before his father, having married Joan Fitzgerald, daughter of the White Knight, by whom he left one son, generally called James Fitzmaurice. James would have succeeded of course, but that the validity of his mother's marriage was disputed. Failing him the next heir would be his grand-uncle, John Fitz-Thomas, who was at this time a very old man. To settle this question, if possible, and also, as Skeffington wrote to the King, 'to execute the succession of your Highness and of your most excellent Queen' Anne Boleyn, the Lord-Deputy issued commissions for all the southern and western counties, and in each Lord Butler was named chief commissioner. But the old artilleryman would not give Butler a single gun, and he continued his journey without the means of taking castles. At Youghal the townsmen received him well, and Parry, who evidently liked good living, notes that claret sold there for fourpence a gallon. Next day they encamped near Midleton, where the Butlers mustered 202 horse, 312 gallowglasses, and 204 kerne, besides a due proportion of the rabble which invariably accompanied Irish armies. Parry's contingent consisted of 78 spearmen, 24 'long boys,' and 5 musketeers—all well horsed. The next day they reached Cork, and Cormac Oge appeared with his host on a hill less than a mile from the city. Drawing up his main body on rising ground fronting the MacCarthies, Butler descended into the hollow with a few followers, and the chief of Muskerry met him there similarly attended. The mayor and aldermen, all in scarlet gowns and velvet tippets, after the English fashion, were very glad to see so many Englishmen, and 'made us,' says Parry, 'the[Pg 191] best cheer that ever we had in our lives.' Next day Cormac Oge came into the town accompanied by the young Earl, who had married his daughter, and who, having been brought up in England, dressed and behaved in approved fashion. He acknowledged that he held all from the King, whom he had never offended; and as a true-born Englishman he was quite ready to go to England and try his title before his Majesty in council, provided his grand-uncle Sir John would do the same. Earl or not, he was at the King's disposal for any service, and to all this Cormac Oge agreed.[166]

Journey of Parry and Lord Butler. The O'Briens.
The youthful Lord Barry, who spoke very good English and was full of complaints against the MacCarthies for keeping him out of his lands, also came to Lord Butler at Cork. Cormac Oge was anxious to have all disputes referred to the Lord-Deputy; but his son-in-law MacCarthy Reagh, the chief of Carbery, who came in upon safe-conduct, said that he would do nothing of the kind, but would hold by the sword what he had won by the sword. Butler was very angry and told him he should repent, but MacCarthy doubtless knew that, however good the will, the power to pursue him into his own country was wanting. Mallow and Kilmallock, which Parry found a very poor town, were next visited; and as the army approached Limerick, O'Brien evacuated two castles in the neighbourhood and obstructed the passes into Thomond with felled trees. Hearing that the invaders had no cannon he restored his garrison, and encamped with a large force three miles from the city walls. At Limerick Parry also found very good cheer, 'but nothing like the cheer that we had at Cork.' They then encamped at Adare, where Donogh O'Brien, the reigning chief of Thomond's eldest son and the husband of Lady Helen Butler, came to meet his brother-in-law. The speech attributed to Donogh seems genuine, and is not without a rude pathos:—'I have married your sister; and for because that I have married your sister, I have forsaken my father, mine uncle, and all my friends, and my country, to come to you to help to do the King service.[Pg 192] I have been sore wounded, and I have no reward, nor nothing to live upon. What would ye have me to do? If that it would please the King's grace to take me unto his service, and that you will come into the country, and bring with you a piece of ordnance to win a castle, the which castle is named Carrigogunnell, and his Grace to give me that, the which never was none Englishman's these 200 year, and I will desire the King no help, nor aid of no man, but this English captain, with his 100 and odd of Englishmen, to go with me upon my father and mine uncle, the which are the King's enemies, and upon the Irishmen that never English man were amongst; and if that I do hurt or harm, or that there be any mistrust, I will put in my pledges, as good as ye shall require, that I shall hurt no Englishman, but upon the wild Irishmen that are the King's enemies. And for all such land as I shall conquer, it shall be at the King's pleasure to set Englishmen in it, to be holden of the King, as his pleasure shall be; and I to refuse all such Irish fashions, and to order myself after the English and all that I can make or conquer. Of this I desire an answer.'

That Donogh in offering his services was going directly against his own family is plain from a letter which his father had written to Charles V. not much more than a year before. 'We have,' he had then said, 'never been subject to English rule, or yielded up our ancient rights and liberties; and there is at this present, and for ever will be, perpetual discord between us, and we will harass them with continual war.' The O'Briens had never sworn fealty to anyone, but he offered full submission to the Emperor, with 100 castles and 18,000 men.[167]

The Desmonds and the Irish.

Old Sir John of Desmond, the rival claimant to the title, also came to Adare and spoke plainly in very good English. 'What should I do in England,' he asked, 'to meet a boy there? Let me have that Irish horson, Cormac Oge, and I will go into England before the King.' Parry thought him as full of mischief as ever; but he agreed to meet the young Earl at Youghal, and also the obnoxious Cormac. It is[Pg 193] curious to see how proud these Desmonds were of their Norman blood, and how they despised the Irish; while often straining every nerve against Henry II.'s successor, offering their allegiance to foreign princes, and boasting to them of their Irish allies.

Parry's observations.

Returning to Clonmel by Kilmallock and Cashel, Parry was despatched to bring Vice-Treasurer Brabazon and Chief Justice Bermingham to a conference with Ossory and his son at Youghal. During the whole long journey from Dungarvan he had met no one who had ever seen an English soldier in those parts. Some days they rode sixteen miles at a stretch over what had once been really, and still remained nominally, Englishmen's ground. The woods, the rivers, and the rich grass lands about them excited his admiration. Nor was there any want of ground suitable for corn, and the ridges showed that it had once been tilled, but not a blade of oats had grown there for twelve years. Parry, who had evidently been very well treated by him, seems to have formed a high idea of Lord Butler's qualifications. If the King would give him artillery there was scarcely any limit to his possible services; for his own marriage with a daughter of Desmond and the marriages of his sisters, no less than his personal character, gave him great influence throughout the South of Ireland.[168]

Lord Leonard Grey made Marshal of the army. He and Skeffington disagree.

Having determined to continue Skeffington in the government of Ireland, notwithstanding his age and bad health, Henry took means to supply him with efficient subordinates. First among them was Lord Leonard Grey, who had returned with a new commission as marshal and with the title of Viscount Grane, which, however, he never chose to assume. The others were Sir John Saintloo, a brave soldier; the Vice-Treasurer Brabazon, who was already well tried; and John Alen, Master of the Rolls, who had been pushing his own interests at Court, and who was entrusted with the royal despatch. Honest musters leading to a reduction of expenses were the King's great object at this time; for Kildare was safe in the Tower, and it seemed that a great army was no[Pg 194] longer necessary. Special care was taken to define Grey's position, and Skeffington, whose supremacy as Henry's representative was fully acknowledged, was reminded that royal blood flowed in the marshal's veins. Discipline had been much relaxed in Ireland, and no doubt reform was wanted; but Grey seems to have used his military authority with undue severity. Thomas Dacre, a member of the great northern family, who came in charge of some spearmen, was imprisoned for eight days, though nothing had been proved against him. Another Dacre was confined for seven weeks without any apparent reason, and during a fortnight he had irons on both arms and legs. Such proceedings certainly gave some grounds for supposing that Grey was not disposed to favour those who had helped to overthrow his rebellious nephew.[169]

Death and character of Skeffington, 1535.

Skeffington died about two months after Grey's return. Though not very brilliant, he had been on the whole successful, and had shown that a private gentleman armed with the King's commission could be more than a match for the greatest of Irish nobles. It was indeed part of Henry's policy, as it had been his father's, to rely much upon persons of far humbler birth. Fox and Wolsey were Churchmen, and the tonsure had been always powerful to counteract plebeian extraction; but Empson the pettifogger, Cromwell the clothier, Stile the scribe, and Tuke, who speculated in kerseys, with many others of no higher original pretensions, were often preferred for important affairs to the chiefs of the English aristocracy. The business was often better done, and the power of the Crown was brought into more prominent relief. Skeffington may be regarded as the first of that long line of able public servants who reduced Ireland to a tardy and unwilling obedience. 'He was,' said Brabazon, 'a very good man of war, but not quick enough for Ireland, and somewhat covetous.' The charge was made by others also, and is easier to make than to refute. But it is certain that Skeffington died in difficulties, and one fact may be set against many opinions.[170]

FOOTNOTES:

[126] Conossius Maguire to the King, Feb. 20, 1534, in Carew. Letter from the five Alens, May 17, 1534. R.O. Ireland.

[127] Examination of Robert Reyley, Aug. 5, 1536, in Carew. Stanihurst.

[128] Stanihurst. Finglas to Cromwell, July 21, 1534. Dowling says Offaly was commonly called 'Thomas sericus.'

[129] The King to the Earl of Ossory, No. 72 in the printed State Papers. Butler's letter is in Stanihurst.

[130] Examination of Robert Reyley in Carew, Aug. 5, 1536; Sir John Rawson to the King, Aug. 7, 1534; Dowling's Annals. Rawson says 'divers of his chaplains and servants' were killed with the Archbishop, and that the murder was in Offaly's presence and 'by his commandment.'

[131] Wine, 20 tuns; beer, 20 tuns; powdered beef, 16 hogsheads; 2,000 dried ling, &c. &c.

[132] Stanihurst.

[133] Stanihurst. Ossory to Walter Cowley, No. 93 in the printed State Papers.

[134] Stanihurst. Brereton and Salisbury to the King, Nov. 4, 1534.

[135] Stanihurst.

[136] Ibid.; Dowling. According to Stanihurst, Salisbury and Brereton did not land until after the fight in which Musgrave fell, but their own letter seems to contradict this.

[137] John Alen to Cromwell, Oct. 4; Brereton and Salisbury to the King, Nov. 4; Skeffington to the King, Nov. 11; Ossory to Mr. Cowley, No. 93 in the printed State Papers.

[138] Brereton and Salisbury to the King, Nov. 4; Skeffington to the King, Nov. 11; Ossory to Mr. Cowley, as above.

[139] John Alen to Cromwell, Dec. 26, 1534, and Feb. 16, 1535; Vice-Treasurer Brabazon to Cromwell, Feb. 16, 1535; Skeffington to Sir Edmund Walsingham, March 13.

[140] The sentence of excommunication is printed in the State Papers, No. 81; see No. 84; Stanihurst. Kildare died Dec. 12, 1534.

[141] Stanihurst; Alen to Cromwell, Dec. 26, 1534.

[142] Ossory to Skeffington, Jan. 17, 1535.

[143] Alen to Cromwell, Feb. 16, 1535; Stanihurst.

[144] Stanihurst; Lord Deputy and Council to the King, March 26.

[145] Ware; Stanihurst; the Lord-Deputy and Council to the King, March 26. The official despatch does not mention the negotiation with Paris, but I see no reason to disbelieve Stanihurst. 'Too late, quoth Boys,' became proverbial.

[146] 'Quæ vulgariter dicitur a saulte.'

[147] Coyne and livery, cuddies, kernaghts, 'vel talia poculenta.'

[148] The indenture is dated July 26, 1535.

[149] Aylmer and Alen to Cromwell, Aug. 21.

[150] Grey to Cromwell, August 15. Aylmer and Alen to Cromwell, Aug. 21 and 26.

[151] Skeffington to the King, Aug. 24; the Council of Ireland to the King, Aug. 27.

[152] Audeley to Cromwell, i. S.P., p. 466; Stanihurst; Four Masters.

[153] The King to Skeffington, ii. S.P., p. 280; Audeley to Cromwell, i. S.P., p. 146; Norfolk to Cromwell, September 9, 1535.

[154] Feb. 3, 1537. The letter to Rothe (enclosing that to O'Brien) is in S.P. ii., p. 402.

[155] Surrey to Wolsey, Nov. 3, 1520; Russell; O'Daly, chap. ix. The latter writer is hopelessly wrong, and makes Thomas Moyle fight on Desmond's side.

[156] He is generally stated to have died June 18, 1529, but he was alive Sept. 12 in that year. For his intrigues with Francis see Wise to Cromwell, July 12, 1534, and the Cotton MS. quoted there; Brewer, vol. iii., No. 3118. The abortive Bill of attainder is calendared under Oct. 1528.

[157] Articles alleged by Ormonde against Kildare, Brewer, vol. iv., No. 1352 (2). Ware; Four Masters, 1523.

[158] James Butler to his father, Brewer, vol. iv., No. 3698; to the King, ib. 3699. Cormac Oge to the King, ib. 5084; to Wolsey, ib. 4933. Sir Thomas Fitzgerald to —— ib. 3922. Archbishop Inge to Wolsey, Feb. 23, 1528.

[159] R. Cowley, ii. S.P., 141; R. Griffiths to Wolsey, in Brewer, vol. iv., Nos. 3372 and 4485.

[160] J. Batcock to —— in Brewer, vol. iv., No. 4878; Sylvester Darius to Wolsey, ib. 4911; Ghinucci and Lee to Wolsey, ib. 4948; Lee to Henry VIII., ib. 5002. The instructions to Fernandez are in Carew, Feb. 24, 1529 (wrongly calendared under 1530).

[161] Fernandez to Charles V. in Brewer, vol. iv. No. 5323; Ghinucci and Lee to Wolsey, ib. 5423; Lee to Wolsey, April 19, 1529, ib. 5469; Desmond's Memorandum for the Emperor, April 28, ib. 5501; Froude's Pilgrim.

[162] Same authorities. Writing later to Charles V. (Sept. 2, Brewer, iv. 5938) Desmond increases his loss by Henry's malpractices to 100,000l., and says he holds the chief power in all Irish harbours from the furthest point of Kerry to Waterford.

[163] In the Pilgrim Wexford is substituted for Waterford. The lists of chiefs in the Pilgrim and in Brewer (vol. iv. No. 5501) are not quite identical.

[164] Brewer, vol. iv. No. 5620; Lee to Henry VIII., July 4, 1529, ib. 5756. For the question of the brief see Brewer, Introd. to vol. iv. pp. ccccxxiii. and ccccxliv., and an excellent article in the Quarterly Review for January 1877.

[165] Stephen Ap Parry to Cromwell, Oct. 6, 1535; Skeffington to the King, Oct. 16.

[166] Stephen Ap Parry to Cromwell, Oct. 6; Lord Butler to Cromwell, Oct. 17.

[167] Parry to Cromwell as before. Con O'Brien to Charles V., July 21, 1534, printed in Froude's Pilgrim, from the Brussels Archives.

[168] Parry to Cromwell, as before.

[169] The King to Skeffington, No. iii. in the printed S.P. Thomas Dacre to Cromwell, Jan. 5, 1536, printed in the Irish Archæological Journal, N.S., ii., 338. Skeffington died December 31.

[170] Brabazon to Cromwell, Sept. 10, 1535. Alen to Cromwell, Feb. 16, 1535.

[Pg 195]

CHAPTER XI.

FROM THE YEAR 1536 TO THE YEAR 1540.

Lord Leonard Grey Deputy, 1536.

Grey was immediately chosen Lord Justice by the Council, and his patent as Deputy was not long delayed. He began badly, his temper involving him in one of those personal difficulties which led to his ruin. He had never been on good terms with his predecessor, and was at no pains to make a decent or politic show of regret. Less than a month after her husband's death Lady Skeffington wrote to Anne Boleyn, declaring that she was overwhelmed with debt through his liberality in advancing money for the public service. She had already complained to Cromwell of Grey's harshness, and her son-in-law Anthony Colley went so far as to accuse him of shortening the late Deputy's life. Aylmer and Alen, afterwards Grey's most unrelenting enemies, were included in Lady Skeffington's complaint. The Council now sustained Grey, but it was not in official documents that the politicians of Dublin were wont to assail a chief governor whose hand might after all be heavy against them. Verbal messages and innuendoes contained in private letters seldom failed to undermine a man whom it might be neither safe nor decent to accuse openly. Grey now contented himself with saying that the late Lord Deputy had died in debt, and that his property was held in pledge for his creditors. But Lady Skeffington replied, and no doubt truly, that the official salary had never been paid, and that she could do nothing without it. Cromwell at least believed her, for he gave orders that her goods should be delivered to her, and that she should be sped on her homeward journey. Grey complied in the most ungracious manner, and had all the luggage and furniture turned out of Maynooth Castle before carts could be provided[Pg 196] to carry it away. It was stored in a church, and there further detained by the new Deputy for a debt to the Crown. Lady Skeffington was unable to leave for eight or nine months after her husband's death, and obstacles were placed in her way to the last. There may have been faults on both sides, but had Grey been either a good-natured or a politic man he might have found means to smooth matters for a widowed lady whose chief desire was the very general one of wishing to get out of Ireland as quickly as possible.[171]

Parliament of 1536.

Grey was commissioned to summon a Parliament, which accordingly met on Monday, May 1, the day before Anne Boleyn was sent to the Tower. In less than three weeks a number of important bills were passed, of which drafts carefully settled by Audeley himself had been sent from England. The succession was secured to the issue of Anne Boleyn, as Brabazon wrote only two days before that unfortunate lady's execution.

Before the letter reached London Jane Seymour had already been Queen a full fortnight, and Cromwell's concern was, if possible, to stop the passing of an Act which would have to be repeated so soon. It was too late to do this, but the Parliament made no difficulty about enacting the same stringent rule of succession for the third as they had done for the second wife. They thus achieved the unique distinction of passing two contradictory Acts of Settlement within eighteen months. This remarkable performance does not adorn the printed statute book, because that compilation was made when Elizabeth was firmly seated on the throne.[172]

The royal supremacy.

The bill declaring the King to be supreme head of the Church encountered some opposition from the proctors of the clergy, two of whom were summoned to Parliament from each diocese. The proctors had only consultative voices, but they now claimed not only to be full members of Parliament, but to form a separate order whose consent would be necessary to[Pg 197] every change in the law. An Act was passed declaring them no members of the body of Parliament, as they had 'temerariously assumed and usurpedly taken upon them to be.' In spite of their opposition and of much secret discontent, a series of Acts were passed to emancipate the Irish Church from Roman influences, or rather for subjecting her to King Stork instead of to King Log. All dues hitherto paid to Rome were forbidden, and the election and consecration of bishops were withdrawn from papal control. Appeals were transferred from the Pope to the King. The payment of first-fruits was imposed on all secular dignitaries and beneficed clergymen, abbots and priors being for the time exempted. The abrogation of this heavy and oppressive tax was reserved for the energy of Swift or the piety of Anne. By Audeley's advice the English heresy laws were not copied in Ireland. An Act was passed to validate the proceedings of this Parliament, though it had been held contrary to Poyning's law, but the spirit if not the letter of that famous measure had been observed by preparing the bills in England. Indeed, the Parliament was as subservient as any official could wish. 'The Common House,' wrote Brabazon, 'is marvellous good for the King's causes, and all the learned men within the same be very good; so that I think all causes concerning the King's grace will take good effect.'[173]

The Act of Absentees.

The weakening of the English power in Ireland by the non-residence of great proprietors had long been recognised. Edward III., on the occasion of his son Lionel's mission, announced by proclamation that the lands of absentees would be granted to Englishmen willing and able to defend them against the Irish. An English Parliament under Richard II. provided that in case of absenteeism the Viceroy and Council might divert two-thirds of the rents and profits to the defence of the country in ordinary cases; one-third in the case of students, of persons absent on the King's service, or of those who had leave of absence under the great seal. Whether or not this English law was ever re-enacted or obeyed in Ireland,[Pg 198] forfeiture was considered an incident of non-residence, and special Acts were passed to protect those who left Ireland on the public service. Henry VI. made a law ordering his subjects of Ireland to return to their own country. By Poyning's Act the statute of Richard II. obtained full force in Ireland, and it was shortly afterwards provided afresh that all licences of absence should be under the great seal of England, exceptions being made in favour of the religious orders and of students. The momentous Act now passed declared that many great proprietors had notoriously failed to defend their lands, whereby the King was forced to incur great expense in bringing an army to Ireland. The persons specially mentioned were Thomas Howard, Duke of Norfolk, and his coparcener Lord Barkley, who claimed and held the seigniories and lordships of Carlow, Old Ross, &c.; George Talbot, Earl of Waterford and Salop, who held the seigniory of Wexford; and the heirs general of the Earl of Ormonde, who held divers possessions and lands. To these were added the Abbots of Furness, Bristol, Osney, and Bath; the Priors of Canterbury, Lanthony, Cartmel, and Keynsham; and the master of St. Thomas of Acon in London. All this property was resumed to the Crown, saving the rights of residents in Ireland, who held under the dispossessed lords. Wexford was at once placed under a royal seneschal, and was so governed till the reign of James I. The Crown thus became one of the greatest of Irish landlords, and the foundations of a reconquest were laid.[174]

The O'Neills.

While Parliament was sitting Phelim O'Neill, chief of Clandeboye, came to Dublin and covenanted with the Lord Deputy to attend all great hostings and to make war upon all enemies of the Government within a day's march of his own country. He promised not to aid or harbour rebels, and to submit all differences between his people and the [Pg 199] King's subjects to peaceful arbitration. The great Leinster chief, Cahir MacEncross Kavanagh, also came to terms, agreed to supply twelve horsemen and twenty kerne in all hostings, and to employ his whole force on journeys of not more than three days' duration. He promised to submit disputes to the arbitration of Ossory and his son. Redmond Savage, the chief of an English family in Down which had long conformed to Celtic usages, made a similar agreement, and also promised to pay the Lord Deputy for his friendship 100 fat cows and a good horse, or fifteen marks Irish. Grey went himself to Dundalk, where Con O'Neill met him. The chief of Tyrone renewed the promises made to Skeffington, binding himself to attend all hostings and do his best against Scotch intruders, but he gave no hostages, and an invasion of his country was not believed to be practicable. The Lord Deputy then returned to Dublin, where a new and very serious danger demanded his presence.[175]

Want of money. Mutiny.

'Lack of money,' as Grey expressed it, 'after the late robbing and spoiling,' was the great difficulty of the English in Ireland during the whole Tudor period. The King now sent 7,000l., but that sum still left the soldiers' pay three months in arrear. There were many differences among the members of Council, but they all agreed in demanding more money. The northern spearmen, on the report that they were not to be paid in full, mutinied openly, declaring that they would have all or none. They refused to hear the King's letter read, threatened the lives of the Vice-Treasurer and Chief Justice, declared that they would not serve without wages, and that if they were not paid they would 'board with the Council at their houses, in spite of their hearts.' The astute borderers carried their point, for they received full payment, while Grey's own retainers were sent empty away. Saintloo's men at Waterford also showed a mutinous spirit, but they were silenced for a time by receiving part of what was due to them.[176]

[Pg 200]

Grey travels southward.

Parliament having adjourned to Kilkenny, Grey followed it thither, the army being victualled for a month. Having made arrangements for restoring the fortifications at Powerscourt, Woodstock, and Athy, Grey left the defence of the Pale to Brabazon, adjourned the Parliament to Limerick, and himself set out for Desmond's country. Besides Ossory and his son and the usual force of the four shires, O'Carroll, MacMurrough, O'Byrne, Lord Roche, and the gentlemen of Wexford and Waterford, accompanied the Lord Deputy. He was also attended by William Body, a confidential servant whom Cromwell had sent over to gather information, and whom he afterwards mentioned in his will. Body travelled to Ireland with George Browne, the new Archbishop of Dublin, and first busied himself in trying to arrange Grey's dispute with Lady Skeffington. He had particular instructions to inquire as to the possibility of increasing the Irish revenue.[177]

The Desmond country. Carrigogunnell.
Marching unopposed across the central plain, Grey found the great Desmond stronghold on Lough Gur undefended, the doors and windows having been carried off and the roof purposely burnt. It was handed over to Lord Butler, who undertook to repair and garrison it at his own expense. Grey then marched to Carrigogunnell, an immense fortress standing in a commanding position over the Shannon. Matthew O'Brien surrendered the place on condition, as was alleged by Body, that it should be garrisoned only by Englishmen. An order was nevertheless given to hand it over to Donogh O'Brien, Ossory's son-in-law. This chief came to Grey and renewed the offers made to Butler. He was ready to serve the King against his father and all others, provided he might have Carrigogunnell; and the Council considered his services more important to them than the castle could be to him. But the English guard restored the place to Matthew O'Brien. Donogh was certainly not an Englishman, and George Woodward, 'an honest and an hardy man,' may have thought himself bound in honour to[Pg 201] restore the original situation, or he may have thought one O'Brien as good as another. Grey merely says that Matthew held out boldly until the battering train was in position, when he was content to depart with bag and baggage.[178]

Grey attacks the O'Briens, August, 1536.
The next undertaking was an attack on O'Brien's Bridge, which had long laid Limerick and Tipperary open to attack. The bridge was of wood, with a castle at each end built in the water. That near the Limerick shore was the strongest, and was of hewn limestone or marble, twelve or fourteen feet thick, and armed with an iron gun carrying shot as big as a man's head, and two small pieces, of which one belonged to some ship, and the other was of Portuguese make. The garrison had also some muskets and hand-guns, and the work was skilfully strengthened with wooden barriers and with hogsheads full of sand. Under Donogh O'Brien's guidance the Lord Deputy marched along the hilly bank of the great river by devious paths, untravelled hitherto, as he believed, by Englishmen or by wheels. The four land-arches had been broken down, and the castle was thus surrounded by water. The royal artillery consisted of one culverin, six falcons, and one half-saker, but these were not heavy enough. In a day and a half all the shot had been fired away, and the walls were almost as sound as ever. No baggage train had been brought, provisions were scarce, and two nights had been spent on the bare ground; it was necessary to retire or to take the castle. Brushwood was abundant, and Grey set his men to make fascines and to throw them into the channel. Ladders were also made, but it

became unnecessary to use them; for Saintloo's men advanced along the frail and shifting path and carried the castle with a rush. The garrison ran out at the other side, and the bridge was then broken down with such tools as were at hand. The army then returned to Limerick, and Lord Butler went to Carrick-on-Suir for more cannon before undertaking the recovery of Carrigogunnell, which the Irish had again seized by stratagem.[179]

[Pg 202]

William Body. His report to Cromwell.

Body, with the insolence of a great man's favourite, had throughout this expedition assumed the character of a Royal Commissioner, to which he had not a shadow of title. He associated with the loosest of boon companions, who disturbed the camp by night and day and swore, with the truth born of alcohol, that he was no Commissioner. At O'Brien's Bridge he blamed Grey for not providing sapping tools, which must have tired out the soldiers, and which would have been quite useless. He was very indignant at having to sleep on the ground 'from Friday inclusive until Tuesday exclusive,' but no one else was better off. Grey, a thorough soldier, was at no pains to conceal his contempt:—

'I desired him to be contented, for I had seen better men than he was, or should be, or any that was there, lodged worse. He was displeased therewith, desiring me not to judge what his fortune might be. Then I said, I was sure he should never be so good as the Duke of Norfolk, and Suffolk, and my lord my brother (the Marquis of Dorset), whom I had seen lodged worse. Whereat he took a great fume for that I should judge any impossibility what he might be; and thereupon leaving us at our coming to Limerick, departed towards Dublin in a great anger. But of his gests by the way the folly of it is such, I will not commit to writing, but, I assure you, like no Commissioner.'

This short experience of Irish campaigning was enough for Body, who returned to Dublin and busied himself in undermining Grey's influence. Few seem to have had his good word, except Ossory and his son, who took care to be civil to Cromwell's confidential man. But Body was perhaps a better judge of a country than of a general's qualifications. 'As far as I have seen it,' he wrote, 'that is to say the counties of Dublin, Kildare, Carlow, Kilkenny, Tipperary, Ormond, Ossory, Desmond, Limerick, and Thomond, if there be any paradise in this world, it may be accounted for one among them, both for beauty and goodness.'[180]

The soldiers refuse to go beyond Shannon.

The army which Grey had at Limerick did not much exceed 2,000 men, including the Butlers and their not very[Pg 203] trustworthy Irish allies. The Pale had been much exhausted by the Kildare rebellion, and it was purposely spared, much to the indignation of Body, who, like many other casual visitors, fancied he understood Ireland better than men who had studied it for years. The Lord Deputy had only 700 men of his own and had no money to pay them. Saintloo's company had received some part of their money at Waterford, but broke out again soon after leaving that city; and it was supposed that two subalterns, Gerbert and Powell, were the true ringleaders. Grey's gunners stood firm, and by threatening to use the guns he kept the mutineers quiet for a time. They behaved, as we have seen, with great gallantry at O'Brien's Bridge; but they refused to go beyond the Shannon, and the idea of a pursuit into Clare was therefore given up. The Council thought Grey's person in danger, and he owned to more peril from his soldiers than from the Irish enemy. He could depend only on his own immediate followers, 100 horse and as many foot, and upon one officer, that Stephen Parry whom we have met before. Whenever the bulk of the troops were called upon to perform a service they all answered together, 'Let us have money, and we will do it.'[181]

The Butlers and O'Briens. Carrigogunnell.
The troops being pacified for the moment and Lord Butler having arrived with another battering piece, the garrison of Carrigogunnell, consisting partly of Desmond men and partly of O'Briens, were summoned to surrender on promise of their lives, and warned that if the castle had to be taken by force no quarter should be shown to man, woman, or child. They detained the messenger and returned no answer. A breach was soon made, and, after more than one failure and the loss of thirty men killed and wounded, the castle was taken by storm. Seventeen of the defenders were killed in the fight, and of forty-six survivors all were put to death on the spot, except certain gentlemen of the O'Briens, for whom large ransoms were refused, and who were taken to Limerick, tried for high treason, and immediately executed. Chief Justice[Pg 204] Aylmer accompanied the army for such purposes. The castle was handed over to Lord Butler, who placed it in his brother-in-law's charge, and Donogh, having gained his great object, became a scourge to the citizens of Limerick.[182]

Grey cannot pay his army.
The troops positively refused to go into Clare without receiving their arrears, and Grey had nothing to give. He therefore proposed to leave them at Limerick, Cork, and Kilmallock; giving his own and the Council's security for their victualling until the King should think proper to send money. They refused; and Butler's men, after twenty days' trial of Lough Gur, would stay there no longer unless the towns had English garrisons. James Fitz-Maurice, whom the King acknowledged as Earl of Desmond, and who had a party in the country, was not at hand, and as no one could take his place the castle was abandoned. The artillery was left at Limerick and Clonmel, and the Lord Deputy went back to meet Parliament at Dublin. His expedition had shown that a small army well led and well paid could go anywhere and do anything in Ireland, and that feudal castles could do nothing against a proper siege train; but it had also shown that the necessary conditions were not likely to be fulfilled under a King who gave away priories while crossing passages, and who staked one of the finest peals of bells in London upon a single throw of the dice.[183]

The Duke of Richmond dies, 1536.
The death of the Duke of Richmond, whom his father no doubt intended to advance and whom Charles V. even thought, or professed to think, destined to succeed him, made no difference to the country which he nominally governed. It was indeed at first supposed that Acts of Parliament passed after his death would be invalid, but the lawyers seem to have decided that this was not the case.[184]

The revenue. Abuses.
The actual revenue of Ireland, derived partly from forfeitures and partly from a parliamentary grant, amounted at[Pg 205] this time to about 5,000l., of which 1,000l. was not paid. Henry, who was of course obliged to supplement this, complained that he got

very little for his money, and wished to reduce the Irish establishment. He declared that he valued an increase of income less for himself than for the common good of Ireland. 'A great sort of you,' he wrote to the Lord Deputy and Council (we must be plain), 'desire nothing else but to reign in estimation and to fleece from time to time all that you may catch from us.' He announced therefore that he was about to send an independent person with ample powers to inquire into Irish affairs. He gave Brabazon detailed instructions for a survey of marsh lands, and bade him go to war no more but apply himself wholly to financial affairs. No salary was to be paid to any officer who acted by deputy, and none but customary fees exacted. Henry said he was determined to reform Ireland, and would value his servants there according to their merits in that behalf. 'If anyone,' he wrote, 'directly or indirectly devised and practised the let, hindrance, or impeachment of this our purpose for any respect, whereunto we will not fail to have a special eye, we shall so look upon him what degree soever he shall be of, as others shall, by his example, beware how they shall misuse their Prince and sovereign Lord, and transgress his most dread commandment.'[185]

Ireland cannot be governed without money.

To this formidable letter Grey and his Council answered that the army had never been properly paid, and had in consequence often mutinied, that they had spent every farthing of revenue on public objects, and had raised large additional sums on their own credit, that credit was now quite exhausted, and that without money to pay off the men it was impossible further to reduce the military establishment. Brabazon had accounted or was ready to account for every penny, 'and as to our desire to reign in estimation, it is to be thought that among civil people there can no name of dignity or honour be in estimation, unless thereunto be annexed rule and riches. Would to God his Majesty did know our gain and riches, which is so great that we of the mean sort of this Council,[Pg 206] being his Grace's officers among us all, we suppose be not worth in money and plate 1,000l. Irish, which is a small substance for us all, being in the rooms that we be under his Grace. We be no such purchasers of possessions, builders, dicers, nor carders, neither yet pompous householders whereby we should consume our profits and gain if we had them.'[186]

Grey attacks the O'Connors, 1537.

Those best acquainted with the country at this time believed that the necessary precedent to its reduction was a thorough conquest of Leinster. The overthrow of the Kildare Geraldines was necessary, but had its inconveniences. They had been a standing menace to the Government, but they had kept the Irish at bay, and their fall left the marches quite open. Without security either of life or title no one would work the forfeited lands, and the margin of waste grew broader every day. Grey's temper and talents made him prefer war to diplomacy, and he resolved to strike at O'Connor, whose hostages were in his hands, and who was under recognizance to deliver 800 cows to the King, but who had regained complete possession of Offaly. His brother Cahir had suffered the not uncommon fate of those who support Irish governments, and had been an exile for two years. Grey, Brabazon, and Aylmer took fourteen days' provisions from Dublin, and were joined on the march by Lords Delvin, Slane, and Killeen, and by William Saintloo, now seneschal of Wexford, with his own company and 100 kerne. They passed along the southern edge of Westmeath to MacGeohegan's country, the modern barony of Moycashel, and took hostages from that chief and from O'Molloy, whose district lay further south. On the same day Brabazon got possession of Brackland Castle through the treachery of an inmate, who acted in Cahir O'Connor's interest, and who was pardoned while the rest of the garrison were beheaded. The soldiers destroyed all that lay in their path, and on the fifth day arrived before Dangan, afterwards Philipstown, which had been fortified with some skill. The march was only of five or six miles, but the ground was boggy, and a road had to[Pg 207] be made with fascines and hurdles. The ditches about the castle were filled in the same way, and the courtyard was forced before nightfall. Three days were spent in waiting for one large and two small pieces of artillery, and on the bright May morning following their arrival fire was opened upon the keep. After four hours' cannonade, resulting as usual in those days with the disabling of the principal gun, a breach was made and the castle at once stormed. The walls were dismantled, and the heads of their twenty-three defenders set on poles 'for a show to the O'Connors.' On the next day Ossory's second son Richard, afterwards created Viscount Mountgarret, came to excuse his father, who had been kept away by ill-health. O'Connor in the meantime had fled into O'Carroll's country, 'which O'Carroll,' Grey carefully notes, 'is the Earl of Ossory's friend.' The punishment of O'Carroll for harbouring the fugitive was nevertheless entrusted to Richard Butler, partly to punish his tardiness, and partly because Grey's fifteen days' provisions were almost gone. It was an absurd expedient, and before the end of the year O'Connor was back and Cahir had fled the country. The sole result of the expedition was to show the force of artillery; yet Henry, unless his language be thought ironical, calls it a notable exploit. 'If, however,' the King added, 'he should be suffered to enter again, it should but add a further courage to that traitorous malice which by all likelihood is so entered, that it will not be removed.'[187]

Grey makes many enemies.

Grey had many enemies, for he was not conciliatory, and his relationship to the Geraldines laid him open to the suspicions of all who had risen on the ruins of the House of Kildare. With Brabazon, the ablest man about him, he had long been on cold terms, and many supposed that the Vice-Treasurer thought he ought to have been Deputy himself. Thomas Agard, Vice-Treasurer of the Mint, a sour but apparently honest Puritan, hated Grey for his attachment to old religious forms, and Archbishop Browne lost no opportunity[Pg 208] of attacking him on the same grounds. Alen, Master of the Rolls, a useful public servant, but with an inborn love of intrigue, gave trouble to every successive chief governor. Robert Cowley and his son were devoted to the House of Ormonde, which Grey thought too powerful. The Deputy did not favour the innovations in religion, and took no pains to hide his dislike to Browne and Agard; but with the rest he was always ready to co-operate. The King, however, found it hard to reconcile conflicting accounts, and resolved to send over Commissioners unconnected with Irish factions to report upon the actual state of affairs. The persons selected were Anthony St. Leger, of Ulcombe in Kent, one of the wisest statesmen who ever represented the English Crown in Ireland; George Paulet, a younger brother of the astute courtier who is best known as Marquis of Winchester, but not equally endowed with prudence; Thomas Moyle, of Gray's Inn, Receiver-General of the Court of Augmentations, and afterwards Speaker of the English House of Commons; and William Berners, auditor of the same court. The Irish Government was directed to treat them with as much deference as if the King were present; and they were ordered to treat Grey with much consideration, and to take his advice when possible. The latter instruction, so well calculated to soothe the Lord Deputy's wounded pride, was not directly made known to him. The Commissioners were ordered to present their credentials to the Lord Deputy as soon as they reached Dublin, and then to summon the Council and read the King's letter, in which he promised to remember their good services. 'If, on the other side,' he added, 'we shall not find you now faithful officers, ministers, and good councillors, but men given more to your own affectes, commodities, and gains, than earnestly bent to our satisfaction, we shall again so look upon the best of you so misusing himself for it, as shall be little cause to rejoice at length of his doings in that behalf.'[188]

The King sends a special Commission.

The first duty imposed on the Commissioners was the reduction of expenditure and the increase of revenue. As a[Pg 209] cheap defence to the Pale, hostages were to be generally taken, and the army was, if possible, to be cut down to 340 picked men, inclusive of garrisons. Horsemen were to receive 8l. yearly, footmen 4l., constables of castles 13l. 6s. 8d., gate-keepers 6l. 13s. 4d., under-warders 4l. 13s. 4d.—all in Irish currency, or about two-thirds of the sterling amounts. The Vice-Treasurer was in future to visit all garrisons quarterly, to see that deserving men received commands, and to provide for frequent musters of all borne on the books. All soldiers in excess of the new establishment were to be paid off with money specially provided, and the King, with a touch of his daughter's temper, gave orders that they should be induced if possible to take less than their due. The Commissioners were to survey waste lands and were authorised to give leases for twenty-one years, with a clause of forfeiture for non-observance of the laws as to English dress and for alliance with Irish rebels—the penalties provided by law being also enforced. After this all offices and officers were to be subjected to rigid scrutiny, with a view to increased efficiency and reduced expense. Detailed instructions were given as to public accounts, and Brabazon was to be repaid all he had spent in annoying the King's rebels.

Powers of this Commission.

The control of legislation was also given to the Commissioners, who were to see various Acts for the establishment of royal authority in Church and State duly passed. They were to inquire as to the claims of clerical proctors to interfere in Parliament, were themselves to have a right of entry as the King's councillors, and were to expound the royal policy 'with all their wit and dexterity, and with such stomach, where they shall perceive any man frowardly, perversely bent to the let and impeachment of the King's purpose in the same, as they may the rather by their wisdom both conduce the thing to effect and reconcile the parties that before would show themselves so wilful and obstinate.' Messages to this effect were sent to both Houses, both Wolsey and Cromwell relying upon a species of intimidation of which Charles I.'s attempt on the five members is the last recorded[Pg 210] example. The Commissioners afterwards exercised the power of dissolving Parliament.

The King has vague good intentions.

The Commissioners were to examine charges of taking money from the rebels which were brought against many men highly placed in Ireland; Henry rightly supposing that many nominal subjects connived at treason, as in the case of O'Brien's Bridge, which had cost much to take and to demolish, and which was now as strong and as troublesome as ever. But he did not choose to see that want of money was the chief cause of this failure. He was indeed, he said, determined to make a full reformation some day, and the information now collected would be very useful when the convenient season arrived. In the meantime, the Commissioners were to reduce the garrison to 340 men.

The Commissioners arrive in Ireland, 1537. Grey's activity against the Irish.

St. Leger and his companions set out early in August, but were detained by adverse winds about Holyhead, and did not arrive at Dublin till the middle of September. Grey had unusually strong reasons for exertions, and he begged hard for money and artillery. The pay of the army was twelve months in arrear. O'Connor was coshering among his friends 'more liker a beggar, than he that ever was a captain or ruler of a country,' and making vain suits daily to the Government. But Grey had not caught him, and he could be submissive enough until what was left of his corn had been saved; his neighbours, English and Irish, thinking it more prudent to shelter an enterprising rebel than to run risks for a Government which could not protect its friends. Grey, who habitually used strong language, characterises these prudent people as 'having as much falsehood remaining in them as all the devils of hell.' Having, as he supposed, made O'Connor 'as low as a dog were for the bone,' he applied himself to the Kavanaghs, whose chief, Cahir MacArt, had married a Geraldine. It had been often proposed to extirpate them and to colonise the country. The Lord Deputy now entered Carlow, burned some castles of the O'Nolans between Newtownbarry and Tullow, forced Cahir MacArt to give hostages, and then turned sharply upon Ely O'Carroll, where O'Connor had first found a refuge. He had now the help of Ossory, who was[Pg 211] always glad to weaken a neighbour, and of Cahir O'Connor, who was as anxious as his brother to divert attention from the Offaly corn. He passed unopposed through the lands of the Fitzpatricks, O'Mores, O'Molloys, and MacGeohegans, received O'Carroll's submission, and then entered Tipperary, where he took a castle belonging to O'Meagher, the chief of Ikerrin. O'Connor came in on safe-conduct, and paid 300 marks for his son, who was given up to him. Grey refused to trust him, and begged Cromwell never to allow his restoration; and the event proved Grey right, though he soon forgot his own advice. He now announced to the minister that he was beginning to understand the Irish nature, and that the King needed only to be in earnest. He was right in blaming constant changes of policy, but like most soldiers he failed to see the real difficulties of the Irish problem.[189]

The O'Donnells. Death of Hugh Oge, 1537.

It was now just a quarter of a century since Hugh Oge O'Donnell, then on his return from Rome, had been received with honour at the Court of Henry VIII. Deeply impressed by what he saw there, and aware of the impossibility of uniting all Irish tribes against the stranger, he had always striven to keep English intruders at bay by remaining on good terms with the Government, and had exerted his strength only to subdue his neighbours on the side furthest removed from the Pale. He had thus extended his sway over the modern counties of Roscommon and Sligo, and over great portions of Fermanagh, Mayo, and Galway, and even of Down and Antrim. He had forced or persuaded the O'Neills to acknowledge his claims to the disputed sovereignty over Innishowen, Raphoe, and Fermanagh; and the Irish generally were so much impressed by his wisdom and prowess that they supposed him to be Hugh the Valiant, the promised Celtic Messiah, who was to redress or avenge the wrongs of Erin. When it seemed clear that this was not so, the dreamers of dreams declared that as he had failed the deliverer would never come. His panegyrists reckon among his titles[Pg 212] to fame that 'the seasons were favourable, so that sea and land were productive:' it is more to the purpose that he executed strict justice and repressed thieves. Like most Irish chiefs, he had difficulties with his children, and his valiant son Manus was discarded at the instance of a mistress whom the old chief had brought into his house. For this and for other sins he made such reparation as he could by a late repentance, donned the cord and cowl of St. Francis, and died in the odour of sanctity. He was buried in his religious dress in the monastery which his father had built at Donegal for friars of the strict observance; and Manus was at once acknowledged both by the tribesmen and by O'Neill, and was inaugurated at Kilmacrenan with the usual ceremonies.[190]

Disturbances in the North.

The new chief at once took up the thread of his father's policy by invading Connaught, and at the same time making loyal professions to Grey. He had, he wrote, been tempted to rebellion by all the disaffected lords in the South and West, but was determined to take no advice but that of the King and his Deputy. As soon as he heard of Hugh O'Donnell's death, Grey at once repaired to the borders of Ulster. The galleys of O'Neill and his Scotch allies had threatened a fortified settlement at Ardglass on the coast of Down, and the Deputy burned to invade Tyrone; but the Council dissuaded him, and the receipt of Manus O'Donnell's letter gave hopes of settling the North by peaceful means. Some thought Grey too fond of making aimless raids, and Alen made some sensible remarks on the subject. 'I would not,' he wrote to St. Leger, 'have the Deputy representing the King's Majesty's person and estate be a common skurrer for every light matter; but, when he should begin a war, begin it upon a just good ground, and when it were so begun, to be so profoundly executed, that all other should take example thereby.' But the King thought only of increasing the revenue and diminishing the army.[191]

[Pg 213]

Grey is baffled by the O'Connors.

Grey had been sanguine enough to believe that his work in Offaly would be lasting, but, as Henry had partly foreseen, O'Connor's return had undone it all. Cahir was a fugitive, and the floods protected Offaly, where the corn had been safely garnered in. At last the waters subsided, and Grey reached Brackland by the old road through Westmeath. O'Connor escaped into O'Doyne's country, the modern barony of Tinnahinch, which Grey and Richard Butler proceeded to ravage. While thus employed the scattered troops were surprised by O'Connor, and some were killed. The Lord Deputy was just able to destroy or carry away the corn stored at Geashill, and to return to Dublin without having seen the enemy. To gain time till the season of long days came round again, Grey gave a safe-conduct to O'Connor, who proposed to visit Dublin. 'But shortly herein to conclude,' as Brabazon puts it, 'the said traitor and his brother Cahir fell to agreement and concord, so that at this presents they both remain in Offaly.' St. Leger, who had a cooler temper than Grey, saw the impossibility of subduing even a single clan by desultory hostings. 'The country,' he said, 'is much easier won than kept.' To overrun Offaly was a small thing, but it could only be united to the Pale by the costly expedient of fixed garrisons. O'Connor had got back his son, and indeed neither he nor any Irishman had much regard for promises or for the fate of hostages.[192]

He continues to attack them.

The O'Connors were weakened by repeated blows, and Alderman Herbert, who had long advised a colonising policy, proposed that Offaly should be peopled with Englishmen once for all. Grey again invaded the doomed district with 800 men, and O'Connor at once declared himself willing to treat, though he utterly refused to trust himself within the Pale. Grey halted at Kinnafad, where a castle built by the Berminghams still overhangs the ford of the Boyne. Having taken precautions against treachery, the Lord Deputy passed about half his men over the river, and then advanced with twelve horsemen to an open field about a quarter of a mile[Pg 214] off, where O'Connor met him similarly attended. The chief submitted to the King's clemency, begged Grey's intercession, and promised to come to Dublin in three days. Cahir sent word that he would come too, but broke his promise. O'Connor kept his tryst, acknowledged himself the King's liegeman, abjured the authority of the Pope for himself and his tribesmen, renounced all Irish exactions, and gave up his black-rents, including a pension of sixty marks from the King. Thanks were in future to be his only reward for service; and he offered to hold legally of the King 'that portion of lands in Offaly which he held by partition after his country's fashion,' undertaking that his brothers and other holders of land there should become entitled in the same way. These lands were to be subject to impositions at so much per ploughland, as if they were situated in the Pale, assessments for the defence of the King's subjects being made as occasion might arise at the Lord Deputy's discretion. For himself he solicited the honour of Baron of Offaly, and begged for such protection as the Government habitually gave to Englishmen. He agreed that the Lord Deputy and all the marchers might cut passes where they pleased, and gave up his son again pending the King's final decision. The crafty Cahir was hunted down, apparently with his brother's help, and brought to Dublin, where he agreed to similar terms and also gave up his son. Yet many sceptics thought the O'Connors would slip the yoke at the first opportunity, and it is evident that nothing had occurred to change their nature, or to attach them to English habits or to English government.[193]

[Pg 215]

Seizure of the five Geraldines.

A main object of Grey's attack both on the O'Connors and the O'Briens may have been to get possession of the heir of Kildare, whose half-sister was married to the chief of Offaly. It is difficult to avoid the thought that Grey had a private as well as a public object in persecuting to the death all members of the fallen family except the children of his own sister. The rebel Earl had five uncles, all men of fair ability and great influence, and Brabazon seems first to have suggested that they ought to be kept in England. Grey asked Sir James Fitzgerald and his brothers Walter and Richard, all of whom had opposed the rebellion, to dine with him at Kilmainham, and in the middle of dinner they were all seized and handcuffed. Sir John and Oliver were arrested before they had heard of their brothers' capture, and the five were lodged in the castle. Grey always plumed himself on this exploit, though he admitted that some of the prisoners were innocent. The Irish Council approved the deed and applauded its secret handling, but none of the Irish officials knew that they were sending these men to the scaffold; the guilt of that must rest on Henry and Cromwell. Aylmer and Alen accompanied them to England, and the chronicler tells us that Richard, who had literary tastes, relieved the tedium of a sea-voyage by singing songs and repeating apophthegms. When he heard that the ship was called 'The Cow,' he was much dismayed, for there was a prophecy that five Earls' brethren should be carried to England in a cow's belly, and should never return. 'Whereat,' says Stanihurst, 'the rest began afresh to howl and lament, which doubtless was pitiful, to behold five valiant gentlemen, that durst meet in the field as sturdy champions as could be picked out in a realm, to be so suddenly terrified with the bare name of a wooden cow, or[Pg 216] to fear like lions a silly coxcomb, being moved (as commonly the whole country is) with a vain and fabulous old wives' dream.' On reaching London they were at once sent to the Tower, and left it only to take the last sad journey to Tyburn.[194]

Survivor of the Kildare family. The 'Fair Geraldine.'

But the family was not destined to extinction. Lady Kildare had accompanied her husband to England, and had her three daughters with her. The eldest was deaf and dumb, and of the youngest nothing particular is recorded, but the second, Lady Elizabeth, has by a strange chance been immortalised as the 'Fair Geraldine.' While yet a child she became maid of honour to the Princess Mary, at whose house at Hunsdon Henry, Earl of Surrey, saw her. She was then only twelve. Four years later she was married to Sir Anthony Browne, Master of the Horse and Knight of the Garter, but also a widower of sixty, whose daughter by his first marriage became her brother Gerald's wife. The unequal match was solemnized in the presence of the King and of the Lady Mary, and Ridley preached on the occasion which drew forth Surrey's sonnet. The situation of the bride's family and the apparent sacrifice of herself sufficiently account for the poetry, and there is no reason to suppose that the poet, who was married, had any regrets for himself. The study of Italian models would naturally lead to rather high-flown language, and poets were always privileged. The romantic fable of the magic mirror in which Cornelius Agrippa, an alchemist living at Florence, showed him the fair one reclining on a bridal couch and reading his sonnet, would not be worth noticing but that it found its way into the 'Lay of the Last Minstrel.' It is refuted by the fact that Surrey never was in Italy. After the death of Browne, who outlived Surrey, Lady Elizabeth was married to the Lord Admiral Clinton, who had been twice a widower. She left no children by either marriage, but her influence at Court may have had much to do with her brother's restoration. A portrait remains to show that she had a sweet face, and that she was not fairer[Pg 217] than many who have had no poet. But canvas, and especially the canvas of Holbein's school, seldom preserves the charm of grace and motion. Three letters remain, creditable so far as they go, and written in a clear, bold hand which contrasts strikingly with the crabbed characters often affected by public men, characters which drew a sarcasm from Shakespeare, and still trouble the historian. A portrait, three letters, and fourteen pretty lines would have hardly preserved the fair Geraldine's memory had it not been for the tragic fates of her father, her brother, and her poet.[195]

Edward Fitzgerald.

Less than two years after her husband's death, and while her rash stepson was lying in the Tower, Lady Kildare came to live at her brother Leonard's house at Beaumanoir in Leicestershire. She found there her son Edward, aged eight, who had been brought by some devoted but unknown friends 'without word, token, nor letter.' With touching humbleness she begged to be allowed the custody of him 'because he is an innocent, to see him brought up in virtue.' The prayer was granted, and the child thus strangely rescued lived to be Lieutenant of Queen Elizabeth's pensioners, and ancestor of the Dukes of Leinster.[196]

Gerald Fitzgerald.

The King was most anxious to get Lady Kildare's eldest son into his power, and St. Leger avers that the King had no object 'but to cherish him as his kinsman in like sort as his other brother is cherished with his mother in the realm of England.' Having disposed of all who were old enough to be dangerous, it was doubtless Henry's intention to bring up the children in English ways and in dependence on him. But Lady Mary O'Connor had other views, and the adventures of Gerald show how inextricably the Geraldines were intermingled with Celtic families. He was ten years old when his half-brother was taken, and was then lying in small-pox at Donore in Kildare. As soon as he could be moved his tutor, Thomas Leverous, who was his father's foster-brother, carried[Pg 218] him off in a basket and brought him safely to his sister in Offaly. Lady Mary procured him a three months' shelter among the O'Doynes, and he was then removed to Clare and placed under the charge of James Delahide. O'Brien, who had the Kildare plate and jewels as well as the heir in his power, refused all offers of the Government; and Leverous and Delahide were allowed to take Gerald to Kilbrittain Castle, and give him up to his aunt, Lady Eleanor MacCarthy, widow of the late and mother of the actual chief of Carbery. Had James Fitzjohn of Desmond wished to surrender the boy MacCarthy could hardly have resisted; but they agreed to amuse the Government with evasive answers, while Gerald employed himself in visiting the old tenants of his family about Adare and Croom. James Fitzjohn offered to take those manors on lease, the real object being to keep off grants to strangers. But Lady Eleanor feared the issue of this unequal contest, and agreed to marry Manus O'Donnell, whom she had rejected some years before. The marriage was desired by the whole Geraldine connection, and Lady Eleanor, accompanied by Leverous, Delahide, and the chaplain Walshe, brought her nephew safely through Thomond, Clanricarde, and Mayo, into Tyrconnell. All the O'Briens and Burkes welcomed and sped them on their journey. As the travellers approached Sligo they were joined by a rhymer named M'Cragh, a native of Tipperary, who was studying his craft in those parts, and through him many details became known to Ormonde. After her marriage with O'Donnell, Lady Eleanor busied herself in forming a confederacy of the Northern chiefs with Desmond and her friends in Leinster and Munster.[197]

Gerald escapes to France, 1540.

But Irish plots are commonly woven in sand, and Grey's activity disconcerted her schemes. Fearing that O'Donnell might be bribed, as Brabazon suggested, to give up the boy, she determined to send him to France. Allen Governor, an English shipowner of St. Malo, happened to be trading in Donegal, and agreed to take the precious passenger. A contract was drawn up before a notary, in which Governor bound[Pg 219] himself to land Gerald and his companions safely in France. Bareheaded, and wearing only the saffron shirt of a humble native, Gerald stole out in a small boat by night and committed himself and his fortunes to the chances of the sea. His aunt had provided him with 140 moidores, and he had also some plate, with part of which his passage was paid. His companions were Leverous, Robert Walshe, a faithful ally but a stern disciplinarian, who did not even spare the rod in the interests of his noble charge, and a young gentleman whose name is not recorded. They arrived safely at Morlaix, where the military governor received Gerald and led him through the town by the hand, taking especial care that no English trader should come near him. Henry's ambassador was nevertheless well informed as to the boy's movements. He re-embarked on the same vessel with a pilot named Jacques Cartier, who brought him to St. Malo, where he was hospitably treated by the Lieutenant-Governor.[198]

Gerald abroad, 1540.

When Chateaubriand, the Governor of Brittany, heard the news, he sent a special messenger to bring the refugees to Rennes. The gossips there would have it that Gerald was the rightful King of Ireland, and that Henry was a mere usurper; and neither he nor his friends could correct them: for they spoke no French. Chateaubriand treated his guest well and forwarded him to Court, where Wallop demanded his surrender as a treaty obligation. Francis did not deny this, but quietly removed the boy to the imperial town of Valenciennes. The faithful Leverous still attended him to watch against English kidnappers who were hanging about, and for greater security sent him to the Emperor at Brussels. But English diplomacy was importunate, and Charles transferred him to the Prince-bishop of Liège, with an allowance of one hundred crowns a month. After six months' residence with the Bishop, his kinsman Reginald Pole sent him to Italy, pensioned him, and provided the best education the peninsula afforded in the houses of the Bishops of Verona and Mantua, and of Gonzago, Duke of Milan, who gave him a further pension. His last patron in Italy was Cosmo de' Medici, who[Pg 220] allowed him three hundred crowns annually; and a three years' residence at Florence doubtless made him a proficient in the arts of courtly dissimulation. Leverous was admitted to the English monastery at Rome, and in Mary's reign became Bishop of Kildare; Robert Walshe went back to Ireland, but I do not find that his attainder was reversed or that he was ever pardoned.[199]

Geraldine pride.

O'Donnell soon made his submission, and was restored to favour. Lady Eleanor had some reason to be afraid, for Alen had proposed to invade Tyrconnell by sea and land with all the forces at the King's disposal. But she had now secured her nephew, and cared nothing for her new husband or his dangers. She called him traitor and many other hard names, said that the only object of her marriage was now gained, and that she had no further occasion for his company. She returned to her son's relations in Munster, but was not pardoned till 1545, seemingly because she did not ask sooner. The Irish Government refused to plead her cause as long as she remained obstinately among the MacCarthies. She came therefore to Malahide on safe-conduct, and thence forwarded a petition to which, as if the Geraldine pride scorned the Irish strain, she affixed her maiden name. After this the frequent reports of a Geraldine invasion ceased, but the head of the family thought it prudent to remain abroad until the death of Henry VIII.[200]

FOOTNOTES:

[171] Lady Skeffington to Anne Boleyn, Jan. 26, 1536; to Cromwell, Aug. 1. Anthony Colley to Cromwell, in Carew, Feb. 13, 1536; Lord Deputy and Council to Cromwell, Nov. 23.

[172] 28 and 29 Henry VIII. The contemporary Schedule of Acts is in the S.P. ii. 526. Brabazon to Cromwell, May 17, 1536; Cromwell to the Lord Deputy and Council, June 3.

[173] Irish Statutes, 28 and 29 Henry VIII. Brabazon to Cromwell, May 17; Grey to Cromwell, May 21.

[174] 25 Henry VI., c. 5 and c. 9, and see Hardiman's Statute of Kilkenny, p. 129; 17 Henry VI., see Carew, vol. iv. p. 457; 12 and 13 Henry VII. For the earlier legislation, see Gilbert's Viceroys, pp. 216, 244. The Act of Absentees is 28 Henry VIII., cap. 3. For the preparation of Bills in England, see Audeley to Cromwell, S.P. vol. ii. p. 439.

[175] Grey to Cromwell, June 24, 1536, for the treaty with Con O'Neill. The other treaties are in Carew, May 4, May 12, and May 31.

[176] Lord Deputy and Council to Cromwell, June 1, 1536; Council of Ireland to Cromwell, June 30; William Wise to Cromwell, July 12.

[177] The Council of Ireland to Cromwell, Aug. 9; Grey to Cromwell, Aug. 10.

[178] The Council of Ireland to Cromwell, Aug. 9; William Body to Cromwell, Aug. 9, in Carew; Grey to Cromwell, Aug. 10.

[179] Same authorities; also Lord Butler to Cromwell, Aug. 11.

[180] Body to Cromwell, Aug. 1536, in Carew; Grey to Cromwell, Nov. 24; Lord Butler to Cromwell, Aug. 11.

[181] Grey to Cromwell, Aug. 10; Body's letter, as above; Lord Deputy and Council to Cromwell, Nov. 23; Grey to Cromwell, same date.

[182] Council of Ireland to Cromwell, Aug. 22, 1536, and the notes; Grey to the King, Aug. 19.

[183] Council of Ireland to Cromwell, Aug. 22. This session of Parliament began Sept. 15, 1536.

[184] See the State Papers, vol. ii. pp. 366, 367. The Duke of Richmond died Aug. 22, 1536.

[185] The King to the Lord Deputy and Council, Feb. 25, 1537.

[186] Lord Deputy and Council to Cromwell, April 20, 1537; to the King, same date.

[187] Grey and Brabazon to Cromwell, June 11, 1537; Council to Cromwell, June 26; Thomas Alen to Cromwell, June 12, in Carew.

[188] The King to St. Leger and others, with the Commission of July 31, 1537; to the Lord Deputy and Council, same date; to Grey, same date.

[189] Lord Deputy and Council to Cromwell, Aug. 12. Grey to Cromwell, Aug. 16, 1537, wrongly printed under 1539 in the S.P.; same to same, Sept. 1.

[190] Four Masters and Annals of Lough Cé, 1512 and 1537. Manus O'Donnell to Grey, Aug. 20, 1537. Ware says that Donegal Friary contained a famous library.

[191] Grey to Cromwell, Sept. 1, 1537; J. Alen to St. Leger and others, No. 183 in the printed S.P.

[192] Brabazon to Cromwell, Dec. 31, 1537. St. Leger to Cromwell, Jan. 2, 1538.

[193] From the light it throws on the land question O'Connor's prayer is worth transcribing:—

'Humiliter petit, quatenus Dominus Rex, ex suâ gratiâ, dignetur concedere sibi, per literas suas patentes, quod ipse, et exitus sui, sint liberi status, et homines legales, more Anglicorum; et quod sit Baro de Offaly, atque habeat sibi et heredibus suis ex regia donatione portionem terrarum in Offaly, quas nunc illic possidet per partitionem, more patriæ, tenendam de Domino Rege secundum leges Anglicanas; ac quod simili auctoritate, fratres sui, et alii possessionarii terrarum ibidem, terras quas nunc possident habeant sibi et heredibus suis; ipse et omnes alii et heredes sui, reddendo Dominio Regi, annuatim, de qualibet carucata terræ, tres solidos et quatuor denarios; et quod carucatæ terræ in Offaly, quotiens Domino Deputato visum fuerit, ac necessitas emergerit, onerantur et assidentur belligeris pro defensione subditorum Domini Regis, eodem modo sicut cæteræ carucatæ terræ inter regios subditos onerantur et assidentur. Igitur humiliter petit, quod Dominus Rex, et Deputati sui, pro tempore existentes, suscipiant suam protectionem et defensionem contra omnes alios, prout suscipiant defensionem Anglicorum.' Submission of O'Connor, March 6, 1538.—Grey to Cromwell, March 17, 1538; Francis Herbert to Cromwell, March 21, 1536, to Norfolk, Jan. 24, 1538; Grey to Cromwell, April 1, 1538.

[194] Brabazon to Cromwell, Sept. 10, 1535; Council of Ireland to Cromwell, Feb. 14, 1536; Stanihurst; Ware; Four Masters, 1535.

[195] Nearly all that is really known about her is contained in a memoir by the Rev. James Graves. See also Hallam's History of Literature and Lodge's Lives of the Earls of Surrey and Kildare.

[196] Lady Kildare to Cromwell, July 16, 1536. Articles by St. Leger and others, Dec. 10, 1537.

[197] St. Leger and others to Cromwell, Jan. 2, 1538; Ormonde to the Irish Council, S.P., vol. iii. p. 44; Stanihurst.

[198] Brabazon to Cromwell, May 26, 1539; Stanihurst.

[199] Sir John Wallop to Essex, April 18, 1540, S.P., vol. viii.; Lord Deputy and Council to the King, July 12, 1542, and Henry's unfavourable answer; Bartholomew Warner to Wallop, May 22, 1540.

[200] Lady Eleanor O'Donnell to the King, May 4, 1545.

[Pg 221]

CHAPTER XII.

END OF GREY'S ADMINISTRATION.

Ormonde proposes to reform his country.
The O'Connors having been quieted for the moment, Ormonde, who had private as well as public reasons for his advice, proposed a temporising policy towards O'Neill and O'Reilly on the north, and towards O'Byrne and O'Toole on the south, side of the Pale. The Government might then easily subdue the Kavanaghs, who were surrounded by settled districts. Their chief, Cahir MacEncross, who has been called the last King of Leinster, had till lately been Constable, and his acceptance of the office seems to have been thought a condescension. Ormonde's son Richard had now succeeded him, and with the aid of Saintloo and his Wexford men might hope to reduce the whole country. To strengthen Kilkenny against a possible counter attack from the O'Mores, Ormonde secured the services of Edmond MacSwiney, a powerful hereditary chief of gallowglasses, whom O'Connor had brought from Donegal. The Earl thought it cheaper to outbid O'Connor than to have MacSwiney's band thrown into the scale of rebellion. Desmond and the rest excused their slowness to reform by saying that they waited for him to begin; and he was anxious to wipe out this reproach, regretting only that he had not the same powers in Kilkenny as in Tipperary. Though not disinterested, Ormonde's was probably the best available plan, and his reforming zeal was certainly serious. 'I have proclaimed,' he said, 'over all the county of Tipperary, that no caines, allyiegs, errikes, Irish Brehons, neither that law, rahowns, and many like exactions and extortions shall cease, with reformation for the grey merchants, and the Liberty court to be duly continued, as the King's laws require.' In Kilkenny he could only exhort; 'howbeit,' he added, 'I have[Pg 222] often persuaded many of them to be converted, which to do I can scarcely have their assents, for the lust they have to caines and other abuses, turning to their profit, as it doth to mine.'[201]

Grey goes to Ulster, 1538.
Taking advantage of O'Connor's quiescent state, Grey cut passes on the borders of Offaly wide enough for several carts abreast. He then turned his eyes to the North, where the MacMahons of Ferney had for three years neglected to pay their tribute of 10l. The borderers of English race were opposed to Grey's raid, and gave the MacMahons warning, but he managed to capture 500 cows, and as many pigs and goats. The expedition was as useless as it was inglorious, for Louth was invaded within a week, and O'Neill, who complained that his black-rent was unpaid, plundered the borders of the Pale and threatened to burn Drogheda. The men of that town and of Dundalk and Ardee rallied at the Lord Deputy's summons, and O'Neill then became quieter in his behaviour. But nothing could keep Grey quiet. He lent soldiers to one Chamberlayne of Athboy, to revenge a private quarrel against O'Reilly. That chief had hitherto been at peace with the Pale; but he lost his brother in this aimless brawl, and a general alliance of the Northern chiefs was with difficulty averted. The MacMahons had done far more harm to Louth than Grey had done to them, and he could gain little reputation by enterprises which had no apparent object but plunder.[202]

The O'Tooles.

While the Lord Deputy was driving cattle in Ulster, the other side of the Pale was in a blaze. John Kelway, Constable of Rathmore, saw some servants of Tirlogh O'Toole eating meat, assumed that it was stolen, and incontinently hanged them. This seems to have been thought unusual even among borderers, and Kelway's conduct found no defen[Pg 223]ders. But the O'Tooles were willing to consider the question of compensation in Irish fashion, and a meeting took place for the purpose. Kelway brought a considerable force, and, on the parley being dissolved without an agreement, he followed the Irish into their mountains. The mountaineers turned to bay on advantageous ground, and drove the English into a small tower. Its thatched roof burned readily, and the whole party had to surrender. The O'Tooles killed Kelway, who deserved nothing better, but held the gentlemen of the Pale to ransom. Chief Justice Aylmer's son was present but escaped, while his brother, Richard Aylmer of Lyons, was taken prisoner. About sixty of the marchers, all householders, fell in this wretched business, and so great a panic followed that an Irishman in Judge Luttrell's service was afraid to travel from Glendalough to Dublin. It is ever thus between races of different degrees of civilisation; if the backward people are beaten it is thought quite natural, but the slightest check is of importance when experienced by members of the higher organisation.[203]

Grey falls out with the Butlers.

The Lord Deputy and the Butlers had never been very good friends, and the dissension now reached such a height as to disturb the whole country. 'I was never,' exclaimed Brabazon, 'in despair in Ireland until now,' and others were not more hopeful. 'My Lord Deputy,' said Lord Butler, 'is the Earl of Kildare born again?' and Luttrell, a keen observer, thought Ormonde hated Grey worse than he had hated Kildare. The Butlers complained that the Lord Deputy systematically slighted their party and favoured the Geraldines; he retorted that they intrigued with Irishmen against his government. One or two of the matters in dispute call for more particular notice.[204]

Ormonde and the O'Carrolls.

After many struggles Fergananim O'Carroll was the acknowledged chief of Ely. His wife was daughter to Kildare[Pg 224] and sister-in-law to O'Connor, and he was ready to submit to Grey as the best means of opposing Ormonde. He promised to hold his land of the King at a rent of twelvepence for every ploughland, to attend the Lord Deputy with a fixed contingent, and to give free quarters for a limited number of the gallowglasses in the royal service. He also undertook to open up his country by cutting passes. O'Carroll at first stipulated that Grey should help him to recover all his father's strongholds; but all those castles were already vested legally in the Crown, and some of them had been granted to Ormonde. The Council therefore objected, and Fergananim seems to have waived his claim without demanding any corresponding concession. The prudence of the Council had prevented the Lord Deputy from concluding an offensive alliance; but he acted as if he had done so, and proceeded to take Birr and Modreeny, both of which Ormonde claimed under a royal grant, and to attack Ballynaclogh. The latter place was held by an O'Kennedy who paid rent to the Earl, and it is within the bounds of Tipperary. O'Carroll boasted that Nenagh and Roscrea would soon be his, and these castles, though long in Irish hands, were part of the old Ormonde inheritance, and had been lately confirmed to the Earl by a new grant.[205]

Grey and the O'Mores.

Connell O'More, chief of Leix, died in 1537, and the inevitable dispute followed between the tanist, his brother Peter, and his sons, Lysaght, Kedagh, and Rory. Grey espoused the cause of the sons, rather, as it seems, because Ormonde sided with Peter than from any preference for hereditary succession. Peter was, however, acknowledged as chief, and met Parry, Grey's confidential man, at Athy. Rory, who was present, assaulted his uncle, and the latter was then seized by Parry and carried to Dublin. Nothing was proved against him, and he was restored on agreeing to pay an annual tribute of twenty marks, and to receive a certain[Pg 225] number of soldiers at free quarters. The young O'Mores resisted the levying of the tribute, and Lysaght, the eldest, was killed in a fray. They had all taken part in the murder of Ormonde's son Thomas five years before, and Kedagh and Rory now plundered one of his villages. Their party consisted of only eight men, but the neighbours pleaded that they dared not resist, because the assailants were aided and abetted by one of the Lord Deputy's servants. The O'Mores pleaded that the Earl had first attacked them, and he rejoined that he had done so in self-defence. There was never a want of excuses for violence on any side. Grey forbade the Earl to retaliate, and it was even said that he shared the plunder. The young O'Mores then attacked Tullow, but the Lord Deputy still held Ormonde's hand, and even sent guns to help his enemies. Hoping to make peace, the Council summoned both uncle and nephews to Dublin. The chief came on Ormonde's advice and practically under his protection, and Kedagh also attended. O'More was at once sent handcuffed to Maynooth, though the whole Council protested, and Kedagh was suffered to depart unhurt. The blow to the Earl's credit was serious, and was not deadened by Grey, who led his prisoner in chains about his own part of the country, much as the Thane of Fife threatened to lead Macbeth. Grey's servants took the cue, and openly in the streets called the Butlers traitors. Lord Butler vowed that unless absolutely forced by his duty he would never wear armour under Grey until he had seen the King, and he cited the example of Count de Rœux, who had made a like vow when the Imperial lieutenant Van Buren had forced him to make peace with France. Even the old Earl meditated a journey to London, though he was so infirm that he could only be carried in a litter. The Irish Council condemned Grey's treatment of O'More; and moreover, said they, 'it is no good policy for the King our master, having no more obedient subjects in this land like unto the said Earl and his son, of reputation in honour, force, and strength, both to preserve and defend the parts where they dwell, and to succour other his subjects in all events, to suppress them which, with all their ancestors, have ever con[Pg 226]tinued their truths to the Crown of England, either upon the accusation of those which for the most part have always done the contrary, or yet in hope to have them now from henceforth true, which hitherto were never true'—remarks which have their practical value in modern Irish politics, as they had in the days of Henry VIII.[206]

Sudden departure of Grey.

Though not too wise in council, Grey was prompt in action, and was never so happy as on horseback surrounded by armed men and free from interference. Perhaps he wished to show how much he could do without Ormonde's help. He left Dublin suddenly, without warning the Council, and attended only by a small force, his companions being under the impression that he was bound only for an eight days' journey into O'Carroll's country. Among them was Lord Gormanston, a son of Lord Delvin, John D'Arcy,

William Bermingham, O'Connor, Rory and Kedagh O'More, and several other Irishmen of note, with a due proportion of kerne and gallowglasses. Of English soldiers Grey had no more than one hundred, and of these the greater part were without armour. A hosting had been proclaimed against the O'Tooles, who still kept some of the prisoners taken in Kelway's raid, and Grey promised to be back in time to lead the expedition. He failed to do so, and a truce was with much difficulty concluded with the mountaineers.[207]

His rash march into Western Munster,
Grey made his first halt at Monasteroris, where O'Connor entertained him in the Franciscan friary. Next day he took Eglish Castle near Birr from the O'Molloys, and was joined by Kedagh O'More, O'Molloy, MacGeohegan, and MacGillapatrick, each of whom brought a few men with him. On the third day he entered Ely, and received the adhesion of Fergananim O'Carroll, who bound himself by indenture on the[Pg 227] usual terms, and gave his son into the Lord Deputy's hands. Grey spent three days in reducing the lands of Birr and Modreeny, the latter of which had to be taken by assault. Ormonde had provided the garrison with arms; but, as he alleged, these were intended only for use against Irish enemies. Grey then entered Tipperary, and on three successive days received the submissions of Dermot O'Kennedy, chief of Ormonde, of MacBrien Arra, and of Dermot O'Mulryan, chief of Owny. Ulick de Burgh, captain of Clanricarde, and Theobald, head of the Clanwilliam Burkes, also submitted; and James Fitzjohn of Desmond, to whom Grey gives the title of Earl, though he was not acknowledged by the Crown, brought a large contingent to the Deputy's help, but refused to enter the gates of Limerick. He had not only procured a safe-conduct, but had solemnly bound O'Connor and others in Grey's train to take his part if any attempt were made against him. The Lord Deputy spent a week in Limerick, where the Mayor and Corporation and the Bishop took the oath of supremacy. Connor O'Brien, the chief of Thomond, met Grey on the Shannon, ten miles from Limerick, and agreed, after a long wrangle, to put his son Tirlogh into the Deputy's hands. He also promised to do all in his power to promote the capture of the castles held by his brother Murrough, the tanist of Thomond. O'Brien's Bridge was once more demolished, Connor led the army through the tanist's district, and everything was destroyed as far as Clare Castle. Here Grey and Desmond had a quarrel about the custody of O'Mulryan's hostages, and there was very near being a pitched battle; but Sir Thomas Butler of Cahir, Ormonde's son-in-law, managed to patch up a truce. Grey was, in fact, quite at O'Brien's mercy, but the family politics saved him. The chief had lately married a second wife, Lady Alice Fitzgerald of Desmond, and Tirlogh, the child of the marriage, was pledged to Grey; but Murrough the tanist and Donough, the chief's eldest son, were both afraid that the issue of the second marriage would be preferred before them. O'Connor, in whom Grey now placed implicit confidence, 'and all sage men of his band, both English and Irish,' begged him not to[Pg 228] venture among the O'Briens, and Edmund Sexton, a noted royalist of Limerick, even conjured him on his allegiance not to cast away the citizens' company, on whom all depended. Grey refused to take advice, and escaped all dangers, chiefly through Donough O'Brien's influence. Donough's loyalty might not have been enough by itself, but he dreaded the aggrandisement of Murrough more than possible dangers from a half-brother who was still in his infancy. Guided by a single gallowglass, who bore a silver axe adorned with silken tassels, the army marched safely into Clanricarde. Ulick de Burgh blamed Grey for his rashness, but he pointed to the guide and said, 'Lo! seest thou not yonder standing before me O'Brien's axe for my protection?' A modern traveller among Arabs must often

be content with some such outward sign of invisible allies, but his trust in O'Brien's axe was made an article in Grey's impeachment.[208]

And into Connaught, 1538.

Ulick was fully acknowledged as chief of Clanricarde, to the prejudice of his uncle Richard. He was believed to be illegitimate, and the De Burghs, however much Hibernicised, had hitherto preserved the English law of succession. The precedent was therefore thought bad by many experienced men, but the relationships of this family are so inextricably confused that it is very hard to say who was legitimate and who was not. The citizens of Galway remembered their origin, and would take no money from the Lord Deputy, and Ulick, who was knighted, took hospitable care of his Irish allies. As at Limerick, the Mayor and Corporation took the oath of supremacy, and so did the Archbishop of Tuam. Grey made several forays into Clanricarde, with the apparent object of strengthening Ulick; and O'Flaherty, two O'Maddens, and Bermingham of Athenry, made their submissions. The Lord Deputy then went towards the Suck in O'Kelly's country, and met O'Connor Roe, who rode with him to Aughrim. Fording the Shannon at Banagher, the army passed through the countries of O'Melaghlin and MacCoghlan, from whom[Pg 229] securities were exacted, and returned unmolested to Maynooth, after an absence of thirty-eight days.[209]

Effects of this journey.

As a military exploit Grey's journey was by no means contemptible, but his critics seem to have been right in thinking it useless. The settled policy had long been to reduce the tribes bordering on the Pale, and not to overrun districts which there was no hope of holding. Many chiefs had come to the Lord Deputy with loyal professions, but they had required safe-conducts, had refused to enter walled towns, and had given children for hostages. They had thus saved their harvest, and the Government could scarcely take vengeance on infants. Grey's supposed partiality for the Geraldines was probably the chief reason that he got back safely. He had no sooner turned his back than James Fitzjohn of Desmond seized Croom and Adare and threatened Ormonde's country. No difficulty had been lessened by an exploit which was obviously open to the reproach of extreme rashness.[210]

Grey's dispute with the Butlers.

Having got back their chief governor, the first care of the Council was to reconcile him with the Butlers. The old Earl's appearance plainly foretold his approaching end, but he came to Dublin and left his son to front the Desmonds and O'Carrolls. Grey wrote to the latter to keep the peace, and Lord Butler at once came to Dublin; but both father and son refused to go to Maynooth, where they would be in the Lord Deputy's power. Kilmainham was at last fixed on as the place of meeting, and Grey took the chair of state, but shook hands with none of the Council, and smiled on no one. The two Butlers offered to abide by the Council's decision, but Grey had already produced a paper reflecting on them for receiving O'Connor after his defeat in the summer of 1537. A Latin confession said to have been made by O'Connor in the presence of Paulet and Berners was relied on, but the chief[Pg 230] was secretly cross-examined by the Council, and so modified his statement as to exonerate the Butlers completely. It was said, for instance, that O'Connor had hired Edmond MacSwiney and his free axes immediately after a conference with Ormonde. O'Connor admitted the hiring, but explained that the gallowglasses were not bound to levy war against the King, and that Ormonde knew nothing at all about the matter. Again, he was charged with retaining Scotch mercenaries, who were allowed a fortnight's free quarters in Ormonde's country. He admitted having brought in the Scots; but the Earl had known nothing of it, and the free quarters had not been given. Ormonde allowed that he had harboured O'Connor, but pleaded the instructions of Grey, who waited for orders from the King, and who was afraid of driving the chief into fresh combinations with Irish enemies. The probability is that O'Connor had at first been ready to confess anything, because absolution was sure to follow, and he is not likely to have been overflowing with Latin, which was his only means of communicating with the English officials.[211]

They accuse each other.

Both Grey and Ormonde gave in long written statements. The Council desired to consider them in the Deputy's absence, and to this he with some hesitation consented. They found that Grey's charges contained nothing new, but only general accusations of slackness; while Ormonde plainly accused Grey of treasonable practices, of shaping his policy to suit young Gerald of Kildare, and of systematically depressing all who opposed the Geraldine faction. The indictment is summed up in the comprehensive statement that 'My Lord Deputy cannot find in his heart to love or favour any man that is preferred, favoured, or put in trust by his Majesty within this his land, and would have none of them, though they be all ready at his commandment, to be toward, or about him, be they never so trusty nor so well meaning; but wholly adhereth to those that were the counsellors, servants, and followers of the disloyal Geraldines, and no men so nigh about him as they, which either of his own prepensed mind,[Pg 231] or being seduced by them, is like to bring this land to perdition again.' On being pressed for proof, Ormonde said that the facts were too notorious to require any.[212]

The Council patch up a reconciliation.

The Council prudently resolved not to let either litigant see the other's charges, and Mr. Justice St. Lawrence having been called in, the originals were burned in his presence. Copies already taken were transmitted to London. Ormonde and his son then swore to serve the Lord Deputy loyally. Grey swore not to use them spitefully nor ask them to perform impossibilities, to deliver Modreeny to the Earl unless O'Carroll could show a better title, and to cause the young O'Mores to restore the plunder of Ormonde's villages, or at least to refer all to the Council. The Council did not believe the agreement would be lasting. 'Neither,' they added, 'can we perceive (whereof we be sorry) that my Lord Deputy is meet to make long abode here, for he is so haughty and chafing that men be afeard to speak to him, doubting his bravish lightness. Nevertheless, it is much pity of him, for he is an active gentleman.'[213]

The Kavanaghs. The O'Reillys.

It was not long before the Butlers had an opportunity of co-operating with Grey. The Kavanaghs threatened the Wexford colony, negotiations failed, and it became necessary to chastise them. Grey entered Carlow in person, and was joined by Saintloo, who, whatever his shortcomings as a governor, was not a bad soldier, and who brought 800 men. After fourteen days' burning and plundering, MacMurrough and his clansmen sued for peace, and agreed to hold their lands of the King. Grey then moved northwards, and provisions for eight days were prepared for a raid against O'Reilly, to be used otherwise by the Deputy in case O'Reilly should make timely submission. O'Reilly did submit, and Grey went to Dundalk with a view of meeting O'Neill, who was now young Gerald Fitzgerald's protector. O'Neill broke his appointment, and he did wisely, for Grey says he was determined to take Gerald if possible, 'and if not, by the oath that I have made to my sovereign lord and master, I would[Pg 232] have taken the said O'Neill and a kept him till he had caused the said Gerald to be delivered to my hands.'[214]

The Savages in Down.

Foiled in this attempt, which can hardly be described as otherwise than treacherous, Grey determined to chastise the Savages, who had refused to pay rent to Brabazon, the King's tenant in Lecale. This old English family had become quite Hibernicised, and were now bringing Scotch mercenaries into the country. Various castles were taken and delivered to Brabazon, who also took charge of Dundrum, an important stronghold belonging to Magennis, which commanded the entry to Lecale on the land side. The Scots fled, leaving corn, butter, and other rural plunder behind. Grey was much struck by the fertility of the district, which is still famous. 'I never,' he said, 'saw a pleasanter plot than Lecale for commodity of the land, and divers islands in the same environed in the sea, which were soon reclaimed and inhabited, the King's pleasure known.'[215]

Labours of St. Leger's Commission.

Sir Anthony St. Leger and his brother Commissioners arrived in Ireland early in September 1537, and lost no time in endeavouring to carry out the King's plan. By November they had surveyed most of the King's lands in Carlow, Kilkenny, Tipperary, Waterford, Dublin, and Kildare. The general result of their observations was that they had seen 'divers goodly manors and castles, the more part of them ruinous, and in great decay, the towns and lands about them depopulate, wasted, and not manured; whereby hath ensued great dearth and scarcity of all manner victuals.' But few applications were made for leases, because there was no security, and they saw the necessity of placing a few castles in a defensible state. Within reach of the walls there was no difficulty in getting tenants. By Christmas the survey was finished, and an increased desire to take leases was quickly manifested; but some lands were still unlet. Two thousand marks in money and securities had been collected for the[Pg 233] King, 'and much more,' the Commissioners reported, 'would have been levied, in case that men had not of late been sore charged with service doing to his Highness here, whereby we be constrained to look on them with more favourable eye.'[216]

The public accounts.

Brabazon reported that the Commissioners had done their work well. The passing of his own three years' account was a yet more difficult matter. They found it tedious and intricate, both from its nature and from the fact that there were no records of the King's ancient inheritance, or of escheats. Brabazon's own arrangements were good, but all before his time was chaos. 'Every keeper,' said the Master of the Rolls, 'for his time, as he favoured, so did either embezzle, or suffer to be embezzled, such muniments as should make against them and their friends, so that we have little to show for any of the King's lands or profits in these parts: it is therefore necessary that from henceforth all the rolls and muniments to be had be put in good order in Bermingham's Tower, and the door thereof to have two locks, and the keys thereof one to be with the Constable, and the other with the Under-Treasurer, which likewise it is necessary to be an Englishman born;

and that no man be suffered to have loan of any of the said muniments, nor to search, view, or read any of them there, but in the presence of one of the keepers aforesaid.' The accounts were nevertheless put in order by March; and having received very gracious thanks from the King, St. Leger and his colleagues returned to England, 'not,' as they were careful to note, 'for that we be weary to serve his Grace, but for because we be very loth to spend any more of his treasure, than we see time to serve him.' Aylmer and Alen, by the King's especial orders, accompanied the High Commissioners to England.[217]

Cromwell and the Irish service.

The official politicians of Ireland generally took care to be on good terms with the virtual ruler of England, and to watch for every sign of change in the distribution of royal[Pg 234] favours. Cromwell was therefore well bespattered with flattery; but there were murmurs, some at least of which reached his ears. St. Leger the discreet may or may not have glanced obliquely at the Lord Privy Seal when he said of himself that 'he had too long abstained from bribery to begin now.' But his colleague George Paulet was more outspoken, and declared openly that 'the Lord Privy Seal drew every day towards his death, and that he escaped very hardly at the last insurrection, and that he was the greatest briber in England, and that he was espied well enough.' Cromwell had given orders that the Commissioners should not interfere with castles in Lord Butler's possession, and to this Paulet objected, hinting that Butler's head as well as Cromwell's might easily be disposed of. His reading of Henry's character was exactly the same as Wolsey's. 'I will,' he said, 'so work matters that the King shall be informed of every penny that he hath spent here; and when that great expense is once in his head, it shall never be forgotten; there is one good point. And then I will inform him how he hath given away to one man 700 marks by year, and then will the King swear "By God's Body, have I spent so much money and have given away my land." I will find the means to put the matter in the King's head, after that wise as shall be to his displeasure; and yet shall he not know which way it came.' Paulet gave Alen a most amusing description of the fashion in which Henry treated the minister to whom he gave such power. 'The King beknaveth him twice a week and sometimes knocks him well about the pate; and yet when he hath been well pommelled about the head, and shaken up as it were a dog, he will come out into the great chamber shaking of his bush with as merry a countenance as though he might rule all the roast.' The appointment of the High Commissioners was a 'flym flawe to stop the imagination of the King and Council' as to Cromwell's object in promoting great grants to Lord Butler. The suggestion of course is that Cromwell was bribed by Butler, and the fact that Paulet was not punished shows that there were limitations to the minister's power. Paulet said as much, or nearly as much, to Grey as[Pg 235] to Alen and Aylmer, and Grey repeated it to the King with some softening of the words. Paulet was evidently hostile to the Butlers; so was Grey, and the fact that they had been on friendly terms was thought evidence of their conspiring in the Geraldine interest.[218]

Charges against Grey. Circuit of the Council in the South, 1539.

Aylmer and Alen were less than two months in London, but they left behind them a mass of accusations against Grey which in time brought forth fruit. Alen soon afterwards received the Great Seal, and during the last days of 1538 proceeded on a tour in the South with the general view of establishing the King's supremacy, of improving the revenue, and of providing for the administration of justice. Archbishop Browne, Brabazon, and Aylmer accompanied the new Chancellor. At Carlow the party enjoyed Lord Butler's Christmas hospitalities, and the old Earl treated them well at Kilkenny, where they spent New Year's day, and where Browne preached to a large congregation. English translations of the Pater Noster, Ave Maria, Articles, and Ten Commandments were published, and copies given to the Bishop and other dignitaries, who were ordered to promulgate them wherever they had jurisdiction. Next morning several felons were hanged, and certain concealed lands sequestrated to the King's use; neither of which proceedings were calculated to increase his Majesty's popularity. The councillors then went to Ross, which they found much decayed through the rivalry of Waterford and the disorders of the Kavanaghs. Here the Archbishop preached again. At Wexford there was another sermon, and the Kilkenny ceremonies were repeated, including the execution of divers malefactors. The Councillors were dissatisfied with Saintloo's conduct as seneschal, and accused him of converting fines and forfeited recognizances to his own use. Badly armed and badly horsed, the soldiers appeared to do the people less good by their protection than they did harm by their extortion. The evils inherent to all palatinate jurisdictions were greatly aggravated by the seneschal's lax administration. It was doubtful whether he had[Pg 236] the right to appoint a deputy at all. He had nevertheless made such an appointment by parole and without any formal record, and his irregular substitute had arrogated all the powers of a Judge of Assize.[219]

The royal supremacy. The Munster Bishops.
From Wexford Alen and his companions went to Waterford, where Browne preached to a great audience, and where the new formularies were again published. The usual hangings followed. Four felons suffered, 'accompanied with another thief, a friar, whom, among the residue, we commanded to be hanged in his habit, and so to remain upon the gallows, for a mirror to all other his brethren to live truly.' The assizes or sessions were attended only by the inhabitants of Lord Power's portion of the county of Waterford. The other and larger division of the shire belonged to Gerald MacShane of Decies, who pretended to hold of the Desmonds, and altogether ignored his tenure of the royal honour of Dungarvan. The Lord of Decies, James Fitzjohn of Desmond, the White Knight, and Sir Thomas Butler of Cahir were summoned with several others. Butler came to Clonmel and made a favourable impression, but the Geraldines sent only 'frivolous, false, feigned excuses, not consonant to their allegiance.' Browne preached again at Clonmel in the presence of two archbishops and eight bishops, all of whom afterwards, before the whole congregation, took the oath of supremacy, and swore to maintain the succession as established by law.[220]

Taxation of southern counties.
After much pressing, the inhabitants of Wexford, Waterford, Kilkenny, and Tipperary consented to pay a yearly subsidy to the King; 100 marks for Wexford, and 50l. for each of the other three. This source of revenue was quite new, and the Council were very proud of inventing it; but they con[Pg 237]fessed to doubts as to its substantial value, especially in Waterford, where Sir Gerald MacShane had power to pay or to withhold. From Clonmel the councillors returned to Dublin by Kilkenny, where they hanged one man more and levied some further fines. They had been absent from the capital five weeks.[221]

Grey in Ulster. The Scots, 1539.

About the time that the Chancellor and his companions were turning homewards, Grey undertook another expedition against O'Neill. Again the ostensible object was to catch young Gerald of Kildare, and in this the Lord Deputy failed. But he very nearly caught O'Neill himself, actually carried off his 'housewife,' and ravaged much of his country. O'Donnell was present, or at least some of his people, for the horse which his standard-bearer rode was taken. James Fitzjohn of Desmond was in alliance with the two great northern chiefs to protect the 'naughty boy,' as Alen called Gerald, and if possible to force the King to restore him. The bastard Geraldines of the Pale were ready to help their natural leader, who grew more dangerous as he grew older. The Antrim Scots were always available for service against the English Government, and Brabazon wished to cripple them by a naval expedition. O'Neill and O'Donnell now sent Roderick O'Donnell, Bishop of Derry, to Scotland for 6,000 Redshanks. In the meantime they professed themselves ready to treat with Grey, and promised to bring young Gerald to meet him on the last day of April at Carrick Bradagh, near Dundalk. They never came, and Grey penetrated to Armagh in spite of bad weather and foul ways. O'Neill still refused to show himself or to give any hostage, but he professed peaceable intentions. The weather made it impossible to advance further, and Aylmer was sent to Blackwater, where he succeeded in making a truce. Again, Grey says that he had intended to seize his nephew by fair means or foul. 'If they had kept pointment with me having young Gerald with them, howsoever the thing had chanced by the oath that I have made unto your Grace, they should have left the young[Pg 238] Gerald behind them quick or dead. If it were the pleasure of God I would that I might once have a sight of him whom as yet I never saw with my eyes.'[222]

The O'Tooles.
The O'Tooles had never been punished for their victory over Kelway, and Grey, who had for the moment no worse enemy than a gouty foot, resolved to chastise them. They proposed to parley near Ballymore Eustace, but did not come. Though in great pain, Grey rode to Powerscourt in a day, entered the mountains and penetrated to Glenmalure, cutting the woods on both sides as he went. 'Before my coming thither,' he said, 'I think there never was Deputy with carts there.' He had some skirmishing with the natives, but took no man of importance, and returned to Maynooth without having improved his gout.[223]

Intrigues concerning Gerald of Kildare.
A confederacy had at this time been formed in favour of young Gerald. His own claims might not have been enough, in spite of Lady Eleanor O'Donnell's efforts, but Henry's ecclesiastical policy was beginning to bear its natural fruit. Priests passed from chief to chief, and communications with Rome were frequent. The Irish said all Englishmen were heretics, and the King the 'most heretic and worst man in the world,' in which perhaps they were not far wrong. They considered Henry a disobedient Papal vassal, and a mere usurper in Ireland. 'When Dr. Nangle, my suffragan,' says Archbishop Browne, 'showed the King's broad seal for justifying of his authority, MacWilliam little esteemed it, but threw it away and vilipended the same.' The plan was that O'Toole, to whom Gerald promised to restore Powerscourt, should harass the Pale from the south, while James Fitzjohn of Desmond, with some Scotch mercenaries, attacked it from the west and O'Neill from the north. If Tara could be reached O'Neill might be proclaimed King of Ireland, and Gerald restored to his own in Kildare. Besides her own[Pg 239]

friends, Lady Eleanor commanded the services of a Bristol captain named Kate, or Cappys, who spoke Irish fluently and owned his own ship. John Lynch, a Galway merchant, met him at Assaroe, on the Donegal coast, and warned some of the confederates that Grey would be too strong for them, and that he was active enough to surprise them when they thought he was amusing himself. But Delahide, Leverous, and others, answered that they had perfect intelligence, that Grey could not ride twenty miles in the Pale without their knowledge, that his army consisted chiefly of churls and ploughmen, of which 300 might easily be vanquished by 100, and that he had no good officers under him. These are the arguments with which the foes of order in Ireland have always deluded their adherents, and sometimes themselves.[224]

Catholic movement.

Wherever Lynch went he found the priests preaching daily 'that every man ought for the salvation of his soul fight and make war against our sovereign lord the King's Majesty and his true subjects; and if any of them which so shall fight against his said Majesty or his subjects, die in the quarrel, his soul that so shall be dead shall go to heaven as the soul of St. Peter, Paul, and others, which suffered death and martyrdom for God's sake.' 'And forasmuch,' Lynch adds, 'as I did traverse somewhat of such words, I was cast out of church and from their masses during a certain time of days for an heretic; and I was greatly afraid.' The result of all this preaching was an invasion of the Pale in the month of August. Lord Butler's policy had kept the O'Briens quiet, and nothing was done on that side. But O'Donnell and O'Neill entered Meath with the greatest army, as some thought, that had ever been seen in Ireland. There was a large contingent of Scots, both from the mainland and the islands, and most of the Northern chiefs added their quotas to the host. O'Neill of Clandeboye, O'Rourke, Maguire, MacQuillin, O'Cahan, Magennis, and MacDermot are among those mentioned. Tara was reached, but no restoration of the ancient kingdom followed. Much[Pg 240] damage was done to the modern kingdom, including the burning of Ardee and of Navan, which was the best market town in the county. The invaders set fire to the standing corn, carried off every portable article of value, and, sweeping all the cattle before them, turned in high spirits northwards. They had met with no enemy, and had probably attained their object of providing funds for a general rising, which was fixed for September 1, and which James of Desmond was expected to join.[225]

Grey routes the O'Neills at Bellahoe, 1539.

Grey summoned the men of Dublin and Drogheda, those citizen soldiers whom the Irish dreaded so much, and hurried after O'Neill. Out of a nominal 350 he could muster no more than 140 of his own men, but he had some help from the gentlemen of the Pale. The marchers, like Rob Roy at Sheriffmuir, waited to see which was the winning side. 'I must help the King,' said Fitzgerald of Osbertstown, to Gerald's messenger, 'but if ye be the strongest we must go with you.' Without waiting for such Laodiceans, the Lord Deputy dashed forward, and, as Lynch had foreseen, caught the Ulstermen quite unprepared. They were encamped at Bellahoe, the ford which divides Meath from Monaghan, on the Farney side of the water, and he routed them before they had time to form. The Irish leaders who knew the country escaped, with the exception of Magennis, whose post was near the ford. He fell into the hands of the Louth men, who were bribed by some of his own clan to kill him, and did so. The only person of note killed on the English side was a gentleman named Mape, who charged up the river bank by Lord

Slane's side, and who was carried by his runaway horse into the midst of the Irish. According to Stanihurst, whose account of this affair is at least highly coloured, the mayors of Dublin and Drogheda and Thomas Talbot of Malahide were dubbed knights on the field by the Lord Deputy. He also says that Black James Fleming, Baron of Slane, led the attack, and called on his hereditary standard-bearer to do his duty in the front. But the standard-bearer, whose name was Robert Halpin or Halfpenny, thought the service desperate,[Pg 241] and refused to advance his banner, preferring 'to sleep in an whole sheepskin his pelt, than to walk in a torn lion his skin.' Calling him a dastardly coward, the Baron ordered Robert Betagh to supply his place, which he cheerfully did: Mape, though he had refused to lead, was fain to follow, and fell fighting in the first rank.[226]

Grey is accused of favouring the Geraldines.

After this great success, which shattered the Irish or Catholic confederacy for a time, Grey remained in the North. A fleet had been collected at Carlingford to chastise the Scots, and the crews had taken part in the fight or pursuit at Bellahoe; but not much could be done against the islanders. The old Earl of Ormonde had just died, and his son was too busy to visit Ulster. He had incurred vast expense in subsidising the O'Briens and the Clanricarde Burkes, who were ready to serve the King with 800 gallowglasses, 800 kerne, and some horse. James Fitzjohn of Desmond was growing daily stronger, while his rival was basking in Court sunshine; and Ormonde attributed this state of affairs to the Lord Deputy, who favoured all Geraldines and depressed all who owed their promotion to Cromwell. James Fitzjohn had seen the Earl's brother, the Archbishop of Cashel, and had promised to meet Ormonde also, but he failed in his appointment, and threatened at every moment to attack Tipperary.[227]

The Desmond heritage. Grey goes to Munster, 1539.

The English Government had in the meantime declared that James FitzMaurice was right heir to the earldom of Desmond. He had been a royal page, and was provided with a force sufficient to guard against any sudden attack. He landed at Cork or Youghal in August, but three months elapsed before any serious effort was made to put him in possession of his own. Leaving Dublin early in November,[Pg 242] Grey joined Ormonde near Roscrea, about which there had been fierce dissensions. The castle was now in the hands of the O'Meaghers, but they gave it up peaceably to the Lord Deputy, and he handed it over to Ormonde. Modreeny, which the Earl now acknowledged as O'Carroll's, was also surrendered. Taking hostages from O'Carroll, MacBrien Arra, O'Kennedy, O'Mulryan, and O'Dwyer to be faithful and pay the King tribute, Grey and Ormonde cut passes through the woods near the Shannon, the inhabitants of which had guided the O'Briens in their raids. They halted two days at Thurles, where Sir Gerald MacShane and the White Knight thought it prudent to submit themselves, and victualled their troops about Cashel and Clonmel. At Youghal they delivered all the castles of Imokilly to the young Earl of Desmond, and two nephews of former Earls accepted him as the head of their House. At Cork Lord Barry, who had held aloof for years, came in and gave security. Hither also came the sons of Cormac Oge, and it was probably on this occasion that their sister Mary MacCarthy married the young Earl. The union was not fated to last long, nor to give an heir to the House of Desmond. The barony of Kerrycurrihy was taken possession of at Kinsale, and MacCarthy Reagh, in whose castle of Kilbrittain Gerald of Kildare had lately found a home, consented to come to Cork and to give his brother as a hostage. He hesitated to sacrifice his cattle, and was easily persuaded by Ormonde, who was now on unusually good terms with Grey. Barry Roe and Barry Oge also gave security. The army then shifted to O'Callaghan's country, and near Dromaneen James Fitzjohn came to the other side of the flooded Blackwater and defied Grey. He would, he said, conclude nothing without the advice of O'Brien, who could dispose of all the Irishry of Ireland. Grey could not pass the river, and returned to Cork. John Travers, a native of Ireland who had learned the art of war elsewhere, had lately been appointed Master of the Ordnance, and accompanied this expedition, in which only 800 men were employed. Travers said that he would go anywhere in Ireland with 2,000 men, and Grey's exploits, no less than Sidney's later, show[Pg 243] that he was right: the difficulty was not to take but to keep. 'Six thousand good men,' Travers added, 'divided in three places as I could give instruction, with certain craftsmen to inhabit the places they win, might make a general reformation in one summer.' The advice was sound, but the Crown could not afford to take it.[228]

Grey's last raid into Ulster.
Once more before young Gerald had left Ireland did Grey turn his attention to the North. For the third time O'Neill promised to meet him, and for the third time he failed to appear. Without victuals, and trusting to plunder for the support of his men, the Lord Deputy then rode 'thirty-four miles of ill way' to Dungannon, and again nearly caught the troublesome chief. But the guides, perhaps intentionally, delayed the soldiers on their night march, and daybreak found them still five miles from Dungannon. O'Neill had time to escape. Six days were spent in promiscuous burnings, during which the soldiers had no bread and lived on freshly killed beef: it is no wonder that disease was rife in the ranks. This was Grey's last warlike expedition; successful in a certain sense, but quite useless as a matter of policy.[229]

Recall of Grey. Consequent confusion.
Grey had often asked leave to go to Court and lay the state of Ireland before the King, begging that his adversaries might not be allowed to ruin him behind his back. His request was now to be granted in an unexpected manner. One of his last acts in Ireland was a quarrel with the Council, in spite of whose remonstrances he sent over Travers, the Master of the Ordnance, with despatches, though he seems to have agreed with them that a man who could be better spared would have done the business just as well. Sir William Brereton, Marshal of the Army, had lately broken his leg, an accident from which he seems never to have fully recovered; Edward Griffiths, another useful officer, was dying of diarrhœa; Travers was the only available officer, and his own department was in bad order. Yet Grey sent him, perhaps because[Pg 244] he thought his talk would be favourable to him. The immediate result of Travers's journey was that the King sent for Grey, professing his anxiety to see him and to send him back to Ireland in time for the fighting season at the end of May. Brereton was to act as Lord Justice during his absence. Henry declared himself willing to raise the wages of soldiers in Ireland, which had been fixed three years before at 5l. 6s. 8d. a year for horsemen and half that sum for footmen, and which had been found quite inadequate. Deplorable disorders had resulted from the necessities of the men. Henry expressed his intention of keeping the troops on the Irish borders instead of in Dublin. Coming events cast their accustomed shadow before, and Grey's recall, for recall it was understood to be, was known to the public sooner than to the officials. It was of course suggested that Grey purposely concealed the truth in order to embarrass the Council; and he refused their prayer to stay until arrangements had been

made for the defence of the Pale. His activity had evidently inspired respect, for he had no sooner crossed the Channel than the O'Tooles made a raid towards Dublin. O'Byrne warned the citizens, and they had time to make ready. The Kavanaghs attacked the Wexford settlers. The O'Connors burned Kildare. Alen and Brabazon had also been called to England, but they were obliged to wait for a fitter time. 'The country,' wrote Brereton in excusing their absence, 'is in very ill case, being assured of no Irishman's peace.'[230]

Trial and execution of Grey.

An enormous number of charges were brought against Grey. He was accused of maintaining the King's enemies and depressing the King's friends, of injustice to Irishmen and others, of violence towards Councillors and others, and of extortion. There is no reason to suppose that he could have taken young Gerald, with whom, in Stanihurst's quaint language, he was accused of 'playing bo-peep;' but no doubt he had been guilty of much injustice, as his unprovoked in[Pg 245]vasion of Ferney and his treatment of O'More sufficiently prove. He cannot be called a man of scrupulous honour, or he would not have arrested the Geraldines at dinner, or professed his intention to capture his nephew by fair means or foul. But Henry VIII. knew how to pardon such conduct, though he could punish his instruments when it suited him. The Irish chiefs felt that they could not trust Grey, and therefore kept no faith with him. He was accused on all sides of greed, and especially of making useless expeditions for the sake of plunder. The usual inquisition made after his arrest shows that he had some private hoards. He was violent in Council, and no doubt it was often hard for a Viceroy, especially for one who suffered from gout, to deal with the Dublin officials, who were independent of him and sometimes spies on his conduct. 'I think,' says Walter Cowley, 'there is not one of the King's Council there but my Lord Deputy successively have sore fallen out with them.' But he was rude and tyrannical to others also, as to Lord Delvin, whose life he was accused of shortening by insults, and especially by calling him traitor, 'which,' says the old Earl of Ormonde, 'shall never be proved.' In any case and whatever his actual guilt, a cloud of witnesses appeared to denounce Grey.[231] He pleaded guilty, rather in hopes of mercy than acknowledging his faults; but no pardon followed. That[Pg 246] he had any treasonable intention is more than doubtful, but there was more against him than against Buckingham; he suffered a year's imprisonment in the Tower, and then underwent the fate to which his treacherous compliance with a tyrant's wishes had condemned his Geraldine kinsmen.

FOOTNOTES:

[201] Ormonde to St. Leger, March 12, 1538. See also the 'Fall of the Clan Kavanagh,' by Hughes, Irish Archæological Journal, 4th series, vol. ii., 1873. Erics were compositions for murder, caines for other felonies. Rahownes may be the same as 'sorohen.' I do not understand allyieg, unless it be 'allying' with the Irish.

[202] Four Masters, 1537; Brabazon to Aylmer and Alen, Whitsuntide, 1538; Council of Ireland to Cromwell, June 10, 1538.

[203] Grey to the King, June 4, 1538; Brabazon to Aylmer and Alen, Whitsuntide; Luttrell to Aylmer, June 5; Council to Aylmer, June 10. All the accounts make out that Kelway was quite wrong.

[204] Justice Luttrell to Chief Justice Aylmer, June 5, 1538; Ormonde's instructions to R. Cowley, June; Lord Butler to his father and to R. Cowley, June.

[205] Lord Butler to his father, June 19, 1538; Ormonde to the Irish Council, June; to R. and W. Cowley, July 16; to R. Cowley, July 20; to the Privy Council, S.P., vol. iii., p. 77; Grey to the King, June 4 and July 26; Council of Ireland to Cromwell, June 10, July 24, and August 22.

[206] Brabazon, Aylmer, and Alen to Cromwell, Aug. 24, 1538. For the treatment of O'More see Ormonde to R. Cowley, June 1538; Aylmer and Alen's articles against Grey, June. Lord Butler to R. Cowley, June 20. Articles alleged on the part of O'More, S.P., vol. iii. p. 26. Council of Ireland to Cromwell, June 10. Luttrell to Aylmer, June 5. The ten years' truce between Charles V. and Francis I. was concluded June 28, so that Lord Butler must refer to some earlier negotiations.

[207] Brabazon, Aylmer, and Alen to Cromwell, July 24, 1538.

[208] Grey to the King, July 26, 1538. Brabazon, Aylmer, and Alen to Cromwell, Aug. 22. Information against Lord Leonard Grey, Oct. 1840, in Carew.

[209] Grey's account has been pretty closely followed; see his letter to the King, July 26, 1538.

[210] For unfavourable strictures on Grey's journey see Brabazon, Aylmer, and Alen to Cromwell, Aug. 22; articles by the Earl of Ormonde in S.P., vol. iii. p. 77; Thomas Agard to Cromwell, July 25, 1538. Agard blames Grey for taking cannon with him; he risked them of course.

[211] Brabazon, Aylmer, and Alen to Cromwell, Aug. 22.

[212] Articles by the Earl of Ormonde, S.P., vol. iii. p. 80.

[213] Brabazon, &c., as above.

[214] Grey to Cromwell, Oct. 31, 1538, in Carew.

[215] Ibid. The 'islands' referred to seem to be the peninsula of Ards, subsequent attempts to colonise which did not meet with much success. The islets in Lough Strangford are very small.

[216] St. Leger and others to Cromwell, Nov. 15, 1537, and Jan. 2, 1538.

[217] J. Alen to St. Leger, S.P., vol. ii. p. 486, 1537. St. Leger and others to Cromwell, Jan. 2, 1538; to Wriothesley, Feb. 11. The King to St. Leger and others, Jan. 17. The Commissioners sailed from Dublin in April.

[218] Interrogatories, with Aylmer and Alen's answers, as to Paulet's conversations, are printed in the S.P., vol. ii. pp. 551-553.

[219] Alen and others to Cromwell, Jan. 18, 1539. In his letter to Cromwell of Sept. 8, 1539, R. Cowley says Saintloo did no service, but kept in a corner like a King, used every kind of extortion, and took no notice of the universal outcry against him. 'Such a liberty,' says Cowley, 'is more like to induce them to plain rebellion than to any civil order.'

[220] Council of Ireland to Cromwell, Feb. 8, 1539, and also the letter of Jan. 18, and Browne to Cromwell, Feb. 16. The letter of Jan. 18 says 'all the Bishops of Munster' were summoned.

[221] The Council of Ireland to Cromwell, Jan. 18 and Feb. 8. Both letters are signed by Alen, Aylmer, and Brabazon; the second by Browne also.

[222] Grey to the King, May 9, 1539; Walter Cowley to Cromwell, Feb. 18, 1539; Thomas Wusle, Constable of Carrick Fergus, to Laurans, Constable of Ardglass, March 1539, in Carew; confession of Connor More O'Connor, servant to young Gerald, April 17, 1539; Brabazon to Cromwell, May 26; Gerot Fleming to Cromwell, April 27.

[223] Grey to Cromwell, June 30, 1539.

[224] Alen to Cromwell, July 10, 1539, and the documents printed in the notes; Robert Cowley to Cromwell, Sept. 8; Archbishop Browne to Cromwell, Feb. 16, 1539.

[225] Four Masters, 1539; R. Cowley to Cromwell, Sept. 8.

[226] Four Masters and Annals of Lough Cé, 1539; Book of Howth; R. Cowley to Cromwell, Sept. 8, 1539. In a letter to Cromwell, dated April 20, 1540 (in Carew), the Dowager Countess of Ormonde mentions the service of her niece's husband Gerald Fleming. In his note to the Four Masters O'Donovan says roundly that Stanihurst's account is 'fabricated;' but it is corroborated by an Irish MS., for which see Shirley's History of Monaghan, p. 36.

[227] R. Cowley to Cromwell, Sept. 8, 1539; James, Earl of Ormonde, and Ossory to Cromwell, Oct. 19; to Wriothesley, Oct. 21.

[228] Ormonde to Cromwell, Dec. 20, 1539; Travers to Mr. Fitzwilliam, same date. Dromaneen is five miles above Mallow.

[229] Lord Deputy and Council to the King, Feb. 13, 1540.

[230] Brereton to Essex, May 17, 1540 and May 7; Council of Ireland to Essex, April 30; Ormonde to Essex, May 1; Alen and Brabazon to Essex, May 8; the King's letter to Grey and Brereton is dated April 1. For the dispute about Travers, see Council of Ireland to Cromwell, March 14.

[231] The charges against Grey may be gathered from the Articles, &c., by Aylmer and Alen in S.P., vol. iii. No. 237, and their letter to St. Leger, June 27, 1538; Ormonde to Cowley, July 16 and 20; the Council of Ireland's Articles, Oct. 1540; Stanihurst. The Articles of the Council seem to have been carefully scrutinised by Wriothesley. In his letter to the King of July 20, 1540, O'Neill says Grey, 'guerras et contentiones in partibus istis seminavit sui lucrandi causâ.' On June 20, 1538, Lord Butler writes to Cowley that 'our governor threatens every man after such a tyrannous sort, as no man dare speak openly or repugn against his appetite;' and on July 20, his father says, 'the Lord Deputy is occupied without the advice of the Council, for his own private lucre and gain.' On the trial of Strafford Oliver St. John—the man who said that 'stone-dead hath no fellow'— cited Grey's case as a precedent for trying in England treasons committed in Ireland. Grey was Viscount Grane in Ireland, but he was declared no peer, and tried as a commoner in England; see Howell's State Trials. As to Grey's private hoards, see a letter from R. Cowley to Norfolk, printed by Ellis, second series, No. 126, and wrongly placed under 1538; it belongs to 1540.

[Pg 247]

CHAPTER XIII.

1540 and 1541.

The O'Neills. Scottish intrigues.

With the usual plundering inroads on the Pale Brereton was able to cope; and the greater chieftains were quiet, for Gerald of Kildare was safe. O'Donnell, who may have resented his treatment by Lady Eleanor, readily reverted to his father's policy, and no difficulty was made about his pardon. O'Neill held aloof, but again professed himself ready to come to Carrick Bradagh. Again he failed to appear, and pleaded that he dared not approach Dundalk through fear of Grey's manifest treachery. He offered to come to Magennis's Castle at Narrowater, a beautiful spot near the mouth of the Newry river and the foot of the Mourne Mountains. Brereton agreed, and a meeting at last took place. O'Neill declared his readiness to perform all that he had promised to Skeffington, to send a trusty messenger to the King, and to leave pardon or punishment for the past to the royal discretion. Till the answer came he was content to be at peace with the Government, and to keep his neighbours quiet. He was at this time intriguing with Scotland, and his secretary was actually at Edinburgh. Cromwell had received information that eight Irishmen had been with the Scottish King, to whom they had brought sealed letters from the principal chiefs, containing offers to take him as their lord and to do homage to him. It was even said that James meditated an invasion of Ireland in person. O'Neill probably waited for the result of these negotiations before sending a confidential servant with a letter to Henry. He begged the King not to send his enemies into his country, where Grey had, as he affirmed, sowed dissensions from selfish motives. He was willing to do anything he was asked unless the new Lord Deputy should prove very[Pg

248] extortionate, and he advised the King not to waste his money in Ulster. Henry answered graciously, and acknowledged some trifling presents which accompanied the chief's letter. Future royal favours, his Majesty was careful to point out, must depend on performance and not on promises. Pardon in the meantime would be granted for the heinous offences committed.[232]

Murder of James FitzMaurice, Earl of Desmond, 1540.

With the sea at hand, and Ormonde ever ready to help him, it was supposed that James FitzMaurice would be able to maintain himself as Earl of Desmond. At first he confined himself to Kerrycurrihy and Imokilly, but after three months he was tempted to go inland towards the Limerick district, in which James Fitzjohn's strength lay. Near Fermoy he was set upon and murdered by his rival's brother, who had earned the title of 'Maurice of the Burnings.' James Fitzjohn, who now believed himself to be undisputed Earl, at once repaired to Youghal, where he was well received and joined by all the chiefs who had lately made such professions to Grey and Ormonde. The garrison had, through over-confidence, withdrawn to Waterford. Gerald of Kildare had just escaped to France, and the web of policy which the English Government had cast over both branches of the Geraldines was torn to pieces for the time.[233]

James Fitzjohn is allowed to succeed him.

There was no evidence of James Fitzjohn's complicity in his cousin's murder, and Ormonde received the King's authority to pardon him, if he could be brought to promise good[Pg 249] behaviour. He preferred to ally himself with O'Brien, and pleaded that Irish confederacies were too strong for him to withstand. To gain his confidence Ormonde risked his own person in the Desmond country for two nights, and passed right through it to parley with O'Brien, who refused to listen to anything. But Desmond would not show himself, and Ormonde then went for a few weeks to England. On his return he found that little harm had been done, and this he attributed solely to O'Brien having been out of his mind. But Desmond claimed the credit of holding his hand. 'In like,' he wrote to Ormonde, 'I desire you, according to my full trust, for to bring me in the King's favour the best ye can; and in case that his Grace will so accept me, I trust we shall both be able to do his Grace acceptable service according to our duty.' On his return from England Ormonde at once resumed negotiations, and St. Leger had been scarcely a month in Ireland before he received friendly letters both from Desmond and O'Brien.[234]

Fall of Cromwell. St. Leger is made Deputy, 1541.

In the meantime Cromwell's head had fallen on the scaffold to which he had sent so many better men. Grey was in the Tower, and Henry found time to appoint a new Lord Deputy. He chose Sir Anthony St. Leger, who already knew much of Ireland, and whose temper would at least save him from his predecessor's chief faults. Sir Patrick Barnewall of Fieldston, an eminent lawyer, had lately enumerated the qualities desirable in a chief governor, and in so doing had drawn a heavy indictment against the last holder of that high office. The King, he said, should provide a Deputy 'faithful, sure, and constant in his promise, and in especial to any concluding of peace; and that he shall be such a person that shall have more regard to his own honour and promise than to any covetous desire of preys or booties of cattle; and that he shall make no wilful war, and when war is made upon a good ground, that the same be followed till a[Pg 250] perfect conclusion thereof be taken, and not left at large, nor yet to take a faint peace; and that the said Deputy shall not be in weighty causes counselled nor guided by such persons as be openly known to be ill-doers, or apt adherents of the ill-doers in their ill-doings against the King's Majesty and his Grace's subjects in time past, for the same hath and may hinder.' In selecting St. Leger, Henry was probably actuated in part by such motives, and in part by hopes of an increased income. With him were associated as Revenue Commissioners Thomas Walsh, Baron, and John Mynne, Auditor of the English Exchequer, and William Cavendish, Treasurer of the Court of Augmentations; but the viceregal authority was not in any way impaired.[235]

St. Leger's policy. The Kavanaghs.

St. Leger seems clearly to have grasped the idea so often put forth and so often neglected, that the pacification of Ireland must begin with the neighbourhood of the Pale, and that distant expeditions were neither lightly to be undertaken nor abandoned without attaining their object. He resolved at once to punish those who had attacked the Pale at Grey's departure, and he turned first to the Kavanaghs. Ormonde had lately ravaged Idrone for a week and taken hostages, reporting that all the mischief was done by Donnell MacCahir, 'who, having nothing to lose, adhereth to Tirlogh O'Toole.' St. Leger now ravaged the territory far and wide, and at the end of ten days the chief came in and submitted. He renounced the name of MacMurrough, and agreed to hold his lands of the Crown by knight-service. After the manner of Deputies in their early days of office, St. Leger believed that he had really made a final settlement. The Kavanaghs were ready enough to make promises, and even to boast their descent from the man who first brought the English to Ireland; but St. Leger was destined to have plenty of trouble with them.[236]

[Pg 251]

The O'Mores and O'Connors, and their neighbours.

Offaly had been so often devastated that the new Lord Deputy could have little to do in that way; but the adjoining district of Leix had been more fortunate, and its turn now came. The O'Doynes, O'Dempseys, and others were separated by St. Leger's policy from O'Connor, whom it was proposed to bridle by establishing fortified posts at Kinnegad in Westmeath, at Kishevan in Kildare, at Castle Jordan in Meath, and at Ballinure in what is now the King's County. A letter arrived from the King with orders to expel O'Connor from his country and to give it to his brother Cahir, if he would behave in a civilised manner, as he had often promised to do. The incorrigible rebel should be made an example to all Ireland by his perpetual exile and just punishment. But this could not be honourably done, for Brereton had made a peace during the difficult days that followed Grey's recall, and O'Connor, whose submission was of the humblest, had done no harm since then. St. Leger indeed showed some inconsistency in the matter, for he thought in September that O'Connor could never be trusted, and in November he advised his restoration to favour. Not only was it proposed to give him a grant of his land, but also to raise him to the peerage as Baron of Offaly, an ancient honour in the eclipsed family of Kildare.[237]

The O'Tooles.

No tribe had hurt the Pale more than the O'Tooles, who could boast of giving a famous saint to Irish hagiology. Originally possessed of the southern half of Kildare, they had been driven into the Wicklow Mountains by Walter de Riddlesford in the early days of the Anglo-Norman occupation. They were afterwards known as lords of Imaile, a small district between Baltinglass and Glendalough, and at one time held nearly all the northern half of Wicklow. The Earls of Kildare expelled them from Powerscourt, and latterly they had led a very precarious life. True children of the mist, they either bivouacked in the open or crept into wretched huts to which Englishmen hesitated to give the[Pg 252] name of houses. They cultivated no land, but levied 300l. a year from their civilised neighbours, partly in black-rent and partly in sheer plunder. The actual chief was Tirlogh O'Toole, who professed himself anxious to mend his ways, and offered to go to England and beg his lands of Henry himself. There was something chivalrous in Tirlogh; for when Grey was hard pressed by the northern confederacy he sent him word that 'since all those great lords were against him he would surely be with him, but whensoever they were all at peace, then he alone would be at war with him and the English Pale.' This simple-minded warrior had kept his word, and he now begged St. Leger to write to Norfolk, in the belief that the Duke would let him want nothing 'when he knew that he had become an Englishman.' In return for his undertaking to forego his exactions and to wear the English dress, he asked for a grant of the district of Fercullen, comprising Powerscourt and about twenty square miles of land, chiefly rocks and woods, but with some fertile spots. St. Leger was anxious to grant Tirlogh's terms, for the lands actually held by him were worthless and would never pay to reclaim, while the O'Tooles were obliged to live on the Pale. The hardy mountaineers had nothing to lose, and they prevented land enough to support 2,000 inhabitants from being cultivated at all. The Lord Deputy accordingly sent over the wild man with a special recommendation to Norfolk, whose Irish experience made him a natural mediator. Tirlogh was so poor that St. Leger had to lend him 20l. for his journey, and he could not even afford decent clothes. 'It shall appear to your Majesty,' wrote the Irish Government, 'that this Tirlogh is but a wretched person and a man of no great power, neither having house to put his head in, nor yet money in his purse to buy him a garment, yet may he well make 200 or 300 men.'[238]

Tirlogh O'Toole at Court.
Tirlogh remained nearly a month at Court, where he was[Pg 253] very well treated; perhaps Henry remembered how well Hugh O'Donnell had requited the kindness shown to him long since. The grant was authorised, and care was taken to make such a fair division among the clansmen as would prevent internal dissensions. Tirlogh became the King's tenant by knight-service at a rent of five marks yearly, and his brother Art Oge, a man of some ability, was gratified with a grant of Castle Kevin. Henry desired that this case should form a precedent, and that in future chiefs received to peace and favour should be treated with on the same basis as the O'Tooles. In doing this he followed the advice of some of his wisest councillors at home. Cranmer, Audeley, and Sadleir did not believe in the possibility of a thorough conquest, and rightly considered that Ireland would be best gained by fair dealing. Pedants and flatterers might argue that the King was actually entitled to most of the land, that the Irish were intruders, and that grants to them were derogatory to the royal dignity. To this it was answered that the intrusions were of very old date, that future rebellions would be more easily punished when they involved a breach of contract, and that the Crown must gain by the mere acknowledgment of its title. The O'Tooles at all events seem to have given up plundering the Pale, and they make little further figure in history. But they could not give up fighting among themselves. The favoured Tirlogh had a grudge against one of his clansmen, and pursued him daily in spite

of orders from the Government. At last the threatened man caught his persecutor asleep, and in the early morning killed him and all his companions; 'and we think,' wrote the Lord Deputy and Council, 'the other would have done to him likewise, if he might have gotten him at like advantage.' Tirlogh left no legitimate children, but St. Leger nevertheless recommended that his son Brian should be allowed to succeed him.[239]

Proposed military order. The King vetoes it.

Finding Leinster in an unusually promising state, the[Pg 254] Irish Council hit upon a strange device for keeping it permanently quiet. In the previous century Thomas, Earl of Kildare, had established the Brotherhood of St. George, an armed confraternity, whose thirteen officers, chosen from among the loyal gentlemen of Dublin, Kildare, Meath, and Louth, elected their own captain annually, but were paid by the State. It was found necessary to dissolve this body by an Act of Parliament, passed in 1494. Its object had been the defence of the Pale against Irish enemies and English rebels. It was now proposed to erect a new order, not named after St. George, but holding its great ceremony on St. George's day. It was to consist of a Grand Master and twelve pensioners, with salaries amounting in the aggregate to 1,000l. The majority were to be Irishmen of family, who might be kept out of mischief by fear of losing their pensions. After seven years, promotion was to depend on knowing English, or having spent two years in the public service in England; the object being to induce Irish gentlemen to cross the Channel and learn manners. As vacancies occurred the persons chosen were to be bound 'not to have any wife or wives.' The Council nominated Brabazon to be first Grand Master; but Ormonde put forth a list of his own, and preferred his brother Richard to the highest place. The Council also proposed to make a pensioner of Lord Kilcullen, and to place him in the castle of Clonmore, which had belonged to his family, but which the King had granted to Ormonde. The Earl naturally ignored this claim, and there were other differences in the rival lists. The Council suggested elaborate machinery by which the Order might be made to work for the reformation of Leinster; but St. Leger does not appear to have been a party to the scheme, and perhaps opposed it quietly. The King, who had just abolished the great military Order, had no idea of creating another, though its patron saint should be St. George instead of St. John. 'We do in no wise,' he said, 'like any part of your device in that behalf.' By minding their business and doing what they were told his Majesty hoped that they[Pg 255] would ultimately succeed in reforming Leinster 'without the new erection of any such fantasies.'[240]

An arrangement is made with Desmond.

James Fitzjohn being now necessarily acknowledged Earl of Desmond, one of St. Leger's first cares was to obtain his submission. Satisfied at last that no treachery was intended, Desmond agreed to meet the Lord Deputy at Cashel. Passing through Carlow and Kilkenny, St. Leger was joined by Ormonde, who took care that the viceregal retinue should be well treated on the journey; but Desmond at first held aloof, and demanded that the chief of the Butlers should give himself up as a hostage before he trusted himself in English hands. This was refused; but Archbishop Browne, Travers, the Master of the Ordnance, and the Deputy's brother Robert consented to run the risk. Desmond then appeared, and said he was ready to do all that loyalty demanded. The proceedings were adjourned to Sir Thomas Butler's house at Cahir, and there Desmond signed a solemn notarial instrument, by which he fully acknowledged the King's supremacy in Church and State. 'I do,' he said, 'utterly deny and forsake the Bishop of Rome, and his usurped primacy and authority, and shall with all my power resist and repress the same and all that shall by any means use and maintain the same.' He renounced the pretensions of his family not to attend Parliament or enter any walled town. He agreed to abide by and to enforce the King's decision as to the Kildare estates, and to pay all such taxes as were paid in the territories of Ormonde, Delvin, and other noblemen of like condition. He constituted himself the defender of the corporate towns, and gave up all claims to the allegiance of the Munster Englishry, with a partial reservation as to men of his own blood, who held their lands under him or his ancestors. Finally, he agreed to send his son to be educated in England. This was Gerald, the ill-starred youth whose folly and vanity were destined to work the final ruin of his House. The Archbishop of Cashel and the Bishops of Limerick and Emly witnessed the instrument, and the manner of the submission was as[Pg 256] satisfactory as a Tudor could wish. 'In presence,' wrote St. Leger to the King, 'of MacWilliam, O'Connor, and divers other Irish gentlemen, to the number of 200 at the least, he kneeled down before me and most humbly delivered his said submission, desiring me to deliver unto him his said pardon, granted by your Majesty; affirming that it was more glad to him to be so reconciled to your favours, than to have any worldly treasure; protesting that no earthly cause should make him from henceforth swerve from your Majesty's obedience. And after that done, I delivered to him your said most gracious pardon, which he most joyfully accepted.' He was immediately sworn of the Council, and St. Leger asked the King's indulgence for having done this without warrant. Care was also taken to prevent a renewal of the quarrel between the new Privy Councillor and Ormonde, who had married the heiress-general of a former Earl of Desmond, and had thus large and indefinite claims on the family estates. The rivals bound themselves in 4,000l. to promote cross-marriages between their children, and to keep the peace. The claims of Ormonde through his wife were nevertheless destined in the next generation to deluge Munster in blood.[241]

Dutiful attitude of Desmond and O'Brien.

Desmond accompanied St. Leger to Kilmallock, 'where, I think, none of your Grace's Deputies came this hundred years before,' and treated him hospitably, openly declaring that he was ready if the Deputy wished it to go to London to see the King. O'Brien came peacefully to Limerick, complaining chiefly that he was not allowed to bridge the Shannon nor to exercise jurisdiction over friendly tribes on the left bank. St. Leger promised him perpetual war unless he would yield on both points, believing that he could do little harm without the concurrence of Desmond, of the Clanricarde Burkes, or of Donogh O'Brien. He was given till Shrovetide to consult his friends, and at last decided to keep quiet and to send agents to watch over his interests in Parliament. A pardon was issued under the Great Seal of Ireland, and towards the[Pg 257] end of the year O'Brien spontaneously addressed a very dutiful letter to the King, begging personal as well as official forgiveness for his many sins. 'My mind,' he said, 'is never satisfied till I have made the same submission to your Grace's own person, whom I most desire to see above all creatures on earth living, now in mine old days; which sight I doubt not but shall prolong my life.'[242]

MacWilliam Burke and MacGillapatrick.

MacWilliam Burke of Clanricarde and MacGillapatrick professed anxiety for the royal favour, and accompanied St. Leger on his tour. He prescribed an earldom for the former, a barony for the latter, and Parliament-robes and other fine clothes for both; in the belief that titles and little acts of civility would weigh more with these rude men than a display of force. He himself had given MacWilliam a silver-gilt cup, and in Limerick Desmond had from vanity or policy worn 'gown, jacket, doublet, hose, shirts, caps, and a velvet riding coat,' from the Lord Deputy's wardrobe. It was very important to conciliate MacWilliam, who could always prevent a junction of the O'Briens and O'Donnells. MacGillapatrick soon afterwards covenanted with the King to live civilly, to act loyally, and to hold his lands of the Crown by knight-service. MacWilliam wrote a letter to Henry confessing and lamenting that his family had degenerated, and belied their English blood, 'which have been brought to Irish and disobedient rule by reason of marriage and nurseing with those Irish, sometime rebels, near adjoining to me.' He placed himself and all his possessions unreservedly in the King's hands, but seems to have let it be known that he would like to be an Earl. Henry refused this unless the repentant Norman would come to Court, but he offered a barony or viscounty without any condition.[243]

Parliament of 1541.

Early in 1541 St. Leger received authority to summon a Parliament. The composition of the House of Commons is[Pg 258] uncertain, for no list of members is extant between 1382 and 1559. In the former of those years eighteen counties or districts and eleven towns were represented. In the latter, ten counties and twenty-eight cities and boroughs returned two members each. Through the action of the royal prerogative the number was progressively increased until the 300 of the eighteenth century was reached. In St. Leger's time the Upper House was the more important of the two, and was attended by four archbishops, nineteen bishops, and twenty temporal peers, of whom Desmond was one. Among the temporal peers was Rawson, late prior of Kilmainham and chief of the Irish Hospitallers, who had just been created Viscount Clontarf. There were four new Barons—Edmund Butler Lord Dunboyne, MacGillapatrick Lord Upper Ossory, Oliver Plunkett Lord Louth, and William Bermingham Lord Carbery. Richard le Poer had been created Baron of Curraghmore six years before. Besides the peers there were present in Dublin Donough O'Brien, MacWilliam Burke, O'Reilly, Cahir MacArt Kavanagh, Phelim Roe O'Neill of Clandeboye, and some of the O'Mores. O'Brien sent agents or deputies. These and other important persons were present at the passing of the Bill which made Henry King of Ireland; but they had no votes and were not considered as members of Parliament.

Henry VIII. is made King of Ireland.

Parliament met on Monday, June 13; but the Munster lords had not yet arrived, and the solemn mass was postponed until Thursday, the feast of Corpus Christi. By that day all had assembled, and they rode in state to the place of meeting. Most of the peers wore their robes. On the morrow the Commons chose a Speaker in the person of Sir Thomas Cusack, a rising lawyer, who afterwards obtained the highest professional honours. He made a set speech at the bar of the Lords, praising the King for many things, but especially for having extirpated the Bishop of Rome's usurped power. Ormonde then gave the substance of what had been said in Irish, to the 'great contentation of those lords who could not understand English.' At the sitting of the House of Lords on the following day, St. Leger proposed that Henry VIII. should be[Pg 259] King of Ireland. A Bill to that effect was read a first time in English and Irish, and was received with acclamation. It was then and there read a second and a third time, and all the Lords subscribed it, lest they should thereafter be tempted to deny their consents. The Bill was then sent down to the

Commons and read three times, and on the morrow, in presence of both Houses, St. Leger pronounced the royal consent—'no less,' he wrote, 'to my comfort, than to be risen again from death to life, that I so poor a wretch should, by your excellent goodness, be put to that honour, that in my time your Majesty should most worthily have another Imperial Crown.' This rapid action is in striking contrast to the long and acrimonious discussion excited by a change of the royal style in our own times.[244]

King and Pope. The royal style.

The question of style was one of considerable practical importance, for the friars had sedulously encouraged the popular notion that the real sovereignty rested in the Pope, and that the King of England was only a sort of viceroy. Alen had recommended the assumption of the royal title four years before; and both Staples and St. Leger had given the like advice. Parliamentary sanction had now been given to the change, and those who acknowledged English law could hardly dispute the principle involved. In the later struggles of Irish parties the contest between the Crown and the Tiara was constantly revived, and the ghost of the controversy is sometimes seen even in our own times. Less than two months before the meeting of St. Leger's Parliament, Paul III. had written to prepare O'Neill for the arrival of a detachment of the Company of Jesus, and before its dissolution the first Jesuits had landed. But for the moment no opposition was visible. The proclamation of the new style was joyously celebrated by the citizens of Dublin. Salutes were fired. Bonfires were lit. Wine casks were broached in the streets; and there was much feasting in private houses. An amnesty was granted to criminals, except traitors, murderers, and[Pg 260] ravishers; but prisoners for debt were not released, lest any creditor should be defrauded. There was some fear lest it should be supposed that the Irish Parliament had elected their King instead of merely declaring his just hereditary right; and many letters were exchanged on the subject. Finally the new style was settled as follows:—'Henry VIII., by the Grace of God, King of England, France, and Ireland, Defender of the Faith, and of the Church of England, and also of Ireland, in earth the Supreme Head.' A new Great Seal had to be sent from England, since there was no competent engraver in Dublin. And thus, after the lapse of nearly four centuries, did Henry II.'s successor repudiate all obligations to Rome, and declare himself King of Ireland by right divine.[245]

Regulations for Munster.

The other Acts passed had no political significance, but followed pretty closely recent domestic legislation in England. After a session of little more than five weeks, Parliament was prorogued with the intention of convoking it again at Limerick. Before the two Houses dispersed, elaborate regulations, which were not embodied in an Act of Parliament, were drawn up for Munster, Thomond, and Connaught. There was no chance of enforcing these ordinances, but some of them are very good. Laymen and minors were disabled from holding ecclesiastical benefices; kernes were ordered to be treated as vagabonds, unless some lord would give bail for them; heads of families were declared responsible for damage done by younger members. Highway robbery and rape were pronounced capital; but by a strange anomaly robberies of above fourteen pence were made punishable by the loss of one ear[Pg 261] for the first offence and of the other ear for the second, while death was fixed as the penalty for the third. A system of fines was promulgated for homicides, invasions, and spoils. The Irish jurisprudence was thus acknowledged, but only as a matter of fact, for the chiefs who indulged in open lawlessness were generally beyond the reach of the law. Saffron shirts were forbidden under penalties, and the permissible quantity of linen was carefully prescribed for each rank. A lord might have twenty cubits, his vassals eighteen, and his servants twelve. A kerne was allowed sixteen and an agricultural labourer ten. Stringent but useless limitations were imposed on coyne and livery, the fact being that great men had usually no other means of protecting their districts. Ormonde was appointed chief executor of these ordinances for Tipperary, Waterford, and Kilkenny, and Desmond for the other counties of Munster. Both were to command the assistance of the Archbishop of Cashel and to be entitled to one-third of all fines levied by them, two-thirds being payable to the King. The regulations for Thomond and Connaught were the same as for Munster, but they were probably even less regarded.[246]

FOOTNOTES:

[232] For the intrigues with Scotland, see Brereton to Essex, May 17, 1540, and the note, S.P. vol. iii., and Layton to Essex, S.P. vol. v. p. 178; O'Neill's letter to Henry was dated July 20; the King's letter to O'Neill is dated Sept. 7—'literas vestras unà cum munusculis grato animo accepimus.' For O'Donnell's submission, see Henry's letter to him of Aug. 20, acknowledging his letters 'per dilectum nobis Johannem Cappis, mercatorem Bristoliensem.' St. Leger brought over O'Neill's pardon.

[233] In a letter to Cromwell of December 23, 1539, in Carew, William Wise, of Waterford, almost foretold the murder, which (according to Mr. Graves's pedigree in the Irish Archæological Journal) took place on March 19 following. The pedigree says the murder was in Kerry, but other accounts, which are evidently correct, point to the neighbourhood of Fermoy or Mitchelstown. Council of Ireland to the King, April 4, 1540; Archdall's Lodge; Russell. O'Daly (chap. xii.) admits that the murder was premeditated.

[234] Ormonde to Brereton from Kilkenny, May 14; to the King, July 26, from Waterford. He had been to England and back between these dates. Desmond to Ormonde, July 8; Lord Deputy St. Leger to the King, Sept. 12, 1540.

[235] P. Barnewall to Essex, May 19; Instructions to St. Leger and the others, and to St. Leger alone, S.P., Aug. 16 and 20. St. Leger landed Aug. 12, 1540.

[236] Walter Cowley to St. Leger, March 15, 1541, 'from the border of Cahir, MacArt's country.' St. Leger to the King, Sept. 12; Council of Ireland to the King, Sept. 22.

[237] Council of Ireland to the King, Sept. 22, 1540; the King to the Lord Deputy and Council, Sept. 7 and 8; Lord Deputy and Council to the King, Nov. 13.

[238] For the O'Tooles, see O'Donovan's Book of Rights, and his notes to the Four Masters, 1180 and 1376; and Lord Deputy and Council to the King Nov. 14, 1540, with the notes. These people had suffered from the Kildare family as much as the Macgregors did from the Campbells. This may partly explain Tirlogh's unwillingness to aid in restoring Gerald.

[239] The King to the Lord Deputy and Council, No. 332 in the S.P., and his very important minute of March 26, 1541; Lord Deputy and Council to the King, Dec. 7, 1542, and May 15, 1543.

[240] For the scheme see S.P., vol. iii. No. 330; the King's answer is No. 337.

[241] St. Leger to the King, Feb. 21, 1541. The submission was signed at Cahir, Jan. 16. For the names of the notaries and of the chief spectators, see Carew, vol. i. No. 153.

[242] St. Leger to the King, Feb. 21, 1541; list of those who attended Parliament, 1541, in S.P., vol. iii. p. 307; O'Brien to the King, vol. iii., No. 352.

[243] St. Leger to the King, Feb. 21, 1541; MacWilliam to the King, March 12, 1541; MacGillapatrick's submission, &c., S.P., vol. iii., No. 336; the King to MacWilliam, May 1.

[244] St. Leger to the King, June 26, 1541; Lord Deputy and Council to the King, June 28; printed Statutes, 33 Henry VIII.; Lodge's Parliamentary Register; Parliamentary lists in Tracts Relating to Ireland, No. 2.

[245] Alen to St. Leger in 1537, S.P., vol. ii., No. 182; Staples to St. Leger, June 17, 1538; Lord Deputy and Council to the King, Dec. 30, 1540. The proclamation of the King's style is in Carew, vol. i., No. 158. The author of the Aphorismical Discovery, who wrote about 1650, says Henry 'revolted from his obedience to the Holy See' by assuming the royal title. There is an abstract of the King's title to Ireland in Carew, vol. i., No. 156; Adrian's grant is mentioned as one of seven titles, some fabulous, some historical. For the proceedings in Dublin, see St. Leger's letters already cited, June 26 and 28, 1541; for the style itself, see the King's letter in S.P., vol. iii., No. 361; for the Seal, see Lord Deputy and Council to the King, June 2, 1542, and Henry's answer.

[246] See the ordinances in Carew, vol. i., No. 157.

[Pg 262]

CHAPTER XIV.

1541 TO THE CLOSE OF THE REIGN OF HENRY VIII.

The O'Carrolls.

The attendance of Irishmen during the session of Parliament was not altogether barren of immediate results. Fergananim O'Carroll, chief of Ely, having become blind, was murdered in Clonlisk Castle by Teige, the son of his old rival Donough, with the help of some of the Molloys. The claimants to the vacant succession voluntarily submitted to the arbitration of the Lord Deputy and Council, and a curious award was given. According to Irish law John O'Carroll, as the eldest, would have been the natural chief. He was set aside as unfit to rule, but received his lands rent free and forty cows annually out of the cattle-tribute payable to the chief. Fergananim's son Teige was also pronounced incompetent, but was nevertheless established as ruler of half the country by way of propitiating Desmond, who was his uncle by marriage. Calvagh or Charles O'Carroll was made lord of the other half, and it was provided that if either procured the other's death he should forfeit all to the sons of the deceased.[247]

Submission of O'Donnell, 1541.

Soon after the prorogation St. Leger went to Cavan to meet O'Donnell. Leaving his boats on Lough Erne, the chieftain came boldly to the appointed place with a dozen followers, and made little difficulty about the terms of peace. He agreed to serve the King on all great hostings, to attend the next Parliament or send duly authorised deputies, to hold his land of the Crown, and to take any title that might be given him. He not only renounced the usurped primacy and authority of Rome, but promised industriously and diligently to expel, eject, and root out from his country all adherents of the Pope, or else to coerce and constrain them to submit to[Pg 263] the King and his successors. He more than once asked to be made Earl of Sligo, and to have Parliament-robes as well as 'that golden instrument or chain which noblemen wear on their necks.' Henry was willing to create O'Donnell Earl of Tyrconnell, but the creation was deferred until the reign of James I.[248]

St. Leger chastises the O'Neills.

O'Neill still refused to come to Dundalk, or in any way to submit to the Lord Deputy. He was, he said, waiting to hear from the King, and he made the curious complaint that St. Leger would not let him send hawks as presents to his Majesty. Diplomacy failing, the Lord Deputy prepared for an invasion of Ulster. He was joined by O'Donnell, O'Hanlon, Magennis, MacMahon, who had lately made submission in the usual form, Phelim Roe O'Neill and Neill Connelagh O'Neill, nephews and opponents of the chief of Tyrone; by the Savages of Ards; and by many others, both English and Irish. Twenty-two days were spent in destroying corn and butter; but no enemy appeared, and the cattle had been driven off into the woods. Meanwhile O'Neill tried the bold but not uncommon experiment of attacking the Pale in the absence of its defenders. The new Lord Louth handled the local force so well that the invaders were ignominiously routed, while O'Donnell ravaged not only Tyrone but a great part of Fermanagh, the very islands in Lough Erne being ransacked by his flotilla.[249]

Success of a winter campaign.

After a month's respite St. Leger made a second raid, and this time captured some hundreds of cows and horses. Another month elapsed, and then a third attack brought O'Neill to his knees. He sent letters to Armagh in which he threw himself on the King's mercy, which he preferred to the Lord Deputy's, gave a son as hostage, and offered to come in person not only to Dundalk but to Drogheda. O'Neill had never been known[Pg 264] to give a hostage before, and great importance was attached to this. Three thousand kine besides horses and sheep were taken in spite of the natives, but not without much suffering on the part of the soldiers, who had to lie without tents on the wet ground. Many horses died, and many more were lamed. The pastime, as St. Leger called it, of a December campaign can never be very pleasant, but he proved, as Sidney proved afterwards, that it was the right way to subdue the O'Neills. There was not grass enough in the woods to keep the cattle alive, and when they came into the fields the soldiers easily captured them.[250]

Submission of O'Neill.

Ultimately O'Neill made a complete submission. He agreed to behave like the Earls of Ormonde and Desmond, praying only that he might not be forced to incur the danger and expense of attending any Parliament sitting to the west of the Barrow. He not only renounced the Pope, but promised to send back future bulls, if ecclesiastics already provided from Rome would do likewise.[251]

The Council advise the King to accept it.

The Council advised Henry to accept O'Neill's submission, seeing that his country was wide and difficult, and now so wasted as to be incapable of supporting an army. It might perhaps be possible to expel Con, but he would certainly be succeeded by a pretender as bad as himself, and extreme courses might lead to despair, and to a universal rebellion. They admitted that the winter war had been proved to be 'the destruction of any Irishmen,' but the loss of men and horses was great, and might lead to risings in other places.[252]

Henry's ideas about Ireland.

The King disliked the wholesale grants of land for small consideration, which were favoured by St. Leger. He rebuked his servants in Ireland for thinking too much of Irish[Pg 265] submissions, and here he saw more clearly than they did. He was now King in Ireland, and required a revenue in proportion. For that purpose he divided Irishmen into two classes, those who were within easy reach of his arm, and those who were not. The former were to be treated sternly, but the latter tenderly, 'lest by extreme demands they should revolt to their former beastliness.' The near neighbours were to be brought to the same terms as Tirlogh O'Toole. A proper rent was to be exacted, and knight-service insisted on for the sake of the wardships and liveries. In the obedient districts monastic lands were to be let on lease for the best possible rent. In more distant quarters the chiefs were to be coaxed into suppressing the religious houses by promising them leases on easy terms.[253]

Ireland at peace, 1542. Submission of many chiefs.

At the beginning of the year 1542 the Council were able to make the strange announcement that Ireland was at peace. They praised St. Leger for his diligence, patience, and justice, and for his liberal entertainment of those on whom, for the public good, it was necessary to make favourable impression. Following up his Dublin success, he now met Parliament again at Limerick, where the principal business was to make terms with the O'Briens. Murrough agreed to give up all claims to the territory of Owney Beg, a poor district lying under Slieve Phelim, which retains its reputation for turbulence to the present day. The possession of this tract had made him master of the western part of Limerick, whence he exacted a black-rent of 80l., and of Tipperary as far as Cashel. The whole country was waste through plunder and extortion, and no one could travel peaceably from Limerick to Waterford through fear of a gang of robbers called the 'old evil children,' who held a castle near the Shannon. Desmond expelled these brigands and handed over their hold to MacBrien Coonagh, who held it at his own expense for two years. St. Leger's observations during the session at Limerick led him to believe that little rent or tribute could be got out of the Irish. The sums promised to Grey were withheld on the ground that[Pg 266] promises had been forcibly extorted. By holding out hopes of gentler treatment, St. Leger brought them to accept his own much easier terms. Tipperary was assessed at 40l. yearly, Kilkenny at 40l., and Waterford at 10l. MacBrien Arra agreed to pay sixpence a year for each ploughland, and to furnish sixty gallowglasses for a month. MacBrien of Coonagh promised 5l., O'Kennedy and MacEgan in Ormonde 10l. each, O'Mulryan forty shillings and sixty gallowglasses for a month, and O'Dwyer eightpence for each ploughland and forty gallowglasses for a month. These sums are small, but seem larger when we reflect that the Government gave no consideration, either by keeping the peace or administering justice, and that the people were extremely poor.[254]

Further submissions.
Several months passed in negotiations with Irish chiefs with the general object of inducing them to submit, to pay rent, and to hold their lands by knight-service; forswearing Irish uses and exactions, and promising to live in a more civilised manner. These terms were accepted by Rory O'More, who had become chief of Leix by the death of his brother Kedagh, by MacDonnell, captain of O'Neill's gallowglasses, by O'Rourke, and by O'Byrne. All except the last named abjured the Pope, as did the MacQuillins, a family of Welsh extraction long settled in the Route, a district between the Bush and the Bann. The MacQuillins were always oppressed by the O'Cahans, who were supposed to be instigated by O'Donnell, and the valuable fishery of the Bann was a perennial source of dissension. Travers, who soon afterwards became lessee of Clandeboye, held this fishery on a Crown lease with the goodwill of the MacQuillins; but in spite of the O'Cahans, who annoyed his fishermen, St. Leger ordered him to help the weaker tribe. Coleraine was taken by Travers, and after a time the neighbours were reconciled, a pension of 10l. being given to each on condition of not molesting those who fished under royal licence. A curious submission was that of Hugh O'Kelly, who seems to have been chief of his[Pg 267] sept as well as hereditary Abbot of the Cistercians at Knockmoy, near Tuam. He renounced the Pope, promised to aid the Lord Deputy with a considerable force in Connaught, and with a smaller one in more distant parts, and to bring certain of his kinsmen to similar terms. In return he was to have custody of the monastic lands and of the rectory of Galway at a rent of 5l., paid down yearly in that town. As if to complete the anomaly this abbot-chieftain gave his son as a hostage for due performance.[255]

Desmond in favour at Court.
Desmond continued to behave loyally. St. Leger received him hospitably in Dublin, and advised the King to do the same. But Alen cautioned his Majesty not to be too free of his grants, especially in such important cases as Croom and Adare. The Chancellor preferred to give the Earl monastic lands in the Pale, by accepting which he would give hostages to the Crown, or among the wild Irish, who would thus certainly be losers though the King might be no direct gainer. Desmond did not linger long in the Court sunshine, for he took leave of the King in little more than a month from the date of his leaving Ireland. Either he really gained the royal goodwill, or Henry thought it wise to take St. Leger's advice, for he gave him money and clothes, made him the bearer of official despatches, and, after due inquiry, accepted his nominee to the bishopric of Emly.[256]

The Munster nobles submit. They abjure the Pope.
With a view to establish order in those portions of Munster under Desmond's influence, St. Leger visited Cork, where the notables readily obeyed his call. They abjured the Pope, and agreed to refer all differences to certain named arbitrators. Henceforth no one was to take the law into his own hands, but to complain to Desmond and to the

Bishops of Cork, Waterford, and Ross, who were to have the power of[Pg 268] summoning parties and witnesses, and of fining contumacious persons. Difficult cases were to be referred to the Lord Deputy and Council, and legal points reserved for qualified commissioners, whom the King was to send into Munster at Easter and Michaelmas. This was part of a scheme for establishing circuits in the southern province, but it was very imperfectly carried out during this and the three succeeding reigns. The state of the country seldom admitted of peaceful assizes, and martial law was too often necessary. The Munster gentry now promised to keep the peace, and to exact no black-rents from Cork or other towns. The Anglo-Norman element was represented by Lord Barrymore and his kinsmen, Barry Roe and Barry Oge, by Lord Roche, and by Sir Gerald MacShane of Dromana. The Irish parties to the contract were MacCarthy More, MacCarthy Reagh, MacCarthy of Muskerry, MacDonough MacCarthy of Duhallow, O'Callaghan, and O'Sullivan Beare. St. Leger himself, Desmond, Brabazon, Travers, and Sir Osborne Echingham, marshal of the army, represented the Crown.[257]

An Earldom for O'Neill.

O'Neill was at last induced to go to Court to receive the Earldom of Tyrone, the title chosen for him by the Irish Government. He would have preferred that of Ulster, but it was in the Crown, and the King refused to part with it. St. Leger did what he could to conciliate O'Neill by attention and hospitality while in Dublin, and rightly attached great importance to the fact that he was the first O'Neill who had ever gone to the King in England. He advised that he should be received with the greatest distinction.

'O'Neill,' say the 'Four Masters,' 'that is, Con the son of Con, went to the King of England, namely, Henry VIII.; and the King created O'Neill an Earl, and enjoined that he should not be called O'Neill any longer. O'Neill received great honour from the King on this occasion.' The acceptance of[Pg 269] a peerage was universally considered a condescension, if not a degradation, for the head of a family who claimed to be princes of Ulster in spite of the Crown. The Irish Government were willing that he should have Tyrone, 'but for the rule of Irishmen, which be at his Grace's peace, we think not best his Highness should grant any such thing to him as yet.'[258]

His submission.

It may be doubted whether O'Neill fully understood the scope of a document which was written in English, and which he signed with a mark; but the form of his submission to his 'most gracious sovereign lord' was as ample as even that sovereign lord could wish:—

'Pleaseth your most Excellent Majesty, I, O'Neill, one of your Majesty's most humble subjects of your realm of Ireland, do confess and acknowledge before your most Excellent Highness, that by ignorance, and for lack of knowledge of my most bounden duty of allegiance, I have most grievously offended your Majesty, for the which I ask your Grace here mercy and forgiveness, most humbly beseeching your Highness of your most gracious pardon; refusing my name and state, which I have usurped upon your Grace against my duty, and requiring your Majesty of your clemency to give me what name, state, title, land, or living it shall please your Highness, which I shall knowledge to take and hold of your Majesty's mere gift, and in all things do hereafter as shall beseem your most true and faithful subject. And God save your Highness.'[259]

He is created Earl of Tyrone. Special remainder.

One week after the delivery of this submission O'Neill was created Earl of Tyrone, with remainder to his son Matthew in tail male: Matthew being at the same time created Baron of Dungannon, with remainder to the eldest son of the Earl of Tyrone for the time being. This patent afterwards gave rise to infinite bloodshed. Con O'Neill certainly acknowledged Matthew as his heir apparent; but it was afterwards stated, not only that he was illegitimate, which might not have[Pg 270] mattered much, but that he was not Con's son at all. There was no doubt about the legitimacy of Shane, and that able savage consistently refused to acknowledge the limitations of the patent. Henry dealt liberally with the new Earl, paying 60l. for a gold chain such as O'Donnell had asked for, 65l. 10s. 2d. for creation fees and robes, and 100 marks as a present in ready money. 'The Queen's closet at Greenwich was richly hanged with cloth of Arras, and well strewed with rushes'—no more was then thought of even in a palace—and Tyrone was led in by the Earls of Hertford and Oxford, the latter of whom was summoned specially for the purpose. Viscount Lisle bore the new Earl's sword. Kneeling in the rushes, the descendant of Niall of the Nine Hostages submitted to be girt by the hands of Henry II.'s descendant. The King then gave him his patent, and he gave thanks in Irish, which his chaplain translated into English. Two of his neighbours, Donnell and Arthur Magennis, were knighted and received gifts from the King. A great dinner followed, to which the lords went in procession with trumpets blowing; and Tyrone carried his own patent. At second course Garter proclaimed the King's style and that of the new Earl. The herald who tells the story is careful to note that Tyrone gave twenty angels to Garter, 10l. to the College of Arms, and 40s. to the trumpeters, with other fees 'according to the old and ancient custom.' Next day Con was taken to pay his respects to the young Prince Edward, and he soon afterwards returned to Ireland.[260]

O'Brien created Earl of Thomond. Special remainder. MacWilliam Earl of Clanricarde. Knights.

Murrough O'Brien, his nephew Donough, MacWilliam of Clanricarde, and many other Irish gentlemen of note, went to Court during the summer of 1543. The three first were raised to the peerage in the same place and with the same ceremonies as O'Neill. Murrough O'Brien was created Earl of Thomond, with remainder to Donough, and Baron of Inchiquin in tail male. Donough's right to succeed as tanist thus[Pg 271] received official sanction. Donough was made Baron of Ibracken in tail male, and, curiously enough, the same patent created him Earl of Thomond for life in case he should survive his uncle. MacWilliam was created Earl of Clanricarde and Baron of Dunkellin. The Earls were introduced by Derby and Ormonde, the Barons by Clinton and Mountjoy, and the King gave a gold chain to each. The presence of the Scottish ambassadors, who had just concluded the abortive treaty of marriage between Edward and Mary Stuart, added to the interest of the ceremony; and no doubt Henry was glad to display his magnificence to the representatives of the poor northern kingdom. Macnamara, the most important person in Clare after the O'Briens, was knighted at the same time; as were O'Shaugnessy, chief of the country about Gort, and his neighbour O'Grady. Many other favours were conferred on these reclaimed Irishmen, and they all agreed to hold their lands of the King.[261]

The MacDonnells in Antrim.

The relations between England and Scotland were at this time much strained. The miserable and mysterious death of James V. left the northern kingdom a battle-field for contending factions, and the restless Beaton had full scope for his intrigues. The Hebridean settlers on the Ulster coast had always been troublesome, since they were ever ready to sell their swords to the highest bidder; and they now became really important. These settlements originated with the Bysets or Bissets, sometimes called Missets, who were said to be of Greek origin and who accompanied the Conqueror to England. They afterwards settled in Scotland, whence they were expelled in 1242 on suspicion of being concerned in the murder of an Earl of Athole, and condemned to take the cross. Preferring Ireland to Palestine, the exiles bought the island of Rathlin from Richard de Burgo, Earl of Ulster. About the close of the fourteenth century, Margaret, the heiress of the Bysets, married John More MacDonnell, a[Pg 272] grandson through his mother of Robert II. of Scotland. This lady is said to have known Richard II. during his second visit to Ireland, and to have recognised him afterwards, crazed and a refugee, in the island of Isla. By Margaret's marriage the estates of the Bysets passed to the MacDonnells, and a close intercourse was thenceforth kept up between the Western Isles and Antrim, which are never out of sight of one another in clear weather. Matrimonial alliances with O'Neills, O'Donnells, and O'Cahans were frequent, and the islemen established themselves so firmly that Rathlin was as late as 1617 claimed as part of Scotland. It has an assured place in Scottish history; for, among the rocks of black basalt and white chalk which give Rathlin its curious piebald look, stand the ruins of the castle where Robert Bruce is said to have learned the lesson of perseverance from a spider. In Henry VIII.'s time the head of the Irish MacDonnells was Alexander or Alaster, whose influence at Court had been great enough to drive Argyle from the western government, but whose common place of residence was on the shore of Ballycastle Bay. Many other Hebrideans were settled in Antrim, but the MacDonnells were always the leading clan.[262]

Contemporary description of them.
John Edgar, a reforming priest of the violent kind which Western Scotland has produced, gave Henry VIII. a graphic account of the islemen in his day. They spent much time in hunting and manly exercises, going barelegged and barefoot though the snow should be waist deep, 'wherefore the tender and delicate gentlemen of Scotland call us Redshanks.' Against exceptional frosts they protected themselves with moccasins made of fresh red-deer hide, secured with thongs and full of holes to let the water in and out. The hairy side being exposed gained them the name of 'rough-footed Scots,' and the whole description recalls a well-known nursery rhyme. The people of the Irish isles of Arran still use cowhide coverings exactly similar, to protect their feet from the sharp lime[Pg 273]stone rocks which are too slippery for soled boots. Edgar is careful to mention that the perones worn by the ancient Latines in Virgil were shoes of the same kind. Travers, who saw a great deal of the Hebrideans, was less struck by their poetic aspect, and simply describes them as 'most vile in their living of any nation next Irishmen.' 'Nevertheless,' says Edgar, who anticipated such criticism, 'when we Redshanks come to the Court waiting on our lords and masters, who also for velvets and silks be right well arrayed, we have as good garments as some of our fellows which give attendance at Court every day.' These hardy islanders were in great request as mercenaries even in the South of Ireland, and it was a far cry to Mull or Isla, where, and where only, the English or Irish Government could seriously injure them.[263]

Fears of Scotland and France, 1543.

St. Leger was uneasy lest a combined Scotch and French attack should be made on Ireland. Two French ships in company with some Scotch galleys were seen off Carrickfergus. There was an English squadron off Lambay, and its appearance had at first had a good effect, but it could not even guard the sixty miles of water between Howth and Holyhead. Frenchmen and Bretons frequented the Irish coast, and even sold Spanish prizes at Cork; for that city claimed the strange privilege of dealing with the King's enemies in time of war. James Delahide was in O'Donnell's country with a servant of the Earl of Argyle, and young Gerald of Kildare might at any moment be made the instrument of fresh disturbances. James MacDonnell, Alaster's eldest son, had been brought up at the Scottish Court, and, alone of his race, had learned to write: he was married—or perhaps only handfasted—to Lady Agnes Campbell, Argyle's sister, and Beaton might at any time turn the connection to account.[264]

St. Leger is successful in Ulster.

In the first flush of the matrimonial treaty Henry announced that he would have Scotsmen treated as friends. But against Frenchmen he had declared war, and he and the[Pg 274] Emperor had bound themselves not to make a separate peace. Yet in thirteen months Charles suddenly came to terms with Francis, leaving Henry to get his army out of France as he best could, and to see the English coast insulted by a French fleet. Whatever the designs of the French party in Scotland, no invasion of Ireland in fact took place. Tyrone, O'Donnell, and some of their neighbours were induced to visit Dublin and to submit their differences to the Lord Deputy. There was a standing dispute as to whether O'Dogherty, chief of Innishowen, owed service and tribute to O'Donnell or to O'Neill. The former established his title, but agreed to pay sixty cows yearly if O'Neill would prevent his men from molesting Innishowen. The contention that O'Donnell himself owed suit and service to O'Neill was not accepted, and both were confined to their own districts. Both made extravagant pretensions, but their documents were worthless, and proceeded for the most part from the imagination of Irish bards and story tellers who would do anything for money, or for love, or from a lively sense of favours to come. St. Leger managed to bring about an amicable arrangement, and even to lay the foundation of an increased revenue in Ulster.[265]

Henry's financial dishonesty.

The reckless extravagance of Henry, his venal courtiers, and useless wars, had sunk him in debt. The plunder of the Church was gone, and there seemed no limit to the calls on the generosity or fears of his subjects. A king who could seek the help of a subservient Parliament to repudiate his debts was not likely to be scrupulous about contract obligations, and he seems to have contemplated resuming by Act of Parliament all Irish lands which had been leased by his authority. St. Leger protested in the strongest manner against thus confiscating the improvements of tenants, who had paid their rent and spent their money on the faith of royal grants. Discontent was already prevalent, for the pay of the soldiers was in arrear. Their number was reduced to 550, but they had not been paid for months, and a sum of less[Pg 275] than 2,500l. was all that the King would send. A full pay was impossible, and the Irish Government were afraid even to make payments on account, lest an invasion or other sudden emergency should find them penniless. They urged the folly of not paying punctually, and their reasoning applies to the frugal Elizabeth as well as to her spendthrift father. The Tudor monarchy had already outgrown the feudal exchequer. 'We assure your Highness your affairs hath often been much hindered in default of money, which being paid at last is no alleviating of charge; and yet by default of monthly payments, half the service is not done that might and should be done. In which case if it might please your Majesty, of your princely bounty, to furnish us for your army beforehand for one whole year, your Highness shall perceive your affairs thereby to be highly advanced.'[266]

St. Leger leaves Ireland, 1544.

Like every other Deputy, St. Leger soon grew heartily sick of Ireland. 'I beseech you,' he wrote to the King, 'to remember your poor slave, that hath now been three years in hell, absent from your Majesty, and call me again to your presence, which is my joy in this world.' Four months after sending this touching appeal he received leave of absence; but he could not then be spared, and he remained in Ireland until the beginning of 1544. Brabazon, who became Lord Justice, remembered what had happened after Grey's departure, and stood well upon his guard. The veteran O'Connor and the new Baron of Upper Ossory were discovered to be in league. They avowed designs against O'More; but Brabazon was not to be deceived, and preserved the peace by imprisoning the Baron. Clanricarde enjoyed his Earldom only a few months, and his life had not been such as to ensure a peaceful succession. 'Whether the late Earl,' the Irish Government wrote, 'hath any heir male, it is not yet known, there were so many marriages and divorces; but no doubt he married this last woman solemnly.' His son Richard by Maude Lacy was ultimately acknowledged as second Earl, and became a con[Pg 276]siderable personage; but his morality or fidelity was not more conspicuous than his father's.[267]

An Irish contingent for the Scotch war, 1544.

Beaton had outwitted Henry, annulled the marriage treaty from which so much had been hoped, and brought his countrymen back to the French alliance. Breathing threatenings and slaughter, the King of England determined to raise an Irish contingent as his predecessors had done. As his object was to destroy the greatest possible quantity of property, he could hardly have done better. One thousand kerne were required for Scotland and 2,000 for France. The order to raise the men only reached Ireland about the beginning of March, and Henry's impatience expected them to be ready in a few days. The Irish nobility were not unwilling to meet the King's views, but they thought six months' notice would have been little enough. Even in England such a sudden levy would have been very difficult, and in Ireland, the King was reminded, 'the idle men were not at such commandment, that willingly they would in such case forthwith obey their governor, nor gladly depart the realm, being never trained to the thing, without some nobleman of these parts had the conduct of them.' Great exertions were made, the Council dividing into a northern and southern recruiting party; but the King was at last obliged to content himself with 1,000 kerne, the proportions to be furnished by different chiefs and noblemen being fixed by Henry himself. Ormonde, who was asked to give 100, sent 200, and Desmond provided 120 instead of 100. The Lords Power, Cahir, and Slane also did more than they were required; but the Irish chiefs were all under the mark, and the O'Briens and others sent none at all. Tyrone, O'Reilly, and O'Connor were pretty well represented, and the deficiencies were supplied from various sources. In Irish warfare every two kerne used to have a 'page or boy, which commonly is nevertheless a man.' That allowance was diminished by one-half, and when all deductions had been made, more than 1,000 fighting men were sent. The ship[Pg 277] which brought treasure for this expedition was chased by the Breton rovers, who then commanded the Channel. There was some difficulty in finding a commander, 'Earls being unwieldy men to go with light kerne,' and the choice of the Council lay practically between Lord Power and Lord Dunboyne. The former, who was Ormonde's nephew, was chosen. The Council were afraid of offending the chiefs by refusing any quotas which might be furnished after the departure of the main body, and they resolved to take all who came. In any case, they said, 'if any ruffle should chance, we be discharged of so many.' They begged Henry to see that they were properly treated for an encouragement to others. The kerne were good soldiers in their way, but the King was warned that they would require some training for regular warfare. The proportion of officers was excessive; but the Council advised their retention, lest disappointment should quench the smoking flax of Irish loyalty.[268]

Irish troops at the siege of Boulogne.
Lord Power's men mustered 700 men in St. James's Park, the rest having been perhaps diverted to the Scottish borders, and they served at the siege of Boulogne, burning all the villages near the beleaguered town, and foraging as much as thirty miles inland. Their plan was to tie a bull to a stake and scorch him with faggots. The poor beast's roars attracted the cattle of the country, 'all which they would lightly lead away, and furnish the camp with store of beef.' They treated Frenchmen no better than their bulls, preferring their heads to any ransom. The French sent to Henry to ask whether he had brought men or devils with him, but he only laughed; and they retaliated by mutilating and torturing every Irishman that they could catch. The Irish gained a more honourable distinction from the[Pg 278] valour of Nicholas Welch, who, when a French challenger defied the English army, swam across the harbour and brought back the boaster's head in his mouth.[269]

Apprehensions from France.
Rumours were afloat at this time about great preparations at Brest for the invasion of Ireland in the interest of Gerald of Kildare. It was supposed that the blow would fall in Cork, Lady Eleanor MacCarthy not having yet been pardoned, and her influence being very great. The Council thought that they could resist 10,000 men with the help of the natives, who would all stand firm against Frenchmen. But if young Gerald once set his foot in Ireland, they could answer for nothing. It was true that he had left Italy and Reginald Pole, but only to serve with the Knights of Malta against the Moslems; and it does not appear that he visited France at all. But the very sound of his name, coupled with Scots one day and with Frenchmen the next, kept the Irish Government in hot water for more than a year. Lady Eleanor received a pardon, and her nephew, who was now nineteen, returned about the same time to Italy. From the time that he entered Cosmo de' Medici's service the rumours in Ireland ceased.[270]

St. Leger returns to Ireland. He falls out with Ormonde.
St. Leger returned to Ireland in August 1544, after the kerne had sailed, and it was probably their absence which kept the island quiet for a time. Like his predecessor, St. Leger found Ormonde's power embarrassing. He knew him to be loyal, and personally both liked and admired him, but could not help being uneasy at his overgrown power. His influence in the Council was so great that St. Leger reported him as having 'the great part of all those that daily frequent the Council here, of his fee.' The King's interest had small chance against the Earl's, 'and as I am true man,' St. Leger wrote, 'I see no man having

learning that will plainly speak in such a case but poor Sir Thomas Cusack.' Ormonde now claimed for his palatinate of Tipperary a larger meaning than had lately been given to it. The undefined boundaries he[Pg 279] stretched to the utmost, and throughout the whole district claimed every sovereign right, except treasure trove and the right of punishing rape, arson, and coining. Men feared to speak openly against him. Cusack was maligned for his independence, and Lord Upper Ossory begged St. Leger to keep his communications secret. The palatinate jurisdiction and the prisage of wines had been taken from the House of Ormonde by Poyning's Parliament; but the Earl could show later documents under the Great Seal, some of which St. Leger suspected to have been forged during the time that Sir Piers Butler was Lord Deputy. St. Leger also complained that Ormonde put obstacles in the way of reforming Leinster, unless he might do it himself and in his own way. He recommended that this mighty subject's wings should be clipped a little, and that he should have no more grants of land in Ireland; he had no objection to the King giving him as much as he pleased in England. To make things pleasant he recommended a garter. After all this he strangely proposed to entrust the Irish Government to a succession of Irish noblemen for two or three years at a time, and to make Ormonde the first Deputy of the new series. The suggestion met with no favour, and seems not to have been thought worthy of an answer. No Irish nobleman received the sword during the remainder of the Tudor period; but when Charles I. was slipping from the throne he committed his interests in Ireland to the charge of another and more famous Ormonde.[271]

Scotch politics. The Lord of the Isles takes Henry's side,

Donnell Dhu, calling himself Earl of Ross and claiming to be Lord of the Isles, having escaped from his almost lifelong imprisonment, was received with open arms by the Hebrideans, who still sighed for their ancient independence. Donnell and seventeen of his principal supporters bound themselves solemnly to be at the command of Lennox, who had declared for Henry VIII. against the regent Arran and the French party, which at this time was also the Scotch party. The confederates gave full treating powers to Rory[Pg 280] MacAlister, Bishop-elect of the Isles, and to Patrick Maclean, Bailie of Iona and Justice Clerk of the South Isles.

and sends agents to Dublin.

A few days after this treaty the bishop and the bailie came to Dublin and asked for 1,000l. Half of this sum, with 100l. worth of provisions, was as much as St. Leger could afford to give them. In the meantime Donnell Dhu had appeared at Carrickfergus with 4,000 men and 180 galleys, having left another force of 4,000 behind him to keep Argyle and Huntley in check. In writing to the King of England he expressed great joy that his Majesty had deigned to look upon so small a person, and either he, or the priest who prompted him, found an extraordinary analogy between the fishers of the Western Isles and those of the Galilean lake, and between Henry VIII. and their Master. At Carrickfergus Donnell Dhu and his friends again bound themselves to do the bidding of Lennox, and 'to fortify after their power the King's Majesty touching the marriage of the Princess of Scotland, and in all other affairs as is commanded them to do by my Lord Earl of Lennox.'[272]

His agreement with St. Leger.

Having done their business in Dublin, Donnell's ambassadors hurried to England and made their terms with the Council. They bound their chief and his friends to be Henry's liege subjects, and to furnish him with 8,000 auxiliaries, who were to co-operate with Lennox and Ormonde, and, if possible, to harry Scotland as far as Stirling. While Lennox remained in Argyle's country all the islemen were to be employed in destroying it; in other places 6,000 were to follow him, but there were never to be less than 2,000 occupied in persecuting the sons of Diarmid. In consideration of this undertaking Henry promised to pay 3,000 of Donnell's men, and to send a force of 2,000 Irish under Ormonde, who was to be subordinate to Lennox.[273]

[Pg 281]

The whole project ends in failure.

St. Leger had considerable difficulty in raising 2,000 men at short notice. Money was scarce with him, and he was not told what pay he might offer. Recruiting was hindered by rumours of casualties among the kerne who had taken part in Hertford's second raid, when they had been specially employed to burn and waste East Teviotdale 'because the borderers would not most willingly burn their neighbours.' The required number was, however, got together by great exertions, one-half being raised by Ormonde. The force when complete consisted of 100 of the Dublin garrison, 400 gallowglasses, and 1,500 kerne. Two hundred and fifty had muskets, or were to some extent trained in the use of artillery, of which there were several pieces. Shipping was collected in the Irish and Welsh ports, and great quantities of munitions put on board. Lennox himself came to Dublin, and sailed with Ormonde for the Clyde. Dumbarton Castle was in the hands of Lord Glencairne, and was to be taken if possible. Should this attempt fail, the plan was to effect a landing in Argyle's country, and to do all the damage possible there. The fleet left Dublin on November 17, and was unlucky from the first, being caught in a storm off Belfast Lough and much damaged. On reaching the Clyde the country was found to be up in arms, the attitude of the islemen was uncertain, a French squadron was on the coast, and Lennox, against the advice of Ormonde, resolved to turn back. Donnell Dhu died at Drogheda just at the critical moment, and was buried in St. Patrick's, Dublin, where an epitaph recorded the mournful fact that he had escaped an exile's life only to die an exile's death.[274]

James MacDonnell offers his services, 1545.

James MacDonnell, the son of Alaster, became Lord of the Isles by general consent. He had been educated at the Scottish Court, and his politics had thus lost something of their insularity. At all events he had learned to write, and that was a rare accomplishment for one of his family in those days. Lady Agnes Campbell had perhaps excited doubts in[Pg 282] his mind as to the desirability of destroying the Argyle power; and others in the isles may have doubted the power of Henry VIII. to protect them against the Campbells and Gordons. But James still professed his readiness to do the King of England's bidding, suggested St. Patrick's day—nearly two months off—for a meeting with Lennox in the island of Sanda, and in the meantime asked for shipping to transport his men. Ragged Scotchmen continued to flock to Dublin, all asking for money; and the Irish Government soon formed an opinion that while the cost of maintaining them was certain, the expectation of service was more than doubtful.[275]

Dissensions between St. Leger and Ormonde.

St. Leger and Ormonde were now at open war. When leaving Gowran for Scotland the latter received an anonymous letter warning him that he was sent there only that he might be the more easily caught and put into the Tower. The writer affirmed that Lennox had said as much, and that the boasting of the Lord Deputy's servants had been to the same effect. The pretext was that the Earl obstructed Irish reforms. Ormonde seems to have partly believed the letter, for he sent a copy to Russell, and begged him to procure an impartial inquiry. He then went to Scotland, declaring that his loyalty was not of that timorous sort which fears inquiry or shuns danger. 'If,' he wrote, 'I saw all the power of the world upon a hill armed against his Majesty, I would rather run to his Grace, though I were slain at his Majesty's heels, than to leave his Highness and save myself.'[276]

They both go to England, 1546.

After his return from Scotland Ormonde wrote several letters to Privy Councillors in England, in which he attacked St. Leger's administration as expensive and wasteful. A graver accusation against a servant of Henry VIII. was that he concealed much which it imported the King to know. The letters were seized on ship-board by the Lord Deputy's brother, and detained for some time in Dublin. Ormonde[Pg 283] refused to state his grievances before the Irish Council, as being necessarily under St. Leger's influence, but preferred to run all the risks of a voyage to England. The Irish Government left all to the Privy Council. St. Leger accordingly went over to state his own case, having first secured certificates of character from the Irish Council, from Desmond, Tyrone, Thomond, and Upper Ossory, and from several Irish chiefs, all of whom willingly came to Dublin at his summons, and 'wept and lamented the departing of so just a governor.'[277]

Intrigues of Irish officials.

Lord Chancellor Alen was not favourable to St. Leger. He quarrelled regularly with every deputy; but there may be some truth in his allegations, which are little more than a statement of the insoluble problem of Irish government. The King's writ did not run much further than in former days. The revenue was almost stationary, and was supplemented annually by 5,000l. of English money. Leinster was not reformed. Irishmen were quiet, but might not long remain so. The chiefs continued to wage private war, and were not to be tamed with abbey-lands in their own countries, or farms in the Pale. 'I cannot,' said Alen, 'learn that ever such barbarous people kept touch any while, or were ever vanquished with fair words. Let Wales be example.' Interrogatories were sent to Irish councillors on these and similar points, and as to whether either St. Leger or the Chancellor had been corrupt in any way. Questions were asked as to the demeanour of every councillor, as to whether Alen's account of St. Leger's overbearing conduct at the Council Board was true, as to the behaviour of Ormonde and others there. In replying to Alen's charges, St. Leger complained of their vagueness, and detailed his strenuous exertions to overcome the inherent difficulties of his task, and here most people will sympathise with him. He thought that Irishmen on the whole kept their word as well as Englishmen, 'and if Irishmen use their own laws, so doth the Earl of Ormonde, and all the Lords Marchers in Ireland.' We have here a line of argument very common in our own day, but very rare in[Pg 284] that of Henry VIII., and St. Leger must be credited with unusual breadth of view. The Irish customs were in truth necessary; for there was then no way of enforcing English law, and the difficulty of applying it fully has not disappeared even in the reign of Queen Victoria. As to mismanagement of the revenue, St. Leger gave

Alen the lie direct, and accused him of conspiring with Walter Cowley to defame him; but this the Chancellor positively denied. The Lord Deputy begged that he might not be wearied with interrogatories, but called before the Council, and confronted with his accusers. 'Then,' he said, 'let me be rid of this hell, wherein I have remained six years, and that some other may serve his Majesty as long as I have done, and I to serve him elsewhere, where he shall command me. Though the same were in Turkey, I will not refuse it.'[278]

St. Leger exonerated from blame. Alen and Cowley imprisoned.

The English Government came to the conclusion that St. Leger deserved no blame. Alen could not be quite acquitted of factious conduct; but he was a faithful servant, and hardly to be spared from Ireland, which had the quality of transmuting wisdom into foolishness and honesty into self-seeking. He suffered a short imprisonment in the Tower, and had to surrender the Great Seal, which, after being refused by two other lawyers, was given to Sir Richard Rede. But his property was restored to him immediately after Edward's accession; he became Lord Chancellor again, and received the constableship of Maynooth, and many other favours. In 1550 he seems still to have been grumbling against St. Leger, who could then afford to speak of him as his old friend. Walter Cowley, the Irish Solicitor-General, was also sent to the Tower. It appears that one William Cantwell held a lease for life of three farms in Kilkenny, and that others had seized them while he was learning English at Oxford. There may have been a question of title, for it was not uncommon in Henry VIII.'s time to grant the same property to several people at once. Believing that he had been kept from his[Pg 285] own by Ormonde, St. Leger espoused Cantwell's cause; and it was to get the Earl out of the way that Cantwell wrote the Gowran letter, and another found at Ross. Cowley, who was more or less under Alen's influence, declared in the Tower that his report against St. Leger had been revised by the Chancellor; but this was solemnly denied. 'I was,' said Alen, 'never of counsel with article of it. God is my Judge, I would be ashamed to be named to be privy to the penning of so lewd a book;' and years afterwards he told Paget that Cowley had confessed the truth of this disclaimer. Perhaps he spoke in fear of the rack; in any case, the Privy Council or the King decided that he was a liar, and he was certainly a plotter like his father before him. The old man was deprived of the office of Master of the Rolls, and the young one of that of Solicitor-General. Both were employed again in the next reign. St. Leger was reconciled to Ormonde, and in spite of his prayers was restored to his government with increased honours and an hereditary pension.[279]

Murder of Ormonde.

Ormonde never saw Ireland again. He kept fifty servants in London, who invited him to sup with them at Limehouse. After supper the whole company sickened, and seventeen in all died. The Earl was carried to Ely House in Holborn, where he lingered for several days, but at last succumbed. There seems to have been no inquiry into this tragedy, and one might suspect that the Government took this means of releasing themselves from a man who had become inconveniently powerful, and whose services were too eminent to attack openly. Henry had no particular scruples about assassination, when, as in Cardinal Beaton's case, he could not reach his enemy by other means; but he would hardly have been likely to poison a subject against whom he could always compass an Act of Attainder. The fact that Ormonde's loyalty was above suspicion may have rendered this course difficult, and Henry may have seen in him a possible Earl of Kildare.

He was ambitious, very powerful, impatient of[Pg 286] interference, and by no means tamely subservient to the ruler of the hour. There is no reason to suppose that Hertford or Wriothesley were capable of such a crime. Warwick was capable of anything; but if he had suspected the Seymours, he would hardly have allowed the matter to be hushed up. An anecdote of Ormonde's son, the famous tenth Earl, perhaps points to a suspicion against Leicester's father; but it is not likely that the mystery will ever be cleared up. The 'Four Masters' say St. Leger had boasted that either he or Ormonde should never return to Ireland; but this is not mentioned by older annalists, nor in the official correspondence, and it is just the sort of story that would have been concocted afterwards. Ormonde's vast estates passed quietly to his heir, a boy of fourteen, who became the most famous and powerful man of his age and country. The boy was educated at the English Court, and 200 marks a year out of his lands in Ireland were assigned for his support.[280]

All Deputies had difficulties with the Butlers and the permanent officials.

Scarcely any Deputy could escape collison with the head of the Butler family, whose influence rested on lasting foundations and not on the favour of the Dublin Government. Moreover, permanent officials, who had powerful connections in the county, knew how to thwart their nominal superior; and, unless he happened to be a man of great tact, difficulties were sure to arise. Grey and Bellingham quarrelled with the Council. Sidney viewed the Ormonde of his day with unconcealed jealousy and suspicion. Strafford was at war with the Lord-Treasurer Cork and with the Vice-Treasurer Mountnorris; and his treatment of the latter contributed to his fall. Lord Fitzwilliam was beaten by a revenue commissioner, Lord Townsend by the boroughmongers; and the lawyers have often been able to make combinations enabling them to dictate their own terms. Australian governors can best appreciate the difficulties of Ireland's rulers in past times.

Henry's Irish policy; why it failed.

Henry VIII.'s plan for the government of Ireland was very different from that which his children pursued. Evidently he did not desire to plant colonists in the country, but rather to civilise the people as they were. By creating some of the[Pg 287] great chiefs Earls, and by insisting on their going to Court for investiture, he hoped gradually to convert them into supporters. Such cases as that of Tirlogh O'Toole show that he knew how to be both gracious and just. On the other hand, the ferocity of his character was exemplified by his treatment of the five Geraldine brethren. He was a thoroughly selfish man, but in matters which did not concern him personally he had many of the qualifications of a statesman. Had England remained in communion with Rome, his tentative and patient policy might have succeeded in Ireland. The Reformation caused its failure, for there never was the slightest chance of native Ireland embracing the new doctrines. The monasteries had not weighed heavily on Ireland, and their destruction made many bitter enemies and few friends. By upsetting the whole ecclesiastical structure, Henry left the field clear for Jesuits and wandering friars; and his children reaped the fruits of a mistake which neutralised every effort to win Ireland.

FOOTNOTES:

[247] Indenture in O'Carroll's case, July 2, 1541, in Carew.

[248] Submission of O'Donnell, Aug. 6, 1541; O'Donnell to the King, April 20, 1542: 'Iterum Vestram Majestatem exortor, mittatis mihi instrumentum illud aureum, quo colla nobilium cinguntur, aut katenam, vestesque congruentes, quibus vestirer decenter, quoties accederem (data opportunitate) ad Parliamentum.'

[249] Lord Deputy and Council to the King, Aug. 28, 1541; Four Masters, 1541: 'he left them without corn for that year.'

[250] St. Leger to the King, Dec. 17, 1541.

[251] Articles binding Con Bacagh O'Neill, in S.P., vol. iii., No. 356: 'Regem recognosco Supremum Caput Ecclesiæ Anglicanæ et Hibernicanæ immediate sub Christo; et imposterum, in quantum potero, compellam omnes degentes sub meo regimine, ut similiter faciant; et si contingat aliquem provisorem aut provisores aliquas facultates sive bullas obtinere de prædicta usurpata auctoritate, illos sursum reddere dictas bullas et facultates cogam, et semetipsos submittere ordinationi Regiæ Majestatis.'

[252] Council of Ireland to the King, S.P., vol. iii., No. 357.

[253] The King to the Lord Deputy and Council, S.P., vol. iii., No. 348.

[254] The session was from Feb. 15 to March 7 or 10; see Lord Deputy in Council to the King, March 31, 1542; for the robbers, see same to same, Nov. 25, 1544.

[255] See the submissions in Carew—MacBrien Coonagh, March 18, 1542; Rory O'More, May 13; MacQuillin, May 18; MacDonnell, May 18; Hugh O'Kelly, May 24; O'Byrnes, July 4; O'Rourke, Sept. 1; MacQuillin and O'Cahan, May 6, 1543. Lord Deputy and Council to the King, July 12, 1542, and Aug. 24.

[256] Desmond's visit to Court was between June 2 and July 5, 1542. Lord Deputy and Council to the King, June 2; J. Alen to the King, June 4; the King to the Lord Deputy and Council, July 5; St. Leger to the King, Aug. 27.

[257] Indentura facta 26 die Septembris, 1542, in S.P. The signatories promised jointly and severally 'usurpatam primatiam et auctoritatem Romani Episcopi annihilare, omnesque suos fautores, adjutores, et suffragatores, ad summum posse illorum precipitare et abolere ... omnes et singulos provisores ... apprehendere et producere ad Regis communem legem,' &c.

[258] Lord Deputy and Council to the Privy Council, Sept. 1, 1542; Four Masters, 1542.

[259] Submission made at Greenwich, Sept. 24, 1542.

[260] The creation was Oct. 1, 1542. The patent is in Rymer; the Herald's account in Carew, Oct. 1. O'Neill was back in Ireland before Dec. 7, when the Irish Government wrote of him to the King. Tyrone's style was—'Du treshaut et puissant Seigneur Con, Conte de Tyrone, en le Royaulme d'Irlande.'

[261] The heraldic account is printed in S.P., vol. iii. p. 473, from the Cotton MSS.; the O'Brien and Burke patents are in Rymer, Conatius being by mistake printed for Donatus; see the King to the Lord Deputy and Council, July 9, 1543; MacWilliam submitted much in the same terms as O'Neill.

[262] Hill's MacDonnells of Antrim, chaps. i. and ii.; Archdall's Lodge's Peerage, Earl of Antrim and Baron MacDonnell; Burton's History of Scotland, vol. iii. p. 149. For the antiquarian controversy in 1617, see Carew, vol. vi., Nos. 183, 188, 189, 190. 191.

[263] Hill, p. 37; John Travers's Devices in S.P., vol. iii. p. 382.

[264] Hill, p. 41; St. Leger to the King, June 4, 1543; Lord Deputy and Council to the King, June 5.

[265] St. Leger to the King, July 18, 1543, and the notes; see also Carew, July 15 and 16.

[266] Lord Deputy and Council to the King, May 15, 1543; same to same, Dec. 7, 1542, and the King's answer.

[267] St. Leger to the King, April 6, 1543; the King to the Lord Deputy and Council, Aug. 9; Lord Justice Brabazon and Council to St. Leger, March 24, 1544.

[268] Lord Justice Brabazon and Council to the King, May 7, 1544; same to St. Leger, March 24, where the kerne are first mentioned in the S.P.; Privy Council to Lord Justice and Council, March 30; Ormonde to the King, May 7. In a letter to the King printed in S.P., vol. iii., No. 437, O'Reilly complains that his contingent cost him 600l., that eight weeks of their wages remained unpaid, and that his chaplain had been taken prisoner in Scotland, and had paid eight nobles for his ransom. This shows that some of the 1,000 kerne went to Scotland.

[269] Stanihurst.

[270] For these rumours, see the S.P. from May 20, 1544, till May 11, 1545, vol. iii., Nos. 407, 408, 411, 414, 415.

[271] St. Leger to Wriothesley, Feb. 26, 1545, with Lord Upper Ossory's letter in a note; to the Privy Council, April 14.

[272] Hill, p. 43. In a letter printed in S.P., vol. v. p. 483, Donnell Dhu speaks of himself as 'in materno utero inimicorum jugo et captivitati astricti, et in hoc pene tempus carceris squalore obruti, et intolerabilibus compedibus truculentissime ligati.' The notarial instrument between the islemen is in S.P., vol. v. p. 477. Lord Deputy and Council of Ireland to the King, Aug. 13, 1545.

[273] Privy Council to Lord Deputy and Council of Ireland, in S.P., vol. iii., No. 422. See S.P., vol. v. pp. 505-7.

[274] Ormonde to Russell, Nov. 15, 1545; Lord Deputy and Council to the King, Nov. 19. Donnell Dhu died before Jan. 20, 1546, the date of a letter from James MacDonnell in S.P., vol. iii. p. 548. Dowling.

[275] Lord Deputy and Council to the Privy Council, Feb. 15, 1546, and a letter in a note from 'Ewyne Allane of Locheld.' James MacDonnell is called Lord of the Isles 'by consent of the nobility,' 'apparent heir,' 'worthy to succeed,' and 'Lord elect.'

[276] Ormonde to Russell, Nov. 15, 1545.

[277] Cusack to Paget, March 28, 1546. See the S.P. from Feb. 20 to March 28, vol. iii., Nos. 431, 433, 434, 435, 438, 439, and 440.

[278] See S.P. 1546, vol. iii., Nos. 441 to 448. No. 439 is a letter from certain Irish chiefs to the King in St. Leger's favour, and they make the reflection, 'Oh si majoribus nostris tales contigissent moderatores.'

[279] Alen's Answer to St. Leger in S.P., vol. iii. No. 446, and W. Cowley's Letter to the Privy Council, No. 448; Alen to Paget, April 21, 1549; St. Leger to Cecil, Dec. 5, 1550.

[280] Stanihurst; Morrin's Patent Rolls, p. 168.

[Pg 288]

MAP OF IRELAND (ECCLESIASTICAL)
CHAPTER XV.

THE IRISH CHURCH UNDER HENRY VIII.

King and Pope.
During the quarter of a century which elapsed between Henry's accession and his final breach with Rome, the King showed great submission to the papal chair. The wishes of such a faithful son could not be lightly regarded, and royal nominations to English bishoprics were invariably confirmed by the Pontiff. Capitular elections still took place; but they had ceased to be free, and preferment was really given by the joint fiat of the Crown and the Tiara. In Ireland the King was less absolute. The popes had not forgotten their original gift of the island; and the clergy, more especially in remote regions, would naturally look to them for promotion, rather than to a King whose power was uncertain and to whom they had a national antipathy. In the year 1520 the united sees of Cork and Cloyne became vacant. Surrey, then Lord-Lieutenant, was besieged with applications, but preferred the claims of Walter Wellesley, head of the great Augustinian house of Conal in Kildare. In right of his priory Wellesley had already a seat in the Irish House of Lords, and Surrey recommended him to Wolsey as 'a famous clerk, noted the best in the land—a man of gravity and virtuous conversation and a singular mind having to English order.' Wellesley was not nominated on this occasion, either because he preferred his priory to a bishopric, or because the Cardinal had other views. In the following year the Bishop of Limerick died, and the Lord-Lieutenant and Council again strongly recommended the

Prior of Conal; but the Pope nevertheless provided John Quin, a Dominican friar, and Wellesley did not become a bishop till 1529. He was then at last consecrated to Kildare,[Pg 289] and allowed to keep his monastery, as in that situation he might very fairly do.[281]

Case of Clonfert.

The points at issue between King and Pope are well illustrated by the case of Clonfert, which fell vacant at the moment of separation. Clement provided the Dean, Roland de Burgo, and Henry appointed Richard Nangle Provincial of the Irish Austinfriars. Nangle was consecrated and took possession of his see. Relying on his family influence, and probably upheld by popular opinion, the Papal prelate, who was armed with the power of granting indulgences and dispensations, defied the royal nominee, and Nangle was afraid to appear in public. It was proposed to bring the Burkes to their senses by laying an embargo on the trade of Galway, but this does not seem to have been done. Ten years after his original provision, and probably after the death of Nangle, De Burgo was confirmed by the King and allowed to hold his deanery and other benefices, of which he had all along kept possession, on condition of renouncing the Pope's bulls and acknowledging that he held from the Crown. The Bishop, who must have had an elastic conscience, died in harness in 1580.[282]

Armagh.

The more important bishoprics were generally given to men whom the English Government could trust, and it is not likely that they were ever filled up in defiance of the King until after his rupture with Rome. Armagh, Dublin, and Meath were rarely entrusted to any but men of English birth. In 1513 John Kite, a Londoner, was appointed by provision to Armagh, but the nomination was certainly agreeable to Henry, who had before employed Kite as a diplomatist in Spain. The temporalities of the diocese were almost immediately restored to him, and he was soon afterwards present in London at the grand reception of Wolsey's red hat. Kite, who received many tokens of royal favour, was translated by the Pope to Carlisle. The Holy See claimed very full rights in the case of a translation; but George Cromer, an English[Pg 290]man, was appointed to Armagh at the King of England's supplication. Such was the form preferred by the Pope, but the supplication was in fact a nomination.[283]

Dublin.

William Rokeby, a Yorkshireman, was translated from Meath to Dublin in 1512. Henry made him his chancellor, and he also was present at the hat ceremony. After his death a Somersetshire man, Hugh Inge, was translated by the Pope from Meath to Dublin. There can be little doubt that this was done with the King's full consent, for Inge acknowledged that he owed all to Wolsey. As a special favour the tax on this occasion was reduced from 1,600 to 1,000 florins, on the suggestion of Campeggio, who reported that certain noblemen had intruded into the diocesan lands and greatly diminished the income. Inge also held the office of chancellor, which at this time was almost invariably given to an archbishop. When Inge died, John Alen, one of Wolsey's chaplains, was provided to Dublin at the King's instance, or supplication as the Pope called it, and immediately received the Great Seal. Alen had been employed by the Cardinal in the suppression of the lesser monasteries, and had incurred great odium in that office.[284]

Meath.

The see of Meath, which has the singular distinction of having never possessed a cathedral, was from its position of especial importance. After being successively filled by[Pg 291] Rokeby and Inge, it was given by the Pope, but probably at Wolsey's instigation, to Richard Wilson, Prior of Drax in Yorkshire. It is remarkable that Wilson, who does not seem ever to have resided in his see, fully acknowledged that the Cardinal's legatine authority extended to Ireland. This was vehemently denied by Primate Cromer and his suffragans, who were able to make their objections good; the whole province of Armagh, except Meath, being situated among the Irishry. On the resignation of Wilson, Edward Staples, a Lincolnshire man, was provided by Clement on the King's nomination. He was allowed to hold St. Bartholomew's Hospital in London, and other benefices, along with his bishopric, and he had a special Papal dispensation for filling offices with incompatible duties. Staples fully embraced the Reformation, and was a principal instrument in carrying out the changed religious policy of the English Crown.[285]

Cashel.

In 1524 Edmund Butler, Prior of Athassel, a natural son of Sir Piers Butler, was appointed by the Pope to Cashel, and by him recommended to the King, who addressed letters in his favour to the Irish Government. Kildare alleged that Butler was opposed by his father, and there was certainly a contest between them. The Archbishop's object was to prevent his father, as acting Earl Palatine of Tipperary, from raising a revenue in that county, the larger part of which was in his diocese. The citizens of Waterford complained that his Grace used every kind of Irish extortion, and his opposition to the palatinate jurisdiction clearly arose from no wish to leave the people untaxed. In one respect indeed the prelate bettered the instruction of the temporal magnates, for he 'retained Dermond Duff for his official and counsellor or commissary, which so entertaineth the King's people by colour of canon law that there can be no more extortion committed by any Irish Brehon, and polleth the King's subjects as he lists, and taketh for fee of sentence of a divorce 10l. or more.' He openly robbed a boat laden with merchandise, and held the owners to ransom. Butler's consecration was delayed for[Pg 292] three years: it is not easy to say why, as there is no trace of a dispute between the Crown and the Pope. Ultimately he became a very important person, and generally acted with the other Butlers in support of the King's authority. He accepted the royal supremacy, and surrendered his monastery when called on to do so.[286]

Tuam.

The western province was so entirely Irish that the King could hardly have interfered effectually with Papal nominees. On the death of the learned Maurice O'Fiehely in 1513, Thomas O'Mullally was provided to Tuam, and lived unmolested by Henry till 1536. But Christopher Bodkin, who had been preferred to Kilmacduagh at the King's request, was translated purely by royal authority to Tuam. The breach with Rome had at this time become irreparable; and Bodkin, whom the Vatican regards as a schismatic but not as a heretic, acknowledged the royal supremacy and held the temporalities of both his sees, as well as the minor ones of Enaghdune and Mayo, until his death in 1572. His astuteness far exceeded that of the Vicar of Bray, for he seems to have kept his preferments and his opinions as well. A rival archbishop was appointed by Clement in 1538, and is now considered the true one by writers on the Papal side. The double line has continued ever since.[287]

Remoter sees.

To the less important and more distant bishoprics appointments were probably very often made by the popes without the King's interference, and even without his notice. But when he did make a recommendation it is hardly likely to have been neglected at Rome. Thus the sees of Clonmacnoise, Clogher, Ardagh, and Kilmore were on particular occasions filled by the King, and the appointments confirmed by the Pope at his request. The case of Clogher is the more remarkable in that a provision of Julius II. had lately declared that church to be immediately subject to the Holy See. In[Pg 293] the yet more remote districts of Down, Dromore, Raphoe, and Derry, the King does not seem to have interfered at all. In providing Edmund O'Gallagher to the see of Raphoe, Clement VII. observed that the diocese was vacant because the King had neglected to nominate any one for seventeen years.[288]

Leinster.

In Leinster the King must generally have had power to prevent any bishop from enjoying the profits of his see. The patronage was very laxly managed, for Kildare lay vacant from 1513 to 1526. In 1523 the Earl of Kildare tried to get the preferment for the dean, Edward Dillon, whom he recommended to Wolsey as of virtuous living and of English name and condition. The application failed, but Thomas Dillon was at last appointed both by King and Pope. This promotion was probably effected in Kildare's interest; for Cowley, a partisan of the Butlers, called Dillon an Irish vagabond, without learning, manners, or other good quality, and not fit to be a holy water clerk. This Irish vagabond had, however, been educated at Oxford. Thomas Halsey was persuaded by Wolsey to accept the bishopric of Leighlin, and Maurice Doran was, at the King's request, provided to the same see. There may be no positive evidence as to Ossory and Ferns, but there is no reason to doubt that the persons appointed were acceptable to the Government.[289]

Munster.

In Munster it is not likely that bishops would be appointed without the consent of the Crown, except perhaps to the remote sees of Killaloe and Kilfenora, in which the succession at this period is almost hopelessly confused. In filling the scarcely less completely Irish bishopric of Ross, the King took a direct part. He called upon the Pope to accept the resignation of Edmund Courcey, and to appoint as his successor the Cistercian John O'Murrilly, with leave to hold the Abbey of Maur in addition. Leo X. complied in every particular; but when O'Murrilly died two years later, the Pope took the strong step of uniting Ross with Dromore in the distant[Pg 294] north. We may infer from this that Henry did not always choose to interfere, but that when he did the Pope paid the greatest attention to his wishes; and that this rule applied to Munster generally. At Waterford and Cork, the strongholds of English law, it was hardly possible for a bishop to enjoy his revenues in defiance of the Government.[290]

Connaught.

In Connaught the popes seem to have provided bishops as a general rule; but they generally avoided a collision when the King's wish was openly expressed. As late as 1533 Christopher Bodkin was appointed to Kilmacduagh at Henry's request; and this is a very strong case, because a purely papal nominee seems to have resigned in his favour. In

Elphin John Max was appointed by the Pope; but as he held the abbeys of Welbeck or Tichfield, or both, along with his bishopric, he can hardly have been distasteful to Henry. The case of Burke and Nangle, already mentioned, shows King and Pope openly at variance. But even at the beginning of that contest the schism was almost complete.[291]

Bad state of the Irish Church.

In the 'Description of Ireland,' written early in Henry VIII.'s reign, there is a story of St. Brigid, who inquired of her good angel of what Christian land most souls were damned. He showed her a land in the west part of the world, where was continually root of hate and envy, and vices contrary to charity, for lack of which souls kept continually falling down into hell as thick as hail showers. It is inferred that the angel spoke of Ireland, 'for,' says the writer, 'there is no land in this world of so long continual war within himself, nor of so great shedding of Christian blood, nor of so great robbing, spoiling, preying, and burning, nor of so great wrongful extortion continually as Ireland.' Among the various causes of this state of things the bishops and clergy are blamed, 'for there is no archbishop nor bishop, abbot nor prior, parson nor vicar, nor any other person of the Church, high or low, great or small, English or Irish, that useth to[Pg 295] preach the Word of God saveing the poor friars' beggars ... Also the Church of this land use not to learn any other science but the law of Canon, for covetyce of lucre transitory; all other science whereof grows none such lucre, the parsons of the Church doth despise. They hold more by the plough rustical than by lucre of the plough celestial, to which they have stretched their hands, and look always backwards. They tend much more to lucre of that plough, whereof groweth slander and rebuke, than to lucre of the souls, that is the plough of Christ. And to the transitory lucre of that rustical plough they tender so much, that little or nought there chargeth to lucre to Christ, the souls of their subjects, of whom they bear the cure, by preaching and teaching of the Word of God, and by their good ensample giveing; which is the plough of worship and of honour, and the plough of grace that ever shall endure.'[292]

State of Ardagh, Ross, Clonmacnoise, and Enaghdune.

This is a heavy indictment, but it is sustained by very many facts which have come down to us. The state of many important churches shows how ill religion was supported. A report to Leo X. on Ardagh Cathedral states that there was no sacristy, no bell nor belfry, no proper appliances for service; and that the walls of the church itself were but just standing. There was only one altar, which was exposed to the weather. Mass was rarely celebrated, and then by a single priest, and the scanty vestments and utensils were kept in a chest in the church. The town consisted of four thatched cabins; and there were few inhabitants, owing to continual wars caused by the conduct of the late Bishop, William O'Ferrall, who had excited the animosity of his neighbours by attempting to exercise temporal power. The bishopric of Ross was in rather better case. The town of 200 houses was walled, and the cathedral church was built of stone in regular cruciform fashion, and with a tiled roof. There was decent provision for the mass. On the other hand, the church was unpaved, and the income of the see no more than sixty marks. At Clonmacnoise, one of the most famous ecclesiastical places in Ireland, things were scarcely better than at Ardagh. The[Pg 296] town could boast but twelve houses, built of wicker and straw. The church was roofless, and half ruined; with a single altar protected by a thatched shed, one vestment, and a cross made of brass. Mass was rarely celebrated, but the body of St. Ciaran was preserved and reverenced. The Pope's informant was an

Irishman, but the saint's name was unknown to him. The ancient see of Enaghdune or Annaghdown on Lough Corrib was in a deplorable state. The church was in ruins, the clergy far out of order, and the revenue not more than 20l., which could only be collected by a steward who had the favour of the country.[293]

Corruption among dignitaries.

The above cases are all of bishoprics situated in remote parts among the Irishry. The state of the Church in the Pale and other obedient districts was of course better, but even in Dublin the metropolitan crozier remained in pawn for eighty years, from 1449 until Archbishop Alen redeemed it by paying one hundred ounces of silver. The clergy were charged with seeking money more than souls; and many acts of violence and extortion are reported on oath against the Archbishop of Cashel and the Bishops of Ferns, Ossory, Leighlin, Waterford, and Limerick; against the Abbots of Tintern, Jerpoint, Kilcooley, Holy Cross, Dusk, and Innislonagh; against the Priors of Kilclogan, Knocktopher, Inistiogue, Kells, Cahir, and Lady Abbey; and against the Prioress of Moylagh. In general bishops and heads of houses were not less extortionate than other gentlemen. They exacted coyne and livery and the other multifarious Irish imposts with neither more nor less severity than the laity. But it should not be forgotten that these ecclesiastical dignitaries were also great landowners, and that they were forced to provide the means of defence in the only possible way. The Archbishop of Cashel and the Bishops of Waterford and Ossory had other means of taxing the people peculiar to their offices; they took excessive fees in all matrimonial and probate cases, and appropriated a portion of every dead man's goods. The Archbishop's lowest[Pg 297] charge for a divorce was 5l., and it was generally double that or more. The citizens of Waterford declared that the canonists were as burdensome as the Irish Brehons.[294]

Parochial clergy no better.

The parochial clergy were no better than the dignitaries. They made charges varying from sixpence to two shillings for all weddings, christenings, churchings, and burials; and at the death of any married person, man or wife, they exacted five shillings, or one-fifth of the personalty, or the best article of apparel, from the survivor. In many places divine service was neglected or was only performed at irregular intervals. The Earl of Kildare, who was not impartial but who probably spoke truly, declared that the churches in Tipperary and Kilkenny were generally in ruins through the system of Papal provisions, 'so as, and if the King's Grace do not see for the hasty remedy of the same, there is like to be no more Christianity there, than in the midst of Turkey.' Henry was just beginning to quarrel with the Pope, and would be ready enough to believe that provisions had ruined the churches. No doubt many bad appointments were thus made, but it may have been impossible to get fit men; for Browne reports the clergy as unlearned persons, who repeated the Latin offices like parrots and without understanding them.[295]

Evils of Papal patronage.

Piers, Earl of Ossory, also adopted the doctrine that the Papal system of patronage had been the chief cause of the utter ruin and destruction 'of cathedral churches, monasteries, parish churches, and all other regular and secular.' Murderers, thieves, and 'light men of war' obtained provisions, ousted the rightful incumbents, ignored the rightful patrons, held livings by force, and wasted them in riotous living. Violence indeed was the rule. John Purcell, Bishop of Ferns, was in close alliance with the dangerous rebel and freebooter, Cahir MacArt Kavanagh, was present when his men sacked the town of Fethard, and himself called loudly for fire to burn the houses. Milo Baron, Bishop of Ossory, was said to be as[Pg 298] bad as the Bishop of Ferns, and to 'have no virtuous quality nor obedience to any good laws.' Archbishop Butler was accused of riotous conduct and of at least one highway robbery, a richly laden boat having been plundered by him on the Suir within four miles of Waterford. Amid the general corruption a bright example was shown by the Franciscan Maurice Doran, Bishop of Leighlin, a learned theologian, an eloquent preacher, and a man of blameless life. Being advised to increase the burdens of his clergy, he replied that he had rather shear his sheep than flay them. Doran was allowed to tend his flock for twenty months only. Having corrected the irregularities of his Archdeacon Maurice Kavanagh, he was treacherously murdered by him. It is some satisfaction to know that Kildare afterwards caught the Archdeacon and his accomplices, and hanged them in chains on the scene of the Bishop's murder.[296]

The Regulars not exempt from censure.

The Regulars by no means escaped censure. The Prior of the Hospitallers of Kilclogan in Wexford was as bad as Bishop Purcell, and 'kept fire in the steeple door of St. John's, until such time as he had out the ward that was within.' James Butler, Cistercian Abbot of Innislonagh and Dean of Lismore, attained a bad eminence. The citizens of Waterford represented him as a man of odious life, who neglected every duty, gave himself up to voluptuosity, and wasted the property of his house to provide for his open and scandalous immoralities. The people of Clonmel repeat the charge, and extend it to the other monks. The Augustinian Canons, in the great monastery of Athassel, of which Archbishop Butler was Prior, were no better. Nor were the mendicants blameless. The Carmelite Prior of Lady Abbey, near Clonmel, which was a parish church, kept a mistress and provided no divine service. The Prior of Knocktopher, also a Carmelite, and the Cistercian Abbot of Dusk, had sons. That secular priests should be fathers of families was of course common both in England and[Pg 299] Ireland; and they may be defended on the ground that they were really married, and that such unions, though condemned by the Church, were not repugnant to the public feeling of the age. But this can hardly be pleaded in favour of monks, and perhaps still less of friars. The Prior of Cahir neglected divine service, but was not accused of immorality. Many enormous crimes were objected against the Abbess of Kilclehin. The canons of St. Catherine's at Waterford had fallen out among themselves, and divided the revenues. All these houses were in south-eastern Ireland, but from what has been said of the state of cathedral churches in Irish districts it may be inferred that proportional irregularities existed elsewhere. The fact that priests were often the sons of priests rests upon less partial evidence than that of Bale, and it was condoned by the Holy See. Leo X. even showed special favour to a monk of Monasterevan, notwithstanding that he was a priest's son. Dispensations on account of defective birth are very common in the Papal correspondence, and were a source of income to the Curia. Archbishop Browne believed that in the Irishry not one parson in five was of legitimate birth. He cannot be considered impartial, but legitimacy was little regarded by the Irish.[297]

The good side of the monastic system.

That some monks were immoral or useless is doubtless true. There were critics who represented them as in every way worse than their English brethren, but some of these were men who desired the destruction of the abbeys that they might divide their lands, and whose indignation had not been excited by abuses until the wishes of the English Court were known. Robert Cowley, for instance, accused them generally of loose living and of 'keeping no hospitality save to themselves.' There is ample evidence that the monks were not all bad. The education of children was almost entirely in their hands. Six houses in Dublin, Kildare, and Kilkenny are mentioned as the only places where the rising generation[Pg 300] might be brought up in virtue, learning, and good behaviour. The boys were cared for by the Cistercians of St. Mary's, Dublin, and of Jerpoint, and by the Augustinian canons of Christ Church, Dublin, and of Kells and Conal. The girls were brought up by the canonesses of Gracedieu, near Swords. St. Mary's was also noted for its hospitality, being the only inn fit for men of rank; and the doors of Christ Church were always open for Parliament, Council, or Conference. To escape dissolution all the monks of these houses were ready to don secular habits. As to the services of the friars in holding stations, in visiting the sick, and in preaching, there can be no doubt whatever. Religion in Ireland was in fact only maintained by them. Most of the friaries had been founded or beautified by great families, who still continued to befriend them, and who reserved a last resting-place within their walls. The Franciscans were especially favoured in this way. Thus, the MacDonnells of Antrim were buried at Bunamargy, the Desmonds at Youghal and Tralee, the O'Briens at Ennis, the O'Donnells at Donegal, the Macnamaras at Quin, the Burkes at Athenry, and the MacCarthies at Irrelagh or Muckross. The Franciscan dress was often assumed in death and burial, and was thought to bespeak the favours of heaven. The Dominicans were planted and cherished in the same way. The Augustinian hermits and the Carmelites had many houses, but were much less important than the other two orders.[298]

Parliament of 1536.

When the Irish Parliament met for the despatch of business in May 1536 many important bills passed without any great difficulty. The proctors of the clergy, who had voices and claimed votes in the Lower House, objected to the King being declared supreme head of the Church; but their opposition was little regarded. Appeals to Rome were forbidden, the jurisdiction of the Pope abolished, and first-fruits vested in the Crown. Grey then prorogued Parliament, first to Kilkenny,[Pg 301] and afterwards to Dublin again. In the meantime Archbishop Browne had landed, and lost no time in recommending the royal supremacy to the people. He had but little success, and incurred some personal danger. Primate Cromer, who was in communication with Rome, took the other side, laying a curse on all who should accept the new system, and reminding his clergy that Ireland was the Pope's gift to England. Browne is said to have made a speech to Parliament, in which he appealed to the example of Christ, who paid tribute to Cæsar, and of the earliest popes, who acknowledged the supremacy of emperors and kings. A bill was then brought in for the suppression of twelve religious houses, and for giving the King a twentieth of all ecclesiastical revenues. A formidable opposition at once arose in both houses, and particularly in the Commons under the leadership of the King's sergeant, Sir Patrick Barnewall, who declared openly that the King's supremacy gave him power to reform abbeys but not to secularise them. He then went to England to lay his views before Henry, and Parliament was again prorogued for nearly four months.[299]

The Reformation makes no progress.

After eighteen months residence in Ireland Browne could report scarcely any progress. The new Head of the Church, by the mouth of his Archbishop, gave the people orders for their spiritual conduct; but they were not well received. All true Christian subjects were ordered to repudiate the Bishop of Rome, and to erase him from their service-books and manuals; but this was never done unless Browne sent his own servants to see to it. The power of binding and loosing and the system of indulgences were called juggling, and the people were reminded that God only could forgive sins. There was no Mediator but Christ, and the so-called Pope's 'great thunderclap of excommunication' could hurt nobody. These exhortations were in vain, while a conditional general indulgence was eagerly taken advantage of. A copy of the paper was even hung up openly in Kilmainham Church. Pilgrimages to Rome were never commoner, and bishops and[Pg 302] priors appointed by provision were received with open arms. The circular which spoke so contemptuously of the Holy See was Browne's composition, but it inculcated at least two doctrines which all modern Protestants reject—the invocation of the Virgin and prayers for the dead.[300]

Troubles of Archbishop Browne.

Lord Deputy Grey was opposed to doctrinal changes, and made no secret of his dislike to Browne, whom he suspected of traducing him. The Archbishop had little help from other officials, and the lawyers opposed him strongly. Lord Butler, Brabazon, Alen, and one or two others of small importance, constituted the whole innovating party. They arrogated to themselves the title of Catholic; they were the right Christians, and their opponents were sectaries. But Browne's antagonists were active and numerous. The Observants took the lead everywhere, and they relied on the support of Grey to defy the Archbishop's authority. Browne had imprisoned one of his own prebendaries. 'Howbeit, spite of my beard, whiles that I was at an house of Observants, to swear them, and also to extinct that name among them, my Lord Deputy hath set him at liberty. I think the simplest holy water clerk is better esteemed than I am.' Most of the clergy were unwilling to acknowledge the royal supremacy, or to denounce the Pope's authority, and they refused to preach at all. The most active preachers now contented themselves with holding forth in corners to select knots of sympathisers, and took no notice either of threats or exhortations. The oath of supremacy had as much effect as oaths taken under pressure usually have. Now and then some bold spirit would openly defy Browne. James Humfrey, the prebendary whom he imprisoned and Grey released, officiated at High Mass in St. Andrew's Church, and omitted to read the Archbishop's circular. The parish priest ascended the pulpit, and began to read the paper; but Humfrey gave a signal to the choir, and the reader's voice was drowned by those of the singers.[301]

[Pg 303]

He cannot agree with Bishop Staples.

By the admission of so zealous a reformer as Brabazon, Staples promoted the Word of God; but the effect of his eloquence was much lessened by the ill-feeling existing between him and the Archbishop. A report of one of Browne's sermons, which, as he alleged, was fabricated by Humfrey, had so excited the wrath of Staples that he denounced it from the pulpit. The Archbishop himself was present, and thought 'the three-mouthed Cerberus of hell could not have uttered it more viperiously.' The scene was in the church of Kilmainham, which was an exempt jurisdiction under the sole charge of Rawson the Prior. Browne also accused Staples of indulging in other 'rabulous revilings' against him, of denying that men should search the Scriptures, and of allowing his suffragan to pray first for the Pope, then for the Emperor, and lastly for the King, in the words, 'I pray God he never depart this world, until that he hath made amends.' Browne imprisoned the suffragan, whom Grey seems to have released without trial. Staples, on the other hand, reported that everyone was weary of the Archbishop's demeanour, and that he himself had never said a word against the King's supremacy, or in favour of the Pope. After an inquiry by Paynswick, Prior of Christ Church, and two others, the quarrel was patched up; but the relations existing between the two chief supporters of the Reformation were not at all conducive to its success.[302]

Lord Leonard Grey obnoxious to both parties.

It was bad enough to be called a heretic by the Bishop of Meath, but worse to be called a poll-shorn knave friar by a Lord Deputy who had soldiers and prisons. Browne said it was no safer to speak against Papal usurpations before Grey than if the Pope had been present. Lord Butler agreed with the Archbishop that Grey had a special zeal for popery, allowed the new system to be openly impugned in his presence, and in fact headed the reactionary party. According to[Pg 304] Browne, he went so far as to maintain a bishop appointed by the Pope against the King's nominee; but this is scarcely credible. Grey, however, had the Corporation of Limerick, and the Bishop and clergy there solemnly sworn to maintain the new order, and renounce the usurpations of Rome. He is said to have burned Down Cathedral, and defaced the tombs of the three saints there; and he was accused on his trial of turning the church into a stable, of pulling down the tower, and of sending the famous peal of bells to England: 'had not God of His justice prevented his iniquity by sinking the vessel and passengers wherein the said bells should have been conveyed.' Grey has himself recorded his proceedings at the Franciscan friary of Killeigh, whence he carried off the organ, the glass windows, and other valuable things. On the other hand, he spared Armagh; and, being at Trim shortly before the destruction of the miraculous Virgin there, 'very devoutly knelt before the idol, and heard three or four masses.' This may have been done from devotional feeling, or through sheer inconsistency, or to annoy Browne, Brabazon, and Alen, who were present, and who refused to enter the chapel, by way of showing an example to the people.[303]

Images, relics, and pilgrimages.

Browne had a conscientious hatred to images, which he called idols, and destroyed them wherever he could. In this case coming events had cast their shadow before, and he at one time thought it prudent to disclaim iconoclasm. 'There goeth,' he wrote in June 1538, 'a common bruit among the Irishmen, that I intend to pluck down our Lady of Trim, with other places of pilgrimages, as the Holy Cross, and such like, which indeed I never attempted, although my conscience would right well serve me to oppress such idols.' Even more[Pg 305] celebrated than the miraculous Virgin was the crozier with which St. Patrick had banished the snakes, and which had been brought from Armagh to Dublin. This wonder-working staff was said to have been delivered by Christ Himself to a hermit in a Mediterranean island, with directions to take it to Ireland, and hand it over to the saint. It was compared to the rod of Moses, and was the chief of a large tribe of croziers upon which people swore in preference to the gospels. The staff was burned publicly, and so was the Virgin of Trim, and a crucifix of peculiar sanctity kept at Ballibogan in Westmeath. The holy cross of Tipperary was probably spared for a time. Browne and his successors nearly put an end to relics, which are now so scarce that a learned member of Parliament in our own times is said to have imported the bones of a more or less authentic foreign saint. But it was beyond the power of Government to put down pilgrimages, which were numerous down to the present century. Of the holy places still remaining, Croagh Patrick in Mayo is probably the most remarkable.[304]

Conformity of Munster Bishops.

When the four Protestant members of Council—Browne, Brabazon, Alen, and Aylmer—visited Clonmel early in 1539, two archbishops and eight bishops took the oath of supremacy before them. The archbishops were Butler of Cashel and Bodkin of Tuam—the first regularly appointed, the second not acknowledged at Rome, but both in undisputed possession. Of the eight bishops, Milo Baron or Fitzgerald of Ossory, Nicholas Comyn of Waterford and Lismore, John Coyne or Quin of Limerick, Thomas Hurley of Emly, Matthew Sanders of Leighlin, and James O'Corrin of Killaloe, appear to have been regularly appointed. The submission of O'Corrin seems to have been resented at Rome; for a Papal administrator was appointed to oust him eighteen months afterwards. He found it necessary to make his peace, and his resignation in 1542 was accepted by the Pope. No[Pg 306] attempt was made to displace Baron, Comyn, Quin, Hurley, or Sanders. The remaining prelates present at Clonmel were probably Dominick Tirrey of Cork and Cloyne, and Richard Nangle of Clonfert. Tirrey was the King's nominee, and continued to hold the temporalities till his decease in 1556. Lewis Macnamara, a Franciscan, was set up against him at Rome, but he soon died, and the Pope did not again interfere for a long time. Nangle, being kept out of Clonfert by his rival, whom Grey was accused of favouring, at this time acted as Browne's suffragan or coadjutor. It is expressly stated that all the Bishops of Munster were present at Clonmel, and all have been mentioned but three. Ross was vacant, and probably Kilfenora. Young James Fitzmaurice, who had been lately provided to Ardfert, may have kept away in Kerry, or very probably he was not in Ireland at all. We must guard against hastily supposing that all, or even any, of these prelates were Protestants. Like Gardiner, Bonner, and Tunstal, they accepted the formulation of the old English principle of national independence, but they had not therefore necessarily any sympathy with the doctrines of Luther.[305]

The Pope makes Wauchop Primate.

Primate Cromer opposed the royal supremacy, but he was none the less accused of heresy at Rome, and Robert Wauchop, a priest of St. Andrews, was appointed to administer the see until the Archbishop should purge himself. Wauchop was a noted theologian, and, in spite of his imperfect sight, had the singular reputation of riding post better than any man in Europe. He had lived chiefly at Rome, and was employed by the Holy See on many missions, including attendance at the diets of Worms, Ratisbon, and Spires. The choice of a purblind man to persuade the sharp-eyed[Pg 307] Germans gave rise to a proverb, and the reputation for riding post may have been gained by the rapidity with which he went from place to place. After Cromer's death Wauchop received the pall, and bore the title of Primate at the Council of Trent, where he attended for eleven sessions, and where he shared with the Archbishop of Upsala the distinction of having never seen his church. In the meantime George Dowdall was appointed by the King on St. Leger's recommendation, and it must be supposed that he took the oath of supremacy. In spite of Dowdall's zeal against the reformed doctrines, he was never acknowledged by the Pope until after Wauchop's death. The latter does not appear to have landed in

Ireland, and his bolts were shot from Scotland or France. When preparing at last in 1551 to visit his diocese, he met a most edifying death in the Jesuit Church at Paris.[306]

The Jesuits sent to Ireland, 1542.

It was by Wauchop's advice that the disciples of Loyola began their work in Ireland. Paul III. addressed a brief to Con O'Neill, as prince of the Irish of Ulster, acknowledging the receipt of letters which he had sent to Rome by the hands of Raymond O'Gallagher, 'by which letters,' wrote the Pope, 'and by his fuller verbal communications, our mind has been variously affected; for we have learned with the pain it calls for how that island is cruelly ravaged by the present King, and to what a pitch of impiety he has brought it, and with what savage ferocity he has spurned the honour of God Almighty. But when, on the other hand, we learned from thy letters and Raymond's words that there existed in thy person a champion of God, and of the Roman Church and of the Catholic religion, we rejoiced greatly in the heavenly Father's love. We praise thee then, beloved son, as thou hast deserved, and commend thee in the Lord; and we give Him thanks for granting thee to us and endowing thee with such virtue and piety for the preservation of that[Pg 308] island at the present time, and we pray Him long to prosper thee, and to preserve thee to us unchanged. We have taken such care as we were bound, and as thou hast asked us to take for thee and for the other champions of the Catholic Faith. We therefore exhort your lordship, and all the peoples of Ireland who follow your authority and piety, to preserve you all as becomes faithful servants of the True Christ, in the Catholic Faith which you have received from your fathers, and preserved with the greatest constancy to this day. For we who embrace that island with singular affection and desire to preserve it in its ancient attachment to the Holy Faith, will never be wanting to your lordship or to your followers in piety.'

The first Jesuit missionaries.

John Codure and Alphonso Salmeron were selected by the Pope as nuncios to Ireland, and another brief was sent to the clergy of Ireland exhorting them to receive the Jesuits with honour and goodwill. Codure died before he could visit Ireland, and Paschal Broet accompanied Salmeron in his stead. Francesco Zapata, not yet admitted to the society, was their secretary. Broet, whom Loyola called the angel of his society, was a native of Picardy. Salmeron was a Spaniard, and one of the original seven companions who took the momentous vow upon the hill of Montmartre. Ignatius himself gave directions to the mission:—

Loyola's instructions to them.

1. They were to use caution in talking, especially with inferiors and equals, to 'take each man's censure but reserve their judgment.' When they could not avoid expressing an opinion, it was to be delivered briefly and with a careless air, so as to avoid further argument.

2. They were to be all things to all men, like St. Paul. An angry man was to be treated with great circumspection.

3. The precept of Basilius was to be observed, that the devil must be fought with his own weapons. To gain favour at first they were to praise virtues rather than denounce

vices. Medicine might then by degrees be administered. Morose men might be won by cheerfulness.

4. In public and private, and especially when performing the duty of peacemakers, they were to remember that 'all[Pg 309] their words and deeds might become known, and that the things done in darkness would be brought to light.'

5. Appointments were to be anticipated rather than deferred, so that there might be plenty of time for the business in hand.

6. In money matters they were to meddle as little as possible. Even the fines which they took for dispensations should be given in alms by the hands of others, so that they might be able to swear that they had not touched one penny.

7. Paschal was to be chief speaker in dealing with great men. In doubtful cases there was to be a consultation, and the opinion of two was to bind the other.

8. They were to correspond with Rome frequently on their journey, immediately on their arrival either in Ireland or Scotland, and at least once a month afterwards.[307]

Their adventures in Scotland and Ireland.

After narrowly escaping imprisonment in France, the three emissaries reached Scotland and saw James V., who gave them a commendatory letter to the Irish nobility and a special one to O'Neill, whom he exhorted so to receive the strangers that they might feel the advantage of his introduction. A brother of Bishop Farquharson of the Isles accompanied them to Ireland, where they found nothing to their liking, either civil or ecclesiastical. The people were savage and the clergy negligent, and neither bishoprics nor parishes were properly served. All the chiefs but one were not only sworn to the royal supremacy, but had declared their readiness to burn the Pope's letters and to deliver his messengers bound to the King or his Deputy. The single exception was about to follow the general example. The Irish chiefs were all afraid to confer with the nuncios, or even to secure them a safe passage out of the island. The Jesuits also complained that the Scottish King had not performed his promises. But if Paschal and his companions could do nothing with the chiefs, they were successful with the people. They changed their place of abode constantly, exhorting men everywhere[Pg 310] in private, hearing confessions, and celebrating the Mass as often as possible. Indulgences were sparingly granted, but they gained goodwill by varying burdensome vows, and by remitting fines and dues. Their personal virtue was evident; they never spared themselves, and they asked for nothing. Any money that came within their reach they diverted through the debtor himself, or through the bishop, to such good work as the repair of churches, the relief of widows, and the care of unprotected girls. After thirty-four days thus spent the pursuit waxed too hot. Rewards were offered for their apprehension, and they escaped to Scotland, where they vainly hoped to find a quieter people. The Scotch chiefs seemed as bad as the Irish, and the foreigners were fain to sail to Dieppe, whence they reached Paris on foot. Zapata remained there for study, and the two Jesuits pursued their journey to Rome in rags, and almost penniless. They were arrested as spies at Lyons, but rescued by Cardinals Tournon and Gaddi, who were passing through and who recognised them. Thus, in apparent, but only apparent, failure ended the first descent of the Jesuits upon Ireland.[308]

The royal supremacy opposed by the friars.

In the days of Henry VIII. the majority of Irish chiefs seem to have cared greatly for land, much less, but still a great deal, for titles and gold chains, and very little for religion. They were, therefore, ready enough to accept the King's ecclesiastical polity; the rather that they hoped to go on exactly as they had done before. But with the people it was different. It was not for their interest that tribal lands should be turned into private estates, nor could they hope for special marks of royal favour. They were barbarous, but they could appreciate virtue, and in the austere self-denial of some friars they could discern glimmerings of a higher light. Against the friars Henry had no available weapon; they could not even be prevented from preaching. Under the very shadow of Dublin Castle the King could give[Pg 311] no peace to his reformed Church, of which the only sincere supporters were a few new comers from England. Except Browne and Staples, who, as we have seen, did not agree, there was no one to preach what Henry wished the people to learn. And neither of them could speak a word of Irish. The lawyers in Dublin heard and disliked the expounders of the new ideas, but the great mass of the population did not even hear them. The friars had it all their own way, and every feeling, national and sentimental, predisposed the Irish to believe their statement of the case. The people were told that Ireland was a fief of the Holy See, and that the vassal had forfeited all by treason to his sovereign lord. The Defender of the Faith had become its assailant, and he was manifestly no longer a Catholic. These were the arguments used daily and never answered. 'In the Irishry,' Staples reported, 'the common voice runneth that the supremacy of our sovereign lord is maintained only by power, and not reasoned by learning.' He recommended that all Irish clerks should have safe-conduct to come and go, and to dispute with himself. 'I trust then,' he added, perhaps with a side cut at the Archbishop, 'to do my master good service, without railing or "frasing," which doth well nowhere, but least in a good cause.' And he strongly urged the assumption of the royal title, as at least one means to disabuse the popular mind. In the meantime the counter reformation had begun. The official Church was to be defended mainly by power, by a few English-speaking ecclesiastics, and by the self-seekers who sought preferment where the sceptre was strong enough to protect them. On the side of Rome was ranged every popular feeling and prejudice, and it was to have the support of crowds of devoted men who could exhort the people in their own tongue, and whose example was sometimes more eloquent than their words.

Irish view of Henry's innovations.

The 'Four Masters' describe Henry's reformation as 'a heresy and new error in England, through pride, vain-glory, avarice, and lust, and through many strange sciences, so that the men of England went into opposition to the Pope and to Rome. They at the same time adopted various opinions and[Pg 312] the old law of Moses, and they styled the King the chief head of the Church of God in his own kingdom. New laws were enacted by the King and Council according to their own will. They destroyed the orders to whom worldly possessions were allowed ... and the four poor orders ...; and the lordships and livings of all these were taken up for the King. They broke down the monasteries, and sold their roofs and bells, so that from Arran of the Saints to the Straits of Dover there was not one monastery that was not broken and shattered, with the exception of a few in Ireland, of which the English took no heed. They afterwards burned the images, shrines, and relics of the saints of Ireland and England.... They also appointed archbishops and sub-bishops for themselves; and though great was the persecution of the Roman emperors against the Church, scarcely had there ever come so great a persecution from Rome as this; so that it is impossible to narrate or tell its description, unless it should be narrated by one who saw it.' There can be no doubt that these were the ideas prevalent in Ireland in the sixteenth century, and they remain essentially unchanged in the nineteenth. That the annalists tell but a small part of the whole truth must be plain to candid students; but it is the only part which the native Irish have ever accepted. In England Anglicanism was the outcome of national independence; in Ireland it was the badge of conquest.

The King resolves to dissolve the religious houses.

Barnewall's mission failed; but he did not lose the King's favour, and was soon promoted: had he been an English lawyer he would have lost his head. While denying the King's right to dissolve monasteries, he made no objection to receiving a grant of their lands, and accepted that very nunnery of Gracedieu where all the young ladies of the Pale had been educated. When the houses met again the clergy opposed all legislation, being perhaps excited by rumours of a Geraldine restoration. The proctors insisted on their right to vote as an estate, and the bishops and abbots, who formed a majority in the Lords, declined to entertain any business until the point was decided. The Council gave a decided opinion that the claim of the proctors was unfounded, and[Pg 313] the spiritual peers at last agreed to proceed to business with or without their consent. The Lords threw out the Bill for confirming the King's title to certain abbeys, most of which had already been suppressed; making an exception only in the case of St. Wolstan's. The Bill for giving the King a twentieth part of all spiritualities was also rejected. After a further prorogation for four months this resistance was at length overcome. An Act was passed declaring the proctors to be no members of Parliament, the first-fruits of abbeys were given to the King, the suppressions were confirmed, the much desired twentieth was granted, and the questions of faculties and testamentary dispositions were arranged in a sense hostile to Rome. As far as an Act of Parliament could do it, the Church in Ireland was now placed on the same footing as the Church in England.[309]

First convent dissolved, 1535. Relative strength of different orders.

The first Irish religious house dissolved by Henry VIII. seems to have been the nunnery of Grane, which gave a title to Lord Leonard Grey; but the nuns were quartered on other houses: this was in 1535. In the latter half of 1536 a commission under the Great Seal not now extant was issued for the suppression of eight Irish abbeys named therein. The earliest victim of the batch was probably St. Wolstan's near Leixlip, a house of canons of the congregation of St. Victor, which was granted to John Alen, the Master of the Rolls. The necessary inquiries into the condition and property of the doomed institutions were too slow for Henry, who chided the Irish Council for remissness. They promised to proceed as speedily as was consistent with his Highness's profit. Before the end of 1537 fifteen more houses had fallen, all within the Pale or in the immediate neighbourhood of walled towns. After this the process of surveying and suppressing went on rapidly, so that by 1541 all, or very nearly all, the houses in Dublin, Kildare, Meath, Louth, Carlow, Kilkenny, Wexford, Tipperary, Waterford, and Limerick city had been[Pg 314] surrendered. A careful calculation makes the whole number about seventy-eight, of which thirty-eight were Canons Regular, eleven Crutched Friars, fifteen Hospitallers, two Benedictines, and twelve Cistercians. Only ten of the number were nunneries, all belonging to Regular Canonesses. To these may be added a few in other districts, such as Aghmacarte in MacGillapatrick's country, and Midleton in the county of Cork.[310]

The Cistercians. Mellifont.

Some monasteries deserve particular mention, and of these Mellifont, the oldest of the Cistercian houses, is perhaps the most famous. It is said to have contained 140 monks, and was called Monastermore, or the Great Monastery. The Cistercians were introduced about 1142 by Donough O'Carroll, Prince of Oriel, at the instance of Malachy, the friend of Bernard of Clairvaux, who wrote his life and in whose arms he died. St. Bernard supplied the new foundation with monks from his own monastery, under the leadership of Christian O'Conarchy, afterwards Bishop of Lismore and papal legate, who presided in that synod of Cashel where the Irish Church was first formally subjected both to Rome and to England. King John afterwards confirmed all grants made before the conquest, and several later sovereigns were benefactors of Mellifont. The abbot was always summoned to Parliament, where he took precedence of all his mitred brethren, and ranked immediately below the bishops. The buildings, of which there are still some remains, are said to have greatly resembled those of Clairvaux. The rich estates[Pg 315] were granted by Elizabeth to Lord Drogheda's ancestor as a reward for defending the northern border of the Pale against the Ulster Irish.[311]

Holy Cross.

Another famous Cistercian abbey was that of Holy Cross on the Suir, whose beautiful ruins recall, though they do not rival, Fountains, Furness, and Rivaulx. This monastery was founded by Donald O'Brien, King of Limerick, shortly before the Anglo-Norman invasion. A fragment of the true cross preserved here attracted many pilgrims, and is thought by some to have been contained in a richly sculptured shrine which still stands. Long after the dissolution pilgrimages continued, and Sir Henry Sidney noted the 'detestable idolatry used to an idol called the Holy Cross, whereunto there is no small confluence of people daily resorting.' The abbots had seats in Parliament, and from the extent of their territorial power were sometimes called Earls.[312]

Dunbrody and Tintern.

Two Cistercian abbeys near one another in Wexford are remarkable from the circumstances of their foundations. Dunbrody was built by the ruthless conqueror, Hervey de Montmorenci, who sought to expiate his cruelties by becoming its abbot and endowing it with all his property. Tintern was founded in fulfilment of a vow made during a storm at sea by William Marshal, Earl of Pembroke, who brought monks and a name from Wales. Tintern was the only Irish abbey which retained the original black dress of Citeaux, thus acknowledging the foundation of Stephen Harding rather than that of Bernard.

Hospitallers. Kilmainham.

Strongbow founded a preceptory for Templars at Kilmainham in 1174, and it became rich and powerful. Under Edward II. the order was suppressed in Ireland with as little pretence of justice as elsewhere, and its possessions granted to the Hospitallers, who showed less charity to the really poor, though their doors were always open to strangers and travellers of importance. The priors of Kilmainham were often[Pg 316] chosen from the greatest families—Talbots, Butlers, and Fitzgeralds—were always summoned to

Parliament, and became very important personages. Being exempt from episcopal jurisdiction they sometimes acted almost like independent princes. In 1444 the Prior, Thomas Fitzgerald, espoused the cause of Archbishop Talbot in his quarrel with the White Earl of Ormonde, and he challenged the latter to trial by combat. The fight was appointed to take place at Smithfield, and both champions were kept in close custody; the Earl being confined in the Tower, of which the Duke of Exeter, inventor of the rack and other gentle instruments, was then constable. The Duke was authorised to allow his distinguished prisoner exercise enough to keep him in good fighting condition, his swordsmanship being evidently thought adequate. The representative of the Church militant was considered wanting in skill, and was detained in the city to receive instructions at the royal expense from Philip Treherne, fishmonger and fencing master. Ormonde's friends cleared his character, and the combat never took place. Many acts of turbulence were charged against Fitzgerald; but he was far outstripped by James Keating, who became prior in 1461, and who defied the King, the Deputy, and his own Grand Master for thirty years. Marmaduke Lumley was sent to supersede him, but died of the ill-treatment which he received. In 1511 Sir John Rawson, the last prior, was appointed. He was an able man and a chief supporter of the Government, but did not think it necessary to observe his vow of chastity. At the dissolution Rawson was created Viscount of Clontarf, where there was a cell of his house, and enjoyed a pension of 500 marks till his death in Edward VI.'s time. Sir William Weston, the English Provincial, was less fortunate, for he was forced to leave his priory and died the same day. The great possessions of Kilmainham were granted to different persons, and the site of the commandery is now fitly occupied by a military hospital, which owes its foundation to the great Duke of Ormonde.[313]

[Pg 317]

Pensions to monks.

Pensions were generally granted to the heads of the dissolved houses and sometimes to the other monks. Thus the Abbot of Mellifont received 40l., and several of the monks from 3l. 6s. 8d. to 20s. The Prior of Fower in Westmeath and the Abbot of St. Mary's, Dublin, received each 50l.; the Prior of St. Thomas's, Dublin, 42l.; and others were paid in proportion to the importance of their convents. In a few cases priors received as little as 3l., and monks as little as 13s. 4d. The ejected brethren often got other preferment. Edmond O'Lonergan, Prior of Cahir, who received a pension of 3l. 6s. 8d., was made vicar of the parish, and William Walsh, Prior of Ballydrohid, had a pension of 6l. 8s. 4d. till he should receive a benefice of greater value. Hugh Doyne, one of the monks of Conal, who had received a pension of 40s., surrendered it on being presented by the Crown to a vicarage. Pensions were charged on the lands of the dissolved houses, and power of distress was sometimes given. The absence of complaints may justify a supposition that payments were pretty regularly made. Great numbers of monks doubtless withdrew to the Continent. Mary herself grumbled at the numerous pensions payable to clerks, and directed her Deputy to make them the first objects of his patronage, so that the pensions might be gradually absorbed.[314]

Titular abbots still appointed. Cistercians.

In the case of the Cistercians at least titular abbots were sometimes appointed for many generations. Alemand, the French historian of Irish monasteries, says that the learned Nicholas Fagan, Bishop of Waterford, was Abbot of Innislonagh, and was buried in the abbey in 1617. According to the same author, who wrote towards the end of the seventeenth century, there were in his time Abbots of Mellifont, Tintern, and Boyle, living in the neighbourhood of their abbeys, but dressing like laymen. They were probably chiefly occupied in receiving novices for education in foreign convents. An important paper drawn up at Waterford in 1646 bears the signature of one prior of Augustinian canons, and of four[Pg 318] Cistercian abbots, to say nothing of Jesuits and mendicants, but some of these may have been appointed after the breaking out of the rebellion. In the reign of James I. some Cistercians certainly lurked in Ireland. The nuncio Rinuccini, who had the charge of Irish patronage from 1645, apologised for preferring so many regulars on the ground that men of family seldom became secular priests.[315]

The dissolution not carried out in remote districts.

In 1541 a commission was issued to the Earl of Desmond and others to survey and dissolve all religious houses in Cork, Limerick, Kerry, and Desmond. In these districts and in the purely Irish regions of Connaught and Ulster, the process of dissolution was slow and uncertain. The title of the Crown was theoretically acknowledged, but in some cases nothing was done for many years. As the native nobility were subdued or reconciled, Henry VIII.'s policy was gradually carried out. In the wildest parts of Ulster the consummation was delayed until after the flight of the Earls in the reign of James I.[316]

Number and wealth of religious foundations. Many are losers by the dissolution.

Without counting the mendicant orders, about 350 religious houses can be traced in Ireland. Many of these had disappeared before the reign of Henry VIII., having become parish churches, or been absorbed in episcopal establishments. Others were dependent on English foundations, and were destroyed by the Act of Absentees; others, again, were cells to more important houses, and followed their fortunes. A yearly income of 32,000l., with personalty to the amount of 100,000l., has been attributed to the Irish monasteries, and their possessions must certainly have been considerable. The monks, and especially the Cistercians, generally chose fertile situations near a river or on the coast, for the sake of fish and water carriage. The most beautiful and convenient sites were in their hands, and their system of cultivation was much superior to that of lay proprietors. The ceaseless wars of Ireland did not entirely spare the religious houses, but they escaped better than other kinds of property. The spoiling of[Pg 319] the Church could never have been considered a great or glorious work. The wealth of the monks is not to be measured by the extent of their lands. It is in the vast number of their houses, orchards, gardens, fishing-weirs, and mills, that we must seek the evidence of accumulated capital. The immense circuit of the walls at Kells or Athassel seems to show that great numbers of artificers and labourers were sheltered within the enclosures, and that the monks knew how to defend their own. The system of corrodies or resident pensions probably reconciled the great nobles, and opposition to the dissolution came partly from those who were impoverished by their abolition. It is to these pensions, which were perhaps often abused, that Cowley probably alludes when he accuses the monks generally of immorality and of showing no hospitality save to themselves and 'certain bell-wedders, which ringleaders have good fees, fat, profitable farms, the finding of their children, with other daily pleasures of the abbeys, and fearing to lose the profit thereof, repugn and resist the suppressing of abbeys, surmising it should be prejudicial to the common weal, which is otherwise.'[317]

The Friaries suppressed. Not before 1541.

In 1541 a commission was issued to Sir Anthony St. Leger and others to survey and suppress all the friaries in Ireland. The total number was rather under two hundred, of which the Franciscans had more than half, the Dominicans forty-three, the Augustinian hermits twenty-four, and the Carmelites twenty-one. As in the case of the older monasteries, the houses within reach were at once dissolved, and the rest were perforce respited. Their possessions were not large, and the friars managed to exist without them. The Dominican historian says there were about six hundred members of his order in Ireland just before Cromwell's conquest, and the Franciscans were probably much more numerous. The houses of Grey Friars had been very generally reformed by the Observants, and it is with these stricter votaries that we generally meet. They swarmed everywhere, and to them is due the[Pg 320] preservation of the Roman tradition until the Jesuits made head in Ireland. Archbishop Browne is never tired of testifying against them, and Thomas Agard, his enthusiastic supporter, calls them crafty bloodsuckers. Almost the only open opposition to the dissolution came from a Franciscan, Dr. Sall, who boldly preached against it at Waterford. During the Cromwellian war and subsequent persecution the Franciscans claim thirty-one martyrs, which shows that they must have been very numerous. In 1645 the Carmelites reckoned twenty-seven houses in Ireland, but most of these were doubtless desecrated and deserted. No candid Protestant can altogether sympathise with Browne and Agard, for we have the most overwhelming proof that but for the friars a large part of the population would have been altogether debarred from the exercise of religion.[318]

All kinds of men share the plunder.

Most of the men who had been useful in carrying out the suppression received a share of the spoils. Brabazon, St. Leger, Sir John Alen, Chief Justice Luttrell, Edmund Sexton, Sir Thomas Cusack, and Robert Dillon, were all enriched in this way. Prime-serjeant Barnewall denied the King's right to dissolve the monasteries, but profited largely by the measure. Celts, Normans, and Saxons, Papists and Protestants alike, showed a fine appetite for the confiscated lands. Desmond had a lease of part of St. Mary Abbey, perhaps to induce him to spend some of his time in Dublin. Three at least of the new peerages—Upper Ossory, Carbery, and Cahir, were partially endowed from similar sources. Edward Power, bastard brother of the first baron of Curraghmore, was granted the possession of Mothel, of which he had been prior. In some cases, as in Clanricarde and Thomond, the Government made a virtue of necessity, and gave monastic lands to lords or chiefs who would have had the power to seize them in any case. It is scarcely necessary to say that the House of Ormonde profited enormously by the dissolution. Sometimes the plunder was too small to excite much cupidity, and then the monks might be spared. Thus the Austinfriars of Dun[Pg 321]more in Galway, who had 'neither land nor profit, but only the small devotion of the people,' were respited during the King's pleasure, on condition of assuming a secular habit. A like indulgence was given to the canons of Toem in Tipperary, which the O'Meaghers had been able to prevent the Royal Commissioners from visiting. Many houses were reasonably granted to the founders' kin, for the dissolution must have been a heavy loss to some families. Most of the corporate towns had founded or fostered monasteries, and Waterford, Drogheda, Kilkenny, Galway, Limerick, Clonmel, and Athenry received a portion of the spoils. All Saints was specially granted to the citizens of Dublin in compensation of their loss during the

Geraldine siege. As a general rule, monastic lands were at first let only on lease, and in succeeding reigns large fines were obtained by the Crown. At the first threat of dissolution some houses hastened to let their lands for long terms, and to cut down their woods and sell their jewels, and thus the plunder actually realised often fell below expectation. I have met with but one case of a charitable foundation being laid immediately upon the ruins of a monastery, and that was owing to private liberality. Henry Walshe, son of a Waterford merchant, bought the Grey Friars from the King, and founded a hospital for sixty or more sick persons. This institution received a royal charter, and still exists on a reduced scale.[319]

No university in Ireland.

No care was taken to supply the place of the monasteries which were devoted to education. There had been three attempts to found a university in Ireland before the reign of Henry VIII. In 1310 John Lech, Archbishop of Dublin, obtained a bull from Clement V., who ordered the establishment of the desired institution, which would, he hoped, 'sprinkle the said land, like a watered garden, to the exaltation of the Catholic faith, the honour of the mother church, and the profit of all the faithful.' Lech died soon after, and[Pg 322] his project was buried with him; but his successor, Alexander de Bicknor, actually made a foundation in connection with St. Patrick's Cathedral, and under the patronage of John XXII. Bicknor's University maintained a very precarious existence till the time of Henry VII., when it finally disappears. The institution was not crushed by the weight of its endowments, for it does not seem to have had any. In 1465 Bicknor's work was ignored by the Parliament of Drogheda, which founded a new university on the ground that there was none in Ireland. But it was not enough to declare that Drogheda should be as Oxford: there was no endowment and no popular support, and this scheme also failed. Very near the end of his reign Henry VIII. made up his mind that one cathedral was enough for Dublin, and he suppressed St. Patrick's. Christ Church had already been acknowledged as the metropolitan church. But it was not till the next reign that Archbishop Browne propounded his abortive plan for restoring the University which had once faintly glimmered.[320]

Archbishop Browne.

The principal instrument by which Henry carried out his ecclesiastical revolution was George Browne, Provincial of the English Austinfriars, who was appointed Archbishop of Dublin in 1535 after regular election by the two chapters. He was consecrated by Cranmer, Fisher, and Shaxton of Salisbury, who were significantly commanded to invest him with the pall. Browne's appointment is ignored at Rome, but no rival prelate was at first set up. He had already distinguished himself by preaching strongly against the invocation of saints, and, whatever his faults were, he was certainly a sincere Protestant. 'The common voice goeth,' said Staples, who had not quite made up his own mind, 'that he doth abhor the Mass.' Browne was married, but whether before or after his consecration does not appear. He zealously promoted the King's supremacy and the destruction of images, and complained bitterly of being thwarted by his colleague of Armagh, by the Irish generally, and even by Lord Deputy Grey. Cromer was in communication with Rome, and circulated a sort of[Pg 323] Papal oath of allegiance among the clergy, in which obedience to heretical powers was denounced and all their acts declared null and void. The old jealousy between Armagh and Dublin may have had something to say to this; for Browne, if we may believe Staples, claimed authority over all the clergy of Ireland. The new Archbishop did not bear himself meekly in his great office, and he received a stinging rebuke, which the writer was pleased to call a gentle advertisement, from the King himself. Henry accused his nominee of neglecting the instruction of the people and the interests of the Crown. 'Such,' he added, 'is your lightness in behaviour and such is the elation of your mind in pride, that glorying in foolish ceremonies, and delighting in we and us, in your dreams comparing yourself so near to a prince in honour and estimation, that all virtue and honesty is almost banished from you. Reform yourself therefore ... and let it sink into your remembrance that we be as able for the not doing thereof to remove you again and to put another man of more virtue and honesty in your place, both for our discharge against God, and for the comfort of our good subjects there, as we were at the beginning to prefer you.' Well might Browne answer that the King's letter made him tremble in body for fear. He defended himself at length, and invoked the fate of Korah should he fail to advance the King's service. His defence seems to have satisfied Henry, but he continued to make many enemies and to excite much criticism. 'His pride and arrogance,' said Staples, 'hath ravished him from the right remembrance of himself.'[321]

Bishop Staples.

Edward Staples, originally a Cambridge man, and afterwards parson of Tamworth and a canon of Cardinal College, was appointed to the see of Meath in 1530 by Papal provision. Either as Bishop or Privy Councillor he incurred the hatred of the Geraldine faction, and fled to England on the breaking out of the rebellion in 1534. Early next year he returned, and was one of the commissioners for suppressing the nunnery[Pg 324] of Grane. Staples did not at first fully embrace the reformed doctrines, for he accused the Archbishop of Dublin of heresy, and appears to have been attached to the Mass; but he was as zealous as Browne for the royal supremacy, and his conversion to thorough Protestantism was gradual like Cranmer's. Staples was a noted preacher, and was promoted for that reason; but the King at one time accused him of slackness and threatened to remove him.[322]

FOOTNOTES:

[281] Surrey to Wolsey, Sept. 6, 1520, and the notes; Pace to Wolsey, April 7, 1521, in Carew; Stubbs, Const. Hist. ii. 317.

[282] Ware's Bishops; Richard Culoke to Brabazon, Nov. 10, 1537; the King to the Lord Deputy and Council, July 10, 1543.

[283] Ware.

[284] Brady's Episcopal Succession, vol. i. p. 325; Ware. Roy's satire against Wolsey, printed in the 9th vol. of the Harleian Miscellany, has the following:

Wat. And who did for the show pay?
Jeff. Truly many a rich abbaye
To be eased of his visitation.
Wat. Doth he in his own person visit?
No, another for him doth it,

That can skill of the occupation.
A fellow neither wise nor sad,
But he was never yet full mad,
Though he be frantic and more.
Dr. Alen he is named,
One that to lie is not ashamed
If he spy advantage therefore.
Wat. Are such with him in any price?
Jeff. Yea, for they do all his advice,
Whether it be wrong or right.

[285] As to the legatine authority, see Brewer, vol. iii., No. 2838, and iv., No. 5131; John Alen to Wolsey, June 1, 1523, in S.P.

[286] Clement VII. to Henry VIII., Oct. 21, 1524, in Brewer and in Rymer; Kildare's Articles against Ormonde in S.P., vol. ii. p. 123; and see Brewer, vol. iv., No. 4277; R. Cowley to Wolsey in 1528, S.P., vol. ii. p. 141; Presentments of Grievances, edited by Graves, p. 203; Council of Ireland to Cromwell, Feb. 8, 1539.

[287] Brady, vol. ii.; Council of Ireland to Cromwell, Feb. 8, 1539.

[288] Theiner's Vetera Monumenta, pp. 515, 516, 521; Brady, Arts, Kilmore, Clogher, and Raphoe.

[289] Kildare to Wolsey, Feb. 8, 1522; R. Cowley to Wolsey, S.P., vol. ii., No. 53; Ware.

[290] For the Ross case, see Theiner, p. 520; for the union of Ross and Dromore 'propter tenuitatem utriusque ecclesiæ,' see Brady, vol. ii. p. 109.

[291] See Brady, under Elphin and Kilmacduagh.

[292] S.P., vol. ii. pp. 11, 15, and 16.

[293] For Ardagh, see Theiner, p. 521; for Ross, p. 529; for Clonmacnoise, p. 518. For Enaghdune, see Ossory to Cromwell in 1532, Carew, vol. i. No. 37.

[294] Presentments of Grievances, ed. Graves; particularly pp. 192 and 203.

[295] Kildare's Articles against Ormonde in 1525, S.P., vol. ii. p. 123; his statement is partially confirmed by the Presentments of Grievances, and see Ossory's own statements in 1534, Carew, vol. i. p. 55; Ware's Life and Death of Archbishop Browne.

[296] Indenture of Remembrance for the Earl of Ossory and Lord Butler, May 31, 1534, in Carew; Presentments of Grievances, pp. 48 and 204; Four Masters, 1525; Dowling's Annals, 1522:—'Mauritius Doran episcopus in jocando ejus adventu quibusdam persuadentibus duplicari subsidium cleri respondit: melius radere oves quam destruere.'

[297] Presentments of Grievances, especially pp. 100, 202, 204, and 248; for the sons of clergy, &c., see Kildare's Articles in S.P., vol. ii. p. 122. In Brewer, Feb. 25, 1521, Leo X. authorises a priest's son to govern the Cistercian Abbey of Rosglas; Browne to Cromwell, Nov. 6, 1538, in S.P.; for Kilclehin (wrongly calendared as Kilcullen), see Hamilton, Oct. 9, 1539.

[298] For the educating monasteries, see Lord Deputy and Council to Cromwell, May 21, 1539, and the petition from St. Mary's, July 31. The value of the friars appears from the whole history of the time. See in particular Presentments of Grievances, p. 130; R. Cowley to Cromwell, Oct. 4, 1536.

[299] Browne to Cromwell, July 15, 1536 (?), in Browne's Life and Death, in Ware, p. 148, and in the Phœnix; R. Cowley to Cromwell, Oct. 4, 1536.

[300] Browne to Cromwell, Jan. 8, May 8, and Aug. 10, 1538. The Form of the Beads in S.P., vol. ii., No. 214; R. Cowley to Cromwell, July 19, 1538 and Aug. 5.

[301] James White to Cromwell, March 28; Lord Butler to the King, March 31; again to Cromwell, April 5; Brabazon to Cromwell, April 30; Browne to Cromwell, Jan. 8, May 8 and 20, 1538.

[302] This quarrel may be traced in detail in the State Papers. Browne to J. Alen, April 15, 1538; to Cromwell, May 8 and 21, and June 20 and 27; Staples to St. Leger, June 17; to Cromwell, June 10 and Aug. 10; Thomas Alen to Cromwell, Oct. 20; Brabazon to Cromwell, April 30.

[303] Grey to Cromwell, Dec. 31, 1537; J. Alen to Cromwell, Oct. 20, 1538; Browne's Letters in S.P. from 1538 to 1540; R. Cowley to Cromwell, July 19, 1538; Lord Butler to Cromwell, Aug. 26. Butler says that at the Lord Deputy's table the vicar of Chester said the King had commanded images to be set up, worshipped, and honoured as much as ever. 'We held us all in silence to see what the Lord Deputy would say thereto. He held his peace, and said nothing; and then my Lord of Dublin, the Master of the Rolls, and I said that if ... he were out of the Deputy's presence, we would put him fast by the heels.... His lordship said nothing all the while. Surely he hath a special zeal to the Papists.' For Down Cathedral, see Stanihurst.

[304] Ware places the destruction of relics in 1538: it was perhaps a little later. For Our Lady of Trim and the Baculum Jesu, see the Four Masters, under 1537, and O'Donovan's notes; also Giraldus Cambrensis, Top. Dist. iii. cap. 33 and 34, and Expug. lib. ii. c. 19, Record Edition. The notice in Campion is perhaps only an echo of Giraldus.

[305] The above paragraph is founded on a careful comparison of the data in Ware, Cotton, and Brady. R. Cowley to Cromwell, Aug. 5, 1538; and see S.P., vol. iii. pp. 110, 117, and 123. A letter from Staples to St. Leger, June 17, 1538, throws some light on Henry's relations with Rome before the divorce question arose: 'Appoint some means how that such bishops as had their bulls of the Bishop of Rome by our sovereign lord's commandment may bring in their bulls, cancelling the same, and to have some remembrance from his Highness, which shall stand them in like effect with the same.'

[306] There are notices of Wauchop in Ware, Brady, Sarpi, ii. 34 (French translation and Courayer's notes), and Moran's Spicilegium Ossoriense, vol. i. p. 13. Twelve letters of Wauchop printed in the last-named work have nothing particular to do with Ireland. He must be regarded as founder of the titular hierarchy in Ireland.

[307] Abstracted from Hogan's Hibernia Ignatiana, p. 4, where Paul's letter may be also read in the original Latin.

[308] Hogan's Hibernia Ignatiana, pp. 3-9. Paul III.'s letter to Con O'Neill is dated April 24, 1541. The Jesuits were in Ireland in February and March, 1542. O'Sullivan Beare, lib. iii. cap. 8. James V. to the Irish chiefs, in S.P., vol. v. p. 202; Paget to Henry VIII. from Lyons, July 13, 1542, in S.P., vol. ix. p. 106.

[309] Calendar of Patent Rolls, p. 73; Grey to Cromwell, Feb. 4, 1537. The last session began Oct. 13, 1537; a detailed account is given by Brabazon in a letter to Cromwell in S.P., vol. ii. p. 524, and in the note there.

[310] Grey and Brabazon to Cromwell, May 18, 1537. The King to the Lord Deputy and Council, S.P., vol. ii. p. 425. Harris's Ware under Staples, Bishop of Meath. For the names of the dissolved houses, see the Statute, 28 Henry VIII. cap. 16, and Calendar of Patent Rolls, p. 38. There were twenty-five mitred abbots and priors in Ireland, ten of Canons Regular, one of Benedictines, one of Hospitallers, and thirteen of Cistercians. Ware, in his Annals, says the heads of St. Mary's and St. Thomas's, Dublin, of Kilmainham, and of Mellifont were regularly summoned to Parliament—the more distant ones very seldom. The Augustinians were the most numerous and probably the richest of the sedentary orders. Their rule was adopted by most of the ancient Irish monasteries, the small residue becoming Benedictine. Alemand, who was originally a Huguenot and who was Voltaire's countryman, remarks that in order to become quickly a bishop in Ireland, it was necessary first to be a Regular Canon.

[311] Chiefly from Alemand; the words of John's grant are 'ante adventum Francorum in Hiberniam.' For the final grant, see Archdall's Lodge. Art. Earl of Drogheda.

[312] Alemand. Sidney to Queen Elizabeth, April 20, 1567, in the Sidney Papers.

[313] Alemand and Archdall. As to the intended combat, see Carew, miscellaneous vol., pp. 446, 447.

[314] Most of the pensions mentioned in the text are traceable in Morrin's Calendar of Patent Rolls. For Cahir, see Archdall's Monasticon. Queen Mary's instructions to Lord Fitzwalter, April 28, 1556, in Carew.

[315] Alemand, passim; Documents in the supplementary volume of King's Primer, No. 66; the Waterford document is in Brennan's Ecclesiastical History, p. 459.

[316] Sir John Davies's Discovery.

[317] In Mant's Church History is an estimate of the monastic property founded on the Loftus MS.; but such calculations must be very rough. R. Cowley to Cromwell, Oct. 4, 1536.

[318] Agard to Cromwell, April 4, 1538. James White to Cromwell, March 28. Spicilegium Ossoriense, vol. i. p. 437. Hibernia Dominicana.

[319] In recommending a grant of Dusk to Ormonde the Council say they 'cannot perceive, as it is situated, that any man can keep it for the King, but only the said Earl or his son.' For Toem and Dunmore, see Calendar of Patent Rolls, pp. 73 and 84. Browne to Cromwell, May 21, 1538.

[320] Ware's Antiquities, by Harris, chap. xxxvii., sec. 3. Lord L. Grey to Cromwell, Jan. 19, 1538.

[321] The King to Browne in S.P., vol. ii. p. 174; Browne's answer, Sept. 27, 1537; Staples to St. Leger, June 17, 1538; Ware's Life and Death of Browne.

[322] Ware's Bishops; Staples to St. Leger, June 17, 1538; Devices by Travers for the Reformation in 1542, S.P., vol. iii., No. 382. The King's rebuke was in 1537, see S.P., vol. ii. p. 174, note.

[Pg 325]

CHAPTER XVI.

FROM THE ACCESSION OF EDWARD VI. TO THE YEAR 1551.

Accession of Edward VI. Ormonde and Desmond.

The death of Henry VIII. made no immediate difference to Ireland, for St. Leger continued to govern as before. There was such a tendency to depress the Ormonde interest that the widowed countess thought it wise to go to London, where she pleaded her own cause with much success. She was supposed to have designs upon the heir of Desmond's hand, and the English statesmen, who naturally dreaded such an alliance, encouraged her to marry Sir Francis Bryan, who was in favour with Somerset as he had been with Henry VIII. The new government directed their attention to economy and the repression of jobbery among the Dublin officials. It was discovered that many who drew the King's pay were serving in the houses of councillors, 'some in the place of a cook, some of a butler, housekeeper, and other like,' so that they were practically useless when called to arms. This was strictly forbidden for the future. The Irish Council were earnestly charged finally to put down 'that intolerable extortion, coyne and livery, having always respect to some recompense to be given to the lords and governors of our countries for the defending of the same.' Desmond was thanked for his services, and the young king offered to have his eldest son brought up as his companion, 'as other noblemen's sons whom we favour are educated with us in learning and other virtuous qualities, whereby hereafter, when we come to just age, we, in remembrance of our childhood spent together, may the rather be moved to prosecute them with our wonted favour, and they all inclined to love and serve us the more faithfully. We shall consent and right glad to have him with us, and shall so cherish him as ye shall have cause to[Pg 326] thank us, and at his return to think the time of his attendance on us to be well employed.' If this offer had been accepted, and if the same results had followed as in the cases of the young Earl of Ormonde and of Barnaby Fitzpatrick, the unspeakable miseries of the Desmond rebellion might have been avoided.[323]

The bastard Geraldines.

The Pale was at this time much disturbed by the depredations of a gang of freebooters, headed by some of the bastard Geraldines who had lost their lands. They overran the southern half of Kildare and the northern half of Carlow, plundering and burning Rathangan, Ballymore Eustace, and Rathvilly. At first they acted with O'Connor, but he was forced to go to Connaught to look for reinforcements, and the MacGeohegans and others were induced by St. Leger to kill his men and drive his cattle. The Fitzgeralds, after defying the Government for a year, were crushed at Blessington in the autumn of 1547. The O'Tooles sided with the English, and thus justified Henry VIII.'s policy towards them. The Irish generally fell away from O'Connor and O'More, to whom they feared to give food and shelter; and the chiefs were obliged to make such a peace as was possible with the Government. The annalists dwell strongly on the strength of the English at this time, on the unexampled bondage in which they held the southern half of Ireland, and on their complete victory over the man who had been 'the head of the happiness and prosperity of that half of Ireland in which he lived, namely, Brian O'Connor.'[324]

Bellingham's first visit to Ireland, 1547.

Sir Edward Bellingham, a gentleman of the bedchamber, was sent over for the first time in the summer of 1547, in charge of reinforcements. This able soldier had been Governor of the Isle of Wight, and had served at Boulogne in[Pg 327] 1546. He had also held diplomatic appointments in Hungary, and at the Emperor's Court. The Privy Council, who expressed themselves satisfied of his military ability, directed the Irish Government to be guided by his advice, and to pay him the unusual salary of forty shillings sterling a day. He was employed by the borderers of the Pale against the O'Mores and O'Connors, and seems to have made his mark from the first. After a short stay Bellingham with difficulty obtained leave to return to England. He must have succeeded in impressing his views on Somerset, to whose religious party he belonged, for St. Leger was recalled in the following spring, and Bellingham was appointed in his stead.[325]

Butlers and Kavanaghs. Bellingham Deputy, 1548.

Bellingham landed at Dalkey on May 18, 1548, and the state of Leinster at once engaged his attention. Moryt Oge Kavanagh had taken a horse and other property from a neighbour, and Bellingham called upon Cahir MacArt to restore it, and to punish the thief. The chief denied all responsibility, on the ground that the culprit was in Sir Richard Butler's suite, and that he could not in any case hang a man for stealing, but only enforce restitution according to the Brehon law. We can now see that in this at least Cahir MacArt was more nearly right than the English lawyers. Moryt Oge had grievances, and said that he was oppressed by one Watkin Powell, but he restored the horse, subject to the Lord Deputy's opinion as to whether he had a right to it as a set off against his own losses. He came to Carlow to plead his own cause, but Sir Richard Butler, who had promised to meet him, did not appear. Butler was accused of showing a bad example in the country by plundering houses, wounding men, and taking gentlewomen prisoners. If this, or even a small part of it, were true of the Earl of Ormonde's brother, it is not surprising that robberies should have been things of every-day occurrence.[326]

[Pg 328]

The Pale constantly threatened.

The defenders of the Pale were fully occupied. Having consulted such men in England as understood Irish affairs, the Privy Council concluded that the principal damage was done 'skulkingly in the winter's nights.' If the Lord Deputy's presence near the border was not enough to prevent incursion, soldiers accustomed to the country were to be quartered there permanently, and nightly watch to be kept, especially on O'Connor's side. Truces were not to last beyond the winter. This border service must have been very disagreeable. John Brereton, who held the office of seneschal of Wexford, of which the duties were very ill discharged by Watkin Powell, was stationed at Kildare, and complained bitterly that he was harassed to death. He could get no leave because he had no second captain, and even in May and June he could scarcely enjoy an undisturbed night. At one time he was roused from his bed by shouts, at another by the announcement that some alarm beacon was blazing. On foot or on horseback he had to march at once, and yet he was unable to answer every summons. A proprietor at Rathangan, who is called Raymond Oge, had his haggard burned by some of the O'Connor kerne. Two English troopers were with him by chance and helped to defend his castle, but the fires which they lit on the roof were not answered. Horses left out in a bog near a wood were carried off and the keepers killed. Nothing was safe unless shut up in a bawn, or fortified courtyard. Owen MacHugh O'Byrne, who was retained permanently by the Government as a captain of kerne, was inclined to do good service, but his men would not advance beyond Lea Castle, saying that 'if Captain Cosby wanted wilfully to lose his life, they did not set so little by their lives.' Cosby was a man of great personal courage. The Constable of Lea, the same James Fitzgerald whose allegiance in Grey's time had been so elastic, required a letter from Bellingham to encourage him. The Lord Deputy himself spent some time at Athy, where eighteen beds were provided for him and his suite; but the border was never quiet for a moment. Fitzgerald and Cosby had no official authority, and their orders carried no weight. If a cow strayed an alarm was raised, and[Pg 329] while soldiers were sent on a fool's errand in one direction, the rebels or brigands had their time to themselves. O'More came to the Barrow and carried off horses and sheep. Owen MacHugh skirmished with him, but the hostile chief, 'like a jolly fellow,' offered the royal kerne 6s. 8d. a fortnight to serve him, and pay to their leaders in proportion. Before Cosby could get his men together the O'Mores had vanished.[327]

Lord Dunboyne.

Other loyal and half loyal partisans were less energetic than Cosby. Lord Dunboyne complained that his manor of Fishmoyne in Tipperary had been plundered by the O'Carrolls and O'Meaghers, and this because he had discharged his men by the Lord Deputy's orders. Bellingham retorted that his lordship lied in his throat; for he had bidden him to entertain true men instead of rebels, and to discharge no one unless it could be done safely. He had particularly cautioned him against 'rashly discharging such as have been malefactors as your gallowglasses were, and naturally as their captains were.'[328]

Pirates.

While the frontiers of the Pale were harassed by robbers, the loyal ports of the south were in constant dread of pirates. A rover named Eagle blockaded Kinsale, which was half depopulated by an epidemic, and another, named Colley, established himself in a castle belonging to Barry Oge, whose aunt he married, so that the poor town was quite shut up. Cork, the citizens told Bellingham, was so well defended by marshes and waters, 'besides walls and towers which we do build daily, that we do not fear all the Irishmen in Ireland and English rebels also, if there be any such, until such time as your wisdom would repair hither for our refuge.' John Tomson, a noted rover, visited both Cork and Waterford. According to the authorities of the latter city he had 'one saker of 16-foot long, having four chambers, so that we do[Pg 330] not see how he may be apprehended.' In an affray between the citizens and an armed French vessel Tomson took part with the foreigner, and the pursuit of them cost Waterford 1,000l. This formidable water-thief was taken by O'Sullivan Bere, who made him pay a large ransom. Afterwards Bellingham rather oddly allowed the Cork men to trade with Tomson, because it seemed possible that he had received pardon, and because the goods then on board did not appear to be stolen. Wine, figs, and sugar were, however, the wares offered by Tomson and his ally Stephenson, and it is most likely that they had been stolen at sea from the Portuguese. Tomson used the occasion to refit and to repair his weapons, and the Waterford men called upon the Mayor of Cork to apprehend the pirates; but that prudent official refused to do so without special orders from Bellingham. Pirates were unpleasant people to deal with. A gang confined at Waterford broke their gyves, nearly murdered a fellow-prisoner, and with many 'cracks' and menaces threatened to burn the gaol.[329]

Their daring outrages.

A pirate named Smith sailed into Youghal, but seems to have taken nothing but loose rigging and spars. He had long infested these waters, seemingly with no more than six men, armed with guns and bows. The Youghal fishermen took heart, and by a combined attack succeeded in capturing Smith. Other pirates named Cole, Butside, and Strangwych are mentioned as active about this time. They were all English, but the trade was by no means confined to any one nation; for Sir Philip Hoby, the English ambassador at the imperial court, was instructed to apply for help to suppress a squadron of twenty sail, manned by lawless desperadoes of all countries, who infested the Irish coast, and robbed the Emperor's subjects. Logan, a Scotch professor of the art, and a survivor from Lennox's expedition, haunted the coast about Howth, and took several vessels. Power and Gough, who robbed a Portuguese ship in Waterford harbour, and ruined[Pg 331] the foreign trade of that port, were probably of Irish birth. Desmond, on whom the honorary office of Lord Treasurer, held by the late Earl of Ormonde, had already been conferred, received a commission from Lord Admiral Seymour to exercise his jurisdiction along the coast from Dungarvan to Galway. The men of the latter town said they could defend themselves against all Irishmen coming by land, but that they had not a single piece of artillery to resist attacks from the sea. They professed unswerving loyalty, as did their neighbours of Limerick, and Bellingham thanked the latter for their efforts to keep the Burkes quiet, 'in whom,' he said, 'the obstinacy is found to break this order, you the King's our own most dear sovereign lord's and master's subjects, the mayor, brethren, and council of Limerick shall proceed to the first and lawful redress and punishment thereof.'[330]

Bellingham's campaign in Leix, 1548.

Before Bellingham came to Ireland a hosting into Leix had been proclaimed, and he carried it out promptly. The men of Drogheda were required to furnish a strong contingent, having 'caused to be mustered all such as are meet for the war without partiality.' They had also to furnish carts, of which it seems the town could only boast three, and there were complaints of the stringency of Bellingham's requisitions; but he said he would rather they were unfurnished than he. The Drogheda men did very good service, and the carts, which were duly paid for, were employed to carry pioneers' tools. The soldiers were thus enabled without excessive fatigue to cut passes through woods, and make causeways over bogs. After a thirty days' campaign in Leix, Bellingham resolved that a town should be built in Leix, and in the meantime was erected Fort Governor or Protector, in the place where Maryborough now stands. The citizens of Dublin were required to assist in making it practicable for soldiers to act upon the border of Kildare; but they made excuses, saying that men could not carry arms and tools as[Pg 332] well. Bellingham sarcastically refuted their argument, 'in which your experience bitterly condemneth my ignorance.' Let them send carts as the Drogheda men had done, and then one man could do the work of two.[331]

Bellingham routs the O'Connors.

In August 1548 Cahir O'Connor, who still kept some force about him, invaded Kildare. Nicholas Bagenal, Marshal of the army, fell in with the marauders, and rescued the cattle taken, though his men were in the proportion of one to sixteen. Cahir retreated with his troop, and with a multitude of camp followers and 'slaves,' who carried their food to what was considered an unassailable position. Bellingham was not far off, and he ordered Saintloo to attack them wherever he could find them. Accompanied by Travers, Brereton, and Cosby, Saintloo tracked them to a spot surrounded by a bog. The soldiers struggled manfully through the moss until they reached hard ground, and a great butchery followed. The oldest man in Ireland had, as Bellingham supposed, never seen so many wood-kerne slain in one day. Such was the slaughter, says this precursor of Cromwell, that none escaped but by mistake, or hiding them in ambush, 'such was the great goodness of God to deliver them into our hands.' The Old Testament in English was beginning to make its mark upon language and upon habits of thought.[332]

Disturbances in Munster. Foreign rumours.

Munster was much disturbed. Edmund Tyrry, the King's bailiff at Cork, had a dispute with some of the Barries about land. The Earl of Desmond was appealed to, and he took Tyrry to Lord Barrymore, desiring the latter to do him justice. Barrymore took the bailiff with him to his court-baron, or 'parliament,' and the case was partly heard and adjourned to a future day. On his return journey towards Cork, Tyrry was waylaid and murdered. Bellingham demanded justice, and Lord Barrymore, after some months' delay, gave up the murderers, who were doubtless duly executed. But the Barry country continued to be the scene of frequent outrages.[Pg 333] Lord Barrymore went out one day in the early winter to drive the cattle of some wild Irishmen, and met with certain other wild Irish who were going to spoil his tenants. A fight followed, and the Barries 'killed incontinently little lack of fourscore of them,' wherewith, said the Corporation of Cork, 'we be glad, and so is the Earl of Desmond.' But Bellingham was not satisfied with Desmond's conduct, nor easy about the future. James Delahide, always the herald of a storm, was in Ireland, and probably with the Earl. Gerald of Kildare might appear again; and there were rumours that the French meditated a descent and the establishment of a fortified port at Skerries to command the passage to Scotland. These fears were not realised; but there were frequent communications between Desmond and the O'Briens, and Bellingham took steps to have everything reported to him. This vigilance perhaps prevented the Munster chiefs from moving.[333]

Anarchy in Connaught. Garrison at Athlone.

The death of the newly-created Earl of Clanricarde revived the normal anarchy of Connaught. Ulick Burke was acknowledged as captain by the Government and by some of the inhabitants during the minority of the Earl's son Richard. But another Richard, the heir's illegitimate brother, gave so much trouble that Sir Dermot O'Shaughnessy, and other well-disposed chiefs, demanded that the young Earl should be settled in possession, and that Commissioners should be sent to Galway for the purpose. The false Richard was, however, allowed to rule his own immediate district, but not without strong hints from Bellingham that what the King gave the King could take away. Burke was reminded that he had apprehended no notable malefactor, and that the Lord Deputy would quarrel with no honest Irishman for his sake. Bellingham had neither time nor force to give to the West, and the towns of Limerick and Galway had very indifferent success in their efforts to keep the peace. But the chief governor's reputation for justice was not without effect even[Pg 334] in Connaught. 'Your lordship's famous proceedings,' wrote the Archbishop of Tuam, 'being divolgated throughout all Ireland, to the great fear of misdoers and malefactors all through the country hereabouts now needing reformation, more than heretofore, all for lack of justice among them to be observed.' Bellingham established a garrison at Athlone, which overawed the O'Kellys and O'Melaghlins; but little progress was made beyond the Shannon. Robert Dillon, the lawyer, was the Lord Deputy's civil substitute, but the sword was necessarily in the Baron of Delvin's hands, who did all he could to prevent Dillon from sending messengers to Dublin. The central districts of Ireland between the Pale and the great river were at this time the theatre of constant war, and in this an English, or Anglo-Norman, adventurer figures conspicuously.[334]

Edmond Fay.

Edmond Fay, who seems to have had property at Cadamstown, in the King's County, and to have claimed more than the natives were willing to allow him, was called into Westmeath by O'Melaghlin to aid him against his enemies. The confederates gained some successes, and occupied, among other places, the historic castle of Kincora. 'Edmond,' say the 'Four Masters,' 'then continued to conquer Delvin in the King's name in opposition to O'Melaghlin; and thus had O'Melaghlin brought a rod into the country to strike himself, for Edmond a Faii expelled and banished himself and all his tribe out of Delvin, just as the young swarm expels the old.' Fay, who was to some extent supported by the Government, and who had soldiers with him, drove the MacCoghlans across the Shannon, and made himself master of most of the country between Athlone and Slievebloom. Not satisfied with this he proposed to attack the O'Carrolls, who joined the MacCoghlans, and expelled him from his recent conquests. Fay called on the Government for help, and the whole county, on both sides of the Brosna, was burned and plundered by the troops, to whom no resistance was attempted. The Irish[Pg 335] demolished Banagher and other castles to prevent their being occupied, and this became a general practice in like cases. Cadamstown was afterwards taken by the O'Carrolls, and Fay returned to his original obscurity. He seems to have had the keep of Thady Roe, or the Red Captain, a noted leader of mercenaries, who held possession of Nenagh. The O'Carrolls burned the monastery and town, but the castle defied their power.[335]

The Pale is freed from rebels.

Towards the close of 1548 Alen was able to report that there were only about a dozen rebels on the borders of the Pale. O'Connor had surrendered at discretion, and his life was spared in the hope of inducing O'More to follow his example. Alen advised that they should be removed from Ireland, and that work should be found for them at Calais or Boulogne. 'There are in all,' he told Paget, 'not twelve persons wherewith your honour to make a maundie, for when Christ ministered at His last supper there were twelve, of whom one was a traitor, and of these ye may have twelve together at one table.'[336]

The coinage. A mint.

The Plantagenet kings had made no difference in the coinage of England and Ireland; but in 1460—when Richard, Duke of York, was Lord Lieutenant—the Parliament of Drogheda, with the express intention of loosening the tie between the two islands, declared that coins intrinsically worth threepence should be struck in Ireland and pass for fourpence. There was afterwards a further degradation, and the money struck by Henry VIII. consisted at last of one-half, or even two-thirds, alloy. 'New coins were introduced into Ireland,' say the 'Four Masters,' with pardonable exaggeration, 'that is, copper, and the men of Ireland were obliged to use it as silver.' Dishonesty had its proverbial reward, for trade was thrown into confusion and general discontent engendered. The Corporation of Galway more than once besought Bellingham to force the new money on the captain of Clanricarde and Donnell O'Flaherty. The Corporation of Kinsale made the same request as to the Courcies,[Pg 336] Barries, and MacCarthies. This was, of course, beyond Bellingham's power, and the Protector went on coining regardless of Irish complaints. Thomas Agard was Treasurer of the Dublin Mint, and exercised his office independently of the Lord Deputy. He was originally in Cromwell's service, and his position not unnaturally brought him into collision with Lord Leonard Grey, who accused him of making mischief. Agard, however, said that Grey, 'which is my heavy lord,' oppressed him out of spite, because he opposed the Geraldine faction, and prevented him from setting up broad looms and dye-works in Dublin. With the politic St. Leger he got on better, but Bellingham, whose temper was quite as despotic as Grey's, was much disgusted at the independence of the Mint. Agard leaned to the Puritan side, and praised Bellingham's godly proceedings. God is with you, he wrote to him, and with all good Christians who love God and their King, with much more of the same sort. But the Lord Deputy was not conciliated, and accused Agard of cooking his accounts, and of embezzling 2,000l. He was not superseded, and was entrusted with the congenial task of melting down chalices and crosses, and of turning them into bad money. The home authorities chose to make Agard independent in his office; but the stronger nature triumphed, and the King's auditor reported that the Treasurer of the Mint dared not for his life speak of his business to any but the Lord Deputy. The debased currency caused much speculation of an undesirable kind. Thus, Francis Digby, who had a licence to export Irish wool, found it pay much better to buy up plate with the current coin and sell it in England for sterling money. Others took the cue, and it became necessary to issue a proclamation. It was, of course, no more possible to prevent the exportation of silver than to change the ebb and flow of the tides.[337]

[Pg 337]

Bellingham's haughty bearing.His rash letters to Somerset,

In November Bellingham paid a short visit to Dublin, where he found Lady Ormonde with her new husband, Sir Francis Bryan, who had a commission as Lord Marshal of Ireland. Bryan, 'the man of youthful conditions,' as Roger Ascham called him, was particularly recommended by the Privy Council to Alen, who could not understand what Henry VIII. had seen in him worthy of great promotion. Bellingham hated him from the first, and Alen thought he would have the same feeling to any one who had married Lady Ormonde. We have no means of knowing whether he was in love with her, or whether he hated her, or whether he merely disliked the alliance as likely to clip his own wings. His idea of the rights and dignity of his position was high and even excessive, and was asserted with a fine disregard of prudence. To Somerset he complained that his credit was bad, and that he was despised in Ireland because he was thought to have no power to reward those who had done good service. He begged that they might be 'fed with some thereof, which no doubt it is great need of, for the wisest sort have ever found that good service in Ireland has been less considered of any place.'

to Warwick,and to Seymour.

In writing to Warwick his words were still stronger, and he complained bitterly at the slight put on him in the matter of the mint. 'I am,' he said, 'at your honourable lordship's commandment; but in respect I am the King's Deputy, your good lordship may determine surely that I will have none exempt from my authority in Ireland's ground, but sore against my will.' He had not spent the King's treasure in gambling or riotous living, nor in buying land for himself. The King's responsible servants in Ireland were neglected, and credit given to backstairs' suitors 'coming in by the windows,' which did more harm than all the rebels and Irishry in the realm. Some of Warwick's letters had hurt him, whereas the true policy would be to let men 'know that I am the King's Deputy, so that they shall think when they have my favours things go well with them, and the contrary when they have them not.' These letters, and another to Seymour, gave great, and not unnatural offence, so that[Pg 338] Bellingham was fain to beg the admiral's pardon and intercession with Warwick. Some measure of the serpent's wisdom is necessary to those who fill great offices.[338]

Bellingham and the Irish.

If Bellingham could thus treat the most powerful men in England, he was not likely to mince matters with those whom he could touch. 'Bring yourself,' said the Lord Deputy to O'Molloy, who had wrongfully detained the property of a kinswoman, 'out of the slander of the people by making prompt restitution, or have your contempt punished as to your deserts shall appertain.' To the Earl of Thomond, who had promised to bring in Calough O'Carroll but had not done so, he wrote a noble letter, but a very imprudent one, considering the character and position of the chief whom he addressed. Calough O'Carroll, he said, had brought his troubles on himself by allowing his men to plunder, and by refusing to give them up; he should be well plagued for it according to promise, until he and his brother found means to come and seek their own pardon. The O'Carrolls submitted and were pardoned.[339]

Bellingham and his Council.

Bellingham was above all things a soldier, and he treated his Council, consisting for the most part of lawyers, in a very high-handed manner. His old friend Alen remonstrated, and there is no reason to doubt him here, though he had a way of quarrelling with successive Deputies. Alen admitted that Bellingham was quite free from pecuniary self-seeking, but thought he had more than his share of the other sin which beset chief governors, ambition namely, and the longing to rule alone. He had said that it would be a good deed to hang the whole Council, and he kept the members waiting for hours among the servants in the ante-room. Alen he accused personally of feigning sickness when bent on mischief. Others he threatened to commit if they offended him, reminding them that he could make or mar their fortunes. When angry he frequently sent men to a prison without any[Pg 339] warrant of law; 'and I myself,' said the Chancellor, 'except I walk warily, look for none other but some time with the King's seal with me to take up my lodging in the castle of Dublin.' The Council had become a lifeless, spiritless corpse, for Bellingham could hear no advice without threats and taunts. It is not surprising that Privy Councillors feared to speak frankly, and forced themselves to wait until this tyranny should be overpast.[340]

Bellingham seizes Desmond.

To a Lord Deputy so jealous for the dignity of his office nothing could be more distasteful than the power of the House of Ormonde, which was now wielded by the Countess and her husband. The Sheriff of Kildare gave a most galling proof of this power by begging that his communications with Bellingham might be kept secret for fear of Lady Ormonde's displeasure. She claimed the right to keep gallowglasses in Kilkenny, and the Lord Deputy infinitely disliked this practice, which had prevailed for centuries. He wished to keep the young Earl in England, lest by living at home he should imbibe exaggerated notions of his own importance. 'His learning and manners,' he said, 'would be nothing amended, and the King's authority thereby be nought the more obeyed.' By remaining in England till he was of discreet years, he might learn willingly to abandon his 'usurped insufferable rule, which I trust he will do yet in time to come.' Any assumption of independence on the part of a subject irritated Bellingham excessively; and when Desmond, whose manners he stigmatised as detestable, neglected his summons, he set out quietly from Leighlin with a small party of horse, rode rapidly into Munster, surprised Desmond sitting by the fire in one of his castles, and carried him off to Dublin. He set himself to instruct the rude noble in civilisation and in the nature of the royal authority, sometimes, if we may believe the chronicler, 'making him kneel upon his knees an hour together before he knew his duty.' This discipline, accompanied doubtless with kind treatment in other ways, seems to have answered so well, that, according to the same authority, Desmond 'thought himself most happy that ever he was acquainted with the[Pg 340] said Deputy, and did for ever after so much honour him, as that continually all his life at every dinner and supper he would pray for the good Sir Edward Bellingham; and at all callings he was so obedient and dutiful, as none more in that land.'[341]

Ireland quiet. Garrison at Leighlin Bridge.

At the beginning of the year 1549 the Privy Council thanked Bellingham for having brought Ireland to a good state. They charged him to aid Tyrone against the Scots, and to be on his guard against French enterprises undertaken under colour of trading. The forts erected where Maryborough and Philipstown now are kept Leix and Offaly quiet.

Breweries were at work under the shadow of both, and it was proposed to start a tan-yard at Fort Protector, as Maryborough was for the moment called. Bellingham established another post, which became very important, to command the road from Dublin to Kilkenny, and thus make the Government less dependent on the House of Ormonde. The suppressed Carmelite convent at Leighlin Bridge required but little alteration, and the Barrow ceased to be a serious obstacle. The Lord Deputy kept twenty or thirty horses here with the greatest difficulty, the hay having to be brought from Carlow through a disturbed country. Irishmen were willing to settle and to make an example of peaceful cultivation, but they were in great fear of Lady Ormonde. Walter Cowley, formerly Solicitor-General and fomenter of discord between St. Leger and the late Earl, had little good to say of the no longer disconsolate widow, but praised Sir Francis Bryan for saying that he would not 'borrow of the law as my Lord of Ormonde did.' The expression was called forth by the action of the Idrone Ryans, who were frightened by the inquiries into tenure, and came to Lady Ormonde offering to convey their lands to her and her heirs; the object being to defeat the Act of Absentees. No doubt the cultivators would have been glad to pay an easy rent to a powerful neighbour, rather than have an active new landlord such as Cosby thrust upon them. Sir Richard Butler, some of whose misdeeds have been already[Pg 341] mentioned, built a castle in O'More's country without any title, and overawed the whole district of Slievemargy.[342]

Progress of the Reformation. Browne and Staples.

Doctrinal Protestantism was not formally promulgated in Bellingham's time; but the recognition of the royal supremacy was pretty general, for he would allow no disobedience. The Treasurer of St. Patrick's, who was refractory, was severely reprimanded, and threatened with condign punishment. A Scot who preached at Kilmainham condemned the Mass, and Archbishop Browne, whose opinions were not perhaps quite fixed, was accused of inveighing against the stranger, and of maintaining that those who sided with him were 'not the King's true subjects.' Means were, however, taken to spread the order of service which Browne had set on foot. The Ten Commandments, the Lord's Prayer, and the Ave Maria were read and circulated in English, but the Mass was retained; a confused arrangement which could not last. Still, the men who controlled the Government and the young King were known to be favourable to the new doctrines, and the Scots emissary soon found a distinguished follower in the Bishop of Meath. Staples had at one time certainly held opinions less advanced than those of Browne, but he now went to Dublin and preached a strong Protestant sermon against the Mass. On returning to his own diocese he found that he had incurred universal hatred. An Irishman, whose infant he had christened and named after himself, desired to have the child re-baptized, 'for he would not have him bear the name of a heretic.' A gentleman refused to have his child confirmed 'by him that denied the sacrament of the altar.' The gossips in the market-place at Navan declared that if the Bishop came to preach there they would stay away, lest they should learn to be heretics. A lawyer in the neighbourhood told a crowd of people that Staples deserved to be burned, 'for if I preached heresy so was I worthy to be burned, and if I preached right yet was I worthy that kept the truth[Pg 342] from knowledge.' 'This gentleman,' Staples quaintly adds, 'loveth no sodden meat, but can skill only of roasting.' Another lawyer, a judge, said it should be proved before the Bishop's face that he preached against learning. The following is too interesting to omit:—'A beneficed man of mine own promotion came unto me weeping and desired me that he might declare his mind unto me without my displeasure. I said I was well content.

My Lord, said he, before ye went last to Dublin ye were the best beloved man in your diocese that ever came in, and now ye are the worst beloved that ever came here. I asked why? "Why," saith he, "ye have taken open part with the State that false heretic, and preached against the sacrament of the altar, and deny saints, and will make us worse than Jews: if the country wist how they would eat you;" and he besought me to take heed of myself, for he feared more than he durst tell me. "Ye have," he said, "more curses than ye have hairs of your head, and I advise you for Christ sake not to preach at the Navan as I hear ye will do." I said it was my charge to preach, and because there was most resort (God willing) I would not fail but preach there. Hereby ye may perceive what case I am in, but I put all to God.' The Bishop spoke as became his office, but he was 'afraid of his life divers ways.'[343]

Bellingham and Dowdall.

Bellingham had information of what was going on in England by private as well as official correspondence. John Issam, a strong Protestant, who was afterwards made seneschal of Wexford, wrote from London an account of the variations of opinion upon the all-important question of the sacrament. 'There is great sticking,' he said, 'about the blessed body and bloode of Jesus Christ, howbeit, I trust that they will conclude well in it, by the help of the Holy Spirit, without which such matters cannot well be tried; but part of our bishops that have been most stiff in opinions of the reality of His body there, as He was here in earth, should be in the[Pg 343] bread, they now confess and say that they were never of that opinion, but by His mighty power in spirit, and leaveth His body sitting on the right hand of His Father, as our common creed testifieth; but yet there is hard hold with some to the contrary, who shall relent when it pleaseth God.' Bellingham certainly did what he could to spread the reformed doctrines, but this was, perhaps, not much. His letter to Primate Dowdall, who had acknowledged the royal supremacy, but was inflexible on the question of the sacrament, is instinct with the spirit of Christian sincerity.

'My Lord Primate,' he says, 'I pray you lovingly and charitably to be circumspect in your doings, and consider how God hath liberally given you divers gifts, and namely, of reputation among the people ... Let all these in part be with the gratuity of setting forth the plain, simple, and naked truth recompensed, and the way to do the same is to know that which, with a mild and humble spirit wished, sought, and prayed for, will most certainly be given, which I pray God grant us both.'[344]

Bellingham advances the royal supremacy.

Bellingham could do nothing with Dowdall; but in the spring of 1549 all the priests in the Kilkenny district not physically incapable of travelling were summoned to meet the Lord Deputy and Council. It was ordered that the Attorney-General should exercise jurisdiction in ecclesiastical matters, and 'abolish idolatry, papistry, the Mass sacrament, and the like.' The Archbishop of Cashel seems to have had no great zeal for the work. Nicholas Fitzwilliam, Treasurer of St. Patrick's, received a stinging rebuke for his hesitation to carry out the royal commands. The innovations were distasteful to most men in Ireland, but Bellingham was recognised as one who would use his patronage conscientiously, and not job in the usual style. John Brereton, a decided Protestant, recommended to him 'for the love of God and the zeal that you have for the education of Christ's flock,' a poor priest who was willing to go into a certain district where he had friends, and where there was no one to declare[Pg 344] the true worship. The suppliant, who was both learned and earnest, could expect favour from no nother's (sic) hand, because he 'is but poor and has no money to give as his adversaries do.' Auditor Brasier told Somerset that 'there was never Deputy in the realm that went the right way, as he doth, both for the setting forth of God's Word to His honour, and to the wealth of the King's Highness' subjects.' But these praises did not serve to prolong his term of office, and he left Ireland without effecting the reforms which he had at heart.[345]

Bellingham leaves Ireland, 1549. His character.

Bellingham's departure from Ireland followed pretty closely on the Protector's eclipse, though it is not quite certain that it was caused by it. Warwick may have borne malice for past lectures, but the Lord Deputy seems to have defended himself successfully, and might have been sent back had he not excused himself on account of ill-health. The malady proved fatal, but he seems to have retained office till his death. There has been a tendency among those who find their ideal realised in a strong man armed, to represent Bellingham as a model ruler. It appears from his letters and from general testimony that he was honest, brave, loyal, and sincerely religious; but his incessant wars were very burdensome, and it is noted that he exacted the unpopular cess more stringently than its inventor St. Leger had done. But he was a true-dealing man, took nothing without punctual payment, and 'could not abide the cry of the poor.' From the love of gain, that common vice of provincial governors, he was absolutely free, and made a point of spending all his official income in hospitality, saying that the meat and drink in his house were not his own, but his dear master's. For the King's honour he paid his own travelling expenses, and insisted on doing the like even when Lord Baltinglass entertained him sumptuously. Alen, who criticised his official conduct so sharply, could not but allow that he was 'the best man of war that ever he had seen in Ireland.' The figure of the Puritan[Pg 345] soldier has its charms; but the sword of the Lord and of Gideon is not a good instrument of civil government. Absolutism may be apparently successful under a beneficent despot, but who is to guarantee that his successor shall not be a villain or a fool? Bellingham's forts did their own work, but his ascendency over lawyers in Dublin and ambitious chiefs in the country was purely personal, and had no lasting effect. There was much to admire in his character, but distance has lent it enchantment, and in practice not much permanent work could be done by a governor of whom the most striking fact recorded is that 'he wore ever his harness, and so did all those whom he liked of.'[346]

Bryan, Lord Justice. Mischief brewing.

As soon as Bellingham had left Ireland the Council unanimously elected Bryan Lord Justice. The Irish, though overawed by the departed Deputy, had been plotting in the usual way, and after all that had passed Lord Thomond and O'Carroll were sworn allies. The Kavanaghs were known to be meditating mischief, and Desmond was not to be depended on. Lady Ormonde had been quarrelling with Lady Desmond, and Alen took credit to himself for having made a truce between them. To the usual elements of discord were added many rumours of Scotch and French invasions. O'Neill, O'Donnell, O'Dogherty, and others proposed to become subjects of France, in consideration of help from thence, and of the most Christian King's good offices with the Pope. Monluc, Bishop of Valence, returning from his mission to the Scottish Court, was directed by Henry to take Ireland on his way, and to gain all the information possible. Sir James Melville, then a boy, accompanied him. 'Before our landing,' he says, 'we sent one George

Paris, who had been sent into Scotland by the great O'Neill and his associates, who landed in the house of a gentleman who had married O'Dogherty's daughter, dwelling at the Loch edge. He came aboard and welcomed us, and conveyed us to his house, which was a great dark tower, where we had cold cheer—as herring and biscuit—for it was Lentroun.' One De Botte, a Breton merchant, was[Pg 346] also sent on secret service to Ireland apparently about the same time.[347]

Death of Bryan, 1550. Lady Ormonde meditates a third marriage.

At this juncture Bryan died at Clonmel under circumstances apparently somewhat suspicious, for there was a post-mortem examination. He had refused to take any medicine, and the doctors, who detected no physical unsoundness, prudently declared that he died of grief; we are not told for what. 'But whereof soever he died,' says Alen, who was present both at the death and the autopsy, 'he departed very godly.' Lady Ormonde, who must have had a rooted dislike to single life, immediately recurred to her plan of marrying Gerald of Desmond, and the Chancellor had to remonstrate on the scandal of so soon supplying the place of two such noble husbands. The danger of putting both the Ormonde and Desmond interests in the same hand was obvious. The Geraldines were already too powerful, and what might not be the consequence of throwing the weight of the Butlers into the same scale, and making them more Irish and less loyal than they had been before? In the end she promised to remain sole for one year. 'Nevertheless,' said Alen, 'I would my lords (if they take her marriage of any moment) trusted a woman's promise no further than in such a case it is to be trusted!' Her marriage took place in the end with beneficial results: for Lady Ormonde was able to keep some sort of peace between her husband and her son, and thus saved much misery and bloodshed. Immediately after her death the quarrel broke out anew, and ended only with the extinction of the House of Desmond.[348]

Brabazon, Lord Justice. Dowdall and Wauchop.

On the day of Bryan's death the Council elected Brabazon to succeed him, and the new Lord Justice soon afterwards went to Limerick to arrange disputes among the O'Briens and between Thomond and Desmond. Before the complicated complaints had been all heard his presence was required in Dublin on account[Pg 347] of the disturbed state of the North; a most dangerous visitor having landed in Tyrconnel. This was the Papal Primate, Robert Wauchop—Dowdall, who had acknowledged the royal supremacy, though without accepting any of the new doctrines, not being acknowledged at Rome. The actual Primate kept himself well informed as to the movements of his rival, whom he understood to be a 'very shrewd spy and great brewer of war and sedition.' There were many French and Scotch ready to attack Ireland, and the former had already manned and armed two castles in Innishowen. Tyrone gave Dowdall letters which he had received from the French king, and the Archbishop, with his consent, forwarded them to the Council. Tyrone swore before the Dean and Chapter of Armagh that he had sent no answers, and that he would remain faithful to the King. He did not acknowledge Wauchop's claims, but merely reported that he called himself Primate, and that he was accompanied by two Frenchmen of rank, who were supposed to be forerunners of countless Scotch and French invaders. The Council warned Tyrone that the French wished to conquer Ireland, and to reduce him and his clan to slavery and insignificance. He was reminded that they had been expelled from Italy and Sicily for their more than Turkish ferocity and rapacity. French messages were also sent to O'Donnell, but no letters, as he had transmitted some formerly received to the Government. He professed his loyalty, and declared that he would not recognise Wauchop unless the Council wished it.[349]

Foreign intrigues. George Paris.

In all these intrigues we find one George Paris, or Parish, engaged. He was a man whose ancestors had held land in Ireland, of which they had been deprived, and he was perhaps related to the traitor of Maynooth. This man came and went between France and Ireland, and though the threatened attack was averted by the peace concluded by England with France and Scotland, his services were not[Pg 348] dispensed with. Henry said that the intrigues had ceased with the peace, but the English ambassador knew that his Majesty had had an interview with Paris less than a week before. Paris told everyone that all the nobility of Ireland were resolved to cast off the English yoke for fear of losing all their lands, as the O'Mores and O'Connors had done. He boasted that he himself had begged Trim Castle of the French king to make up for the lands which the English had deprived him of. The Constable spoke as smoothly and not much more truly than the King. Monluc was still employed in the matter, had interviews with Paris, and gave him money.[350]

St. Leger again Deputy. Alen displaced, 1550.

After Bellingham's death it was determined to send St. Leger over again, though he disliked the service, and though the Irish Chancellor continued to indite bulky minutes against him. It was felt that the two could hardly agree, and Alen was turned out of the Council and deprived of the great seal, which was given to Cusack. His advice was nevertheless occasionally asked. A year later he received 200 marks pension from the date of his dismissal, though he had only asked for 100l. Many charges were made against him, the truest, though he indignantly denied it, being that he could not agree with others. But after careful search no fault of any moment could be found in him, and he had served very industriously in Ireland for twenty-two years. With all his opportunities he declared that he had gained only nine and a half acres of Irish land. St. Leger and his friends, who were for conciliating rather than repressing the Irish, naturally disliked Alen. He had a decided taste for intrigue; but if we regard him as a mere English official, diligent and useful, though narrow and touchy, he must be allowed to have had his value.[351]

[Pg 349]

St. Leger adopts a conciliatory policy.

The new Lord Deputy's salary was fixed at 1,000l. a year from his predecessor's death, though St. Leger, who alleged that he was already 500l. the poorer for Ireland, fought hard for 1,500l. He retained his old privilege of importing 1,000 quarters of wheat and 1,000 quarters of malt yearly, to be consumed only in Ireland. The appointment was evidently intended to restore some confidence among the natives, who had been scared by Bellingham's high-handed policy. St. Leger having suggested that Irishmen should be 'handled with the more humanity lest they by extremity should adhere to other foreign Powers,' he was directed to 'use gentleness to such as shall show themselves conformable,' that great Roman maxim of empire which has been so often neglected in Ireland. Encouraging letters were to be sent to Desmond, Thomond, and Clanricarde; and to MacWilliam, the O'Donnells, O'Reilly, O'Kane, and MacQuillin. Pieces of scarlet cloth and silver cups to the value of 100l. were to be distributed to the best advantage among them. Particular instructions were given for reforming the military establishments, and officers were not to be allowed to have more than 10 per cent. of Irish among their men. Coyne and livery, the most fertile source of licence and disorder, was to be eschewed as far as possible. Irish noblemen were to be encouraged to exchange some of their lands for property in England, and thus to give pledges for good behaviour. In Leix and Offaly leases for twenty-one years were to be given; and religious reform was everywhere to be taken in hand. One very curious power was given to the Lord Deputy. When England was at war with France or the Empire, he was authorised to license subjects of those Powers to import merchandise under royal protection, excepting such articles as were under a special embargo.[352]

Hesitation about pressing the Reformation forward.

St. Leger was ordered to set forth the Church service in English, according to the royal ordinances, in all places where it was possible to muster a congregation who understood the language. Elsewhere the words were to be translated truly[Pg 350] into Irish, until such time as the people should be brought to a knowledge of English. But small pains were taken to carry out the latter design, and the Venetian agent reported, with practical accuracy, that the Form of Common Prayer and Administration of the Sacraments was not enforced in Ireland or other islands subject to England where English was not understood. The book still remains that of the English colony, and of no one else in Ireland. Cranmer and Elizabeth both saw the necessity of attempting to reach the Irish through their own tongue, but neither were able to do it. When Bedell, at a later period, threw himself heart and soul into the cause, he received not only no encouragement, but positive opposition, from the Government; and in any case the breach was probably then past mending. Protestantism had become identified in the Irish mind with conquest and confiscation, a view of the case which was sedulously encouraged by Jesuits and other foreign emissaries.[353]

Bad state of the garrisons.

St. Leger lost no time in visiting the forts in Leix and Offaly, and he found there the disorder natural to, and perhaps pardonable in, an ill-paid soldiery. Bellingham had complained more than a year before that so many women of the country—Moabitish women he would have called them had he lived a century later—were received into Fort Protector. Some officers indignantly denied this, 'and as to our misdemeanour in any point,' they added, 'we put that to the honestest men and women in the fort.' If this report was true, discipline had been much relaxed in a year and nine months, for St. Leger found as many women of bad character as there were soldiers in the forts. Divine service there had been none for three years, and only one sermon. Staples, who was the preacher on that solitary occasion, 'had so little reverence as he had no great haste eftsoons to preach there.' There was also a want of garrison artillery; and eight pieces of cannon, with forty smaller pieces called bases, were demanded by the Master of the Ordnance. He also asked for 400 harquebusses, and for bows, which the Dugald[Pg 351] Dalgettys of the day had not yet learned to despise. There were rumours of a French invasion, and it was proposed to send a strong expedition to Ireland—six ships with attendant galleys, 1,000 men, including many artificers to be employed in fortifying Baltimore, Berehaven, and other places in the south-west, and the mouths of the Bann and of Lough Larne in the north-east. The Constables of Carrickfergus and Olderfleet were ordered to put those castles in order for fear of Scots. Lord Cobham was designated as leader of the expedition, and the Irish Government were directed at once to survey Cork, Kinsale, and other southern harbours.[354]

St. George's Channel unsafe. Want of money.

Martin Pirry, Comptroller of the Mint, who brought over bullion collected in France and Flanders, had to stay seven days at Holyhead for fear of five great ships which he saw drifting about in the tideway. In the end he secured a quick and safe passage by hiring a twenty-five ton pinnace with sixteen oars, into which he put twenty-five well-armed men. St. Leger had been complaining bitterly that he could get no money out of the mint, although 2,000l. was owing. Pirry seems to have had only a limited authority, for though over 7,000l. was delivered by him on the Lord Deputy's warrant, St. Leger still objected that he had to make bricks without straw, and to put port towns in a posture of defence without being allowed to draw for the necessary expenses.[355]

Abortive scheme for fortifying in Munster. Apprehensions of French invasion.

The expedition did not take place, but Sir James Croft was sent over with instructions to inspect all the harbours between Berehaven and Cork, to make plans of the most important, and to select sites for fortification; utilising existing buildings as much as possible, and taking steps for the acquisition of the necessary land. He was then to extend his operations as far east as Waterford, acting in all things in concert with the Lord Deputy. It is evident that things were in a state quite unfit to resist a powerful French armament;[Pg 352] but the weather as usual was on the side of England, and of eighteen French vessels laden with provisions, more than one-half were lost in a storm off the Irish coast. This fleet was, no doubt, destined only for the relief of the French party in Scotland, and there does not seem to have been any real intention of breaking the peace with England. But the Irish exiles were unwilling to believe this. George Paris, who had been despatched from Blois about Christmas 1550, returned to France in the following spring, bringing with him an Irishman of importance. The Irish offered Ireland to Henry, and begged him to defend his own, saying that Wales would also rise as soon as foreign aid appeared. Their avowed object was 'the maintenance of religion, and for the continuance of God's service in such sort as they had received from their fathers. In the which quarrel they were determined either to stand or to die.' It would be better to invade England than Ireland; for the English Catholics would receive an invader with open arms. Paris spoke much of the frequent conquests of England. No outward enemy, once landed, had ever been repulsed, and the thing was easier now than ever. The sanguine plotter talked loudly of all that had been promised him, and professed to believe that the Dauphin would soon be King of Ireland and Scotland at the very least. 'With these brags, and such others, he filleth every man's ears that he chanceth to talk withal.' He had constant interviews with the Nuncio, but the French grew every day cooler. The English ambassador perceived that the Irish envoy was 'not so brag,' and at last reported that he had been denied help. He attributed this change of policy entirely to the fear of increasing the difficulties in which the Queen Dowager of Scotland already found herself.[356]

Difficulties in Ulster. Andrew Brereton.

While Scots and Frenchmen threatened its shores, Ulster furnished more even than its normal share of home-grown strife. Captain Andrew Brereton, who seems to have been a son or grandson of Sir William Brereton, held Lecale as a Crown tenant at will. He was a man singularly unfit to deal[Pg 353] with a high-spirited race like the O'Neills. When Tyrone, according to ancient Irish custom, sent a party to distrain for rent among the MacCartans, Brereton set upon them and killed several men, including two brothers of the Countess. To the Earl's remonstrances he replied by calling him a traitor, and threatening to treat him as he had treated O'Hanlon—that is, to spoil him, slay his men, and burn his country. It is clear that Brereton was not actuated by any special love of the MacCartans, for he beheaded a gentleman of that clan—without trial. He forcibly expelled Prior Magennis from his farm on the church lands of Down; and Roger Broke, a congenial spirit, shut up the Prior in Dundrum Castle. Tyrone went to Dublin to welcome St. Leger on his arrival, and Brereton openly called him a traitor at the Council Board, in the presence of the Lord Deputy and of the Earls of Thomond and Clanricarde. The proud O'Neill of course took the accusation 'very unkindly.' St. Leger was of opinion that such handling of wild men had done much harm in Ireland; and the Council, while admitting that Tyrone was 'a frail man, and not the perfectest of subjects,' thought that this was not the way to make the best of him. Brereton had no better justification for his conduct than the gossip of one of MacQuillin's kerne, who said that Tyrone had sent a messenger to the King of France to say that he would take his part against King Edward, and would send him Brereton and Bagenal as prisoners. Brereton was very properly relieved of his command in Lecale, on the nominal ground that he had refused to hold the Crown land there upon the Lord Deputy's terms; which St. Leger evidently thought more likely to have weight with the English Council than any amount of outrages committed against the Irish. He was afterwards restored, and gave trouble to later governors.[357]

FOOTNOTES:

[323] Lord Protector and Privy Council to Lord Deputy St. Leger and Council, March 25, 1547; the King to the same, April 7; King Edward VI. to the Earl of Desmond, Oct. 6. In a letter dated Lambeth, July 6, to her 'assured loving friend Mr. Cecil, Master of Requests,' Lady Ormonde begs that Abbeyleix may not be granted to Barnaby Fitzpatrick to her son's detriment, and she refers to Cecil's 'former friendship.' Here we see the beginning of a most important connection.

[324] Four Masters, 1546, 1547.

[325] Introduction to Carew, vol. ii. p. lxxxv.; Archbishop Butler to the Lord Protector, Feb. 25, 1548; Calendar of Patent Rolls, p. 154.

[326] Calendar of Patent Rolls, p. 66. For Butler and Powell, see three letters calendared under April and May 1548, Nos. 16, 17, and 19.

[327] Privy Council to Lord Deputy and Council, Nov. 2, 1547; John Brereton to Bellingham, May 1548 (No. 20), and July (Nos. 44 and 45); Cosby to Bellingham, July (Nos. 48 and 50). Bellingham dated a letter from Athy, Aug. 19, 1548. The eighteen beds are mentioned by John Plunket and Thomas Alen in a letter to him of the 18th.

[328] Lord Dunboyne to Bellingham, June 21, 1548, and the answer (No. 25).

[329] Sovereign and Council of Kinsale to Bellingham, July 15, 1548; Mayor, &c., of Cork to same, July 24, Aug. 27, Dec. 29, and the answer, Jan. 10, 1549; Mayor, &c., of Waterford to Bellingham, Sept. 5, 1548.

[330] Mayor, &c., of Youghal to Bellingham, July 8, 1548; Deputy Mayor and Council of Galway to same, Aug. 13; Bellingham to Limerick, Aug. (No. 63); John Goldsmith to Bellingham, Aug. 22; Kyng to Wyse, Sept. 5. Sir Philip Hoby's letter is calendared among the foreign S.P., April 17, 1549.

[331] Bellingham to Alen, July 1548 (No. 39); Mayor, &c., of Drogheda to Alen, Aug. 8; Bellingham to Privy Council, Aug. (No. 84), and to the Mayor of Dublin (No. 67). For the fort, which became Maryborough, see the notes to O'Donovan's Four Masters under 1548 and 1553.

[332] Bellingham to the Privy Council, Aug. 1548 (No. 84).

[333] Bellingham to the Mayor of Cork, Aug. 1548 (No. 80); Mayor, &c., of Cork to Bellingham, Nov. 18; Alen to Somerset, Nov. 21; Bellingham to Arthur, Dec. (No. 145).

[334] Archbishop Bodkin to Bellingham, July 25, 1548; Bellingham to Richard Burke, Aug. (No. 83), and to the Mayor of Limerick, Sept. 18; Ulick Burke to Bellingham, Sept. 22.

[335] Four Masters, 1548 and 1549.

[336] Alen to Paget, Nov. 21, 1548.

[337] Harris's Ware, pp. 211-217; S.P., vol. iii. p. 534; Four Masters, 1546; Mayor, &c., of Galway to Bellingham, July 27 and Aug. 13, 1548; Sovereign and Council of Kinsale to same, July 16; Agard to same, Sept. 23; Richard Brasier to same, Oct. 8; Memoranda by Bellingham, Nov. 14; Bellingham to Warwick, November (No. 132, i.); Privy Council to Bellingham, Jan. 6, 1549.

[338] Bellingham to Somerset, Nov. 22, 1548, which encloses a copy of the letter to Warwick; to Issam, Dec. (No. 163).

[339] Bellingham to O'Molloy, Nov. 24, 1548; to O'Carroll (No. 138); to Thomond (No. 137).

[340] Alen to Paget, April 1549 (No. 32).

[341] Bellingham to John Issam, Nov. 1548 (No. 140). Hooker's Chronicle in Holinshed. The capture of Desmond was about Christmas 1548.

[342] Richard Brasier to Somerset, Nov. 14, 1548; John Moorton to same, April 15, 1549; Anthony Colcloght to same, Feb. 1 and 13, and to Cahir MacArt, Jan. 27; Walter Cowley to Bellingham, March 14; Brian Jones to same, April (No. 35).

227

[343] Staples to —— between Dec. 22 and 29, 1548. The letter is not addressed to Bellingham, but he must have seen it, as it is endorsed by his clerk. See also Walter Palatyne to Bellingham, Nov. 23, 1547, and Interrogatories for Archbishop Browne at the end of that year. The first Book of Common Prayer was not printed till 1550.

[344] Bellingham to Dowdall, Dec. 1548; John Issam to Bellingham, Dec. 22; Richard Brasier to Somerset, Nov. 14.

[345] Sovereign of Kilkenny to the Lord Deputy, April 26, 1549; Walter Cowley to same, June 25; Brasier to Somerset, Nov. 14, 1548; John Brereton to Bellingham, 1548 (No. 174).

[346] Book of Howth; Ware; Hooker in Holinshed; Lodge's Patentee Officer in Liber Hiberniæ. Bellingham embarked at Howth, Dec. 16, 1549.

[347] Patrick Fraser Tytler's England under Edward VI. and Mary. He quotes Melville's Memoirs. See in particular the letter of Sir John Mason to the Privy Council, June 16, 1550. The 'Loch' mentioned by Melville must be Lough Foyle or Lough Swilly.

[348] Instructions from Lord Chancellor Alen to Thomas Alen, Feb. 1550. Bryan died, Feb. 2, 1550.

[349] Lord Chancellor and Council to Tyrone, March 17, 1550:—'Tam ferox est illius nationis nobilitas ut sub Turcâ (quantumvis barbaro) mitius viveres quam sub illorum regimine ... summo conatu libertatem patriæ, sanguinis libertatem et personæ vestræ dignitatem abolebunt.' Dowdall to Alen, March 22; Brabazon to the Privy Council, March 26, with enclosures.

[350] Sir John Mason to the Privy Council, June 14, 1550; Foreign Calendar and Fraser Tytler, ut supra.

[351] Letters of Croft and the two Bagenals, July 31, 1551; Alen to Cecil, April 5, 1551, and to the Privy Council, Aug. 10. The grant is calendared after the latter date. Having been chief of the commission for the dissolution of abbeys, Alen thought it prudent to go to England during Mary's reign, but made his peace, became again a member of Council, and lived to congratulate Cecil on becoming once more Secretary of State.

[352] Instructions to Lord Deputy St. Leger, July 1550; Mr. St. Leger's Remembrances for Ireland, same date. He was sworn in on Sept. 10.

[353] Instructions to St. Leger; Barbaro's 'Report on England' in 1551, in the Venetian Calendar.

[354] St. Leger to the Lord High Treasurer, Sept. 27, 1550; Henry Wise and John Moorton, officers at Fort Protector, to Bellingham, Jan. 6, 1549; Articles for an expedition into Ireland, Jan. 7, 1551; St. Leger to Somerset, Feb. 18; Privy Council to Lord Deputy and Council, Jan. 26.

[355] Martin Pirry to the Privy Council, Feb. 21, 1551; St. Leger to the same, March 23.

[356] Instructions to Sir James Croft, Feb. 25, 1551, in Carew; Sir John Mason to the Privy Council, April 18, printed by Fraser Tytler.

[357] Articles against Andrew Brereton, Nov. 1550; St. Leger to Cecil, Jan. 19, 1551. The Council in Ireland to the Privy Council, May 20.

[Pg 354]

CHAPTER XVII.

FROM THE YEAR 1551 TO THE DEATH OF EDWARD VI.

The Reformation officially promulgated, 1551.

No Parliament was held in Ireland during Edward VI.'s reign; and the official establishment of Protestantism is generally supposed to date from a royal order, dated Feb. 6, 1551, and promulgated by the Lord Deputy on the first day of the following month. But the new Liturgy had been already introduced, and copies had been forwarded to Limerick, and perhaps to other places. St. Leger, who felt that the Communion Service was the really important thing, had it translated into Latin for the benefit of those who had some tincture of letters, but who could not read English. The citizens of Limerick made no difficulty about receiving the new formulary; but the Bishop, John Quin, refused, and was therefore forced to resign. Quin, who was old and blind, had been willing to acknowledge the royal supremacy, but very naturally refused to embrace a new faith. It has often been stated that Quin accepted the Reformation; but it is not easy to see how this can be reconciled with the facts. His successor was William Casey, whose consecrators were Archbishop Browne, Lancaster of Kildare, and Devereux of Ferns. The two last had been consecrated by Browne and by Travers of Leighlin. Travers had only just been appointed himself, and was probably in pretty nearly the same condition.[358]

Doctrinal conference in Dublin.

Immediately after the arrival of the momentous order, St. Leger summoned the clergy to meet him in Dublin. To this assembly the royal mandate was read, as well as the opinions of certain English divines in favour of the proposed changes. Primate Dowdall at once protested. 'For the general benefit of our well-beloved subjects,' the King was made to say,[Pg 355] 'whenever assembled and met together in the several parish churches, either to pray or hear prayers read, that they may the better join therein in unity, hearts and voices, we have caused the Liturgy and prayers of the Church to be translated into our mother tongue of this realm of England.' 'Then,' observed the Primate, 'shall every illiterate fellow read Mass?' 'No,' answered St. Leger with much force, 'your Grace is mistaken; for we have too many illiterate priests among us already, who neither can pronounce the Latin nor know what it means, no more than the common people that hear them; but when the people hear the Liturgy in English, they and the priest will then understand what they pray for.' This last observation might be true enough in Dublin, but it was singularly inapplicable to Ireland generally. The key-note of the controversy had,

229

however, been struck, and it was clear that the Primate and the Lord Deputy occupied very different standpoints. Finding St. Leger a formidable antagonist, and seeing that the case was virtually prejudged, Dowdall somewhat forgot his habitual dignity, and threatened the Viceroy with the clergy's curse. 'I fear,' was the answer, 'no strange curse, so long as I have the blessing of that Church which I believe to be the true one.' There was some further altercation about the Petrine claims to supremacy; and Dowdall, finding that he made no impression, left the hall with all his suffragans except Staples, and repaired to his own diocese. St. Leger then handed the King's order to Browne, who received it standing. 'This order, good brethren,' said the Protestant Archbishop, 'is from our gracious King, and from the rest of our brethren, the fathers and clergy of England, who have consulted herein, and compared the Holy Scriptures with what they have done; unto whom I submit, as Jesus did to Cæsar, in all things just and lawful, making no question why or wherefore, as we own him our true and lawful King.'[359]

[Pg 356]

St. Leger, Browne, and Dowdall.

The above proceedings show that St. Leger was at least in general agreement with the Protestant party, but he had certainly no wish to force the reformed doctrines on the reluctant Irish. Browne complained that he had publicly offered the sacrifice of the Mass in Christ Church, 'after the old sort, to the altar then of stone, to the comfort of his too many like Papists, and the discouragement of the professors of God's Word.' The Archbishop found it convenient to forget that this was strictly according to law; and that the royal order, even admitting that it had all the power claimed for it, had not yet gone forth to alter the state of things established under Henry VIII. Browne could not deny that the Lord Deputy had made due proclamation of 'the King's Majesty's most godly proceeding;' but alleged that it was only for show, 'while massing, holy water, Candlemas candles, and such like, continued under the Primate and elsewhere,' without let or hindrance from the chief governor. Dowdall, he said, was 'the next father in word and deed of Popery;' the Viceroy a Gallio who did not scruple to say, 'Go to, your matters of religion will mar all.' St. Leger seems in good truth to have been laughing at the ex-friar. 'My Lord of Dublin,' he said, 'I have books for your Lordship.' Browne found them on examination 'so poisoned to maintain the Mass with Transubstantiation, and other naughtiness (as at no time I have seen such a summary of Scriptures collected to establish the idolatry), clean contrary the sincere meaning of the Word of God and the King's most godly proceedings.' The Archbishop had copies taken, which he sent to the Privy Council. St. Leger was angry at this, and Browne says he threatened to do him harm, even should it cost 1,000l. The Archbishop intimated that the 1,000l. would be nothing to him, for that he had enriched himself by peculation, and attributed to him a degree of vindictiveness which does not seem really to have belonged to his character. Browne admits that the Lord Deputy called Dowdall before the Council for practising the old ritual, 'who came and disputed plainly the massing and other things, contrary the King's proceedings; and that he would not embrace them: whereat the Deputy said nothing.[Pg 357]' Sir Ralph Bagenal called the Primate an arrant traitor. 'No traitor, Mr. Bagenal,' said Lord Chancellor Cusack, who was Dowdall's cousin; and the Primate continued in his old ways as long as St. Leger held the reins of government. The Lord Deputy even recommended Tyrone to 'follow the counsel of that good father, sage senator, and godly bishop, my Lord Primate, in everything, and so ye shall do well.' He made indeed no secret of his regard for Dowdall, whose high character was admitted by all but fanatics. 'He is,' he declared openly before more than a dozen persons in the hall of Dublin Castle, 'a good man, and I would that all the Irishmen in Ireland spake so good English as he, and if they do no worse than he the King had been the better served.'[360]

St. Leger has some idea of toleration.

It was impossible that any secret policy could go on without Alen having a hand in it. St. Leger told him that the danger from both France and from the Emperor was much increased by the religious sympathies of the Irish, who, in civil matters, would like foreigners only in so far as they could profit by them. He ridiculed the notion of France annexing Ireland, though he thought it possible that Henry II. might make a diversion there to prevent England from interfering with him in Scotland or on the Continent. He thought the Emperor would be friendly for old acquaintance sake, but that he disliked the new fashions in religion; 'and no wonder, seeing that in that matter daily at home among ourselves one of us is offended with another.' St. Leger, in short, was a statesman who could admire moral excellence in men of different opinions; and Browne was a fanatic. 'God help me!' said the Deputy. 'For my own part, knowing the manners and ignorance of the people, when my lords of the Council willed me to set forth the matters of religion here, which to my power I have done, I had rather they had called me into Spain or any other place where the King should have had cause to make war, than burdensome to sit further here. I told my lords no less before my coming away.' Alen had refused to put this conversation in writing, though[Pg 358] urged to do so by Browne; saying that he wished St. Leger no harm, though he had lost all through him. He said as little as might be against him even when questioned afterwards by the Council. After his interview with the Lord Deputy, Alen went to sup with Lockwood, Dean of Christ Church, and found there the Archbishop and Basnet, late Dean of St. Patrick's. When the servants had gone the conversation turned upon St. Leger, whom Browne attacked on the grounds already mentioned, saying that he was but a 'dissimular in religion.' He was, in fact, a thoroughly secular politician, wise and resolute, and willing to carry out orders from the Government; but not pretending to like the plan of forcing an English-made religion upon the Irish, and administering it in practice as gently as possible. He was really in advance of his time, and had formed some notion of religious liberty. That he sympathised with the old creed there is not the smallest reason to suppose. 'They name me a Papist,' he said. 'I would to God I were to try it with them that so nameth me;' and he was accused in Mary's reign of writing satirical verses against Transubstantiation, which shows that his opinions were not supposed to be anti-Protestant. He would have had things stay as they were under Henry VIII; the royal supremacy acknowledged, and doctrinal changes left to the action of time, persuasion, and increased enlightenment.[361]

These views not in favour in England.

But these ideas did not recommend themselves to the English Council, which had now come under Warwick's influence. Neither the bishopric of Leighlin nor that of Ossory was granted to St. Leger's chaplain, James Bicton; though his patron strenuously defended him against the charge of Papal leanings, declaring that there was no more competent man in Ireland, nor one who had better set forth God's Word. Bicton, who had been formerly chaplain to the Earl of[Pg 359] Ormonde, was of Irish birth, though educated at Oxford, and was at all events not one of the very ignorant priests whom St. Leger cast up against his friend the Primate. He became Dean of Ossory, and had a large chest of books at Kilkenny, besides a wine cask full at Bristol, for which he had paid 40l.; and he seems to have supported a poor Irish scholar at Oxford. It would be difficult to say anything so good of Travers, who was preferred before him at Leighlin. Travers owed his promotion to his cousin the Master of the Ordnance, whose chaplain he had been; but he did no credit to his blood, scarcely anything being recorded of him but that he oppressed his clergy and made money out of his see.[362]

Sir James Croft succeeds St. Leger, 1551.

Whatever was the exact cause of St. Leger's recall, it is likely that he was glad to escape from the thankless Irish service. Sir James Croft, his successor-designate, was already in Ireland, and he handed him the reins without waiting for his patent. Croft was directed to put the seaports of Munster and Ulster into a defensible state; but the English Government showed a bad example, for though Argyle was plotting in the North and MacCarthy in the South, the artillery was sent over in charge of a clerk only. MacCarthy was to be apprehended if possible, and also George Paris, who was 'a common post between Ireland and France,' sailing in French ships which were to be overhauled in search of him. When the thousand men who had been promised arrived at Cork there was no money to pay them. Croft and his advisers begged and borrowed till both credit and provisions were well-nigh exhausted in the barren wilds of West Cork. Soldiers unpunctually paid could not but be dangerous, and there was no sort of justice to be obtained in the country districts. 'If in England,' said Crofts, using an apt illustration, 'the place of justice were appointed only at Dover, I think no man doubts but the people would soon grow out of order.' A thorough reform in the official circle, head and members, was necessary before any great improvement could be expected in the people. Before leaving Cork, Croft did what he could to secure local justice by drawing up[Pg 360] regulations for maintaining the peace of the district under Desmond's general superintendence, not greatly differing from those already supposed to be in force, but with a clause which shows how the Puritan spirit was working. The Earl and those joined in authority with him were to have a special care to 'set forth divine service according to the King's proceeding, and diligently to look for the punishment of harlots, for which purposes they may call for the bishops and ministers within their circuit, giving them warning of their duties to see them punished according to the orders taken in that behalf.' MacCarthy More, who had submitted, was required with his clansmen to swear allegiance to Edward VI. as King, and also as 'supreme head of the Church in England and Ireland, and clearly to renounce the Bishop of Rome and all his authority,' and take his 'oath on the Bible' to obey all laws, civil and ecclesiastical, set forth by the King and his successors.

Croft proposes to colonise in West Munster.

Archbishop Browne, having got rid of St. Leger, was loud in praise of his successor's activity, who was the first governor to visit Baltimore (Ballagheyntymore). Crofts proposed to the Council that a colony of married Englishmen with their wives and families should be planted in this remote place, who, after serving as soldiers for a time, would be able to protect themselves as others had done at Calais. But the King blamed Croft for visiting Baltimore at all, since he had not the power to do anything there. In August the time for fortifying was already past; and there was a danger that Spanish fishermen might discover the Lord Deputy's intentions, and even find means to forestall them.[363]

The Ulster Scots attacked. Failure at Rathlin, 1551.

The affairs of Ulster next engaged the attention of Croft. The Scots had lately made themselves supreme from the Giant's Causeway to Belfast; and it was determined to attack them there, and, if possible, to capture the island stronghold of Rathlin, whither the MacDonnells had transported all the cattle and horses taken by them in their late raid. A hosting was accordingly proclaimed for thirty-one days, and the army mustered at Carrickfergus. The roads being impassable for[Pg 361] carts, everything had to be carried on pack horses or by sea. The Lord Deputy himself went by land through the country of several Irish chiefs, of whose intelligence Chancellor Cusack, who tells the story, formed a favourable opinion. Some of them joined the expedition. Meat was abundant throughout the four days' journey, at the rate of 10s. a beef and 16d. a mutton; much less than the prices of the Pale. Leaving the heavy baggage at Carrickfergus, Croft advanced to Glenarm, where he encamped. No Scots appeared, and but few cattle; but immense stores of corn were found. There lay at Ballycastle four small vessels which the English men-of-war had captured, and some of the prisoners from the Scots were brought before the Lord Deputy. The result of their examination was a resolution at once to attack Rathlin, where James MacDonnell and his brethren were. It was found that the captured boats would only carry 200 men, and it was therefore resolved not to risk a landing unless some more of the Scots vessels could be taken, or unless the men in the island yielded to the fear of the cannon upon the English ships. Sir Ralph Bagenal and Captain Cuffe approached the island with about 100 men, but the galleys which they wished to seize were at once driven in shore, and a threatening crowd of Scots hung about the landing-place, and took no notice of the fire from the ships, which was probably too vague to endanger them much. The tide was ebbing, and the invaders seemed to run no great risk; but the Race of Rathlin, even in the finest weather, is never quite calm, and a sudden reflux wave lifted Cuffe's boat high and dry on to the rocks. The men, about twenty-five, were slain on the spot, the officers taken and held by James MacDonnell as pledges for the return of the goods taken from him about Glenarm, and for the release of his brother Sorley Boy, who was a prisoner in Dublin. Croft was obliged to yield on both points, and the whole expedition ended in failure. The threat of complaining to the Scots Government was not likely to weigh much with MacDonnell, who was on good terms with the anti-English party.[364]

[Pg 362]

Disturbed state of Ulster.The O'Neills consider wheat a dangerous innovation.

Most of the chiefs of Ulster, who feared the Scots more than they hated the English, paid their respects to Croft at Carrickfergus, and were glad to submit their grievances to his arbitration. Tyrone, O'Donnell—with his two rebellious sons, Calvagh and Hugh—Maguire, the Baron of Dungannon, MacQuillin, O'Neill of Clandeboye, MacCartan, the Savages, Magenis, and others, had complaints to make, and the Lord Deputy patched up their differences for a time; most of them agreeing to pay some rent or tribute to the King for their lands, and not to employ Scots mercenaries. Maguire was declared independent both of O'Neill and O'Donnell, and sheriffs were appointed both in Ards and Clandeboye, which, being part of the Earldom of Ulster, had once had a feudal organisation. A garrison was left in Carrickfergus, and a commission charged with abolishing the Irish laws, 'so as by God's grace,' says the sanguine Cusack, 'that country since the time of the Earl of March was not so like to prosper and do well as now.' A garrison was also left at Armagh, under command of the Marshal Nicholas Bagenal, who was joined in commission with the Baron of Dungannon for the purpose of re-establishing order in Tyrone, which was utterly wasted through the dissensions of the Earl and his sons. There were not ten ploughs in the whole country. Hundreds had died of hunger in the fields. The Baron's lands were better off; for he felt that he owed his position to King Henry's patent, and to please the English Government he had caused wheat to be largely sown. Tyrone did his best to burn the Saxon crop, and the people declared that they would grow it no more; 'for that was the chief cause (as they said) that the Earl did destroy their corn, for bringing new things to his country other than hath been used before. And what the Earl will promise now, within two hours after he will not abide by the same.' Most of this unstable chief's fighting men had gone over to his son Shane, who abused his powers dreadfully. Cusack thought the people would prefer to have the Baron over them, 'for that he is indifferent, sober, and discreet, and is a hardy gentleman of honest conversation and towardness,' whose country[Pg 363] was as well ordered as the Pale. Tyrone had no capacity for government, and was ruled by his wife; but he so far yielded to the Deputy's persuasion as to accept a garrison for Armagh, and to go first to Drogheda and then to Dublin. Having been once enticed into the Pale, Tyrone was detained there against his will. This was done by Cecil's advice, who agreed with Cusack that Tyrone was quite useless in his own country, and quite unable to control Shane.[365]

Shane O'Neill and his brother Matthew.

Tyrone had, or might have had, a son by Alison Kelly, the wife of a smith in Dundalk. The mother brought her boy Matthew at the age of sixteen to the chief, who acknowledged him as his own, and thus, according to the ancient Irish law, made him equal with his children of less doubtful origin. Shane, on the other hand, was the offspring of an undisputed marriage. Matthew was certainly acknowledged as an O'Neill when he was made Baron of Dungannon and heir to the earldom, but Shane explained the difficulty by saying that his father was a gentleman, and never denied any son that was sworn on him, and that he had plenty of them. Whether there was any election to the chieftainship we do not know, but Shane was, by the practical adhesion of the clansmen, in a better position than most Irish tanists. Thus it strangely happened that Matthew, who was confessedly born in adultery, was heir to the feudal title, while Shane, who was certainly legitimate, claimed the reversion of the tribal sovereignty. The influence of the clergy had probably weakened or destroyed the old Irish principle that an adulterine bastard could be brought into the real father's lawful family by acknowledgment, nor could English law have been altogether without effect; but it is strange to see one in such a position as Matthew O'Neill, or Kelly, maintained by statesmen and lawyers against Shane and his brothers.[366]

Invasion of Tyrone.

Whether O'Neill or Kelly, the Baron of Dungannon was[Pg 364] a man of resolution and ability. He accompanied Bagenal on an expedition against Shane, which the Dean of Armagh, Terence Daniel, or O'Donnell, tried to prevent by exaggerated accounts of the distance. The bridge over the Blackwater was broken down, and the castles at Dungannon were also dismantled. This became a regular practice in Irish warfare, in order to prevent the English from placing permanent garrisons in strong places; and any disposition on their part to repair such a building was generally frustrated by the length of time necessary, the difficulty of obtaining labour, and the want of provisions. When the danger was past the chief would re-occupy his stronghold, and soon made it serviceable for raising a revenue, or resisting sudden attacks of neighbouring tribes. Bagenal met with little resistance during his raid. Shane appeared on a hill with eighteen horsemen and sixty kerne, and the Baron of Dungannon advanced against him with only four followers. 'An the King were there where thou art,' said Shane, 'he were mine.' The Baron, nothing daunted, answered, 'I am here but the King's man, and that thou shalt well know,' and spurred his horse forward. Shane, who was never remarkable for dashing courage, retired into the wood closely followed by his brother, who was prevented by the thick covert from using spear or sword, and who tried to close, but was caught by a branch at the critical moment, and nearly lost his own seat. Shane escaped on foot, leaving his horse and arms to the Baron, and afterwards came to Bagenal on parole, when a truce was patched up.[367]

The Scots attempt a settlement in Down.

Emboldened by success, the Scots extended their operations to the south of Belfast, slew John White, landlord of Dufferin, and proposed to make a settlement on the western shores of Lough Strangford. Hugh MacNeill Oge, who held the district between that inlet and Belfast Lough, took their part, and the Prior Magennis and his kinsman, the Bishop of Dromore, were authorised to make large offers with a view of detaching him from his allies; but he refused to come to Bagenal. The Baron of Dungannon had some trifling success against the[Pg 365] Scots, and another officer drove some of their cattle through Ards to Strangford, apparently crossing the ferry there, and thence into the Pale. One thousand cows were also taken from Hugh MacNeill Oge; but he promptly recouped himself from the herds of his neighbours on every side, so that the balance was soon again in his favour. The expedition was evidently a failure, and the 'Four Masters' represent it as a disastrous one; the English and their allies losing 200 men.[368]

Another doctrinal conference.

The general directions to Croft for his conduct in ecclesiastical matters was much the same as those given to St. Leger. Public worship in English was to be made general, and a translation to be made into Irish for use in such places as required it. He was sworn in on May 23, and on June 16 he wrote to Dowdall, who was at St. Mary's Abbey, inviting him to take part in a conference concerning the disputed points in religion. The Lord Deputy said much about what was due to Cæsar, hinted that he should be sorry to see the Primate removed from his great office, and entreated an answer by the hands of the Bishop of Meath, who, as chief of his suffragan, seemed the fittest intermediary. Dowdall answered very truly that no discussion could bring about agreement between those who differed as to fundamentals, and excused himself from waiting on his lordship, as he had for some time withdrawn from public affairs. Mohammed decided to go to the mountain, and the discussion took place in the hall of St. Mary's Abbey, Croft being supported by two bishops, Staples of Meath, who conducted the case for the Crown, and Lancaster of Kildare. The debate first turned on the new liturgy, Dowdall treating it as an innovation, and his opponent as the Mass purified from gross corruptions. The following is the most remarkable part of what was said:—

Dowdall. Was not the Mass from the Apostles' days? How can it be proved that the Church of Rome has altered it?[Pg 366]

Staples. It is easily proved by our records of England. For Celestinus, Bishop of Rome, in the fourth century after Christ, gave the first introit of the Mass which the clergy were to use for preparation, even the psalm, Judica me, Deus, &c., Rome not owning the word Mass till then.

D. Yes, long before that time; for there was a mass called St. Ambrose's Mass.

S. St. Ambrose was before Celestinus; but the two prayers, which the Church of Rome had foisted and added unto St. Ambrose's works, are not in his general works; which hath caused a wise and a learned man lately to write that these two prayers were forged, and not to be really St. Ambrose's.

D. What writer dares write or doth say so?

S. Erasmus, a man who may well be compared to either of us, or the standers by. Nay, my lord, no disparagement if I say so to yourself; for he was a wise and a judicious man, otherwise I would not have been so bold as to parallel your lordship with him.

Lord Deputy. As for Erasmus's parts, would I were such another: for his parts may parallel him a companion for a prince.

D. Pray, my lord, do not hinder our discourse; for I have a question or two to ask Mr. Staples.

L. D. By all means, reverend father, proceed.

D. Is Erasmus's writings more powerful than the precepts of the Mother Church?

S. Not more than the Holy Catholic one, yet more than the Church of Rome, as that Church hath run into several errors since St. Ambrose's days.

D. How hath the Church erred since St. Ambrose's days? Take heed lest you be not excommunicated.

S. I have excommunicated myself already from thence.

Opposite opinions were then given about the Virgin and her power to mediate; and the Primate finally appealed to the consecration oath, which Staples had taken as well as he. The Bishop of Meath said he held it safer for his conscience to break it than to keep it, and he praised the oath of supre[Pg 367]macy. And thus, without any approach to an understanding, but with many mutual expressions of courtesy and goodwill, the champions of Rome and of England measured swords and parted.[369]

Dowdall goes away. The Primacy removed to Dublin.
A few days after this the Primate disappeared, and it was understood that he had gone abroad like a traitor, as Browne said, who with indecent haste demanded that the old contest between Armagh and Dublin should be finally decided in his favour. Dowdall, he

said, claimed by the 'Bishop of Rome's bulls and I by the King's majesty and his most noble progenitors' grants and gifts.' He recounted the services of his predecessors in supporting the Government of the Pale, and asked not only for the empty title and honours of Primate of all Ireland, but for 'all and every the spiritual profits, living, and commodities,' belonging to Armagh. The King granted the chief place to Browne, who in the Anglican succession remained Primate of all Ireland till deprived by Queen Mary. Those who adhere to Rome of course ignore the interruption in Dowdall's primacy, but his withdrawal beyond seas was considered as a resignation by the English Government.[370]

Church patronage. Bale.

The sees of Armagh, Cashel, and Ossory being vacant, Croft recommended that they should be filled with peculiar care. The negligence of the Bishops and other ministers allowed the old ceremonies to remain in many places. It was necessary to send over good, zealous men to fill up the bishoprics as they fell vacant. If this could not be done, Croft begged that at least he might have a competent adviser in ecclesiastical matters to enable him to direct the bishops, who were blind, obstinate, negligent, and very seldom learned. For Armagh it would be well to choose a divine with some property in England, who might act as a commissioner for deciding the daily quarrels arising in the North. For the bishopric of Ossory, Croft, Protestant as he was, ventured to recommend Leverous, Gerald of Kildare's old tutor, who had been pardoned for his offence in carrying him out of the realm. For[Pg 368] learning, discretion, and decorous life there was no one superior in Ireland, and Croft had heard him 'preach such a sermon, as in his simple opinion he heard not many years.' Personally unobjectionable, Leverous was known to be attached to the old doctrines, and Croft's advocacy failed, as he himself expected. The see of Ossory was conferred after some delay upon John Bale, a Carmelite friar, born in Suffolk and educated at Jesus College, Cambridge. The arguments of a layman, Lord Wentworth, according to his own account, enforced by the charms of a young lady, according to the account of his enemies, converted Bale to the Reformation. He married a wife, who was his companion in all his wanderings and vicissitudes, and became a professed Protestant. It was not in his nature to hide his light under a bushel; he preached openly against the Roman doctrine, and suffered imprisonment in consequence. Having been released through Cromwell's intercession, he spent eight years in Germany. Returning to England on Edward's accession, he became Poynet's chaplain, and obtained the living of Bishopstoke. The King happening to see and hear him at Southampton, of his own accord promoted him to Ossory. Bale was a multifarious writer, a man of learning and eloquence, and unquestionably sincere; but coarse and violent, with no respect whatever for the feelings of others, and remarkably unfit for the task of persuading an unwilling people to embrace the Reformation.

Edward's opinions about patronage.

Though partially shorn of its glories, the see of Armagh, claiming as it did to be founded by the national apostle, was still of great importance. Pending an appointment in England, Croft proposed that Basnet, late Dean of St. Patrick's, should enjoy the first-fruits of the vacant see along with the revenues of his old deanery. The Lord Deputy was moved to this by the curious practical consideration that Basnet was 'experimented in the wars of the country.' Make it worth his while to live at Armagh, and he would be most useful to Bagenal and the Baron of Dungannon. But the young King, who had already opinions of his own, was scandalised at the idea, and shrunk from making bishops of any but ministers earnest in setting forth God's glory. He directed that Deans and[Pg 369] Chapters should maintain divine service and preach the gospel in vacant sees, declaring that he minded the education of his people above all things. If the dignitaries proved negligent the Lord Deputy might appoint occasional ministers to do the duty.[371]

Cranmer's difficulties about Irish patronage.

Cranmer named four persons as fit for the archbishopric of Armagh, but none of them were in haste to go to Ireland. Of these the King selected Richard Turner, a Staffordshire man, but vicar of Chartam in Kent. Cranmer described him as an earnest preacher, merry and witty withal, who wanted nothing, loved nothing, dreamed of nothing but Christ only. He had shown courage in the late Kentish insurrection, and that would be a useful quality in Ireland. 'He preached,' says Cranmer, 'twice in the camp that was by Canterbury; for the which the rebels would have hanged him, and he seemed then more glad to go to hanging, than he doth now to go to Armachane, he allegeth so many excuses, but the chief is this, that he shall preach to the walls and stalls, for the people understand no English. I bear him in hand Yes, and yet I doubt whether they speak English in the diocese of Armachane. But if they do not then I say, that if he will take the pain to learn the Irish tongue (which with diligence he may do in a year or two) then both his doctrine shall be more acceptable not only unto his diocese, but also throughout all Ireland.' But Turner would not go. Perhaps he estimated more correctly than Cranmer the difficulty of learning Irish, and his wit and liveliness would only enable him to forecast the misery of a man who should preach to unwilling congregations in halting and uncertain language. Cranmer's other three nominees also failed him; and he then recommended Hugh Goodacre, who was induced to accept the unenviable post. The archbishopric of Cashel had not even the dignity of Armagh to make it attractive, and it remained vacant during the rest of Edward's reign.[372]

Pluralities.

The King had a reasonable dislike to pluralities, and[Pg 370] resisted the union of Clonfert and Elphin in the hands of Clanricarde's uncle, Rowland Burke. 'A good pastor,' he said, 'cannot nourish two flocks at once, and it agreeth not with our religion.' But he gave in when it was proved to him that the sees were small and poor, and that their union would be likely to further rather than to hinder religion.[373]

The coinage.

It would have been well if Edward or his advisers had paid as much attention to honesty in civil government. The attempt to give a forced course to bad coin had had its usual evil effects. The Irish currency had always been less pure than that of England, but practically little difficulty had occurred until the late changes. An English groat was worth sixpence Irish, and everyone understood what he was doing. But now the country was flooded with base coin of uncertain value, and men bargained, as they do still at Cairo, for sterling money, foreign crowns, and livres Tournois. Trade with England was necessarily conducted by means of a reputable currency; and the whole of the new Irish coinage being only available for local use, felt the effects of inflation as well as of its own intrinsic baseness. There was great confusion in every trade, and all was attributed to the coin, which every one thought would be cried down, and therefore feared to have in possession. 'Being put to sale of all men,' said Croft, 'and no man desirous to buy it, it must needs be good cheap.' It was urged that, coins being only counters for exchange, they should be taken at the proclaimed price, but Croft rightly argued that gold and silver had been chosen on account of their fitness for the purpose and also for their intrinsic value. The effect of laws against usury is to raise the rate of interest, and the effect of putting an artificial value on coin, in conjunction probably with other causes, was to raise necessaries to a famine price. Corn that had been worth 6s. 8d. had risen to 40s.; leather, iron, boots and shoes, wine and hops, had all become dear. Six herrings sold for a groat. Englishmen, and especially officials with fixed salaries, could not live in Ireland. The native Irishman was somewhat better off, for 'he careth[Pg 371] only for his belly, and that not delicately.' 'We that are stipendiaries,' said the Lord Deputy, 'must live upon our stipends, and buy with our money which no man esteemeth.' The native lords used coyne and livery, and did what they could to make their vassals keep all provisions in the country, so that the markets were unsupplied, and the Government had scarcely any alternative but to practise like extortions.[374]

Evils of a debased currency.

The inhabitants of Dublin, Waterford, Limerick, Cork, Drogheda, and Galway were consulted, and they all attributed the state of trade to the currency. A petition signed by the attorneys of those communities, by seven peers, and by many others of high position was sent to the King; and the petitioners prayed that the coin might be of the same weight, value, and fineness in both kingdoms. 'By the whole consent of the world,' said the Lord Deputy and Council, 'gold and silver have gotten the estimation above all other metals, as metest to make money and be conserved as a treasure, which estimation cannot be altered by a part or little corner of the world, though the estimation were had but on a fanciful opinion, where indeed it is grounded upon good reason, according to the gifts that nature hath wrought in those metals whereby they be metest to use for exchange, and to be kept for a treasure. So as in that kind they have gotten the sovereignty, like as for other purposes other metals do excel; and so is everything good, as God said at the beginning, whereof followeth that the thing which we count naught cometh of the misuse.' No laws or proclamation could prevent the value of money from depending on the quantity of bullion it contained, and without money exchanges could not be made. Men saw that an artificial scarceness was created, and blamed the Government for not taking the obvious step of crying down the coin. Croft apologised for his importunity in pressing the currency question, observing that one string would put a harp out of tune, and that the tuner would naturally strike that the oftenest. The King's advisers did not deny the facts, but hesitated to make the necessary sacrifice. Next year, however, they found it absolutely necessary[Pg 372] to act. Two of the despised groats were proclaimed equivalent to fourpence English, and an immediate revival of trade was the result.[375]

The Revenue. Attempts at mining.

The hope of making some profit out of Ireland to set against the cost of governing her had attracted the attention of Henry VIII.'s ministers to her mineral resources. Traces of lead, tin, copper, iron, and alum had been found, and St. Leger hoped to turn them to account. In the last year of his reign Henry authorised an advance of 1,000 marks sterling, and it was thought that the mines would soon be self-supporting. The only serious attempt made was at Clonmines, near Bannow, in Wexford. Silver was found mixed with lead, and much expense was incurred. Germans were employed in the work under the direction of Joachim Gundelfinger, and a large mass of ore was raised. A smelting-house was built at Ross, both wood and coal being used, and there were stores at Newtown Barry and Ballyhack. There was some jealousy of the foreigners, who received very high wages, and it was thought that Englishmen would be better and cheaper. The English surveyor reported that the strangers cost 260l. a month, and scarcely earned 40l., and he proposed to dismiss them, at least until the work of sinking deep shafts had been completed by less expensive labour. The Germans retorted that the surveyor himself was to blame. But there was sickness among the miners, and some of them died; and after some further trial the Germans were sent home and the works stopped. It was found that the King had lost nearly 6,000l. in two years.[376]

[Pg 373]

French and Scotch intrigues. The O'Connors. 1552.

The early part of the new year was disturbed by rumours of invasion. Wauchop had just died at Paris, but his spirit still animated Ulster, and help was confidently expected from Scotland. The French were trying to recruit in Ireland, and some of those who held the seaports might as well have been Frenchmen or Spaniards so far as the State was concerned. Old O'Connor, who had received messages and tokens from the ubiquitous George Paris, managed to escape from the Tower, but was caught near the border and brought back. Walter Garrett, a soldier of Berwick, probably an Irishman, who had deserted and gone as far south as Newcastle, was taken trying to cross the Tweed or the Solway in a boat without oars. He confessed his knowledge of O'Connor's movements, and this roused suspicion as to the fidelity of the great frontier garrison. Leix and Offaly were still unleased, the forts cost 7,000 marks yearly without any return, and a rising among the friends of the old chief might undo the little that had been done. The garrisons were most oppressive, taking 1l. worth of wheat for five shillings, and 4l. of beef for twelve shillings, and the people were ready to rebel on the mere chance of shaking them off.[377]

Tyrone is detained in Dublin.

Tyrone and his countess were detained in Dublin, while Shane continued his fire-raisings in Ulster. The Earl complained bitterly of his own treatment, of Bagenal's incursions, and of Cusack's intrigues. The Marshal had taken 1,000 kine and 300 mares from him, and had billeted himself and his army at Armagh. O'Donnell had suffered from similar extortions. In St. Leger's time, he said, all had been quiet, and he sent a statement of his grievances to the late Lord Deputy, who, very wisely, sent it to Northumberland with the seals unbroken. Against the Chancellor Tyrone could[Pg 374] find no better accusation than that he had twice dissuaded him from sending hawks as presents to the King. Cusack maintained that Tyrone's arrest was justified by his negligent and savage behaviour. 'If there were but one plough in the country,' the candid barbarian had boasted, 'he would spend upon the same, with many other indecent words for a captain of a country to say.'[378]

Anarchy in Connaught.

The fort at Athlone remained a memorial of Bellingham's military plans, and under its shelter Westmeath submitted to the government of a sheriff; but it cannot be said that the garrison kept Connaught quiet, either by force or example. They sacked Clonmacnoise, and took away the bells from O'Rourke's Tower, and left neither bell, image, book, gem, nor window-glass in the whole place. 'Lamentable was this deed,' say the annalists, 'the plundering of the city of Ciaran, the holy saint,' and by no means calculated to increase the popularity of the King's religion. Whether on account of this outrage or not, Croft found it necessary to visit Athlone himself, and try to establish some order in Connaught. The dissensions of the young Earl of Clanricarde with his kinsman Ulick, who was loth to part with his authority, had laid the whole country waste. Cusack with a small force succeeded, after a few executions, in placing the Earl quietly, and swearing the gentry of the district to obey him. Agriculture again flourished, and Cusack boasted that he had increased the ploughs in use from 40 to 200, and that both ploughs and cattle could be left safely in the open field. Clanricarde made use of his new power to seize Roscommon, about which O'Connor Roe and O'Connor Don were disputing, and to hand it over to Cusack for the reception of a garrison. The warlike Chancellor brought O'Kelly to terms, and then succeeded in getting a promise from the chiefs that they would assemble a force of 1,500 men to support the Earl in chastising MacDermot of Moylurg, who had been plundering the O'Connors' cattle. Cusack thought there should be a presi[Pg 375]dent to govern Connaught in conjunction with Clanricarde and MacWilliam of Mayo, who was well disposed.[379]

Government of Leinster. Gerald of Kildare comes to England.

Leaving Cusack in the West, the Lord Deputy went into Leinster, and made successful arrangements for maintaining peace there. He gave a lamentable account of the state of the country. The Kavanaghs were indeed quiet, and the O'Byrnes supported soldiers without grumbling; but the poor in the towns were starving, and their cry sounded continually in his ears. They were too wretched even to state their own grievances, and this was done for them by the neighbouring gentry. Croft's regulations for the garrisons at Carlow and Leighlin show considerable forethought. The constables were prohibited from levying contributions themselves, but might obtain the necessary supplies from the country through four 'cessers,' chosen by the freeholders for each garrison. No kerne were to be quartered on the people, except thirty, which William Keating covenanted to keep always ready for police purposes, and these were to be billeted as the 'cessers' should appoint. Under the circumstances the young Earl of Ormonde's rents were not very well paid, but Croft managed to send him 400l. The state of the currency was such that the Earl would lose one half if it were paid in Ireland. Gerald of Kildare, who was now in England, was less fortunate, and the Lord Deputy declared that he could get nothing for him. At a masque given by the King this adventurous young man, who was now twenty-seven years old, and very handsome, had met Mabel Browne, step-daughter to the fair Geraldine. According to the family historian she fell in love with him. They were married, and her father's influence procured the honour of knighthood for the returned exile, and a patent restoring his estate. He did not, however, come to Ireland till the next reign.[380]

Cusack's attempts to conciliate the Irish.

Passing eastwards again, Cusack found the O'Farrells peacefully paying rent and supporting soldiers, but O'Reilly,[Pg 376] who had seven warlike sons and 1,600 men, was less submissive. With 1,200 followers he met the Chancellor, who had only 200, and agreed to give hostages for the restoration of spoils taken out of the Pale, and to pay a fine of 200l. Cusack made it a rule to impose a fine, since the Brehon code required restitution only; but as the fines were seldom paid, the chiefs made little real concession.

O'Reilly refused to go to Dublin, lest he should be imprisoned like Tyrone, but admitted that that chief deserved his bonds if he had behaved as Cusack reported, and that he should deserve them also in like case. The MacMahons and the O'Hanlons were found equally well disposed, and Magennis kept house like an English gentleman, and exercised the office of sheriff of Down. From this point the Scots' handiwork began to be visible. John White, the farmer of Dufferin, had been murdered by them, and the murderers kept possession of the district. The fertile lands of Lecale seemed to invite settlers, but the neighbouring region of Ards warned them off, being laid waste by the invasions of the islanders. Hugh MacNeill Boy, the chief of Clandeboye, had agreed to meet Cusack, but, hearing of the landing of some six or seven score Scots archers, he broke his appointment. Through his frequent conflicts with Bagenal there was scarcely anything left in the country worth destroying, and the Chancellor was fain to leave a small party of soldiers behind him, and to await the action of the Council in Dublin. Permanent garrisons at Belfast and Castlereagh were the means he proposed for bridling this part of the North. The O'Cahans and MacQuillins in northern Antrim were willing to obey the Baron of Dungannon, but were coerced by the Scots, who disposed of their force as they pleased. Cusack had a fruitless interview with the formidable Shane O'Neill, and Shane went straight from the meeting to burn his father's house at Dungannon, which was only four miles off. Led by the light, Cusack's horsemen were able to save the building, and he afterwards succeeded in capturing 700 of Shane's kine, and many horses. The Baron of Dungannon took charge of the castle, and 300 gallowglasses were quartered on the county,[Pg 377] but Cusack saw plainly that nothing permanent could be done without a resident governor. The Chancellor was somewhat more successful with O'Donnell and his rebellious son Calvagh, both of whom came to Dublin and bound themselves to keep the peace.[381]

Unsuccessful attack on the Ulster Scots. Death of Brabazon.

Soon after this the Lord Deputy made another attempt to punish the Scots for the Rathlin disaster, and Hugh Oge O'Neill for supporting them. O'Neill attacked the advanced guard at Belfast, then 'an old castle standing on a ford,' and killed Savage of Ards, with fifty others. The main body crossed the Laggan safely, and proceeded to fortify the old stronghold. Meanwhile the Baron of Dungannon had brought up his forces, but incautiously encamped in the open field before effecting a junction with Croft. There he was set upon by the sleepless Shane, and utterly routed, so that the whole expedition ended in failure. Sir William Brabazon, the Vice-Treasurer, who had served so long and so well in Ireland, died on the march. His body was buried in Christ Church, Dublin, but his heart, according to the annalists, was 'sent to the King, in token of his loyalty and truth towards him.'[382]

Tyrone is released.

Tyrone complained to the King of his continued detention. His country, he said, suffered by his absence, and he offered either to plead his own cause in England, or to submit unreservedly to Commissioners sent from thence. Danger was still feared from Scotland, but the English party there procured the arrest of George Paris, on the information of one of O'Connor's sons. On the whole it was thought better to release Tyrone, his countess and her son remaining as pledges for him, and Shane's brother for that troublesome person. The Earl bound himself in 6,000l. to keep the peace towards the

King's adherents, the Baron of Dungannon, Calvagh O'Donnell, Maguire, and Tirlogh Luineach O'Neill.[383]

[Pg 378]

Desmond.

The Corporation of Waterford praised Desmond for visiting remote parts of his district, and training the wild people; a task for which few, if any, of his ancestors had shown any taste. Cusack wrote in the same strain, and advised that Dungarvan should be taken from the Butlers, and restored to him. The Chancellor's pet idea was to have a President at Limerick, less as a governor than as a general referee in all disputes, and he believed that by such peaceful means permanent civilisation might be cheaply attained.[384]

Croft recalled, 1552.

At this time the King granted leave of absence to Croft, whom he apparently intended to send back; but the O'Connors became uneasy, and Sir Henry Knollys was sent to stop the Lord Deputy. The clouds blew over, and Croft was able to go before the end of the year, leaving the government to Cusack and Chief Justice Aylmer. Tyrone was released a few days later, and followed Croft to London; and Hugh O'Neill submitted, apologising for the past, and making promises for the future. The latter chief received certain monastic lands rent free, especially stipulating for the friary at Carrickfergus, where his ancestors were buried. Belfast Castle was restored to him. The Government had in fact been unable to chastise him, and put the best face they could upon matters. It can hardly be doubted that the three secular priests whom Hugh intended to maintain at the family burying place were not likely to advance the King's views in religion.[385]

Character of Croft. St. Leger returns to Ireland.

Sir James Croft bears a fair character among Irish governors. He did nothing very striking, nor did he contribute much towards a final pacification; but he was considered a just man, and he made no personal enemies. He was at least no bigot, for he received warm praise from Archbishop Browne, though he did not hesitate to recommend Leverous for a bishopric. It was, however, decided that St. Leger should return to Ireland in his stead. Sir Anthony's government[Pg 379] had been cheap, and not ineffectual. During the last five years of Henry's reign there had been a small annual surplus; but since his death there had been a constantly growing deficit, which could only be met by increasing the taxation of the obedient shires, by employing Irish soldiers almost exclusively, and by maintaining such troops as were necessary at free quarters upon the country. Miserable expedients certainly; but the English Government could devise nothing better, and they were determined to keep down the expenses. It was resolved not to increase the existing force of 2,024, and to make no attempt at a thorough conquest. The arrangement with Tyrone was dishonourable, but was to be adhered to, lest a breach of faith should lead to war, and consequent expenditure. The King's death prevented a full return to his father's policy, and those who had lately governed in his name immediately lost all influence.[386]

Protestant Bishops.

Goodacre was consecrated to Armagh and Bale to Ossory on the same day by Browne, Lancaster of Kildare, and Eugene Magennis of Down. Where Bale was there was sure to be controversy, and a fierce one arose about the ritual proper to the occasion. The Archbishop would have postponed the ceremony, and Bale, who frequently denounces him as an epicure, declares that his object was to 'take up the proxies of any bishopric to his own gluttonous use.' Lockwood, Dean of Christ Church, was supreme in his own cathedral, and his timidity led him to wish for the pontifical order. Bale accordingly stigmatises him as an ass-headed dean, a blockhead who cared only for his kitchen and his belly. But Lockwood had the law on his side; for King Edward's first book only had been proclaimed in Ireland, and it contained no form for consecration. Browne and Cusack also wished to stand on the old way. Goodacre was for the form contained in the second book, and now used in England, but he[Pg 380] was willing to waive his own opinion. Bale, however, positively refused to be consecrated according to the old usage, boldly maintaining that one king makes one law, and that Ireland must necessarily follow England. His vehemence carried the day, and the consecrations took place according to the new Anglican use. The Communion Service followed, and Bale rejected the consecrated wafer, successfully arguing that common bread should be used. He afterwards preached twelve strong Protestant sermons in Dublin, insisting particularly on the marriage of priests; and he flattered himself that he had established the people 'in the doctrines of repentance, and necessary belief in the gospel.'[387]

Goodacre.
Goodacre seems never to have seen his cathedral, to which access was barred by Shane O'Neill. Bale says he was a man of remarkable sincerity and integrity, and a zealous and eloquent preacher. He also informs us that he was poisoned by the procurement of certain priests of his diocese, 'for preaching God's verity, and rebuking common vices.' This contemporary statement has been doubted, on account of Bale's prejudices, but it is repeated by Burnet on the authority of Goodacre's fourth lineal descendant. Burnet's informant received the story from his grandfather, who was Goodacre's grandson. According to this tradition the actual murderer was a monk, who pledged Goodacre in poisoned wine, and died himself of the effects. Bale says he was himself warned by letter to beware of the Archbishop's fate. Whether the joint authority of Ossory and Sarum is to be rejected or not will much depend upon the reader's opinion of two learned, and in some respects not dissimilar divines.

Bale.
Bale soon proceeded to Kilkenny. On his journey from Waterford to Dublin he had already passed through part of his diocese, and had been much scandalised by what he saw and heard. The parish priest of Knocktopher boasted that he was a son of William, late prior of the Carmelites there—not the legitimate son, as he was careful to point out. The marriage of a friar would have been a heinous offence, but an irregular connection was venial, and it was thought honour[Pg 381]able to be the offspring of a spiritual man, whether bishop, abbot, monk, friar, or secular priest. Bale, who had himself been a Carmelite, and who had married a wife, rebuked this candid ecclesiastic, and resolved to set himself as bishop to the work of reform. He admits that he had no success; and none could be expected where public opinion sanctioned the pleasant vices of the clergy.[388]

Proceedings of Bale.

Far more questionable was Bale's zeal against images, the destruction of which will never make men Protestants. His opinions were hopelessly at variance with those in vogue in Ireland, as may be judged from the following autobiographical passage:—

'Many abominable idolatries maintained by the epicurist priests, for their wicked bellies' sake. The Communion or Supper of the Lord was there altogether used like a popish mass, with the old apish toys of Antichrist in bowings and beckings, kneelings and knockings; the Lord's death after St. Paul's doctrine neither preached nor yet spoken of. There wawled they over the dead, with prodigious howlings and patterings, as though their souls had not been quieted in Christ and redeemed by His passion; but that they must come after and help at a pinch with requiem æternam to deliver them out of hell by their sorrowful sorceries. When I had beholden these heathenish behavers, I said unto a senator of that city that I well perceived that Christ had there no bishop, neither yet the King's Majesty of England any faithful officer of the mayor in suffering so horrible blasphemies.'

This was at Waterford. At Kilkenny things were no better, and on his arrival Bale proceeded to show his zeal for reform. All the statues of saints were turned out of St. Canice's Cathedral, but the Bishop had the good taste to preserve the fine painted windows erected in the fourteenth century by his high-handed predecessor Ledred. The less artistic Cromwellians afterwards destroyed what Bale had spared, and some fragments were dug up in 1846. Bale had some supporters, chiefly laymen. The clergy, whose moral failings he had lashed so mercilessly, were not convinced by[Pg 382] hearing the host called a 'white god of their own making,' nor easily persuaded that the lucrative practice of saying masses for the dead was useless, nor inclined to admit a liturgy which condemned all that they most valued. The deanery was in the hands of Bishop Lancaster, who could give no help, and among the prebendaries there was either obstructive apathy or violent opposition to change. Bale was certainly wrong in trying to impose King Edward's second book without legal warrant; but he had gained his point with Browne, and disdained to yield to the inferior clergy. The latter pleaded that they had no books, and quoted the Archbishop against their own diocesan, who says he was 'always slack in things appertaining to God's glory.' Bale's sincerity is unquestionable, but he had set himself an impossible task, and his violence made him enemies who showed no quarter when their turn came. The most patient of men might have done nothing in such a position, but his reputation would have been better had he shown some Christian moderation. Bedell afterwards fell into the hands of his opponents, but his imprisonment was relieved by expressions of sympathy and admiration from the most unlikely quarters, and he must have felt that he had not worked in vain. Bale could have no such consolation.[389]

Catholic reaction at Edward's death.

On the first rumour of Edward's death it became evident that the Bishop of Ossory's authority was at an end. Oddly enough the priests hastened amid general rejoicing to proclaim Queen Jane. They were eager for change, and probably knew little of the fair saint whose innocent life was sacrificed to the ambition of others. Justice Howth, who had been Bale's strongest opponent, censured him for not being present at the ceremony; 'for indeed,' says the Bishop, 'I much doubted that matter.' In order, he adds, to 'cause the wild people to bear the more hate to our nation,' the priests also propagated a report that the young Earl of Ormonde and[Pg 383] Barnaby Fitzpatrick had been slain in London. The forts were attacked, and many Englishmen killed. Mrs. Matthew King, the clerk of the check's wife, was robbed 'to her very petticoat' on the highway by the Fitzpatricks and Butlers. But rumour and uncertainty were soon at an end, and the priests and people of Kilkenny learned that Catherine of Arragon's daughter was Queen of England.[390]

FOOTNOTES:

[358] St. Leger to Cecil, Jan. 19, 1551; Brady's Episcopal Succession.

[359] This conference is detailed in Mant's Church History, pp. 194, 199. See also Ware's Life of Browne. The conference was held in St. Mary's Abbey, the residence of Dowdall, he having refused to attend the Lord Deputy at Kilmainham.

[360] Browne to Warwick, ut supra. Examination of Oliver Sutton, March 23, 1552.

[361] St. Leger to Cecil, Jan. 19, 1551. Deposition of Sir John Alen, March 19, in the deponent's own hand. 'The Bishop of Kildare (Lancaster),' he says, 'came to me persuading me on his behalf to put in writing the words Mr. St. Leger spoke to me in Kilmainham, to whom I made this answer, "Show my lord that albeit I love his little toe better than all Mr. St. Leger's body, yet I will do nothing against truth."'

[362] Bicton's curious will is printed in Cotton's Fasti, vol. ii. Appendix.

[363] Croft to Warwick, May 1551; Instructions to Desmond and others July 1; Archbishop Browne to Warwick, Aug. 6.

[364] Cusack to Warwick, Sept. 27, 1551.

[365] Cusack to Warwick, Sept. 27, 1551; Instructions to Mr. Wood, Sept. 29, with Cecil's notes, 'Keep him (Tyrone) still, participating the cause thereof to the nobility;' Hill's MacDonnells of Antrim, chap. iii.

[366] Ancient Laws and Institutes of Ireland, vol. iii. p. 146; Maine's Early History of Institutions, p. 53.

[367] Bagenal to Croft, Oct. 27, 1551.

[368] Bagenal to Croft, Nov. 11, 1551; Sir Thomas Cusack's Book, May 8, 1552; Four Masters, ad ann. 1551.

[369] Mant, pp. 209-210, from a Clarendon MS. The letters which passed between Croft and Dowdall are given by Mant from the Harris MSS.

[370] Browne to Warwick, Aug. 6, 1551; Ware's Browne.

[371] Instructions for Mr. Thomas Wood, July 28, 1551; and the King's answer, Aug. 17.

[372] Strype's Cranmer, book ii. chap. xxviii., and Appendices 65 and 66.

[373] Instructions for Mr. Wood, Sept. 29, 1551. Cecil wrote on the margin 'denied for the King liketh no union.' The King's amended answer, Nov. 26.

[374] Croft to Cecil, March 14, 1552; to the Marquis of Winchester, March 22.

[375] W. Crofton to Cecil, April 12, 1551; Lord Deputy and Council to Privy Council, Aug. 30, and the answer in Nov.; Croft to Northumberland, Dec. 22; Lord Deputy and Council to the Privy Council, Jan. 27, 1552—'idleness decayeth nobility, one of the principal "kayes" of a commonwealth, and bringeth magistrates in contempt and hatred of the people,' and the petition enclosed. Croft to Cecil, March 14, and to Winchester, March 22. Ware's Annals.

[376] Wicklow tinstone has never been thought workable, see Kane's Industrial Resources, p. 210. Dr. Kane does not seem to have known anything of the Clonmines venture. Lord Deputy St. Leger and Council to Henry VIII., Oct. 24, 1541, and June 4, 1543. St. Leger acted on the advice of Thomas Agard, a mining expert. Minute of Council in S.P., 1546. St. Leger, Croft, and others to the Privy Council, May 20, 1551; Robert Record, surveyor of mines to the Privy Council, Feb. 1552. Harman's certificate, same date. Joachim Gundelfinger to the Privy Council, May 15. Reports on the mines, Aug. 1552, and Feb. and April, 1553. Instructions to St. Leger in Carew, July 1550, p. 228, as to alum. The MSS. contains many details interesting to specialists, especially the certificate of Gerrard Harman, a German.

[377] Privy Council to Croft, Feb. 23, and May 29, 1552. Sir Thomas Cusack's 'Book,' in Carew, 1553, p. 241.

[378] The Earl of Tyrone's articles, Feb. 9, 1552; St. Leger to Northumberland, March 10. Sir Thomas Cusack's 'Book,' in Carew.

[379] Cusack's 'Book' in Carew. Four Masters, 1552.

[380] Earls of Kildare. The patent of restoration is dated April 25, 1552. Orders for Leighlin and Carlow in Carew, April 30. Croft to the Privy Council, April 16, May 1, and May 31.

[381] Cusack's 'Book' in Carew, No. 200. It is there wrongly dated 1553.

[382] The facts of this expedition (June and July 1552) are given by the Four Masters; and see Ware's Annals.

[383] Tyrone's complaint, July 1552; Privy Council to George Paris, Oct. 25; to Croft, Dec. 10; Cusack to Privy Council, Dec. 22; Memorandum concerning Tyrone, Dec. 30, in Carew.

[384] Mayor, &c., of Waterford to the Privy Council, Dec. 18; Cusack and Aylmer to the Privy Council, Dec. 22 and 30; Declaration of Desmond's title, Dec. 30; Cusack in Carew, ut supra.

[385] Northumberland to Cecil, Nov. 25, 1552; Cusack's 'Book' in Carew, vol. i. p. 236; King's letter in Lodge's Patent Officers; Ware's Annals.

[386] A paper calendared under Jan. 1553 (No. 75) calculates the average expenses from 33 to 38 Hen. VIII. at 8,500l. a year. In the six years of Edward's reign they rose by regular gradation from 17,000l. to 52,000l. The average revenue for the former period was 9,000l., for the latter, 11,000l. See also No. 83, 'a device how to keep Ireland in the stay it now remaineth upon the revenues only.'

[387] The consecrations took place on Feb. 2, 1553.

[388] Bale's 'Vocation,' in the Harleian Miscellany.

[389] Church histories of Mant, Killen, Brennan, and Reid. Graves's History of St. Canice. They all derive their chief inspiration from Bale's own 'Vocation.' Fuller has preserved the nickname of 'biliosus Balæus,' given to the Bishop in contemporary controversy.

[390] Browne and Bale were friars; yet Protestants will not blame them for entering the holy estate of matrimony, any vows to the contrary notwithstanding. To modern England a married clergy seems quite natural, but the scandal was great during the transition period, and Queen Elizabeth felt the awkwardness herself. The following statement of Harpsfield may be true or false, but it shows what could be said by a contemporary. It should be remembered that Harpsfield was Archdeacon of Canterbury. 'Against these kind of marriages, and maintenance of the same, King Henry, in his latter days, made very sharp laws, whereupon many so married put over their women to their servants and other friends, who kept them at bed and board as their own wives. And after the death of King Henry they received them again (as love money) with usury; that is, the children in the mean season begotten by the said friends, whom they took, called and brought up as their own, as it was well known, as well in other as in Browne, Archbishop of Dublin. It would now pity a man at the heart to hear of the naughty and dissolute life of these yoked priests,' &c.

[Pg 384]

CHAPTER XVIII.

THE REIGN OF MARY.

The succession to the crown.
Lawyers and casuists might dispute about the succession. Logically, Mary and Elizabeth could not both be legitimate; but the people of England swept these cobwebs away. Catherine had for twenty-two years borne the title of Queen, and in that great place

she was not known to have done anything worthy of blame, but much deserving the highest praise. And then there was the will of Henry VIII. Its execution had perhaps been informal, but the people cared nothing for that; it was his will, and he had been authorised by Parliament to make it. The sick-room fancies of a boy of sixteen were not to be allowed to alter such a settlement.

Mary proclaimed.

The struggle for the crown was short, and was little felt at the distance at which Ireland then was, though the Dudley party took care that Queen Jane's accession should be officially known there. On the thirteenth day after her brother's death Mary was proclaimed by the Council in London, on the fourteenth the baffled Northumberland renewed the proclamation at Cambridge, on the fifteenth the grand conspirator himself was arrested. On the very day of the Cambridge proclamation the Privy Council wrote to Aylmer, the acting Lord Justice cancelling the former communication, and directing that Mary should be proclaimed 'Queen of England, France, and Ireland, Defender of the Faith, and on earth supreme head of the churches of England and Ireland.'[391]

St. Leger is Deputy, 1553.

Besides twelve Privy Councillors, six individuals connected with Ireland, who happened to be in England, signed these letters—Cusack, the Chancellor; Lord Gormanston; Staples, Bishop of Meath; Thomas Luttrell, Chief Justice of the[Pg 385] Common Pleas; James Bathe, Chief Baron; and the veteran John Alen. The object probably was to show the men in Dublin that this time at least there was no mistake as to which Queen they were to obey. Cusack, Aylmer, Luttrell, and Bathe were confirmed in their offices with increased emoluments, and no immediate change was made in the general management of Irish affairs. Some disturbances amongst the O'Connors were easily put down, and the citizens of Dublin repulsed a raid of the O'Neills near Dundalk. In the meantime Northumberland had expiated his crimes on the scaffold. Gardiner, Bonner, Tunstall, and others had been restored, and Cranmer, Latimer, and Hooper imprisoned; and there was time to think of the affairs of Ireland. In October, soon after the coronation, St. Leger was appointed Lord Deputy in fulfilment of the late King's intention. He landed at Dalkey on November 11, and on the 19th took the oath and received the sword in Christ Church.

His instructions.

St. Leger's instructions show the policy which Mary had adopted. As regards temporal affairs it did not greatly differ from that of her father. The Scots in Ulster were not to be molested unless they gave fresh trouble. The army was to be reduced to 500 regular soldiers, of which not more than ten per cent. were to be Irishmen. Extraordinary garrisons were to be discharged at the next general pay day, and if possible induced to go back to England without raising riots. The Lord Deputy might employ kerne and gallowglasses where necessary, and the usual private bands were to be continued; but coyne and livery were to be eschewed as much as possible. St. Leger found it impossible to carry out the reduction of the army lower than 1,100 men, besides kerne. The question as to the desirability of a Presidency for Munster was to be carefully considered in all its bearings. Leix and Offaly being in great measure waste, the Lord Deputy was to grant lands in fee simple at a small quit-rent either to Englishmen or Irishmen, binding them to erect and maintain farm buildings, and to till a certain portion of land. By this means it was hoped that these unfortunate districts would soon be made like the English Pale. Leases for twenty-one years were to be[Pg 386] given to Crown tenants generally, including holders of monastic lands. Goodacre had just died, so that there was no difficulty about Armagh, to which, as well as to the Primacy of all Ireland, Dowdall was immediately restored, with the additional grant of the priory of Ards rent free for life. The Mass and the rest of the old religion was to be restored as nearly as possible.[392]

> Mary maintains the rights of the Crown.

But Mary, though zealous for orthodoxy, had no intention of yielding the rights of the Crown to the Pope, and this was no doubt well understood. One of St. Leger's earliest duties was to go to Drogheda and place the government of Eastern Ulster in the hands of Eugene Magennis, who specially covenanted not to admit any provisor from Rome. An Irish-born priest named Connor MacCarthy asked Mary for a letter of licence to go to Rome, there to obtain certain benefices from the Pope, fearing lest some should be in the Queen's gift, 'and also considering the statute of Premunire.' Nor was the fear an idle one, for when Tyrone afterwards obtained a Papal bull for the appointment of his chaplain to the restored priory of Down, the Queen sharply reminded him that she intended to maintain the prerogative in that behalf which she had received from her progenitors. MacCarthy was not the only Irish ecclesiastic of the reign who thought it necessary to petition for relief from the consequences of the dreaded statute.[393]

> Catholicism restored. Bale refuses to give way. Bale's religious dramas.

In some places the old religion was restored without waiting for any formal order. As soon as Edward's death was known Justice Howth and Lord Mountgarret, the Earl of Ormonde's uncle, went to Kilkenny and desired to have the sacrament celebrated in honour of St. Anne. The priest said the Bishop had forbidden celebrations on week days; 'as indeed I had,' says Bale, 'for the abominable idolatry that I had seen therein.' The learned judge, who seems to have had no commission, then discharged the clergy from obedience to their[Pg 387] Bishop, and commanded them to proceed in the old way. On August 20 Mary was proclaimed at Kilkenny with much solemnity. Bale strongly objected to wear cope or mitre, or to have the crozier borne before him; not from any opposition to the Queen's title, but from dislike to vain ceremonies. Taking a New Testament in his hand, he went to the market-cross followed by a great crowd, to whom he preached from the 13th chapter of Romans, on the reverence due to magistrates. But the clergy of the cathedral, who had no sympathy with the Bishop's doctrines, provided two disguised priests to carry mitre and crozier before him against his will. The people were amused, instructed, or scandalised, as the case might be, by the representation of a tragedy concerning God's promises in the old law, and by a comedy of St. John the Baptist. The baptism and temptation of Christ were brought upon the stage, and the young men of the town acted both at the morning and evening performance. Both dramas were written by Bale himself, and in a literary point of view they are far from contemptible. They mark the transition between the mystery plays of the middle ages and the compositions of Shakespeare's immediate precursors. Personified abstractions as well as historical characters appear on the stage; nor did Bale shrink from a representation which seems impossible to us, for he boldly introduces the first person in the Trinity under the name of Pater Cælestis. Justification by faith is the great doctrine inculcated, and where the author speaks in person he loses no opportunity of attacking the Church of Rome. In an epilogue he exhorts the people to

'Hear neither Francis, Benedict, nor Bruno,
Albert nor Dominic, for they new rules invent,
Believe neither Pope nor Priest of his consent,
Follow Christ's gospel,' &c.
In another play on the instructive story of King John, 'Ynglond vidua' says:—

'Such lubbers as hath disguised heads in their hoods,
Which in idleness do live by other men's goods,
Monks, chanons, and nones.'
[Pg 388]

In his other works Bale throughout shows the same spirit. Thus he calls that very questionable hero, Sir John Oldcastle, 'a blessed martyr not canonised by the Pope, but in the precious blood of his Lord Jesus Christ.' St. Paul is the great object of Bale's admiration, and he seems to have thought that he was like him. The points of resemblance are similar to those which Captain Fluelen discovered between himself and Alexander the Great. Thus, Paul was tossed up and down between Candia and Melita, Bale between Milford and Waterford. There was a river in Monmouth and a river in Macedon, and there were salmon in both.[394]

Opposition to Bale in his diocese.
Sir Richard Howth, Treasurer of St. Canice's, and his friend Sir James Joys, were among Bale's most energetic opponents. To annoy him they suggested solemn exequies and prayers for the soul of Edward VI. The Bishop argued that it would be better to wait for orders from Dublin. The ceremony had already once been postponed to see the devil dance at Thomastown—a Sunday amusement which the mob perhaps preferred to the Bishop's plays. Bale found another enemy in one whom he calls Bishop of Galway, and who was probably John Moore, Bishop of Enaghdune, the ancient diocese in which Galway stands. This Moore was commissioned, along with other prelates not acknowledged in the Roman succession, to consecrate Patrick Walsh Bishop of Waterford. He was no credit to the Reformation, for Bale represents him as spending his nights in drinking and his days in confirming children at twopence a head. A gallowglass brought a dog in a sheet with twopence hanging round his neck to be confirmed with his neighbours' children; in this, says Bale, 'noting this beastly Bishop more fit to confirm dogs than Christian men's children.' The soldier may have regarded him as a schismatic, but it is not easy to understand how such a man can have attained episcopal orders.[395]

[Pg 389]

He is forced to fly.
Ten days after the proclamation of Mary there was a general revolt against Bale, incited by Howth, whose position in legal circles gave him ample means of knowing how the wind blew at Court, but who was rather horrified at the length to which the clergy and their adherents went. In Bale's absence they rang the bells of St. Canice's and of all the other churches, flinging their caps to the battlements of the cathedral with shouts of laughter, but doing no actual violence. A little later the mob was not so good-humoured. The Fitzpatrick and Butler kerne, and especially the 'furious family of Mountgarret,'

annoyed Bale in many ways. Barnaby Bolger, an enterprising tradesmen who had formerly aroused great indignation by forestalling Kilkenny market, and whose young daughter was married to 'Grace Graceless,' an adherent of the Fitzpatricks, headed a tumultuous attack on the Bishop's house outside the town. He and his friend Mr. Cooper, the parson of Callan, were robbed of all their horses, and thus deprived of the means of escape. Five of Bale's servants, one of them a girl of sixteen, were caught haymaking, and all murdered. He managed to close the portcullis and defend himself until rescued by Robert Shee, the sovereign of Kilkenny, 'a man sober, wise, and godly, which is a rare thing in this land.' Shee, who could command the services of 100 horse and 300 foot, sent Bale by night to Dublin, and no doubt he thought of St. Paul's journey under somewhat similar circumstances. But there was no safety in the Irish capital, and the Bishop escaped by sea in a sailor's dress. He was captured at St. Ives and brought before the justices, but was released when nothing was found to connect him with Wyatt's or any other plot. He was again captured by pirates and had to pay a ransom, but ultimately succeeded in reaching Holland. For five years he lived at Basel, where he continued to write with an acrimony which had not been lessened by his recent troubles. When Elizabeth became Queen, Bale made no attempt to regain his bishopric. At sixty-three he was disinclined to face the Kilkenny people again, or perhaps he had learned that he was unfit to govern men. He became a prebendary of Canterbury, and devoted his remaining years[Pg 390] to literature. His hurried flight from Ireland had forced him to leave books and manuscripts behind, and the Queen ordered them to be sent over to him. 'He had,' she said, 'been studious in the search of the history and antiquities of this our realm,' and might probably do something for their illustration. Whether Bale ever got back his library or not, he was certainly not silenced for want of materials; for the extent and variety of his learning were considered most remarkable.[396]

Wyatt's rebellion. Croft, Cheeke, and Carew, 1554.

The abortive insurrection of Wyatt had the usual effect of setting Mary more firmly on the throne, and at the same time of exasperating her against some whom she might have been willing to spare. Sir James Croft, the late Lord Deputy, was arrested before he had time to raise his tenants in Herefordshire: he was convicted, but afterwards pardoned. Sir Peter Carew, who afterwards played an important part in Irish affairs, was also accused of complicity, and thought it prudent to go abroad, where his companion was no less a personage than Sir John Cheeke. Venturing to Brussels, where Paget was ambassador, they were led to suppose that there was no danger, but that crafty diplomatist had them kidnapped near Antwerp, and carried to England in a fishing boat. Their captors were the Flemish and Spanish officials; and Philip, while expressing becoming indignation at the breach of hospitality, took care not to hear of it until the prisoners were safe beyond seas. The passage can hardly have been pleasant, for they were blindfolded and chained, one at each end of the boat. Poor Sir John Cheeke, who afterwards showed his unfitness for the crown of martyrdom, and who perhaps saw a vision of the stake, did not conceal his misery. 'Although very well learned, but not acquainted with the cross of troubles, he was still in great despair, great anguish, and heaviness, and would not be comforted, so great was his sorrow; but Sir Peter Carew, whose heart could not be broken nor mind overthrown with any adversities, and yielding to no such matter,[Pg 391] comforted the other, and encouraged him to be of a good stomach, persuading him (as though he had been a divine) to patience and good contentation.' The man of action, as is not seldom the case, showed that he had more philosophy than the philosopher. Sir Peter, whose guilt, if he was guilty, was much less clear than that of Croft, was pardoned by the Queen, and afterwards served her well at St. Quentin. Sir John Cheeke lived to undergo a worse humiliation than that of Cranmer, to be made an instrument in the persecution of those with whom he secretly agreed, to suffer in the few months which his pusillanimity had gained him a thousand martyrdoms of grief and shame, and then to die heart-broken and dishonoured. Sir Nicholas Arnold, afterwards employed by Elizabeth in Ireland, was another of the conspirators. Lady Jane, the innocent victim of so many intrigues, laid her beautiful neck upon the block, and fivescore Kentishmen suffered death for their zeal to the Reformation or their hatred of Spanish influence. Gerald of Kildare and the young Earl of Ormonde both served with distinction against Wyatt, and the orthodox Queen rewarded both with goodly grants of abbey lands. Ormonde had been captain of one of the bands of Whitecoats sent by the city into Kent, where many of his men deserted to the insurgents.[397]

The primacy is restored to Dowdall.

The insurrection being at an end, the Queen lost no time in forcing Browne to surrender his patent of precedence, and restoring Dowdall to the primacy, and a commission was issued to him and to Drs. Walsh and Leverous for re-establishing the old religion, and punishing those who had violated the law of clerical celibacy. Browne, who had a wife, was accordingly deprived, and, pending the appointment of a successor, the temporalities of his see handed over to Lockwood, the pliant Dean of Christ Church. Staples of Meath, who was likewise married, and was besides personally obnoxious to Dowdall, was also deprived in favour of one of the Commissioners who sentenced him, the learned William Walsh,[Pg 392] formerly a Cistercian monk of Bective Abbey. Curiously enough, Walsh, who was appointed by Pole in virtue of his legatine authority, did not receive a Papal provision till 1564, some time after Elizabeth had expelled him from his see. The same treatment for the same offence was inflicted on Lancaster, Bishop of Kildare, who was succeeded by Leverous, already Bishop of Leighlin by Papal provision. A fourth married bishop was Travers of Leighlin, who was succeeded by Thomas O'Fihel or Field, an Augustinian friar. A fifth, Casey of Limerick, had to make way for his aged predecessor Quin. On Bale, who had left the field clear, no legal sentence of deprivation was passed; but his successor, John Thonory, was already appointed. Thonory has an evil name for having corruptly wasted the property of his see, and is said to have died of grief at the loss of some of his ill-gotten gains. Of the deprived prelates, Lancaster lived to be Archbishop of Armagh, and Casey, who survived two successors, and saw another expelled, regained his see in 1571. Browne, Travers, and Lancaster are supposed to have died before the accession of Elizabeth, and Staples soon after it.[398]

Kildare returns to Ireland, 1554.

This year was memorable for the return of Gerald of Kildare, whose titles and estates were restored to him. The attainder, however, was not renewed till 1569. Old Brian O'Connor was released from the Tower, and allowed to revisit Offaly, an indulgence which he owed to the exertions of his daughter Margaret, who was Kildare's aunt, and who relied upon the number of her connections at Court, as well as her own knowledge of the English language. Barnaby Fitzpatrick, Lord of Upper Ossory, King Edward's bosom friend, returned about the same time, and so did a far more important personage, the young Earl of Ormonde. 'There was great rejoicing,' say the 'Four Masters,' 'throughout the greater part of Leath-Mhogha because of their arrival; for it was thought that not one of the descendants of the Earls of Kildare, or of the O'Connors Faly, would ever come to Ireland.'

Constant war among the Irish.

While the obedient shires were busy with the restoration[Pg 393] of the ancient religion, the native Irish made war among themselves, with but little interference from the Government. Donough O'Brien, the second Earl of Thomond, and a firm friend of the Crown, was killed in April 1553 by his brother Donnell, leaving the earldom to Connor, his eldest son, by Lady Helen Butler, who survived him. Donnell, however, assumed the title of O'Brien, and the clansmen were divided between the representatives of the old and new order. Donnell petitioned that, having been nominated according to the ancient custom, he might be acknowledged as chief. St. Leger was unable to grant this, but offered to write to the Queen in his favour. In the meantime other controversies were submitted to the arbitration of O'Carroll, O'Mulrian, and MacBrien Arra, on the part of Donnell; and of the barons of Mountgarret, Cahir, and Dunboyne, all Butlers, on the part of the Earl. The umpires in case of disagreement were the Lord Deputy, the Lord Chancellor, and the Earl of Desmond. It is very hard to make out the exact sequence of events, but either just before or just after this negotiation, Donnell attacked one of his nephew's castles, and was driven off by the arrival of the Earl of Ormonde. He then turned his attention to the plunder of Clanricarde. The Baron of Delvin continued to ravage MacCoghlan's country, and one of the Nugents, who was foster-brother of Kildare, being killed, the newly restored Earl, who lost no time in showing that he meant to keep up the family traditions, exacted 340 cows as an eric. The O'Carrolls in the south, the MacSweenys in the north, killed each other in the old fashion. Shane O'Neill persuaded the Earl of Kildare and the Baron of Delvin to take his part in a quarrel with one sept of his name, and old Tyrone was defeated by another sept, supported by the MacDonnells, who were also intriguing with Calvagh O'Donnell.[399]

The Pope and the 'Rex Hiberniæ,' 1555.

We have seen that the Queen had no intention of yielding any part of the dignity which had belonged to her predecessors. Notwithstanding the Papal pretension to suzerainty,[Pg 394] she had as a matter of course assumed the royal title created by her father in Ireland. The Holy See found it necessary to respect accomplished facts, and had not Julius III. abandoned all claims to the monastic lands, Pole would never have been allowed into England. Paul IV.'s pretensions were boundless, but he could not afford to quarrel about a mere trifle both with England and Spain. He considered it a great glory for his pontificate that its opening should be signalised by the arrival of an English ambassador. Whether he wished it or not, Philip and Mary were, and would remain, King and Queen of Ireland. He therefore ignored all that Henry had done, and, as if of his own mere notion, erected Ireland into a kingdom. The world might perhaps suppose that Mary took it from his hand, and not in right of blood. 'The Popes,' says the sarcastic Venetian, 'have often given that which they could not take from the possessors, and, to avoid contentions, some have received their own goods as gifts, and some have dissembled the knowledge of the gift, or of the pretence of the giver.' But in Ireland, where distance cast a halo of enchantment over Papal politics, and where Franciscans and Jesuits swayed the popular mind, the bull which announced the gracious gift was taken by many for what it pretended to be, and not for what it really was.[400]

The Queen maintains her prerogative.

Mary gave evidence of her desire to restore the splendour of religion by re-establishing St. Patrick's as a cathedral. Leverous was the first Dean of the new foundation, and was allowed to hold the preferment along with the see of Kildare. The man selected to undo Browne's work was Hugh Curwin, Dean of Hereford, a native of Westmoreland, and one of the Queen's chaplains. He had become known as a preacher in favour of Henry's marriage with Anne Boleyn, in opposition to the Franciscan Peto. The deanery of Hereford had been his reward. Peto, on the other hand, had become the Queen's confessor, and was the chosen instrument of Paul IV., when that Pope in a fit of anger appointed a legate to supersede[Pg 395] Pole. Mary so valued the royal authority that she resented the irregular honour intended for her confessor, though he had been the champion of her own legitimacy, stopped the red hat at the gates of Calais, and never allowed Peto any benefit from the Pope's irritability. On the whole, Anne's advocate fared better than Catherine's. Curwin, whose first article of belief enjoined submission to principalities and powers, no doubt knew how to turn the Queen's love of power, as he had done her father's, to his own advantage. He was treated with exceptional favour, and gained practical control of the temporalities even before his consecration, which was performed in London by Bonner, Thirlby, and Griffin. Immediately afterwards he received the Great Seal of Ireland. Curwin had the pall from Rome, and in the Papal record of his appointment Philip and Mary are said to have supplicated for it, Browne being ignored, and Curwin made successor to Alen. But the King and Queen only acknowledged that Curwin was preferred on their recommendation, and he had to renounce on oath all things prejudicial to the Crown, whether contained in the Papal bull or not. Curwin held a provincial synod soon after his arrival in Ireland, at which the principal business was the restoration of the ancient rites.[401]

No progress made in Ulster. St. Leger has no money, 1555.

Ulster was in a state of more than usual confusion. Manus O'Donnell, who had been constantly at war with his father, was opposed by his son Calvagh, who had the help of the Scots. They addressed him as illustrious lord, and he went over to Scotland to claim the proffered aid. Returning with a large force, and with a piece of ordnance which the annalists inexplicably call a crooked gun, he entered Lough Swilly, took his father prisoner, and battered Greencastle and another fortress on Lough Foyle. Calvagh thenceforth assumed practical control of his clan. The Scots slew Hugh MacNeill Oge, and St. Leger divided his territory between Phelim O'Neill and the sons of Phelim Bacagh. The hardy interlopers had even designs on Carrickfergus, which St. Leger says were frustrated 'by the help of God and Mr. Parker;[Pg 396]' but in a campaign of six weeks the Lord Deputy could gain no real advantage. As in the case of most Irish governors, his detractors, among whom Sir William Fitzwilliam was conspicuous, were busy at Court. They accused him, among other things, of falsifying estimates in favour of Andrew Wyse, the late Vice-Treasurer, whose accounts had been found unsatisfactory. 'I am now in case,' he said, 'as the poet's fame. I have meat to the surlip and drink to the netherlip, and can reach neither of them.' His position made it impossible for him to economise, and no money came to pay his hungry retinue. A friendly chronicler has remarked that St. Leger, like all other Irish governors, was hated chiefly for his good deeds; like a good apple tree, which, the more fruit it bears, the more stones are thrown at it.[402]

Lord Fitzwalter (Sussex) Lord Deputy, 1556.

The Lord Deputy's entreaties for release were heard at last, and the government was conferred on Sir Thomas Radcliffe, Lord Fitzwalter, afterwards created Earl of Sussex, who, but for his Irish service, would bear one of the fairest characters in our history. Mary rejoiced that the true Catholic faith had by God's great goodness and special grace been recovered in England and Ireland, and she directed her representative 'to set forth the honour and dignity of the Pope's Holiness and See Apostolic of Rome, and from time to time to be ready with our aid and secular force, at the request of all spiritual ministers and ordinaries there, to punish and repress all heretics and Lollards and their damnable sects, opinions, and errors.' Cardinal Pole, she added, was about to send over a legatine commission to visit the Irish Church, and official assistance was to be given 'in all and everything belonging to the function and office legatine, for the advancement of God's glory and the honour of the See Apostolic.' The new governor was reminded that he lay under an obligation to execute justice, and was exhorted at much greater length to exert himself for the improvement of the revenue. A Parliament was to be held, chiefly as a means of restoring[Pg 397] religion according to the Queen's ideas, of settling her marriage and succession, and of voting a subsidy. Sir Henry Sidney, who now makes his first appearance in Irish history, accompanied the Lord Deputy as Vice-Treasurer. He brought with him a sum of 25,000l.[403]

A warlike mayor of Dublin.

About the time of the new Lord Deputy's arrival, the Kavanaghs made a raid into the neighbourhood of Dublin. Sir George Stanley took command of the citizens, and drove 140 of the assailants into Powerscourt, where they had to surrender at discretion. Seventy-four were hanged. John Challoner, who was Mayor of Dublin at the time, provided the civic force with arms, which he had brought at his own expense from Spain. This martial magistrate was offered knighthood, but he excused himself. 'My Lord,' he said, 'it will be more to my credit and my posterity's to have it said that John Challoner served the Queen upon occasion, than to say that Sir John Challoner did it.'[404]

Sussex makes a journey into Ulster, 1556.

Sussex landed at Dublin towards the end of May, and received the sword from St. Leger's willing hands. The religious ceremonies were of a kind entirely satisfactory to the Queen. After a month's stay in the capital he set out for the North, and appeared in church both at Drogheda and Dundalk. The force mustered on this occasion was very considerable, for besides the regular soldiers and Ormonde's followers, the gentlemen of the Pale were called on to serve with from one to six horsemen each. The Plunkets contributed twenty-four horse, the Nugents eighteen horse and twenty-four foot. Dublin sent sixty horsemen and gunners, and Drogheda forty men well appointed. 'The Byrnes and the Tooles' wastes' in Wicklow were expected to send twelve horse each, and other Irish contingents joined on the march. The first Sunday was spent at a mill beyond Newry, where Dowdall said Mass, and where O'Hanlon, whose chiefry seems to have been disputed, was solemnly proclaimed. Mention is made of a great hill of stones, which[Pg 398] was, perhaps, the traditional spot for the election of an O'Hanlon. Passing along the right bank of the Newry river, which he crossed near Tanderagee, Sussex reached the Laggan valley near Moira, and passing Belfast, reached Carrickfergus on the ninth day after leaving Dublin. From this the army marched across the central districts of Antrim, and, at last, on the twenty-fourth day from Dublin, Sussex reached Glenarm, and found that James MacDonnell had fled before him into Scotland. The fugitive sent to France for help, but his envoy's proceedings were counteracted by Paget's vigilance. A quantity of cattle were captured, besides butter and other produce hid in a cave. This seems to have been the only result of an expedition which lasted thirty-seven days. Sussex dismissed his allies at their old rendezvous near Newry, and on the very next day, as if in ridicule of his efforts, a messenger arrived to say that the Scots had attacked the rear guard. Sidney afterwards said that he had slain James MacConnell, a mighty Scots captain, during this expedition. Some Scots of name were certainly killed, and one of them may have been called James; but the real James MacDonnell was back at Glenarm before the end of the year.[405]

His failure.

The moral which Sussex drew from this inglorious expedition was that the North could only be held by a chain of forts along the coast from Dundalk to Lough Foyle. Some part at least of the expense would be paid by the salmon fisheries of the Foyle, the Bann, and the Bush; and by the herring, cod, ling, and hake fisheries, of which Carlingford was the chief seat. A good English bishop would also, he thought, be a means to civilise the country. It had not yet been discovered that making the Church a badge of conquest only served to make religion itself odious. The dislike of the Irish to English ecclesiastics had been marked throughout the middle ages, and even if England had remained in communion with Rome, bishops who were Government officials first and chief pastors afterwards, could scarcely[Pg 399] have ministered successfully to the wants of O'Neills and O'Donnells.[406]

The King's and Queen's Counties. The natives.

The settlement of Leix was in outward form completed, and Sussex received the Queen's thanks for it. The arrangements were not without a show of equity; but the old inhabitants could not reconcile themselves to the intrusion of a colony, and their pertinacious opposition forced the Government to treat them with far more rigour than had been at first intended. The western half of the new Queen's County was originally reserved for the O'Mores, each head of a sept becoming a landlord holding an estate in tail by knight-service. The chiefs were prohibited from keeping any idlemen except of their own sept, or more than one for every 100 acres. They were to attend the constable of the fort when required, to repair bridges, and at all times to keep the passes open between their districts and those occupied by the English. They were to dress like Englishmen, except when riding, and to teach their children to speak English, to attend the Deputy annually, and to use only the Common Law. All above twelve were required to take the oath of allegiance. Forfeiture was prescribed for a persistent refusal to keep the passes open; for retaining superfluous idlemen; for keeping more than one set of harness; for interrupting communication with the English; for making a private way; for marrying and fostering with the Irish, and for absenteeism. The Deputy's licence removed the penalty in all these cases. For keeping unlicensed firearms the first offence was to be punished by forfeiture, and the second by death.

The settlers.

The eastern district was assigned to the English, to hold on similar terms, and twelve places, among which Stradbally and Abbeyleix are the best known, were to be kept in a defensible state as satellites to the royal fort of Maryborough. The duties of the settlers were in general the same as those assigned to the O'Mores; but whereas the latter were restrained in the matter of arms, the possession of them was made obligatory on the former. A good bow and sheaf of[Pg 400] arrows, or one hand-gun at least, was to be kept in every house. Forfeiture was to be incurred in the same way as by the Irish, and in addition for falling away from the use of the English tongue, for holding more than 300 acres in demesne, or for entertaining Irishmen, except so far as they were necessary for husbandry. A few natives, whose services as captains of kerne had deserved special recognition, were to have grants in the English territory, and it was suggested that a large territory should be offered to the Earl of Kildare. A constable, resident at the fort, was to have the same powers locally as the Lord Deputy had generally. Stringent rules were made as to free quarters and purveyance. The constable or president on his annual circuit was to have his own expenses and those of four men and five horses borne for one night only by each town; and each sept of the O'Mores was to bear the like burden, and no more. Finally, a church was to be built in each of the twelve settlements within three years, and a parson, of English birth, was to have the tithe.[407]

The natives cling to their land.
Whatever the intentions of the Queen or her Deputy might be towards Leix and Offaly, there was sure to be plenty of opposition on the part of the natives, who were, however, as usual, divided among themselves. The old chief, Brian O'Connor, was still alive, and his son Donough carried on the old feud and killed his cousin, the son of Cahir Roe. Both Donough and Connell O'More, the chief of Leix, fell into the hands of Sussex in the course of the year, but to the surprise of the Irish in general were released in deference to Kildare and Ormonde, who had become in some measure responsible for them. The O'Mores remained quiet for a time on the lands reserved to them. Donough and others of the O'Connors afterward came to Sussex at Philipstown, as the fort of Offaly must henceforth be called, and made their submission, giving promises of good behaviour, which they immediately broke.[408]

[Pg 401]

They are again attacked, 1557.
After the meeting at Philipstown, Sussex and his Council repaired to Leighlin, where the principal O'Connors neglected to appear as they had promised. A leader of the Kavanaghs, who had not taken warning by the recent fate of his clansmen, was executed, and Connel O'More, who had once more broken into rebellion, was hanged in chains at Leighlin about the same time. Offaly was next invaded and hostages taken, who were executed on a further outbreak taking place, with the exception of O'Connor himself, who was detained prisoner in Dublin.[409]

Parliament of 1557. The monastic lands are not restored.
The Parliament, from which Mary expected much for the Church of which she was so faithful a daughter, met at last and enacted all the laws made in England against the Protestants. The old statutes against Lollardry, which prescribed death by fire as the punishment for obstinate or relapsed heretics, were declared to be in full force. A communication from Pole was read by Curwin as Chancellor, kneeling down in open session, in which the Cardinal urged the assembly to restore Ireland to full communion with the Church. All Acts derogatory to the Pope which had been passed since the

twentieth year of Henry VIII. were accordingly repealed. The Queen was declared a legitimate, absolute sovereign, and all laws and sentences to the contrary were abrogated. On the other hand, grants of monastic land were confirmed. There could be no doubt of Mary's wish to restore the religious houses, but this does not appear to have been done except in the single case of Kilmainham. Oswald Massingberd, who during the Puritan ascendency had led a wandering life in the woods, was appointed Prior by Pole, and the nomination was confirmed by the Queen. Massingberd was sworn of the Council, and assumed the position of his predecessors; but he seems to have had no belief in the stability of the new system. He gave long leases and sold all that was saleable, and he took no thought for the morrow. There appears to have been no intention of specially favouring the obsolete[Pg 402] order of St. John, for no attempt was made to restore it in England; but in Ireland it happened that the Crown had not parted with the house and lands. In the same way, since it could be done without offending vested interests, Mary re-established the Benedictines at Westminster, the Carthusians at Sheen, and the Observants at Greenwich. There are indications that she wished to examine titles closely, and to restore the monks where defects appeared; but she granted and confirmed grants of abbey lands as freely as her father and brother. Ninety years later, when the confederate Catholics had military possession of the greater part of Ireland, and the Nuncio Rinuccini was apparently all-powerful, the claim of the regulars to their old possessions was met by the nobility and gentry with anger and scorn.[410]

>Sussex makes an abortive expedition westward;

When released from his Parliamentary duties, Sussex marched westward against the O'Connors, who, under Donough, had possessed themselves of Meelick Castle, on the Shannon. The line of march lay through Offaly, by Killeigh, Ballyboy, and Cloghan, no opposition being offered by the O'Molloys or O'Maddens. The Shannon was reached on the third day. Clanricarde must have been in a tolerably peaceful state, for Athlone pursuivant seems to have had no difficulty in going to Galway to seek ammunition and provisions. Cannon were brought by water from Athlone and planted in the grounds of the friary, on an island or peninsula on the Galway side of the stream. The castle was summoned, and a cautionary shot fired without effect. Next day the cannonade began, and at the sixteenth shot a large piece of the courtyard wall fell down. The O'Connors escaped by a postern gate, and were proclaimed traitors. Clanricarde, Thomond, O'Carroll, and other chiefs, came to pay their respects to Sussex, and may well have laughed at the small results achieved by the display of irresistible force. A garri[Pg 403]son was placed in the castle, and, hostages having been taken from the neighbouring clans, the army returned through MacCoghlan's country, led by the chief himself. The Lord Deputy had the pleasure of seeing the night lit up by fires which the rebels kindled within a mile of his camp. The outlying buildings at Philipstown were all burnt, and arrows shot into the fort itself. Such was the practical outcome of a nine days' expedition, during which, as the annalists say, it is not easy to state or enumerate all that was destroyed.[411]

>and another into Ulster.

An expedition into Ulster, undertaken three months later, had the same lame and impotent conclusion. The annalists say compendiously that Armagh was burned twice in one month by Thomas Sussex. His horsemen encamped in the cathedral, and no enemy opposed the destroyer, who returned after a week to Dundalk only to hear that Shane O'Neill was burning and plundering within four miles of the town. Being pursued, Shane retreated to his woods, whither those who knew the country declined to follow him. Sussex then returned to Dublin; the Queen being richer by a few cows, and Sir James Garland poorer by the village which O'Neill had burned.[412]

The central districts still disturbed.

Not much impressed by the late invasion, the O'Connors who had escaped from Meelick stationed themselves at Leap Castle, about which there had been so much fighting in bygone days. Sussex took the castle without trouble, but Donough again escaped by the speed of his horse, and the stronghold was seized by O'Carroll as soon as the army had left. Sidney afterwards made two separate inroads into the same district. O'Molloy was proclaimed a traitor, and everything destroyed. It is not easy to see how there could be anything combustible left in the devoted country. The O'Carrolls were also engaged about this time in opposition to the Government, and in support of the O'Mores and O'Connors, and the annalists are again at a loss to enumerate[Pg 404] the preys and slaughter which were made from the Shannon to the Nore.[413]

War between the O'Neills and O'Donnells.

A local war of considerable importance took place this year between the O'Neills and O'Donnells. Manus, the old chief of Tyrconnel, had been kept a prisoner for the last two years by his son Calvagh, who assumed the leadership. This claim was disputed by his brother Hugh, who, with his immediate adherents, had deserted to Shane O'Neill. Shane was delighted at the opportunity of interfering, and declared that not one cow should escape, though the O'Donnells should carry away their cattle into Leinster or Munster. He himself would in future be the sole King of Ulster. Shane pitched his camp at Carriglea, near Strabane, just above the junction of the Finn and the Mourne. It was more a fair than an encampment, and the time was gaily passed in buying, and no doubt in drinking wine and mead, as well as fine clothes and merchandise. Calvagh, who lay five miles off with a few followers, sent two trusty spies to the camp, who mingled boldly with the throng of camp followers and soldiers belonging to many different clans. In front of Shane's tent they found a great central fire, and a huge torch as thick as a man's body blazing brightly. Sixty gallowglasses with their axes, and as many Scots, with heavy broadswords drawn, stood ready to guard the chief. When the time came for serving out supper, the spies claimed their share with the rest, and received a helmet full of meal and a corresponding quantity of butter. Not staying to make cakes, they carried back the trophy to Calvagh, who immediately got his men under arms. He had but two companies of the MacSweeney gallowglasses and thirty horsemen. No look-out was apparently kept at the camp, which they entered at once. There they had little to do but to kill till their arms were tired, the deficiency of force being much more than counterbalanced by the totally unprepared state of the O'Neills. Shane, whose reputation for courage is not high, slipped out at the back of his tent with only two companions, leaving his men to their fate. The three fugitives threaded the passes of the neigh[Pg 405]bouring mountains, and passed the Finn, the Deel, and the Derg by swimming. At Termonamongan, near the latter river, Shane bought a horse, and never rested till he reached the neighbourhood of Clogher. Calvagh remained in possession of the camp, and his men spent the rest of the night in drinking the wine which the O'Neills had provided for themselves. The extent of the plunder may be estimated from the fact that Con, Calvagh's young son, who had given up his horse to his father and fought on foot, now had eighty steeds for his share, including a celebrated charger of Shane's called the Eagle's Son.[414]

Sidney, Lord-Justice. No money.

Sussex had not been very long in Ireland before he asked for a holiday, and he was allowed to spend Christmas at home; Curwin and Sidney, and afterwards Sidney only, being appointed Lords Justices. War had been declared with France at midsummer, and one of the first letters received by the new governor announced the loss of Calais, and the Queen's vain hope of recovering it. In the storm of St. Quentin and the defence of Guisnes, English soldiers had shown that they were made of the same stuff as the victors of Agincourt, but the war was unpopular. Mary's subjects felt that they were sacrificed to Philip, and this jealousy of Spain both caused the fall of Calais and prevented its recovery. But the national vanity was sorely hurt, and Sidney thought it a good opportunity to point out that James MacDonnell was expected in Ulster with many French and Scots allies, and that the natives would join him or fall upon the Pale, which was itself heartily sick of English rule, of soldiers at free quarters, and of purveyors, who paid, if they paid at all, something very much less than market prices. The army was reduced to a little over 1,000 men, and the people of the Pale, though well disposed, could afford no effective help. Credit was extinct, and the bad money caused great misery. Yet even bad coin was scarce. 'Help us, my lord,' he wrote openly to Sussex, 'help us to money at this pinch, though it be as base as counters.'

Men, money, and provisions were alike wanting, and the[Pg 406] outlook was as dark as could be. Desmond proposed that the Queen should send special commissioners, independent of the Government, to inquire into the state of Ireland, and point out means of reformation. He himself had perhaps sinned through ignorance, and he thought justice and fair dealing more likely to do the work of civilisation than a new conquest. 'We neither think it meet, nor intend,' answered Mary, with a touch of her father's humour, 'to make any new conquest of our own, nor to use any force when justice may be showed.' She proposed to do all that was necessary by fair means.[415]

Hatred of the English Government.

Sidney's fears of foreign complications were not unfounded. He had no ship of war at his disposal, and he feared that Dublin might be blockaded. George Paris was in France, declaring that the wild Irish were quite ready to transfer their allegiance, and Sidney had reason to believe that Kildare was playing his hereditary game. There can be no doubt that this great nobleman, whose estates lay between the capital and the disturbed midland districts, was a thorn in the side of each successive governor. It was thought he wanted to be Deputy himself, and all the principal lawyers in Dublin had a retaining fee from him. William Piers, Constable of Carrickfergus, the vigilant guardian of the North, was told by one of his men who was present, that Sorley Boy MacDonnell, in the careless after-supper hour, said plainly 'that Englishmen had no right to Ireland, and they would never trust Englishmen more, but would trust the Earl of Kildare, "who," quoth Sorley, "hath more right to the country...." The nature of these people is they will speak what is in their hearts when the drink is in their heads.' The love of claret, inherent both in Scottish and Irish chiefs, tended to keep up constant communication with France. The hereditary hatred of England might at any moment counterbalance the jealousy which Scotland felt for the French regent and king matrimonial, and an invasion of Ireland might[Pg 407] seem less dangerous than that from which the caution of the Scots lords had just saved England. The recollection of Dundalk was not so fresh as that of Flodden.[416]

Attempts at conciliation.

Lady Tyrone had been closely imprisoned, apparently by Shane, for urging her husband to hold fast to his allegiance. 'I will not,' says Sidney's informant, 'you make this known to the Primate, or Kildare, or any Geraldine in Ireland.' To the Queen the Lord Justice wrote that the coast was infested by hostile cruisers, that he dreaded a French attack on castles which could not resist artillery, and that he could scarcely be answerable for the defence of the country. The effect of Sussex's advice while at Court may be gathered from the number of letters which Mary addressed to great men in Ireland. Tyrone and O'Reilly were thanked for past services, the former being charged to help the Deputy with a contingent, and the latter to dismiss the Scots in his pay. Calvagh O'Donnell was reminded of his duty, and encouraged to hope for a peerage and other rewards. Barnaby Fitzpatrick, whose courtly education was not forgotten by his friend's sister, was exhorted to behave like one who regards the service and weal of his natural country. His neighbour O'Carroll might look forward to a peerage for life if he would give help in season. Desmond and Clanricarde were directed to put Thomond in possession of his earldom and estates, the care of the coast being particularly recommended to the former. Desmond and Ormonde were thanked, and advised to refer all their differences to the arbitration of the Lord Deputy and Council.[417]

A spirited policy.

The Queen did not limit her care for Ireland to writing letters. She doubled the army; 800 men being sent over, and directions given for raising 200 more in Ireland. Every foot soldier was to receive twopence a day, and every horseman threepence a day, in addition to the old wages. The Deputy's salary was raised from 1,000l. to 1,500l., with the usual allowances, and he was directed to move constantly to and[Pg 408] fro, residences being maintained for him at Roscommon, Athlone, Monasterevan, Maryborough, Philipstown, Ferns, Enniscorthy, and Carlow. The O'Mores and O'Connors were to be still further chastised, and as much as possible effected against the Scots. In most other matters the former instructions were to remain in force. The restored Deputy was not expected to make bricks without straw, more than 200l. having been spent on the carriage of munitions to Chester for the Irish service.[418]

Sussex returns to Ireland, 1558.

Sussex left London on March 21, and we are told that he travelled post; but he did not leave Holyhead till the 26th of the following month. The actual passage only occupied a few hours. Detraction, the usual lot of Irish governors, followed him on his journey, his accuser being no less a person than Primate Dowdall, who was summoned over to tell his own story, and who died in London some three months before the Queen. Sidney and his Council declared that the Archbishop was actuated by personal malice, and that there was no foundation for his statements. There was, however, some excuse for a prelate who saw his metropolis and three churches burned by the viceregal army. Sussex believed that Dowdall was in league with his predecessor. Were it not, he said, for his set purpose to serve the Queen, he might find occupation enough in avoiding the nets spread on all sides, the catch line whereof he could not prove but by looking into Mr. St. Leger's bosom.[419]

The O'Connors still troublesome. Sussex goes to Munster.

Sussex had left Leix and Offaly in confusion, and he returned to find them in the same state, his brother, Sir Henry Radecliffe, being actually besieged in Maryborough by the natives, under Donogh and another O'Connor, accompanied by Richard Oge, one of the bastard Geraldines who had so long been troublesome. The garrison beat off their assailants after a hard fight, Richard Oge falling by the hand of Francis Cosby; but Donough again escaped. The first matter which[Pg 409] demanded the personal attention of Sussex after his return was the state of Thomond, where Sir Donnell More O'Brien—who had slain his brother, the second Earl, five years before—was now disputing the title of his young nephew Connor, whose principal castles he held. Ormonde, whose aunt was the young lord's mother, was of course interested in his favour, and the same reason was enough to make Desmond incline to Sir Donnell. It became necessary for Sussex himself to go in force and establish some kind of order. Taking the familiar line through Offaly and Ely, Leap Castle being abandoned at their approach, the Lord Deputy and his troops, strengthened on the route by the adhesion of Barnaby Fitzpatrick and a considerable force, marched across North Tipperary by Newport and Cahirconlish to Limerick, which was reached on the seventh day after leaving Dublin. At a point a few miles from the city Ormonde and his brother Edmund appeared with a large party. The young lord of Cahir, Gerald the heir of Desmond, with all the forces of his house, MacCarthy More, who received the honour of knighthood and a gold chain and gilded spurs, and William Burke, chief of the district, joined on the same day. At the gate of Limerick the mayor and aldermen in scarlet robes delivered to Sussex the keys and mace, which he returned to the mayor. With the civic insignia and sword of state borne before him, the Lord Deputy rode to the door of the cathedral, where the Marian bishop, Hugh Lacy, met him, and where he was censed and sprinkled with holy water. Sussex kissed the cross both here and at the rood, where the same ceremonies were repeated, and knelt devoutly at the high altar while the Te Deum was sung. Salutes were fired after church.

The Desmonds at Limerick.

The Lord Deputy rested ten days at Limerick, during which time was performed the rite of 'bishoping' Desmond's youngest child, the old Earl being present himself. This was a first or second baptism, for the little Fitzgerald was not old enough to be confirmed, and the Lord Deputy stood sponsor and gave his god-child his own name, and presented him at the same time with a gold chain. The career of James[Pg 410] Sussex Fitzgerald thus auspiciously begun was destined to end in a traitor's death on the scaffold.

The O'Briens.

Sir Donnell O'Brien failed to appear, and was thrice proclaimed traitor at Limerick. Sussex then issued forth into Thomond. Clare Castle and Ennis made no resistance, but a few cannon shot had to be fired at Bunratty before it surrendered. The Earl of Thomond, having been placed in possession of his country, was sworn upon the sacraments and on the relics of the Church with bell, book, and candle, to forsake the name of O'Brien, and to be true to the King and Queen. All the freeholders of the district swore in the same solemn way to obey him as their captain.

O'Shaughnessy.

On his journey westward from Limerick, Sussex spent a night with O'Shaughnessy at Gort, where he 'dined so worshipfully as divers wondered at it, for the like was not seen in an Irishman's house.' At Galway he was received with the same civic, military, and religious ceremonies as at Limerick, and, after staying four or five days, returned by Athenry and Meelick into Offaly, and thence to Dublin.[420]

Expedition against the Hebridean Scots. It ends in failure.

Sidney's apprehensions were partially realised, for James MacDonnell landed before Sussex with 600 islemen and two guns. But Carrickfergus had been reinforced, and the greater part of the Scots returned to their own country. Colla MacDonnell, one of the chief's five brothers and the resident guardian of his clan's Irish interests, died soon afterwards, and, his brother Angus having refused to take his place, Sorley Boy, the youngest and ablest of the family, filled the vacant post. It was decided to attack the Redshanks in their own islands, and a fleet assembled at Lambay from which great things were evidently expected. Sussex urged despatch; but the delays of the supply service were inveterate, and nothing was done for nearly three weeks. The Lord Deputy landed first in Cantire, and began operations by burning James MacDonnell's 'chief house called Sandell, a fair pile and a strong.'

The fleet is in danger,

He boasted that in three days he burned everything from[Pg 411] sea to sea in a district twenty miles long, and this without meeting any opposition worth notice. Isla was the great object of the expedition; but the wind was unfavourable, and the incendiary's work could be carried on elsewhere. Arran was accordingly devastated, the army dividing into two, so as to make the damage more complete. Isla being still inaccessible, the same fate was intended for Bute, but just as the boats were about to be manned a sudden gale sprung up, 'and that being then the weather shore the wind wheeled suddenly and made it the lee shore, whereby we being very near the shore were forced to ride it out for life and death in such a place as if any tackle had slipped or broken the ship whose tackle had so slipped or broken must needs have perished.' The cable of a Dublin transport parted, and she foundered with a loss of twenty-eight men. Most of the small vessels got into harbour, 'but the masters of H.M.'s ships I think thought scorn thereof.' The fine gentlemen who commanded men-of-war in those days were unwilling to take advice from the old seamen who acted as their sailing masters or pilots. With loss of boats, running rigging, and anchors, the fleet escaped, and the captains, whose courage was 'somewhat cooled,' were content after this to be controlled by their professional associates.

and is forced to retire.

The poor little Cumbrays having been ravaged, the disabled vessels were just able to reach Carrickfergus after a dead beat against a stiff north-wester. Sussex landed, and was nearly lost in regaining his flag-ship, the 'Mary Willoughby.' A council of war was then held, and it was found that there were provisions for only three weeks more, and that damages could not be properly repaired in Ireland. Only three ships were at all fit for service; and, moreover, 'the new bark is a ship of such length and unwieldliness in steerage as she is not to be ventured among the isles in such stormy weather, where there be many deep and narrow channels and strong tides.' It was feared that the ships might be becalmed or otherwise delayed in the isles, there was now no spare tackle in case of future storms, and it was by no means impossible that the crews and troops might starve. The hope of visiting Isla was therefore abandoned, and Sussex landed the soldiers with the[Pg 412] less ambitious intention of attacking the Scots in the Route. An English fleet and army carefully equipped and commanded by many gallant gentlemen had just succeeded in burning some barren islands, not without considerable loss to themselves, and had returned disabled without striking a blow. Sussex was conscious of his failure, and begged the Queen 'not to impute any lack in me, but to consider that whatever I wrote of was feasible, is feasible, and shall with grace of God be put in execution with a great deal more than I wrote of,' &c. The expedition is not even noticed in the Scots correspondence of the time, nor was anything done to retrieve matters on land. Out of 1,100 soldiers, but 400 were fit for service, the rest being prostrated by illness caused by the foul water on board ship.[421]

Activity of Sussex. He leaves Ireland at Mary's death.

Want of activity at least could not be charged against Sussex, who carried out strictly the spirit of the Queen's instructions, which desired him to be constantly on the move. He was at Leighlin a few days after his return from Scotland, and then returned to Dublin, where the affairs of Munster occupied his attention. The old Earl of Desmond was dead, and his son Gerald, destined to a disturbed life and a miserable death, succeeded to the splendid but troublesome inheritance of the Southern Geraldines. He promised fair, and was knighted by the Lord Deputy's hands, who went to Waterford to receive his homage and to admit him to the earldom. Sir Maurice Fitzgerald of Decies, who ruled about one half of the county of Waterford, also made his submission, promising to obey the law and make others obey it, to give his help to all judges, commissioners, and tax-gatherers, and to secure free admission for all to the markets at Waterford, Dungarvan, and elsewhere. The news of Mary's death reached Ireland soon after this, and Sussex, who had already obtained leave to go to England, hurried away to pay his court to the new sovereign. He left Ireland tolerably quiet.[422]

[Pg 413]

Story as to an intended Marian persecution in Ireland.

Mary did all she could to efface her father's anti-Roman policy; but no Irish persecution took place. This may have been less from the Queen's want of will than from the insignificance of the Protestants in Ireland. It is said that many people fled from the western parts of England in hope of sharing the comparative immunity enjoyed by the small Protestant congregation in Dublin. One story seems to show that this had attracted attention, and that Dublin would not have long escaped. It rests on the testimony of Henry Usher, one of the fathers of Trinity College and afterwards Archbishop of Armagh, and was repeated by his more famous nephew James Usher, and by other public men of repute. Henry Usher died at a great age in 1613, and was Treasurer of St. Patrick's as early as 1573. In the absence of anything to rebut it, such evidence can hardly be rejected. The story is that a Protestant citizen of Dublin named John Edmonds had a sister living at Chester married to one Mattershed, who kept an inn or lodging-house in which Cole, Dean of St. Paul's, slept when on his way to purge the Irish Church. 'Here,' said Cole, in the hearing of his hostess, 'is a commission that shall lash the heretics of Ireland.' The good woman watched her opportunity, possessed herself of the doctor's wallet, and substituted a pack of cards for the commission—a service for which she received a pension of 40l. from Queen Elizabeth. On reaching Dublin, Cole went straight to the Castle, where the Lord Deputy, who had just returned from his Scotch expedition, was sitting in council. Cole declared his business in a set speech; but when the secretary opened his wallet he found only the cards, with the knave of clubs uppermost. Sussex had conformed to the dominant creed, but had probably no wish to be a persecutor, and may have rejoiced at Cole's discomfiture. 'Let us have another commission,' he said, 'and we will shuffle the cards in the meanwhile.' A new scourge for the heretics was despatched, but before it came to hand Mary's unhappy career had closed.[423]

[Pg 414]

Death of Mary and Reginald Pole.

The weak enthusiast who, far more than Gardiner or Bonner, must share the responsibility for the persecution with which this Queen's name is inseparably connected, was not long divided from her in death. Reginald Pole survived his kinswoman some twenty-two hours, and almost the last sounds to reach his ears were the cheers with which a people that breathed freely once more greeted the accession of Queen Elizabeth.

FOOTNOTES:

[391] Morrin's Patent Rolls, p. 304.

[392] Instructions for Sir A. St. Leger, Oct. 1553; Morrin's Patent Rolls, pp. 300-304.

[393] Petition of Connor MacCarthy, 1553. The Queen to Sussex, July 6, 1558. Orders taken at Drogheda, Dec. 6, 1553, in Carew.

[394] Bale's select works, Parker Society; King Johan, a play, ed. J. Payne Collier, Camden Society; 'God's promises in all ages of the old law,' in Dodsley's Old Plays, vol. i.; a brief comedy or interlude of John Baptist in Harl. Misc. vol. i.

[395] Bale's Vocation; Cotton's Fasti, vol. i. p. 123.

[396] Bale's Vocation; Ware's Annals. Queen Elizabeth to the two St. Legers, calendared under 1559 (No. 85). Dr. Reid printed the following contemporary epigram:—

'Plurima Lutherus patefecit, Platina multa,
Quædam Vergerius, cuncta Balæus habet.'

[397] Hook's Life of Pole, vol. iii. p. 359, note; Machyn's Diary, Jan. 27, 1554; Life of Sir Peter Carew, ed. by Macleane, and also printed in Carew, vol. i.

[398] Brady; Cotton. Dowling says of Thonory: 'Pro dolore amissionis thesauri sui per fures mortuus. Fures confitebantur et executi.'

[399] Indentures with the O'Briens, Sept. 1554, in Carew; Four Masters, 1554.

[400] Sarpi's Council of Trent, trans. by Courayer, lib. v. cap. 15, and the notes. Dr. Lingard, vol. v. end of chap. v., objects to Fra Paolo's account, but I cannot see that his own much differs.

[401] Brady; Hook's Life of Pole; Ware's Life of Curwin; Rymer, Feb. 22, and April 25, 1555; Morrin's Patent Rolls, p. 339.

[402] Hooker in Holinshed; St. Leger to Petre, Dec. 18, 1555; Four Masters, 1555. James MacDonnell's agents to Calvagh O'Donnell, calendared under 1554 (No. 7).

[403] Instructions to Lord Fitzwalter, April 28, 1556, in Carew. Sidney Papers, i. p. 85.

[404] Ware's Annals.

[405] Sussex's Journal, Aug. 8, 1556, in Carew; Sidney's Relation, in Carew; 1583; Lord Deputy Fitzwalter to the Queen, Jan. 2, 1557; Calendar of Foreign State Papers, Oct. 28, 1556.

[406] Opinions of Lord Fitzwalter, Jan. 2, 1557. He mentions hake as 'a kind of salt fish much eaten in Ireland.'

[407] Privy Council to Lord Deputy, Sept. 30, 1556; Orders for Leix, Dec.; Lord Deputy to the Queen, Jan. 2, 1557. An Act of Parliament was passed in 1557, entitling the Crown to Leix and Offaly, and authorising the Lord Deputy to make grants under the Great Seal.

[408] Proceedings of the Deputy and Council, Feb. 25, 1557, in Carew. Four Masters for 1555 and 1556.

[409] Four Masters, 1555 and 1556. Proceedings of Deputy and Council, Feb. 25, 1557, in Carew. Dowling says Connel O'More was 'apud pontem Leighlin cruci affixus.' Ware's Annals.

[410] Thomas Alen to Cecil, Dec. 18, 1558; Letters of Queen Mary, calendared under 1557 (Nos. 63 and 64), and petitions (Nos. 65 and 66). For grants of abbey-lands, see Morrin's Patent Rolls, passim. Mary's only Irish Parliament (3 and 4 Phil. et Mar.), met June 1, 1557, in Dublin. There were adjournments to Limerick and Drogheda. See Stuart's Armagh, p. 244, and Rymer, Dec. 1, 1556.

[411] July 1557; Journal by Sussex of that date in Carew; Four Masters, 1557.

[412] October; Four Masters, 1557.

[413] Four Masters. This was towards the end of 1557.

[414] Four Masters, 1557.

[415] Lord Justice Sidney and Council to the Privy Council, Feb. 8, 1558; Desmond to the Queen, Feb. 5 and Feb. 23, and her answer, April 19; Sidney to Sussex, Feb. 26, and to the Queen, March 1.

[416] Piers to Curwin, Feb. 14, 1558; Sussex to Boxoll, June 8; Articles by an Irishman, 1558 (No. 15).

[417] The Queen's letters are all dated March 12.

[418] See instructions in Carew, March 20; Estimate for munitions, March 13.

[419] Machyn's Diary; Sussex to Privy Council, April 7, with inclosures; Dowdall to Heath, Nov. 17, 1557.

[420] This tour is in Carew, i. 274-277; the date in the end of July 1558.

[421] For the expedition to the isles, see Sussex to the Queen, Oct. 3, Oct. 6, and Oct. 31, 1558.

[422] Journeys by the Earl of Sussex, July and Nov. 1558, in Carew; oath of Gerald Earl of Desmond, Nov. 28.

[423] Ware's Life of Browne. In their instructions to the Lord Deputy and Council, Philip and Mary say:—'Lord Cardinal Poole, being sent unto us from the Pope's Holiness and the said See Apostolic Legate of our said realms, mindeth in brief time to despatch into Ireland certain his commissioners and officials to visit the clergy and other members of the said realm of Ireland,' &c., Carew, April 28, 1556.

Printed in Great Britain
by Amazon